North Korea and Northeast Asia

Asia in World Politics
Series Editor: Samuel S. Kim

Cooperation or Conflict in the Taiwan Strait?
by Ralph N. Clough

Pacific Asia? Prospects for Security and Cooperation in East Asia
by Mel Gurtov

East Asia and Globalization
edited by Samuel S. Kim

In the Eyes of the Dragon: China Views the World
edited by Yong Deng and Fei-Ling Wang

North Korea and Northeast Asia

Edited by Samuel S. Kim and Tai Hwan Lee

ROWMAN & LITTLEFIELD PUBLISHERS, INC.
Lanham • Boulder • New York • Oxford

ROWMAN & LITTLEFIELD PUBLISHERS, INC.

Published in the United States of America
by Rowman & Littlefield Publishers, Inc.
A Member of the Rowman & Littlefield Publishing Group
4720 Boston Way, Lanham, Maryland 20706
www.rowmanlittlefield.com

12 Hid's Copse Road
Cumnor Hill, Oxford OX2 9JJ, England

Written under the auspices of the Sejong Institute, Seoul, Korea

British Library Cataloguing in Publication Information Available

Library of Congress Cataloging-in-Publication Data

Kim, Samuel S., 1935–
North Korea and Northeast Asia / Samuel S. Kim and Tai Hwan Lee.
p. cm. — (Asia in the world)
Includes bibliographical references and index.
ISBN 0-7425-1710-1 (cloth : alk. paper) — ISBN 0-7425-1711-X (pbk. : alk. paper)
1. Korea (North)—Foreign relations. 2. National Security—Korea (North) 3. East Asia—Foreign relations. 4. World politics—1945– I. Lee, Tai Hwan. II. Title. III. Series.
DS935.65 .K579 2002
327.5193—dc21

2002004591

Printed in the United States of America

∞™ The paper used in this publication meets the minimum requirements of American National Standard for Information Sciences—Permanence of Paper for Printed Library Materials, ANSI/NISO Z39.48-1992.

Contents

Tables and Figures

TABLES

FIGURES

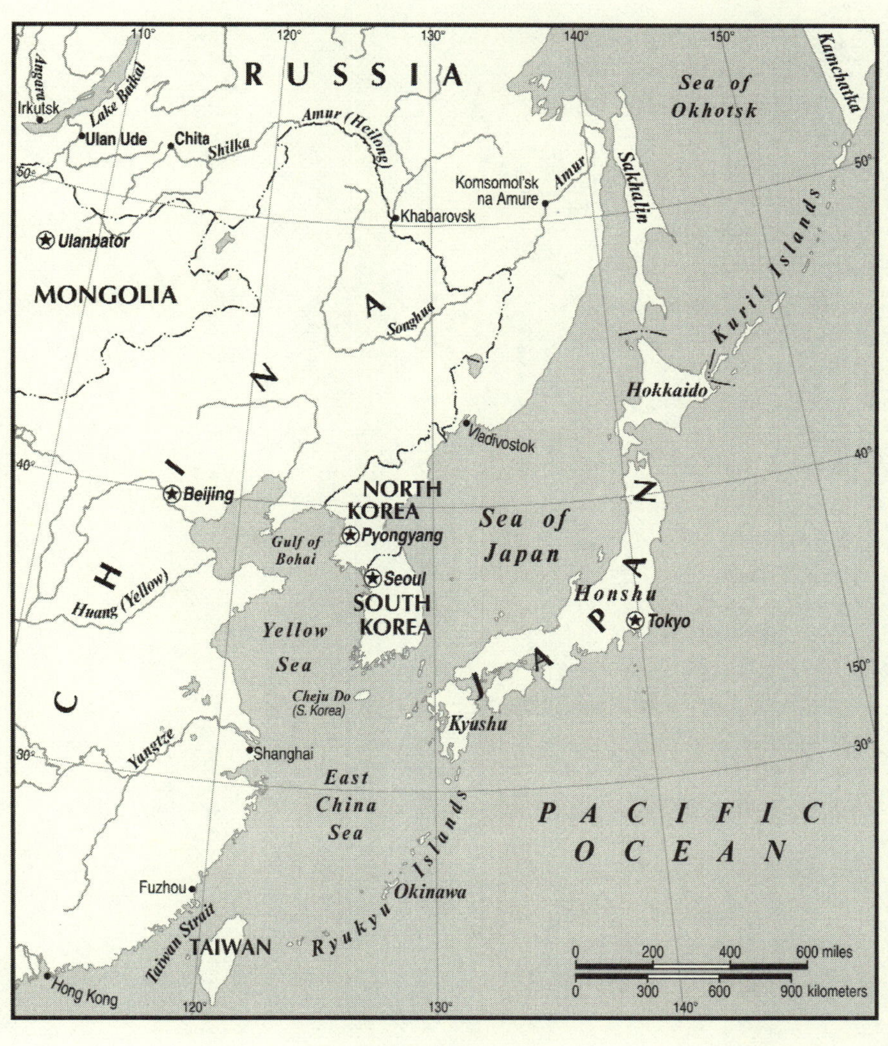
RUSSIA
Sea of Okhotsk
Kamchatka
Angara
Irkutsk
Lake Baikal
Ulan Ude
Chita
Shilka
Amur (Heilong)
Komsomol'sk na Amure
Amur
Sakhalin
Khabarovsk
Ulanbator
MONGOLIA
Songhua
Kuril Islands
Hokkaido
Vladivostok
NORTH KOREA
Beijing
Pyongyang
Sea of Japan
Gulf of Bohai
Seoul
SOUTH KOREA
Honshu
Tokyo
Huang (Yellow)
Yellow Sea
JAPAN
CHINA
Cheju Do (S. Korea)
Kyushu
Yangtze
Shanghai
East China Sea
PACIFIC OCEAN
Ryukyu Islands
Okinawa
Fuzhou
Taiwan Strait
TAIWAN
Hong Kong
0 200 400 600 miles
0 300 600 900 kilometers
110°
120°
130°
140°
150°
50°
40°
30°

Preface

A glance at a map of Northeast Asia quickly reveals why this region is viewed by many as among the most important and dangerous places in the post–Cold War world. Geography and region-specific fault lines, especially the potential of implosion or explosion in North Korea, have given rise to a highly complex interdependence of security in the Northeast Asian region. North Korea, surrounded by the Big Four (China, Russia, Japan, and the United States) plus South Korea, is the region's geostrategic pivot point and its most critical flash point. Through its conventional and nonconventional (asymmetrical) military capabilities and threats, an unstable North Korea could destabilize the region. Consequently each of the Big Four regards the Korean peninsula as falling within its own geostrategic ambit, albeit in varying degrees.

The threat of a North Korean collapse, with regional spillover costs in the form of refugees, has become a strategic nightmare, especially for Beijing and Seoul, while simultaneously increasing North Korea's leverage from its position of relative weakness. Managing the North Korean threat in its multiple and mutating forms has become an integral part of the problem and the solution for both the future of the Korean peninsula and the future of Northeast Asian geopolitics.

North Korea's uncanny resilience in the face of seemingly fatal internal contradictions raises several puzzles and paradoxes of theoretical and real-world significance. This book is divided into three main parts to address these puzzles and paradoxes. The first part (consisting of chapter 1) considers, in broad strokes, North Korean–Northeast Asian relations in both theoretical and practical terms. The second part (chapters 2 through 5) examines the complex interplay of global, regional, and national forces that have influenced and shaped the changing patterns of conflict and cooperation in North Korea's relationships with its three neighboring Northeast Asian powers (China, Russia, and Japan) and with the United States, Pyongyang's de facto neighbor and the reigning superpower in Northeast Asia. The third part (chapters 6 through 8) tracks, explains, and assesses North Korea's survival strategies in both the security and economic domains in the context of Northeast Asian geopolitics.

Each contributor has been asked to address essential and enduring questions within the framework of a specific topic. Adopting a variety of theoretical perspectives (asymmetrical conflict theory, mercantile neorealism, and prospect theory, to name a few) in the context of interaction-specific and issue-specific case studies, the authors assess North Korea's system-maintaining survival strategies in the setting of Northeast Asian geopolitics. In doing so, they seek to identify the changes and continuities that have characterized North Korean foreign relations over the years and the reasons why North Koreans behave as they do in the conduct of their international relations, with a particular emphasis on the post–Kim Il Sung years (1995 through 2001).

This book would not have seen the light of day without the intellectual initiative and financial support of the Sejong Institute, where the project was conceived in mid-2000, when the first-ever inter-Korean summit was taking place in Pyongyang. The key rationale was to stimulate and support timely exchange of scholarly discourse between the South Korean and American experts on North Korean affairs, especially with respect to Pyongyang's renormalization efforts with Beijing and Moscow and the normalization talks with Washington and Tokyo before and after the Pyongyang summit. The chapters of *North Korea and Northeast Asia* represent revised versions of the papers presented at twin panels of the 2001 International Studies Association (ISA) held in Chicago in February of 2001, which were organized by Samuel Kim with a research grant from the Sejong Institute. We wish to thank our chapter authors for their acuity, hard work, and patience, often beyond the call of duty, to meet our many demands for revisions. Samuel Kim wishes to thank the Center for Korean Research at the East Asian Institute of Columbia University for continuing encouragement and support, and especially his graduate research assistants—Ingrid Davis and Abraham Kim—for their characteristically skillful, efficient, and multitasking work in library and online research and for stage-managing the preparation of the book manuscript. Tai Hwan Lee wishes to thank his colleagues at the Sejong Institute for their abiding support and encouragement for this and other projects.

Finally, it was our pleasure to work with Rowman & Littlefield Publishers in the production of this book. We are particularly grateful to Susan McEachern for her unflagging support and encouragement and for her role as an invisible collaborator and invaluable navigator. Special thanks are also due to Alden Perkins and Carrie Obry for their efficient steering of the manuscript through the various stages of production. The usual disclaimer still applies: the editors and chapter authors alone are responsible for any remaining errors in fact or interpretation.

Samuel S. Kim
Tai Hwan Lee

I

THEORY AND PRACTICE

1

North Korea and Northeast Asia in World Politics

Samuel S. Kim

A recent satellite photo of the Korean peninsula and its surroundings at night is perhaps more telling than a thousand words. Northeast China and South Korea are ablaze with light, but North Korea—officially known as the Democratic People's Republic of Korea (DPRK)—is totally dark outside the single dot of the capital city, Pyongyang. Many see North Korea as Northeast Asia's time bomb, seemingly ripe for implosion or explosion. Yet as the new millennium begins, not only does the DPRK still exist, but it has somehow managed to muddle through despite a downward spiral of declining production, spreading famine and triage, and deepening socialist alienation. The consensus in South Korean and U.S. intelligence communities in early 2000 was that North Korea would survive for at least the next fifteen years (to 2015).[1]

The paradox of survival in the face of seemingly fatal internal contradictions raises several key questions for scholars and policymakers concerned about the future of North Korea in the Northeast Asian context. They also provide the focus and theme that this books seeks to address with interaction-specific and issue-specific case studies. How can we explain Pyongyang's uncanny resilience and ability to survive in defiance of all the gloomy predictions? What has made it possible for North Korea to defy the classical realist axiom "the strong do what they have the power to do and the weak accept what they have to accept"[2] in obtaining almost everything it wanted from the United States through the asymmetrical nuclear negotiations in 1993 and 1994? What accounts for the equally remarkable paradox of North Korea becoming America's largest aid recipient in Asia, even as it remains on the United States' blacklist of terror-sponsoring states? What is the nature of the North Korean threat in post–Cold War Northeast Asia? What kind of coercive bargaining leverage did Pyongyang exercise in system-maintaining survival strategies? What are North Korea's prospects for sustaining such survival strategies in the uncertain years ahead, especially with the advent of the hard-line Bush administration in Washington and the more nationalistic Koizumi government in Tokyo?

In pursuit of these lines of inquiry, this introductory chapter is organized into six sections. The first two sections depict in broad strokes *sui generis* regional characteristics and contending theoretical perspectives in international relations for a contextual analysis of North Korean foreign relations in the post–Cold War era. The third section, drawing from chapters 2 through 5, examines the complex interplay of global, regional, and national forces that have influenced and shaped the changing patterns of relationship between North Korea and its three neighboring Northeast Asian powers (China, Russia, and Japan), as well as its relationship with the United States, Korea's de facto neighbor and the reigning superpower in Northeast Asia. The fourth section, drawing from chapters 6 through 8, assesses Pyongyang's survival strategy in both the security and economic domains in the Northeast Asian context. The fifth section presents an overall assessment of North Korea's survival strategy. The sixth and final section briefly addresses the most vexing double-edged question of how and whether North Korea can rise to the challenge of moving from system-maintaining coping strategies to a system-reforming direction without triggering a cataclysmic system collapse.

THE NORTHEAST ASIAN ENVIRONMENT

Northeast Asia is more than a simple geographical referent. It is a region that encompasses China, Mongolia, the two Koreas, Japan, and the Russian Far East, and also involves the United States as the extraterritorial, lone superpower. It is claimed as a region of vital importance for America's security and economic interests, and the role of the United States remains a crucial component (perhaps the most crucial) of the regional geostrategic and geoeconomic equation. The world's heaviest concentration of military and economic capabilities is in Northeast Asia, with the world's three largest nuclear weapons states, three threshold nuclear weapons states (North Korea, South Korea, and Japan), and the world's three largest economies.[3] With every country in the region now both a consumer and a producer of missiles, the dangerous and unsettling reality is missile proliferation and an arms race.[4] The United States, by dint of its deep involvement in Northeast Asian geopolitics and geoeconomics, provides more than 80 percent of the one hundred thousand troops deployed in the Asia-Pacific region, concentrated mostly in Japan and South Korea.

Following the reunification of both Vietnam and Germany, Northeast Asia has the world's highest concentration of divided polities: divided China and divided Korea, the two most prominent potential flashpoints. It is also worth noting the numerous seemingly intractable territorial and maritime disputes: the Tokdo/Takeshima Islands (Seoul versus Tokyo), the Diaoyu/Senkaku Islands (Beijing versus Tokyo), the Northern Territories (Tokyo versus Moscow), the Northern Limit Line on the Yellow/West Sea (Seoul versus Pyongyang), and the Spratly Islands (China versus six other East Asian states). With the entry into force of the United Nations Convention on the Law of the Sea (UNCLOS) in 1994, the enlarged exclusive economic zones (EEZs) pose a clear and present danger of a new pattern of maritime conflict in the region. The June 2001 fishing dispute between Seoul and Tokyo, with Moscow as a third player, may be a wake-up call in terms of geoeconomic maritime conflict in Northeast Asia.

In the middle of this precarious and tough neighborhood, divided Korea stands as a strategic pivot. For over a century, history and geography have consigned Korea to the position of a highly contested strategic crossroads, the site of wider great-power geopolitical struggles and wars that have involved, to varying degrees, czarist Russia, the Soviet Union, Qing China, the Republic of China, the People's Republic of China, Japan, and the United States. Consider how the emerging Cold War turned into a hot war in Korea, with some three million human casualties on both sides. Even today, almost half a century after the Korean War "ended" with an armistice accord, the so-called demilitarized zone (DMZ) remains the most heavily fortified conflict zone in the post–Cold War world, where more than 1.8 million military personnel confront each other, armed to the teeth with the latest weapons systems. In the latter half of the 1990s, the volcano of potential crisis in North Korea seemed to have become more active than ever before. The possibility of an unstable or collapsing North Korea with inordinate asymmetrical (nonconventional) military capabilities has extraordinary refractory ramifications for great-power politics in Northeast Asia and beyond. Each of the Big Four (the United States, Japan, China, and Russia) considers the Korean peninsula to be within its own geostrategic ambit. Koreans, for their part, have long recognized their own security predicament, likening it to being "a shrimp among whales."

However, the external environment of states in Northeast Asia has not been stagnant in the post–Cold War era. The momentous changes of the late 1980s and the 1990s are unprecedented in their nature, scope, and rapidity. The received wisdom about the traditional Korean security predicament—that Korea is a weak country in a region where so many countries are strong—is no longer a reliable guide to the peace process on the Korean peninsula. For the first time in many years, the Korean peninsula is no longer a site of traditional confrontational great-power rivalry. All four major external powers have now expressed their shared interest in seeking peace and stability on the Korean peninsula. The two Koreas may now be experiencing greater security sovereignty than at any time since the opening of the "hermit kingdom" in the 1870s.

There are at least three sets of momentous forces reshaping the international relations of Northeast Asia. First, the normalization of Moscow-Seoul relations in 1990 and Beijing-Seoul relations in 1992 has knocked out one of the Cold War alliance systems in the region. Second, in the last two decades, with a rising China and a declining post-Soviet Russia, along with a rising South Korea and declining North Korea, the greatest shifts in power, at least as defined and measured in conventional terms, have taken place in this region. Third, the forces of globalization in the 1990s have transformed both the context and the conditions in which Northeast Asian regional geopolitics are played out. From this perspective on post–Cold War Northeast Asian international relations, geopolitics is no longer the only game in town, now coexisting and even competing with geoeconomics and geogovernance.

As a result of the uneasy juxtaposition of continuities and changes and in place of the clarity, simplicity, and apparent stability of the former structure of East-West conflict, a new Northeast Asian regional order is emerging, with multiple complexities and uncertainties and of indeterminate shape and content. The end of global bipolarity and the U.S.-China-U.S.S.R. strategic triangle has not brought a new global and regional order. Although great-power conflict and rivalries in traditional form have dissipated, uncertainties abound about the shape of the Northeast Asian regional order to come.

Indeed, it is this unique, combustible cocktail of *sui generis* regional characteristics—high capability, abiding animus, entanglement of the Big Four in Korean affairs, North Korea's recent emergence as a loose cannon, and the absence of multilateral security institutions—that challenge scholars and policymakers alike in divining the shape of things to come in the emerging regional order. To a significant degree, the shaping of post–Cold War Northeast Asian politics has become path-dependent, since unexpected events such as the attacks on America of September 11, 2001, can easily force movement along quite different trajectories.

CONTENDING THEORETICAL PERSPECTIVES

All the new world-order challenges are concentrated in Northeast Asia, pivoting around two central issues: the source of possible threats to the region's stability and the feasible and desirable conflict-management models needed to establish peace and stability in the region. There are at least four contending theoretical perspectives of real-world significance for Northeast Asian international relations: balance of power realism, neoliberal institutionalism, social constructivism, and globalization.

Balance-of-Power Realism and the Rise of China

The debate about Northeast Asian security has been dominated by realists who argue that states, as unitary rational actors in international anarchy, are driven to seek power or security. The assumption is that continuity in the basic nature of world politics is shaped by the structure of the international system (i.e., the distribution of material power at the systemic level) and by the perennial struggle for power and plenty. The realist concern for relative power gains at the unit level has led many to argue that Northeast Asia is primed for the revival of a classical great-power rivalry and balance-of-power realpolitik. The end of the Cold War is understood as a return to multipolar systems, or at least to the uneasy juxtaposition of global unipolarity and regional multipolarity that is said to be more prone to instability and conflict than bipolar systems.[5]

The most influential trend that realists fear will shape the future of Northeast Asia, however, is the political dynamics associated with power transitions. In an argument that draws insights from Thucydides' explanation of the Peloponnesian war, fast rising powers are believed almost invariably to be revisionist challengers seeking to change the existing international order and to supplant the dominant power. Realists have argued that signs of a power transition process in post–Cold War Northeast Asia during the 1990s—the rise of China, a declining Russia, a stagnant Japan, and a retreating hegemon (the United States)—indicate that it will be as difficult to achieve a stable, lasting peace in this region as it was in Europe over the past several centuries. These dynamics will make the political environment ripe for Sino-American and Sino-Japanese rivalry. Applying the thesis of the clash of civilizations to the debate on the rise of China, Huntington argues that Asian countries will be more likely to join China than to balance against it, and that Asia's Sinocentric past, not Europe's multipolar past, "will be Asia's future," even as "China is resuming its place as regional hegemon."[6] Realist anxiety is growing and debate is widening in Washington as well as among China's East Asian neighbors, especially Tokyo, on the feasibility and desirability of various strategies—for example, balancing, bandwagoning, capitulating, or ignoring—to manage the rise of Chinese power.[7] Europe's half-millennium history of rivalry and major war may be Asia's future.

By the logic of realist power transition theory, belligerent preemptive or preventive actions are motivated less by aggressive intentions than by fear and a fundamental dissatisfaction with the status quo, largely as a result of closing windows of opportunity and increasing vulnerability brought on by relative power shifts.[8] It is in this region that a rising China, a declining post-Soviet Russia, a rising South Korea, and declining North Korea have brought about the greatest swings in power in the last half-century. As shown in table 1.1, U.S. and Japanese shares of global gross national product (GNP) and industrial production from 1980 to 1997 have declined only slightly. The most dramatic changes are seen in the rapid rise and decline of China's and Russia's shares of global GNP and industrial production: for China a jump from 3.3 percent to 10.7 percent in global GNP and from 3.0 percent to 15.3 percent in global production, and for Russia a drop from 7.0 percent to 1.7 percent in global GNP and from 9.0 percent to 1.8 percent in global production. For most realists, the "back to the future" correlation between rapid internal growth and external expansionism has troubling implications for the future of Northeast Asian regional order. Tables 1.2 and 1.3 show the structure of the Northeast Asian international system in realist/material terms in the 1990s.

What would a system-maintaining China and a unified Korea look like by the year 2015? If we accept the projections of a 1995 RAND Corporation study, by 2015 China will have caught up with the United States, with its gross domestic product (GDP) reaching $11 to 12 trillion (in 1994 dollars) compared to $4.5 trillion for Japan, $3.7 billion for India, and $2 trillion for a unified Korea. However, its military capital will be less than half that of the U.S., as shown in table 1.4.[9]

Table 1.1. Changing Shares of the Major Powers of Global GNP and Global Industrial Production, 1980–1997

	1980	*1990*	*1995*	*1997*
Shares of Global GNP (%)				
USSR/Russia	7.0	5.6	1.9	1.7
U.S.	22.3	22.5	20.8	20.6
China	3.3	6.6	10.7	10.7
Japan	8.1	9.0	7.7	7.7
Shares of Global Industrial Production (%)				
USSR/Russia	9.0	7.0	2.0	1.8
U.S.	18.7	17.4	16.9	16.6
China	3.0	8.0	14.1	15.3
Japan	7.3	8.7	7.1	6.9

Source: Adapted from Viktor N. Paviatenko, "Russian Security in the Pacific Asian Region: The Dangers of Isolation," in Gilbert Rozman, Mikhail G. Nosov, and Koji Watanabe, eds., *Russia and East Asia: The Twenty-First Century Security Environment* (Armonk, NY: M. E. Sharpe, 1999), 20–1.

Table 1.2. Amounts, Ranks, and Shares of Material Power Resources, 1990s

	China	*Russia*	*Japan*	*U.S.*
Basic Resource				
Population (1995)	1st 21.2%	6th 2.6%	8th 2.2%	3rd 4.7%
Territory (1994)	2nd 7.3%	1st 13.2%	59th 0.3%	4th 7.1%
Economy				
GNP in $billion (bn) (1997)	1,055 (7th) 3.5%	403.5 (12th) 1.3%	4,772.3 (2nd) 15.9%	7,690 (1st) 25.7%
GNP at PPP in $bn (1997)	4,382.5 (2nd) 11.9%	618.4 (14th) 1.7%	2,950.7 (3rd) 8.0%	7,691.1 (1st) 20.8%
Manufacturing (1995)	7th 3.0%	8th 3.1%	1st 25.4%	2nd 22.6%
High-tech Exports as % of Merchandise Exports (1996)	21%	–	39%	1st 44%
Merchandise Exports in $bn (1996)	151.0 (10th) 2.8%	81.4 (15th) 1.5%	410.5 (3rd) 7.6%	575.5 (1st) 10.7%
Military				
Nuclear Weapons (1996)	4th 2.5%	2nd 46.1%	– –	1st 46.8%
Military Expenditure in $bn (1999)	39.9 (7th) 4.1%	56.8 (6th) 4.3%	40.4 (2nd) 5.9%	292.1 (1st) 41.1%
Military Personnel (1999)	2,820,000 (1st) 12.9%	1,004,300 (5th) 4.6%	242,600 (22nd) 1.1%	1,365,800 (2nd) 6.2%

Sources: Robert A. Pastor, "The Great Powers in the Twentieth Century: From Dawn to Dusk," in Robert A. Pastor, ed., A *Century's Journey: How the Great Powers Shape the World* (New York: Basic Books, 1999), 19; World Bank, *World Development Report 1998–1999* (New York: Oxford University Press, 1999), 226–27; International Institute of Strategic Studies (IISS), *The Military Balance 2000–2001* (London: IISS, 2000), table 38.

Some optimistic realists flatly reject the ascendant-China thesis. For example, William Wohlforth argues that the post–Cold War international system is unprecedentedly and unambiguously unipolar. The United States enjoys "a much larger margin of superiority over the next most powerful states or, indeed, all other great powers combined than any leading states in the last two centuries," in all the underlying economic, military, technological and geopolitical components of power. He argues further that the current unipolarity is not only peaceful and stable, but durable as well. It minimizes strategic peer competition among the other great powers, and the second-tier powers have an incentive to bandwagon with the unipolar superpower rather than to balance against it.[10] Thus Wohlforth rejects the "unipolar moment" thesis as profoundly mistaken and pessimistic and the ascendant-China thesis as profoundly mistaken and optimistic.[11] For Gerald Segal, China is no more

Table 1.3. Military Expenditures of Major Military Powers in Northeast Asia, 1999

Classification	*GDP (U.S.$bn)*	*Defense Budget (U.S.$bn)*	*Defense Budget as percent of GDP*	*Military Manpower (1,000 persons)*	*Military Expenditure per capita (U.S.$)*
U.S.	9,200 (27%)	283	3.1	1,371	1,036
Japan	4,300 (12.8%)	40.4	0.9	242	319
Russia	1,000 (2.9%)	56	5.1	1,004	380
China	732 (2.2%)	39.9	5.4	2,820	32
Taiwan	288 (0.85%)	15.0	5.2	370	687
South Korea	407 (1.2%)	12.0	3.0	672	257
North Korea	14.7 (0.04%)	2.1	14.3	1,055	98
Regional Total	15,942	448.4	5.3 (average)	7,534	401.3 (average)
% of Global Total	47.3%	56%	4.1 (global average)	35%	221 (global average)

Source: International Institute of Strategic Studies (IISS), *The Military Balance 2000–2001* (London: IISS, 2000).
Note: Based on 1999 constant prices.

than a "middle power" and a largely "theatrical power"; "China matters in the same way any middle-power adversary matters: it is a problem to be circumvented or moved."[12]

There are several problems with the mainstream realist visions of post–Cold War Northeast Asian international relations. First, the historically derived correlation between system transition and war causation may no longer apply. There are many differences between a rising China and the rise

Table 1.4. Projections of Asia and the United States in 2015

Country	*GDP (trillions)**	*Military Capital (billions)**
China	11–12	410
Japan	4-5	173
India	4	353
(United) Korea	2	129
Indonesia	1.5–2.0	60
United States	11–12	895

*In 1997 U.S. dollars.
Source: Charles Wolf Jr., "Asia in 2015," *Wall Street Journal*, March 20, 1997, A16.

of Wilhelmine Germany, and furthermore world history may well be in a different normative (anti-imperial) cycle.[13] Indeed, what distinguishes the post-1945 international system is the extent to which international organizations have become prominent and permanent parts of a complex, increasingly interdependent global system. In the post–Cold War era, thanks to globalization dynamics, the games that nation-states play have lost much of the realist simplicity of the struggle for power and plenty. Colonialism and imperialism have been consigned to the dustbin. Moreover, with the third wave of democratization, "democracies seem able to influence international norms and institutions, thereby affecting the probability that force will be used even by states that are not themselves particularly democratic."[14] Past generalizations, and much of conventional realist wisdom, can no longer provide a sure guide for the future, and the future of world politics will not necessarily resemble the past if the extrapolated generalizations themselves are no longer valid.[15]

In a rapidly globalizing world, the very notion of "great power" is subject to continuing redefinition and reassessment. What constitutes power has changed significantly with the demise of the socialist superpower and the diffusion and multiplicity of power in all its varying forms, whether hard or soft, material or nonmaterial. The traditional military and strategic concept of power pays too much attention to a state's aggregate power (power potential as inferred from its as yet unconverted resources and possessions) and too little to the more dynamic and interdependent notions of power in an issue-specific domain—that is, power defined in terms of control over outcomes. As David Baldwin argued some two decades ago, "the notion of a single overall international power structure unrelated to any particular issue-area is based on a concept of power that is virtually meaningless."[16] Despite the sudden "third worldization" of the former Soviet Union (South Korea's GNP has already surpassed Russia's), Russia's strong cards include its territory (still the world's largest), its science and technology, its natural resources, its permanent membership in the United Nations Security Council, and above all its status as the only nuclear superpower that can effectively destroy the United States (see tables 1.2 and 1.3).

The ascendant-China thesis comes at a time when the coherence of the Chinese state is deteriorating. The domestic social, demographic, and environmental problems encountered by Beijing in its march to great powerdom are legion.[17] By conventional measurements of the rise and fall of great powers (in terms of shifts in international military and economic power balances), China is a rising great power. Yet it remains an incomplete great power in a rapidly changing world where transnational nonmilitary challenges to power and soft sources of power are becoming increasingly important.[18] China's emerging role in world affairs—its future capabilities, intentions, and foreign policy behavior—remains the major source of uncertainty in the transition from Cold War to post–Cold War order. China is a major regional power with myriad world-class domestic problems. In the coming years, the way Beijing manages its economic reforms, rampant corruption, and leadership transitions may be influential factors that will shape China's future. A weak and fragmenting China would be the worst of all possible scenarios, a disaster not only for China but also for peace and stability in the region and beyond.

The realist unipolarity thesis is a variation on hegemonic stability theory and an extension of the bipolarity thesis as a sure recipe for international peace. Though there was no global war or nuclear war during the Cold War era of bipolarity, East Asia was the site of sanguinary armed conflicts with more human fatalities than any other region of the world: the Korean War (three million), the Vietnam War (two million), the Chinese Civil War (one million), and the Pol Pot genocide (one to two million).[19]

Moreover, diplomatic and military history does not support the core assumption of the realist peer competitor argument that power parity (bipolarity) and the preponderance of power buy peace and stability because weaker powers will not challenge the security interests of the stronger states. The literature on asymmetric conflicts shows that weaker powers have engaged in wars against stronger adversaries more often than not, and big powers frequently lose wars in asymmetric conflicts (e.g., the Vietnam War).[20] According to a recent study, weak states were victorious in nearly 30 percent of all asymmetric wars in the approximately two-hundred-year period covered in the *Correlates of War* data set. More tellingly, weak states have won with increasing frequency over time.[21]

In reviewing fifty years of Chinese diplomacy, Beijing still calls the Korean War a war of aggression that the imperialists launched to strangle the new People's Republic; the Chinese performance in Korea is still publicly exalted as "a world miracle in which the weak vanquished the strong," even as "the signing of the Korean armistice rewrote the history of Chinese diplomatic negotiations which [prior to the coming of the PRC (People's Republic of China)] had always ended with sacrifice of China's national interests."[22] Weaker states have also initiated many brinksmanship crises that fell short of war,[23] with the most recent example being North Korea.

Shying away from the polar extremes of the pessimistic or alarmist realists and the complacent or optimistic realists, Thomas Christensen argues a third way. A substantial military force, the unique political geography of Sino-centric East Asia, and a highly charged nationalist Chinese government could pose major challenges for American security interests in East Asia. For example, China and the United States could clash violently, especially over the issue of Taiwan, without the slightest pretense on Beijing's part of having caught up with the United States in overall national military power or technology.[24]

In a real-world situation, it is not so much the overall aggregate military power across Northeast Asia that will shape the emerging Northeast Asian order as it is the complex and dynamic interplay of domestic politics, elite perceptions, and diplomatic and security strategies in the capitals of the Big Four, involving specific military capabilities in specific geographic and political contexts. Ultimately, the critical issue in assessing China as a great power or as a rising power is behavior. What matters most is not the growth of Chinese power, but how and for what purposes a rising China will actually wield its power in the conduct of its international relations.

Neoliberal Internationalism and Constrained Regionalism

While acknowledging both conflict and cooperation as basic features of international life, neoliberal internationalism represents a more positive collective response to the perennial question of whether international peace is possible through multilateral institutions in the absence of a world government. Mainstream institutional liberals accept some of the core assumptions of structural realism (neorealism) but reject the realist claims that cooperative security via multilateral institutions is a mirage and that international law is nothing more than a reflection of the interests of world powers.

The core assumption of liberal institutional theory is that multilateral institutions help states to cope with uncertainty and to pursue their interests cost-effectively. Through international institutions, regulative norms, rules, and governing procedures are established to provide member states with convergent expectations, transparency of actions, and improved communication. Multilateral institutions, including security institutions, represent a response to the problems of international cooperation created by large numbers of actors, and such institutions can affect the "national interests" cost-benefit calculations of states through their information generating and disseminating functions, thus increasing the likelihood of international cooperation in N-person games.[25]

Other liberals argue that international politics are best explained by domestic sources: a state's foreign policy behavior in general and its war-prone behavior in particular depends more on its specific type of national government or social system than on the structure of the international system. Proceeding from sharply divergent premises, Wilson and Lenin both identified the cause of war and the conditions for peace in the nature of the social and political systems of the state. More recently, the second-image theory of democratic peace—that liberal democracies rarely fight against each other—has gained wide if not paradigmatic acceptance in international relations theory.[26]

Kantian liberals argue that a stable peace can be achieved through the expansion of economic interdependence, the enlargement of democracy, and the formation of a security community. Bruce Russett and John Oneal advance the empirically grounded argument that Immanuel Kant's perpetual peace is no longer utopia, but a living reality.[27]

Absent widespread liberal democracies, extensive economic interdependence, and multilateral security institutions—the three liberal/Kantian conditions for international peace—many view Northeast Asia as primed more for international conflict than for international cooperation.[28] The Northeast Asian region duplicates the global North-South divide with its sharp bifurcation between wealthy capitalist states (Japan, South Korea, and the United States) and poor countries that are either socialist or developing in transition (China, Russia, Mongolia, and North Korea). Viewed in this light, the absence of regional multilateral institutions is hardly surprising.

However, mainstream neoliberal institutionalism does not fully take into account the "Asian way"—or the ASEAN way—to international cooperation, an informal consultative and networking model that emphasizes multilateral dialogue and consensus-building rather than formal regimes with a high degree of institutionalization. Indeed, the prevalence of informal bi-multilateral or minilateral institutions is one of the defining features of East Asia in general and Northeast Asia in particular. Despite the myriad interconnections in a wide range of issue areas in the past decade, Northeast Asia spawned only a handful of such minilateral institutions. With the exception of the Association of Southeast Asian Nations (ASEAN) Regional Forum (ARF), which is more Southeast Asian than Northeast Asian in structure and orientation, and the APEC (Asia Pacific Economic Cooperation), none of the remaining six minilateral institutions have all Big Four in membership, as shown in table 1.5.

Table 1.5. Northeast Asian Participants in "Regional" Minilateral Institutions, 2001

	ARF (23)	*Four-Party Talks (4)*	*TCOG (3)*	*KEDO (3+10)*	*APEC (21)*	*TRADP (5)*	*TEMM (3)*	*ASEAN Plus Three (13)*
DPRK	X	X				X		
ROK	X	X	X	X	X	X	X	X
U.S.	X	X	X	X	X			
Japan	X		X	X	X		X	X
China	X	X			X	X	X	X
Russia	X				X	X		
Mongolia	X					X		
Taiwan					X			
Hong Kong					X			

X=Participating member state.

Japan and Russia are excluded from the currently stalled Four-Party Peace Talks. China and Russia are excluded from the Trilateral Coordination and Oversight Group (TCOG) and the Korean Peninsula Energy Development Organization (KEDO). Japan and the United States are not participating member states of the Tumen River Area Development Programme (TRADP). The United States and Russia are not involved in the Tripartite Environment Ministers' Meeting (TEMM) and the ASEAN Plus Three Group. The track record of these minilateral institutions in meeting the crucial challenge of achieving Northeast Asian geopolitical and geoeconomic integration is hardly encouraging for the future of multilateral cooperation in Northeast Asia.

Of the eight minilateral institutions, the TRADP is perhaps best for testing neoliberal institutionalism in the Northeast Asian setting. Nearly a decade old, the TRADP, in which China, North and South Korea, Russia, and Mongolia have all been involved, seems tailor-made for exploring the possibilities and limitations of a multilateral Northeast Asian economic regime. The TRADP presents a unique case of regime formation involving multiple sets of actors—provincial, national, and international—all engaged in bargaining over the nature, scope, and direction of Northeast Asian economic development. As originally conceived, the TRADP was an ambitious project to turn the sleepy backwaters of Rajin in North Korea, Hunchun in China, and Posyet in Russia's Far East into a Northeast Asian Hong Kong, with estimated costs of thirty billion dollars over a fifteen- to twenty-year period. The six participating member states—the earlier five plus Japan—were meant to complement one another. Japan and South Korea would provide investment capital, modern technologies, and management and marketing skills; North Korea and the PRC would provide cheap labor; and China and Russia would supply the coal, timber, minerals, and other raw materials. China needed a port outlet to the Sea of Japan. Russia wanted to integrate the political economy of its Far Eastern region into the dynamics of the Northeast Asian economy. Mongolia, as a landlocked country, obviously wanted access to an international port. North Korea apparently wanted to turn the Tumen River into a Chinese-style special economic zone (SEZ), and South Korea finally saw another gateway to North Korea.

By the end of 2000, the original grandiose multilateral infrastructure project had not collapsed so much as downsized into smaller bilateral or trilateral projects. As shown in table 1.6, cumulative foreign direct investment (FDI) for 1991 through 2000 was only $1.6 billion, less than one-eighteenth of the $30 billion originally envisioned, with a highly skewed distribution: $519 million for China (Yanbian Korean Autonomous Prefecture); $576 million for Russia (Primorsky Territory); $392 million for Mongolia (Eastern), and $88 million for North Korea (Rajin-Sonbong Economic and Trade Zone).[29]

Table 1.6. The Tumen River Area Development Programme (TRADP) Characteristics and Indicators, 2000

	Yanbian Korean Autonomous Prefecture China	*Rajin-Sonbong Economic and Trade Zone DPRK*	*Eastern Mongolia*	*Prmorsky Territory Russian Federation*
Area	42,700 km^2	746 km^2	287,600 km^2	165,900 km^2
Population	2,185,000	150,000	223,000	2,200,000
Major City (Population)	Yanji (340,000)	Rajin (67,000)	Choibalsan (46,000)	Vladivostok (650,000)
International Arrivals	57,000	81,175	7,600	120,000
Main Industries	Light industry; forest products; tourism; agriculture; food processing; pharmaceuticals	Light industry; aquaculture; wood and seafood processing; tourism; transport services	Mining; agriculture; agro-processing; tourism	Aquaculture; food processing; forest products; engineering; mining; tourism
Labor costs	$60	$80	$60	$70–100
GDP per capita	$619	$491	$417	$1,398
GDP growth	4.4%	N/A	-4.6%	3.5%
Cumulative foreign direct investment (FDI) (1991 through 2000)	$519 million	$88 million	$392 million	$576 million

Source: Adapted from TRADP at www.tumenprogramme.org

What went wrong? The feasibility of the TRADP as originally conceived was closely keyed to the economic and political context of the Soviet Union, Mongolia, and North Korea in the late 1980s and the assumed willingness of Japan and South Korea to provide the lion's share of the capital needed to launch the project. With the collapse of the Soviet economy, and consequently North Korea's, the initial conditions and context dramatically changed. Japan's interest in the Tumen project had been limited; from the outset, Tokyo refused to become a participating member state. Beijing's somewhat unusual activism suggests that China stood to gain the most from the project. China saw the project's potential to expand subregional economic cooperation between the two Koreas and provide access to the Sea of Japan.

The TRADP, which involved both central and local decision makers from its five participating states plus the United Nations Development Programme (UNDP), shows that international cooperation becomes more difficult as the number of actors increases, while historical, civilizational, and national-identity fault lines remain intact. This is because international cooperation requires both recognition of opportunities for the advancement of mutual interests and policy coordination once such opportunities have been identified and recognized. As the number of actors with conflicting identities and interests increases, however, the likelihood of defection also increases, while the feasibility of sanctioning defectors diminishes. Likewise, transaction costs rise with the multiplicity and complexity of each player's payoff structure and mutual interests, thus militating against any easy identification and realization of common interests.[30]

Constructivism and Identity Politics

Mainstream structural realists and the vast majority of neoliberals and rational choice theorists have slighted the impact of ideational variables (i.e., norms, culture, and identity) in international relations. They have assumed that state identities and interests are either permanently fixed or merely derivative of their perennial struggle for power and plenty. The end of the Cold War and the collapse of the Soviet Union opened up considerable space for cultural and sociological perspectives in international relations scholarship; it is no coincidence that almost all major studies of national identity have been published in the post–Cold War era.[31] This is further testimony to the empirical anomalies in state behavior and in the dominant structural realist paradigm.

Constructivists shift their primary attention away from power and security to show not only that ideational variables are important but also why and how identity politics matter in post–Cold War global politics. Unlike primordialists, social constructivists argue that national identity is formed and changed through repeated interactions with significant international reference groups.

The identity of a state (national identity) more than anything else provides a cognitive framework for shaping its interests, preferences, worldviews, and consequent foreign-policy actions; understanding of this identity will therefore contribute to more accurate accounts of state behavior. A state actor in the international system understands other states based on the identity it ascribes to them and often responds accordingly. International structures are shaped and reshaped by what state actors actually do in the course of enacting their identities. Hence, the distribution of identities of relevant states, rather than the international power structure (structural realism) or international regimes (neoliberal institutionalism), would better explain and predict whether international cooperation is possible. Collective memory of the past is central to the constructivist thesis.[32]

The shifting roles of the major powers in Korean affairs have much to do with the difficulties of adjusting national identities in a new post–Cold War era. At no time has the challenge of redefining national identity seemed more urgent and open-ended than it did in the 1990s, particularly in Russia, China, and North Korea. With the Cold-War overlay of stark bipolarity lifted, East and Northeast Asia reemerged as the sites of civilizational divides—between Russia and China and between Russia and Japan—and of historical and national identity animus—between North and South Korea, China and Taiwan, China and Vietnam, Korea and Japan, China and Japan, Russia and Japan, and so on. Unlike in post–World War II Europe, history has always cast a long shadow in Northeast Asian international relations, often serving as a major source of fodder for national-identity animus.

Although China, Russia, and Japan, as the three Northeast Asian powers, share common interests in maintaining the peace and stability of the region, a high degree of distrust born of historical and contemporary concerns stands in the way of restructuring this trilateral relationship on a stable footing. With the end of the shared Soviet threat, longstanding differences regarding questions of past aggression, territorial and commercial disputes, human rights, and competing foreign policy goals have often been exposed and exacerbated by the rise of unstable domestic politics in Moscow, Tokyo, and Beijing. Indeed, there is little that binds the Chinese, Japanese, and Russian states and societies together, but much that divides them.[33] "Of China, Russia, and Japan's six images of each other," according to one major recent study, "not one could properly be called positive."[34]

A major multinational citizens' opinion survey, jointly sponsored by two leading newspapers in South Korea and Japan—*Tong-a Ilbo* (Seoul) and *Asahi Shimbun* (Tokyo)—was conducted in October and November 2000 in the full glow of the inter-Korean summit. This survey, involving national samples of 2,000 people in South Korea, 3,000 in Japan, 1,024 in the United

States, and 1,000 in China, shows with disturbing clarity why Northeast Asia has little if any social and psychological foundation to forge truly cooperative multilateral institutions (see tables 1.7–1.9).

As shown in table 1.7, of the six Northeast Asian countries and peoples involved in the survey—the United States, Russia, China, Japan, South Korea, and North Korea—none elicited a majority positive ("like") perception. The United States received the highest positive perception on average from South Koreans (30.7%), Japanese (29.4%), and Chinese (33.0%) and North Korea the lowest positive perception (1.9 percent), again from Japanese respondents. North Korea elicited the highest negative ("dislike") perception (56.7 percent from Japanese respondents), followed by Japan, which was perceived negatively by 43.2 percent of Chinese respondents and by 42.2 percent of South Korean respondents.

Two caveats need mentioning. First, thanks in part to the afterglow of the inter-Korean summit that took place a few months earlier, the psychological distance between South Koreans and Japanese had been narrowed by about 23 percent compared to three years earlier, when 65 percent of South Koreans answered that they "dislike" Japan. Second, this joint survey was conducted in October 2000, more than a half-year before the sudden deterioration of Japan–Republic of Korea (ROK) relations and the eruption of one of the most vitriolic anti-Japanese demonstrations in South Korea in recent years. If a similar public opinion survey had been conducted in mid-2001, the negative perception among South Koreans toward Japan might easily have exceeded the 65 percent response of 1997. Another interesting finding is that the United States, as a nonresidential superpower and a de facto neighbor, scores better than any Northeast Asian country in a positive if not impressive perception response in South Korea (30.7 percent), Japan (29.4 percent), and China (33 percent).

People's threat perceptions, in answer to the question "By which country do you feel most militarily threatened?," show a sharp bifurcation (see table 1.8). While North Korea elicits a high threat perception from South Koreans (53.7 percent) and Japanese (44.2 percent), the United States receives the highest in threat perception, from 62.8 percent of Chinese respondents. When the question is rephrased and focused on North Korea—"Do you feel threatened by North Korea?"—North Korea wins the threat sweepstakes by huge majorities: 86.8 percent in South Korea, 71.5 percent in Japan, and 94 percent in the United States say they feel threatened by North Korea, (if we combine the "strongly" and "to a certain extent" categories of responses), probably much to the delight of Pyongyang, given its coercive leverage diplomacy and the fact that threat has become a fungible asset in Pyongyang's foreign relations.

It is in the question of national influence perception that we begin to see the popularity of the ascendant-China perspective. As shown in table 1.9,

Table 1.7. Multinational Citizens' Perceptions of Other Northeast Asian Countries, late 2000

		ROK	*Japan*	*U.S.*	*China*
Q-1: (ROK, Japan, China) Do you like or dislike, or neither like nor dislike, the **United States?**	1. Like	30.7	29.4		33.0
	2. Dislike	18.7	7.6		31.0
	3. Neither like nor dislike	50.6	60.9		33.4
	4. Do not know/No response	–	2.1		2.6
Q-2: Then, do you like or dislike, or neither like nor dislike, **Russia?**	1. Like	11.0	3.7	17.2	38.3
	2. Dislike	26.4	40.4	21.4	15.4
	3. Neither like nor dislike	62.6	52.8	58.4	42.4
	4. Do not know/No response	–	3.1	3.0	3.9
Q-3: (ROK, Japan, U.S.) Then, do you like or dislike, or neither like nor dislike, **China?**	1. Like	22.6	17.1	12.6	
	2. Dislike	20.6	20.1	39.6	
	3. Neither like nor dislike	56.8	59.4	45.5	
	4. Do not know/No response	–	3.4	2.3	
Q-4: (ROK, U.S., China) Then, do you like or dislike, or neither like nor dislike, **Japan?**	1. Like	17.1		47.0	18.8
	2. Dislike	42.2		10.6	43.2
	3. Neither like nor dislike	40.7		40.3	33.6
	4. Do not know/No response	–		2.1	4.4
Q-5: (Japan, U.S., China) Then, do you like or dislike, or neither like nor dislike, **South Korea?**	1. Like		20.4	22.7	34.5
	2. Dislike		16.8	14.5	15.8
	3. Neither like nor dislike		60.0	59.7	44.8
	4. Do not know/No response		2.8	3.1	4.9
Q-6: Then, do you like or dislike, or neither like nor dislike, **North Korea?**	1. Like	29.5	1.9	7.1	37.4
	2. Dislike	21.9	56.7	32.7	16.7
	3. Neither like nor dislike	48.6	36.9	57.2	41.2
	4. Do not know/No response	–	4.5	3.0	4.7

Source: "Multinational Citizens' Poll on Current States Surrounding Korean Peninsula," *Tong-a Ilbo* (Seoul), December 4, 2000.
Note: South Korea: N=2000, survey conducted 10/25–11/18/2000. Japan: N=3000, 11/19–11/20/2000. U.S.: N=1024, 11/13–11/18/2000. China: N=1000, 11/1–11/10/2000.

Table 1.8. Multinational Citizens' Perceptions of Threat in Northeast Asia, late 2000

		ROK	*Japan*	*U.S.*	*China*
Q-1: By which country do you feel most militarily threatened? Please select one country	1. U.S.	12.4	13.2	–	62.8
	2. Russia	4.0	9.5	20.9	1.2
	3. China	7.7	9.4	38.1	–
	4. Japan	20.7	–	2.5	12.4
	5. ROK	–	1.1	0.1	0.4
	6. North Korea	53.7	44.2	6.0	0.2
	7. Do not know/No response	0.3	8.0	10.0	13.7
Q-2: Do you think the U.S.-Japan security agreement is helpful or is not helpful in maintaining peace and security in the Asia-Pacific region	1. Helpful	54.5	66.4	53.6	4.1
	2. Not helpful	43.5	15.0	19.8	54.8
	3. Neither way	–	–	–	–
	4. Do not know/No response	2.0	18.6	26.6	41.1
Q-3: (ROK, Japan, U.S.) Do you feel threatened by North Korea? How strongly do you feel threatened?	1. Strongly	11.1	11.7	38.2	
	2. To a certain extent	75.7	59.8	55.8	
	3. Not threatened				
	4. Do not know/No	13.2	22.0	6.0	
	response	–	6.5	–	

Source: "Multinational Citizens' Poll on Current States Surrounding Korean Pennsula," *Tong-a Ilbo* (Seoul), December 4, 2000.
Note: South Korea: N=2000, survey conducted 10/25–11/18/2000. Japan: N=3000, 11/19–11/20/2000, U.S.: N=1024, 11/13–11/18/2000. China: N=1000, 11/1–11/10/1000.

Table 1.9. Multinational Citizens' Perceptions of the Most Influential Power in Asia, late 2000

		ROK	*Japan*	*U.S.*	*China*
Q-1: Which country do you think will become the most influential in Asia in ten years? Please select one country, whether it is an Asian country or not.	1. U.S.	8.1	13.7	54.9	9.6
	2. Russia	2.1	1.1	4.7	1.4
	3. China	52.6	47.2	18.9	73.2
	4. Japan	23.3	8.4	3.8	7.7
	5. ROK	10.7	4.3	0.9	1.1
	6. North Korea	1.0	2.3	2.1	0.1
	7. India	0.1	0.9	1.8	0.4
	8. Vietnam	–	0.3	1.3	–
	9. Other	1.2	0.6	2.0	1.9
	10. None	0.1	7.3	–	–
	11. Do not know/No response	0.8	13.9	9.6	4.6
Q-2: (ROK, Japan, China) In the global economy, do you think the importance of Asia will grow in the future, remain the same, or diminish?	1. Grow	65.3	57.6		75.5
	2. Remain the same	29.3	26.8		18.3
	3. Diminish	5.4	4.1		4.4
	4. Do not know/No response	–	11.5		1.8

Source: "Multinational Citizens' Poll on Current States Surrounding Korean Pennsula," *Tong-a Ilbo* (Seoul), December 4, 2000.
Note: South Korea: N=2000, survey conducted 10/25–11/18/2000. Japan: N=3000, 11/19–11/20/2000, U.S.: N=1024, 11/13–11/18/2000. China: N=1000, 11/1–11/10/1000.

China is expected to be the most influential country in Asia by 2010 by 52.6 percent of South Koreans, 47.2 percent of Japanese, and 73.2 percent of Chinese, but only 18.9 percent of Americans. In contrast, Russia was chosen by a paltry 1.1 percent of Japanese, 1.4 percent of Chinese, 2.1 percent of South Koreans, and 4.7 percent of Americans, and Japan by a surprising 8.4 percent of Japanese, 3.8 percent of Americans, 7.7 percent of Chinese, and 23.3 percent of South Koreans.

There seems as yet no social and psychological foundation for establishing a more comprehensive and stable security architecture in the Northeast Asian region, owing to the absence of common or shared identities, rules, norms, and governing procedures around which state actors' expectations could converge. This is not to say that public opinion is the key determinant of state policy in the region. One of the most important findings to emerge from a collaborative project on learning in Soviet and American foreign policy is that a change in beliefs and perceptions does not necessarily result in a change of foreign policy; rather, policy change often takes place in the absence of a prior change in beliefs and perceptions, when political leaders pragmatically redefine their national interest with little or no reassessment of basic beliefs and goals.[35]

Globalization Challenges

What does it mean for Northeast Asian countries and peoples to feel secure in an era of globalization? In the 1990s, both the agency and the sources of threat have become more complex and diverse than ever before. The scope, intensity, speed, sheer number, modality, and impact of human relations and transactions have radically increased regionally and globally, eroding the boundaries between hitherto separate economic, political, and sociocultural entities throughout the world. As a consequence, the traditional boundaries delimiting international and domestic threats have been substantially blurred, if not completely erased. The forces of globalization of the 1990s have transformed both the context and the conditions under which Northeast Asian regional geopolitics can be played out. Northeast Asian states now must worry not only about their military power but also about the economic power, cultural power, and knowledge power needed to survive and prosper in a world that is becoming increasingly globalized and competitive.[36]

Contemporary globalization is said to be accelerating both the rise and fall of the effective state and the frequent changes in the status ranking of the state within the world system, as the state waxes and wanes in its power to attract the identification of its citizenry. Viewed in this light, the main challenges of post-international relations are associated with the destabilizing dynamics of the weak states, not the rising powers. The emergent threat emanates from the breakdown of the domestic public order of weak or incoherent states. Contrary to the theses of "hyperglobalization" and "globaloney," the state is not obsolete, let alone disappearing, but neither is it as robust as it once was. Instead, globalization functions as a double-edged sword, promising opportunities while also posing dangers, thereby undermining the certainties associated with the state-centric, self-help realpolitik. The requirements for a competent and effective state are constantly being redefined in this rapidly globalizing world. Thus, the greatest challenge confronting the world community, including the United States, is not so much how to cope with the rise of China as how to manage the weaknesses of China: its growing internal security, legitimation, social, environmental, and ethnonational deficits.

For years, "Asian values" have been touted as the reigning force behind the East Asian miracle. But the Asian financial crisis of 1997 and 1998 has not only put to rest claims that the frenzy about globalization amounted to nothing more than "globaloney," but has also punctured cultural-relativist claims about "Asian values" or any single Asian developmental model. The fact that some East Asian countries were severely hit while others escaped the crisis relatively unscathed, and their differing prospects and pace of recovery are better explained by country-specific circumstances and the pressures of globalization than by Asian values or an Asian "situational uniqueness." Not every East Asian country contracted the Asian financial flu, nor has every infected, crisis-ridden country rebounded with the same speed.

Despite globalization, or perhaps even because of it, all politics are local. Differences in internal constructions and resulting domestic politics have a substantial impact on how states define threats and vulnerabilities, and therefore on the whole reconceptualization of the security problematique.[37] With the recent changes of political leadership in 2000 and 2001—the more realpolitik Putin in Moscow, the more unilateral Bush administration in Washington, and the more nationalistic governments in Tokyo and Beijing—the foreign policies of Northeast Asian states and the United States have become increasingly symptomatic of highly charged, nationalistic domestic politics. By any reckoning, all the countries involved in the management of the emerging engagement process on the divided Korean peninsula are experiencing, albeit to varying degrees, corresponding disorientation and readjustment of their Korean policies and international roles.

THE NORTHEAST ASIAN POWERS AND NORTH KOREA

The remarkable DPRK–European Union (EU) normalization process of 2000 and 2001 only spotlights the extent of Pyongyang's diplomatic isolation. Unlike the first half of the 1970s—*la belle époque* of Pyongyang's Third World diplomacy—North Korean foreign policy in the post–Cold War era has been confined largely to its neighboring powers: China, Russia, Japan, the United States, and South Korea. China, Japan, and South Korea alone easily account for about three-fourths of Pyongyang's foreign trade. There is little doubt that the Big Four, especially the United States, loom ever larger in Pyongyang's foreign policy, as is shown in chapters 2 through 5.

The Pyongyang summit of June 2000, the first of its kind in the half-century history of the divided peninsula, has generated opportunities and risks for both Koreas and the Big Four. The opportunity for greater inter-Korean cooperation lies in the demise of great-power rivalry and the corresponding opening of more autonomous space for both Koreas. The Pyongyang summit was remarkable because it was initiated and executed by Koreans themselves with no external shock or great-power sponsorship. The previous inter-Korean accords had been responses to major structural changes external to the Korean peninsula. The South-North Joint Communiqué of July 4, 1972, was a product of the panicked reaction of both Koreas to the "Nixon-in-China" shock. The Basic Agreement—officially the Agreement on Reconciliation, Nonaggression, Exchanges, and Cooperation, which took effect on February 19, 1992—was Pyongyang's grudging response to Seoul's *Nordpolitik*. It followed a rapid succession of external shocks in 1990 and 1991: Moscow-Seoul normalization, German reunification, and the collapse of the Soviet Union. Even the scheduled inter-Korean summit that had to be aborted because of the sudden death of Kim Il Sung in July 1994 was a stepchild of Jimmy Carter's personal diplomacy. In the latter half of 2000, the notion that the Pyongyang summit had improved prospects for thawing the remains of the Cold War on the Korean peninsula seemed to have intensified the needs and efforts of the Big Four to readjust their Korean policies to the rapidly changing realities on the ground.

That said, however, the Big Four inevitably compete, clash, and coalesce with each other in various issue areas as they pursue their national interests and ideals in Northeast Asia and the Korean peninsula. North Korea per se is seldom all that important to any of the Big Four. Its importance is closely keyed to and shaped by the overall foreign policy goals of each of the Big Four and how North Korea is seen as part of the problem or part of the solution for the shape of international life to come in Northeast Asia.

The United States and North Korea

By any reckoning, the United States remains the most powerful external power in inter-Korean affairs. In the post–Cold War era, the United States has come to play the rather unusual role of the "honest broker" in the resolution of the Korean conflict, without first dismantling its Cold War U.S.-ROK alliance system, addressing U.S. troop presence in South Korea, or normalizing its relations with North Korea. Indeed, one of the most striking features of the great-power politics on the Korean peninsula is that none of the three neighboring powers has a military presence on the peninsula. Only the United States, the lone superpower, maintains some 37,000 troops on South Korean soil. With the Pacific Ocean becoming an "American lake,"[38] the United States is widely perceived and acted upon as a de facto "neighboring" power in Korean affairs.

Writing in early 1999 for *Foreign Affairs*, perhaps the most influential foreign policy magazine for policy makers in Washington and elsewhere, Harvard political scientist Samuel Huntington offered a trenchant cultural realist critique of America's creeping unilateralism: "On issue after issue, the United States has found itself increasingly alone, with one or a few partners, opposing most of the rest of the world's states and peoples. . . . On these and other issues, much of the international community is on one side and the United States is on the other."[39] In its first six months, the Bush administration seems to have accomplished a diplomatic mission impossible by turning creeping unilateralism into rampant unilateralism, trashing multilateral treaties or treaties-in-the-making one after another (the anti-ballistic missile [ABM] treaty, the Biological Weapons Convention, the Comprehensive Test Ban Treaty, the Kyoto Protocol, the International Criminal Court [ICC], a draft treaty on international small arms sales, and the like). As a consequence, U.S. relations with both allies and adversaries, including the ROK and the DPRK, seemed to be in worse shape in mid-2001, at least until the terrorist attack on America of September 11, 2001, than ever before in the post–Cold War era.

With the demise of the Soviet Union and diminishing Chinese aid to North Korea, the United States has become *faute de mieux* the functional equivalent of China and the Soviet Union combined, in Pyongyang's strategic thinking and behavior. During the Cold War, Pyongyang demonstrated a remarkable unilateral zigzag balancing strategy in its relations with Beijing and Moscow, always attempting to extract maximum payoffs in economic, technical, and military aid, and taking sides if necessary on particular issues, but never completely casting its lot with one against the other.

This Cold-War habit dies hard. In the post–Cold War era, as Robert A. Manning argues in chapter 2, the United States has become "the focal point of Pyongyang's efforts at regime survival, the key to enhancing international legitimacy, obtaining economic aid, investment and increased trade, as well as tactical benefits in its relations with South Korea." Such a shift in tactics was endorsed by Kim Il Sung himself as early as 1990 or 1991. Yet its successful execution has encountered a host of problems all stemming from the different priorities and incentive structures that drive each party's respective policies toward the other.

For Washington, the central concern has remained the same: how to deal with Pyongyang's asymmetrical threats in an alliance-friendly and cost-effective way. The North Korea policy of the United States, as the lone superpower in the post–Cold War era, is shaped by global concerns (such as maintaining the integrity of the Non-Proliferation Treaty regime), but also by East Asian regional and U.S.-ROK bilateral concerns and by fractious partisan politics at home.

Since the mid-1990s, North Korea's growing weakness and instability, combined with the dangerous asymmetry of power on the Korean peninsula, has paradoxically set in motion an agonizing reappraisal of American policy on North Korea. It has become increasingly clear that America's deterrence policy alone is no longer sufficient for coping with the clear and continuing danger of a North Korean "hard landing" (i.e., a reunification-via-collapse leading to an absorption of North Korea by South Korea). America's North Korea policy shifted in the late 1990s from deterrence to "deterrence-plus." The logic of the deterrence-plus policy, associated with the Perry process, is to neither prop up the North Korean system nor seek its collapse, but to promote a process of dialogue and confidence-building relations that move beyond deterrence. With the deterrence-plus policy has come a shift from a reactive to a more active role in the management of inter-Korean affairs. And yet it has not been easy to pursue the deterrence-plus policy because of a mismatch between desirability and feasibility in two scenarios: the hard landing scenario is the least desirable but most likely outcome, while the "soft landing" is the most desirable but least likely outcome.

At the same time, Pyongyang's normalization efforts are best seen as part of a Cold-War habit of manipulating major powers to gain maximum security and economic benefits. It is becoming increasingly clear that Kim Jong Il's agreement to hold the historic inter-Korean summit in June 2000 was a major concession not so much to Seoul as to Washington. Pyongyang was exploiting the new connection with Seoul to speed up normalization talks with the United States and to gain access to bilateral and multilateral aid and foreign direct investment.[40] Indeed, the second half of 2000 witnessed a flurry of Pyongyang-Washington interactions, including two quasi summit meetings—one between President Clinton and Vice Marshal Jo Myong-Rok in Washington and another between Secretary of State Madeleine Albright and Chairman Kim Jong Il in Pyongyang. Despite significant progress toward a U.S.-DPRK missile accord, at the end of the year Pyongyang stopped short of diplomatic success, due partly to on-site verification issues and partly to rapidly changing U.S. political circumstances beyond its control.

Pyongyang has tellingly held Washington's new hard-line administration hostage to the resumption of inter-Korean dialogue. This America-centric effort not only breaches the letter and the spirit of the North-South Joint Declaration (Article 1), but also contradicts North Korea's own longstanding party line that Korean affairs should be handled without foreign intervention or interference. DPRK-U.S. relations are once again at a crossroads. Does Washington still figure prominently in Pyongyang's calculations to place the world's lone superpower in the economic and security role previously played by the Soviet Union and China during the Cold War? Or has there been a subtle but significant reorientation in Pyongyang's great-power strategy, as showcased in the rejuvenation of Sino-DPRK and Russia-DPRK relations since 1999? Is Pyongyang playing multiple cards—the China card, the Russia card, and the U.S. card—in the multiple games of Northeast Asian international relations? Or does the United States still remain, as Manning aptly puts it, "a strategic life raft" and "a mortal threat," calling for an ever larger array of threats (asymmetrical military capabilities) as bargaining chips, and for existential deterrence? One thing remains clear: the greatest challenge facing Pyongyang's survival strategy in the post–Cold War world is how and whether to play the America card.

Japan and North Korea

Of the Big Four involved in Korean affairs, Japan has made the least progress in normalizing its relations with North Korea in the post–Cold War era. As earlier noted and as shown in table 1.7, North Korea commands the dubious distinction, among Japanese respondents, of eliciting the lowest positive ("like") perception (1.9 percent) and the highest negative ("dislike") perception (56.7 percent). Also, as shown in table 1.8, 71.5 percent of Japanese respondents said they feel threatened by North Korea.

North Korea is one of the major external factors in the rise of Japan's assertive rising-sun nationalism in recent years. In a move that spoke of strong nationalist sentiment among Japan's politicians, in August 1999 the upper house of the Diet voted resoundingly (166 to 71) to officially designate the rising-sun flag and longtime unofficial anthem as legal symbols of the nation.[41] Of course, such right-wing nationalism in Japan can only rattle its regional rivals, including Pyongyang. In Northeast Asia, Prime Minister Junichiro Koizumi is widely perceived as a right-wing nationalist; his popularity among younger politicians and citizens does not augur well for the future of cooperative Northeast Asian international relations in general, nor for DPRK-Japan normalization talks in particular.

Viewed in this light, North Korea's test firing of the Taepodong-I missile over Japan on August 31, 1998, was at once a surprise, a crisis, and perhaps even a blessing for Japan's born-again rising-sun nationalism. Indeed, no single event is said to have impacted and reshaped Japanese public opinion as much as that missile launch. The widely expected test launch of a new long-range missile, Taepodong-II in late August 1999 is also said to have supplied the necessary justification for the passage of the rising-sun flag and anthem legislation.

For Japanese security planners, the intermediate-range Rodong missiles are far more threatening than the long-range Taepodong missiles. While the Taepodong missile program is still in the development and testing stage and is still subject to the 1999 Berlin Agreement and self-imposed moratorium, North Korea has successfully tested and deployed Rodong missiles in substantial numbers at various sites inland and along the northern borders. With an estimated range of 1,000 to 1,300 kilometers, more than half of Japan is within range of the Rodong. The mere possibility that North Korea might develop the capability to load its weapons of mass destruction (WMD)—chemical, biological, and nuclear—on its intermediate-range ballistic missiles makes the Rodong a greater threat than the Taepodong. Moreover, the Rodong is among the DPRK's most developed asymmetrical military capabilities, a credible weapon of terror against large cities in western Japan and a trump card for system maintenance and survival. North Korea is not likely to give it up. So far the United States has concentrated its attention on the issue of the longer-range Taepodong missile, but the strategic threat posed against Japan by the Rodong missiles, not to mention recent Chinese missile advances, remains real.[42] As detailed by Myonwoo Lee in chapter 3, after a hiatus of seven years, Japan-DPRK normalization talks started gaining momentum only in the wake of the 1999 Berlin Agreement and the easing of U.S. sanctions. Japan's officially chosen course regarding North Korea was

> to make efforts to redress abnormal post-war relations with North Korea in close coordination with the United States and the ROK, in a manner that can contribute to the peace and stability of the Northeast Asian region; and to strike a balance between dialogue and deterrence in the execution of these policies.[43]

However, this official policy pronouncement glosses over two nagging issues: the colonial past and the alleged abductions of eleven Japanese nationals by North Korean security agents in the 1970s and 1980s.

At first glance, the abduction issue seems easier to settle than the colonial past. In actuality, it is the more intractable problem, as it excites national identity politics in both countries in a zero-sum, winner-take-all manner. At the tenth round of normalization talks in Tokyo, for example, Japan's chief delegate, Takano Kojiro, underscored the importance of finding a satisfactory solution for the abduction issue by explaining its links to Japan's domestic politics.

Any normalization treaty that might come of the talks, he argued, must receive the approval of the Diet; such approval would not be forthcoming without public support, which in turn would hinge upon whether the abduction issue had been resolved. With a surge of new publicity, the abduction issue has become a hot topic in Japanese domestic politics. A citizens' group that has long campaigned for the disappeared persons has stepped up a petition drive that had already collected 1.3 million signatures for stronger government action. The Japanese government is caught in a dilemma as it tries to keep pace with Seoul and Washington in dealing with Pyongyang, while at the same time encountering mounting public outcry at home for being too soft on North Korea.

For Pyongyang to yield on the abduction issue is to admit it is a terrorist state, which would be a self-delegitimating act of a high order. A quick fix for this problem outside the global media spotlight no longer seems possible. On the eve of the tenth round of normalization talks in mid-2000, Pyongyang went ballistic, savaging Tokyo for calling it "North Korea" instead of using the official name, "Democratic People's Republic of Korea," which is claimed to be "the sacred name of the sovereign country recognized by the world,"[44] underscoring the continuation of the Japan-DPRK legitimation war.

On the question of settling the past, there have been a few developments of a potentially positive nature. At the tenth round of normalization talks in mid-2000, Japan is reported to have advanced for the first time a proposal to apply the same formula it had used in normalizing relations with South Korea in 1965—that is, "economic cooperation" aid consisting of a grant of $300 million and a loan of $200 million in lieu of "compensation." North Korea also made a concession of sorts by no longer insisting on "reparations" from Japan, settling instead for "compensation." It was against this seemingly hopeful backdrop and in advance of the eleventh round of normalization talks in Beijing that the Japanese government announced in October 2000 its decision to donate five hundred thousand tons of rice to North Korea via the World Food Program (WFP), a five-fold increase over past contributions.

Nonetheless, the eleventh round of normalization talks in Beijing in October 2000 lasted only two days, without any agreement on the next round of talks. What is most notable about the eleventh round is that Japanese negotiators put forth a proposal for a nine billion dollar "economic aid" package (60 percent in grant aid and 40 percent in loans) as quid pro quo for North Korea's moderation of the missile threat and satisfactory resolution of the abduction issue. Contrary to Japanese expectations, Pyongyang responded that such attempts to short-circuit an admission of repentance and compensation for the colonial past were unacceptable. The eleventh round of normalization talks thus collapsed, with each side saying, in effect, that the ball was in the other's court.

Apart from the continued asymmetry between the demands of the two sides, Pyongyang was apparently counting on the fully established Washington connection, which would inevitably force Tokyo to accommodate North Korea's "just demands" for a Japanese apology for past wrongs as well as both economic aid and compensation for the colonial period. Pyongyang was banking on the "Clinton-in-Pyongyang" shock to bring Tokyo back into negotiations. On the other hand, as Myonwoo Lee argues in chapter 3, Tokyo is increasingly pressured by domestic politics, and public opinion is opposed to rushing to normalization, especially when it is viewed as cost-ineffective.

For the near future, Japanese policymakers seem to have quietly concluded that their wisest course is to maintain the status quo as long as possible. For Japan, Korean reunification poses a dilemma. While a strong, united, and nationalistic Korea could pose a formidable challenge or even threat to Japan, the continuation of a divided Korea with an unpredictable state in the North is no less threatening to Japan's security.[45] The challenge, therefore, is to navigate between the Scylla of a unified Korea, with all its uncertainties, potential instability, and new challenges, and the Charybdis of a divided Korea, with the continuing danger of implosion or explosion in the North.

China and North Korea

China has managed to maintain a relatively stable two-Koreas policy more so than any of the other neighboring powers during the post–Cold War era. The most notable accomplishment has been a reconfirmation of Sino-DPRK geopolitical ties since 1999. In the wake of the North Atlantic Treaty Organization (NATO) air war against Yugoslavia, the NATO/U.S. bombing of the Chinese embassy in Belgrade, and the rapid deterioration of Sino-American relations in 1999, China made a subtle readjustment to its Korea policy at a time when Pyongyang was launching a diplomatic outreach in unprecedented fashion. As a result, Beijing's displeasure with its unruly socialist ally in the strategic buffer zone was largely put aside as the Chinese leadership began to see the United States as the greater challenge to its strategic interests in the region.

Against this backdrop, Beijing's relations with North Korea began to be renormalized beginning in the spring of 1999 through the exchange of high-powered delegations. Beijing seems to have taken the initiative in jumpstarting the process of renormalization with Chinese Foreign Minister Tang Jiaxuan's five-day visit to Pyongyang in April 1999. Two months later, in early June 1999, a fifty-member North Korean delegation led by Supreme People's Assembly (SPA) President Kim Yong Nam made a high-profile state visit to China. For Pyongyang, the visit was a success not only as a turning point in the Sino–North Korean strategic partnership, but also for obtaining China's promise of an additional one hundred fifty thousand tons of grain and four hundred thousand tons of coal.[46] In October of the same year, on the occasion of the fiftieth anniversary of the establishment of diplomatic relations, Chinese Foreign Minister Tang Jiaxuan traveled to Pyongyang to discuss ways of expanding bilateral ties.

Kim Jong Il's choice of Beijing for his first-ever unofficial state visit, May 29 through 31, 2000, spotlights China's place in Pyongyang's diplomatic outreach. Unlike Kim Yong Nam's state visit a year earlier, Kim Jong Il's China trip led Pyongyang to praise the emergent Sino-DPRK renormalization process. By achieving a "consensus of views on all the matters discussed," we are told, the Beijing summit advanced the cause of socialism and further consolidated the DPRK-China friendship—a relationship sealed in the blood of the Korean War—at a time when the international situation was becoming increasingly complicated.[47] For the first time in the post–Cold War era, *Rodong Sinmun*, the official organ of the Korean Workers' Party (KWP), declared that the two leaders had expressed their solidarity and support for each other's unification policy and construction of socialism during the Kim-Jiang summit in Beijing. It claimed also that there have been significant achievements in China's socialist modernization, and that these achievements were possible only under the leadership of the Chinese Communist Party.[48]

More than any other major power, China has the most to gain, at least in the short run, from the inter-Korean rapprochement process that the June 2000 Pyongyang summit has reflected and effected. As Kim Jong Il's visit to Beijing a couple of weeks before the summit underscores, Beijing was back in the center of peninsular affairs as facilitator and cheerleader, if not honest broker. Yet the rapid pace of post-summit events and developments revealed Beijing's geopolitical crisis (*weiji*) in the Chinese usage of the term, indicating not only danger (*weixian*) but also an opportunity (*jihui*) to be seized. Beijing welcomed the summit as a first, giant step in the inter-Korean peace process while simultaneously worrying about the adverse consequences of too rapid an improvement of U.S.-DPRK relations.

As if determined to showcase its multitasking balancing act, Beijing dispatched two high-powered delegations in October 2000: a military delegation to Pyongyang headed by Defense Minister Chi Haotian to reaffirm Sino-DPRK military ties, and a civilian delegation to Seoul headed by Prime Minister Zhu Rongji to elevate Sino-ROK relations from a "cooperative partnership" to a "full-scale cooperative partnership," pushing the United States and Japan to the sidelines. China's proactive balancing strategy may have contributed to the uncharacteristically hasty move by the Clinton administration to accelerate its normalization talks with the DPRK, stemming from worries about losing control over the rapidly moving Korean target, and also about China's rising role in the region.

Yet Beijing was greatly surprised and even unnerved by the extent to which Secretary of State Madeleine Albright's quasi-summit meeting with Kim Jong Il overshadowed Chi Haotian's presence in the city. Such a reaction is hardly surprising considering the rapid pace of unprecedented diplomatic events, especially the U.S.-DPRK normalization talks. The emerging inter-Korean peace process in the latter half of 2000 immediately put into play several plausible scenarios for reshaping the regional security architecture in Northeast Asia. One possibility was that the United States might take command over the emerging reconciliation process that would redound to the disadvantage of China's influence on peninsular affairs. Indeed, Beijing's role in Korean affairs seemed ever closely keyed to Sino-American relations, watching the development of any U.S.-DPRK warming process with a sharp, realpolitik eye.

In January 2001, Kim Jong Il's second "secret" visit to China (Shanghai and Beijing) in less than eight months was designed as a more extensive personal inspection of "capitalism with Shanghai characteristics." During the widely publicized trip, Kim Jong Il was reported to have visited the Shanghai stock market and economic export zones in and around Shanghai, accompanied by tutoring Premier Zhu Rongji, underscoring the need for "new thinking" that had been emphasized by the North Korean media in preceding weeks. Is this not evidence enough of *juche* (the North Korean ideology of self-reliance) being shanghaied? However, a simple reality check suggests that post–Kim Il Sung North Korea is no post-Mao China, and that the initial conditions of post-Mao China are inapplicable and not readily reproducible in post–Kim Il Sung North Korea (see chapters 4 and 6).

For the first time in eleven years, Chinese President Jiang Zemin made a three-day official visit to Pyongyang, from September 3 to 5, 2001, capping the flurry of renormalizing political and diplomatic exchanges and efforts since mid-1999. Yet there seems to have been far more behind-the-scenes realpolitik maneuvering than met the public eye in the Jiang-Kim summit in Pyongyang. In a sudden policy reversal on September 2, a day before Jiang's official state visit was to begin, North Korea launched a unilateral diplomatic preemptive strike, proposing that the stalled inter-Korean talks be resumed as soon as possible. The message seems loud and clear—that North Korea makes such decisions on an independent footing, not relying on China's sympathy, advice, or pressure. The Jiang-Kim summit is also notable for the absence of a joint communiqué or declaration. This may suggest China's realpolitik refusal to play with North Korea on variations of the anti-American DPRK-Russia Moscow Declaration of August 4, 2001, which capped the

Putin-Kim summit a month earlier (in regard to such issues as the ABM Treaty, the presence of U.S. troops in South Korea, and antihegemonic, multipolar world order).

As can be seen in chapter 4 and chapter 6, China remains North Korea's largest trade partner. Beijing has allowed Pyongyang to run annual bilateral deficits of approximately a half-billion dollars since 1995. China's role in North Korea's trade would be even larger if barter transactions and aid were factored into these figures. If North Korea's trade with China is regarded as politically determined, as Noland argues in chapter 6, it is financing more than half of the North Korean balance of payments deficit. Sino-DPRK trade registered a 32 percent increase in 2000 (to $488 million) and a whopping 80 percent increase in the first half of 2001 ($311 million) after two years' consecutive decreases in 1998 to 1999.

Nonetheless, a highly asymmetrical Beijing-Pyongyang-Seoul triangular trade relationship has emerged. The Sino-DPRK trade of $488 million represented 20 percent of its overall foreign trade (down from 29 percent in 1998), but only about 0.5 percent of China's global trade, 0.15 percent of South Korea's global trade, and 1.6 percent of South Korea's trade with China. More revealing, South Korea's trade with China in 2000 generated a huge trade surplus of $5.7 billion, while North Korea's trade with China generated a trade deficit of $414 million.

Recent developments in Sino–North Korean relations, however, have not been all positive. As it has provided more aid in a wider variety of forms—direct government-to-government aid, subsidized cross-border trade, and private barter transactions—Beijing has become more deeply involved, playing an active role in the politics of regime survival in the North. Although the exact amount and terms of China's aid to North Korea remain unclear, it is generally estimated at one-quarter to one-third of China's overall foreign aid. Paradoxically, Pyongyang's growing dependence on Beijing for its economic and political survival has also bred mutual distrust and resentment. Pyongyang has taken a sleight-of-hand approach by privately asking for more and more aid even as North Korean diplomats habitually deny that they have ever asked for or received any Chinese aid. In every high-level meeting between the two governments, according to one Chinese scholar, the North Korean request for economic aid dominates the agenda.[49] Nonetheless, Beijing provides "humanitarian aid" in order to lessen flows of refugees to China, to delay a possible North Korean collapse, and to enhance China's own leverage in Pyongyang and Seoul. However, as North Koreans rightly perceive that China's aid is given as a result of Beijing's own self-interest, the aid has not increased China's leverage with Pyongyang, to Beijing's growing frustration.

The rapid growth of Sino-Korean interaction at all levels, involving political, economic, educational, religious, and humanitarian (human rights) actors, has also created a variety of emerging challenges for identity politics in the complex triangle of asymmetrical interdependence. There has already emerged a Pyongyang-Beijing-Seoul triangle of human movement and friction involving flows of some one hundred thousand to three hundred thousand refugees from North Korea to northeast China; more than four hundred thousand Chinese middle-class tourists and about 135,000 Chinese-Korean (*chosonjok*) illegal migrant workers from China to South Korea; and almost a million South Korean tourists to China in 2000.

Against this backdrop, the North Korean refugee question, hitherto much ignored but a potential time bomb for both Koreas, has brought into sharp focus how easily and quickly such incidents as two cause célèbre cases in January 2000 and June 2001 can throw China's delicate two-Koreas policy into a tailspin. Even before the eruption of the second North Korean refugee incident, China had already launched its Strike Hard campaign at the end of May 2001. The campaign resulted in a dramatic increase in the number of humanitarian aid workers arrested and fined, and North Korean refugees forcefully repatriated.

Central to Beijing's two-Koreas realpolitik is growing concern about the possibility of Korean reunification by southern absorption. There is far more to Beijing's status quo, antiunification policy than is immediately apparent. While this policy seeks to maximize China's leverage as a balancer in Northeast Asian politics, China also genuinely fears that North Korea could come to feel cornered and see no choice but to fight back. Beijing does not doubt that Pyongyang would fight rather than succumb to German-style hegemonic unification. Even if the system in the North were simply to collapse, the likely result is a bloody civil war rather than immediate absorption by the South. The alternative scenario is no more comforting: fearing both the ideological and strategic consequences of a united Korea, Beijing might intervene to rescue the post–Kim Il Sung system from collapse as a way of maintaining a strategic shield in the northern half of the Korean peninsula, or as a way of arresting a massive exodus of refugees into China's northeastern provinces.

To whatever extent possible, Beijing will continue to invest the minimum necessary political and economic capital in its difficult relationship with Pyongyang in order to maximize its influence in Northeast Asian affairs. That said, however, China's multitasking two-Koreas strategy is more reactive than proactive. It is concentrated on the challenge of maximizing short-term gains and minimizing or avoiding short-term constraints. It does not appear, however, to include a long-term strategic vision for the Korean peninsula other than to keep it a buffer zone and to slow down the Korean reunification process as much as possible in order to maintain the two-Koreas status quo.

Russia and North Korea

What is most striking about Moscow's relations with Pyongyang is not that there were abrupt vicissitudes and fluctuations throughout the 1990s—for indeed there were many—but that the downward spiral of Russia-DPRK relations that resulted from a series of domestic and external shocks has been reversed and put back on a renormalization track since the mid-1990s. As Elizabeth Wishnick argues in chapter 5, the renormalization process gained momentum when Vladimir Putin's vigorous pursuit of realpolitik intersected with Kim Jong Il's new diplomatic opening to the outside world. In July 2000, Putin became not only the first Kremlin leader ever to visit the neighboring communist country, but also the first among the Big Four to make an official state visit to North Korea. A year later, Kim made a twenty-four-day train journey through Russia's vast expanse for a two-day summit meeting, the longest and strangest trip made by any head of state in our time.

Moscow's skewed two-Koreas policy started with a bang in 1990 but ended with a whimper. Ironically, if Moscow was the chief catalyst for transforming the political and strategic landscape of Northeast Asia, including the initiation of cross-recognition and the entry of the two Koreas into the United Nations, Beijing became the major beneficiary, occupying the pivotal position from which it could exert greater influence over Seoul and Pyongyang. As if to emulate Beijing's much-touted equidistance policy, since the mid-1990s Moscow has retreated significantly from its skewed policy, moving toward a more balanced policy as a way of reassuring, and thus enhancing its leverage in, Pyongyang and resuming its great-power role in the politics of divided Korea. Nonetheless, the precipitous and traumatic decline of Russia from great power status to that of a poor and powerless state, and the lack of a widely accepted "national" identity go a long way in explaining the turbulence of Russia's Korea policy in the 1990s.

Against this backdrop, Vladimir Putin, upon assuming office as President of Russia in May 2000, reaffirmed his pledge to restore Russia as a great power. His state visit to Pyongyang on July 20 and 21, 2000, coincided with the completion and ratification of three national security and foreign policy blueprint documents that year: a new national security concept (January 10), a new military doctrine (April 21), and a new foreign policy concept (July 10). Together, these blueprints put inordinate stress on safeguarding Russia's "national" interests, defined in terms of Russian exceptionalism, great power prerogatives, and economic interests. The period of 1998 to 1999 was a turning point in Moscow's agonizing reappraisal of the rapidly changing and threatening international environment and the reconstruction of its ruling coalition. The liberal-statist balance of political elite interests was shattered by the August 1998 financial crisis and, more importantly, by the NATO/U.S. war in Kosovo.[50]

Russian exceptionalism is said to stem from the ineluctable geographical fact that post-Soviet Russia still has the largest territory in the post–Cold War world, and from Russia's status as the only truly Eurasian continental power. Even in an era of globalization, size matters in the mobilization and projection of Russia's identity as a great power. It also expresses Moscow's inability and unwillingness to define its identity as anything but a great power, and "great powers seldom operate under the same rules and constraints as lesser powers."[51]

The new foreign policy concept also makes a reference to the Korean peninsula, expressing Russia's desire to play an important role in the inter-Korean peace process and to seek balanced relations with the two Koreas:

> The situation on the Korean peninsula gives rise to the greatest concern. Russia's efforts will be concentrated on ensuring our country's full and equal participation in efforts to settle the Korean problem and on maintaining balanced relations with both Korean states.[52]

Stripped to the core, power-balancing, interest-maximizing, result-oriented realpolitik has come back with a vengeance.

What were the specific measures taken to enhance Russia's great-power role in inter-Korean affairs? In February 2000, Russian Foreign Minister Igor Ivanov traveled to Pyongyang to sign a new treaty—the DPRK-Russia Treaty on Friendship, Good Neighborliness, and Cooperation—as a fresh start to replace the 1961 security pact that was scrapped in 1996. The new treaty, which took effect in late October 2000 with an exchange of certificates of ratification, was hailed as providing political and legal guarantees to boost cooperation and exchange in all aspects of the DPRK-Russia relationship. The automatic military intervention clause of the 1961 treaty (Article 1) was replaced by a more ambiguous "immediate contact" clause in case of a security crisis in the new treaty (Article 2):

> In the event of the emergence of the danger of an aggression against one of the countries or a situation jeopardizing peace and security, and in the event there is a necessity for consultations and cooperation, the [two] sides enter into contact with each other immediately.[53]

On April 27, 2001, for the first time since the collapse of the Soviet Union in 1991, North Korean Defense Minister Kim Il Chol made an official state visit to Moscow. During this visit, the two governments signed two "military technological cooperation" agreements that Moscow would modernize North

Korea's aging Soviet-era weapons systems, provide regular security consultations, and train North Korean military personnel to upgrade and refurbish North Korean military facilities.

Putin's personal diplomacy in 2000 and 2001 is a dramatic step not only toward bringing Moscow back into the rapidly changing Korean peninsular equation in order to reassert Russia's great-power identity, but also to counter troublesome American policies. The United States loomed large in the first Putin-Kim summit. In the DPRK-Russia Moscow Declaration of August 4, 2001, replete with Soviet-style lingo,[54] both parties addressed "international" (read: "the United States") and bilateral issues. Four of the eight points seem designed to send a strong message to the United States: "a just new world order" (point one); the 1972 ABM Treaty as a cornerstone of global strategic stability (point two); a Korean reunification process by independent means and without foreign interference (point seven); and the pullout of U.S. forces from South Korea as a "pressing issue," regarding which Putin expressed his "understanding" (point eight). The remaining points have to do with the promotion of bilateral political and economic cooperation, especially "the plan for building railways linking the north and the south of the Korean peninsula, Russia and Europe on the principle of the mutual interests recognized in the worldwide practice" (point six).

This joint declaration was far more muscular and provocative than the South-North Joint Declaration, and it included trenchant attacks against infringement of state sovereignty under the pretext of humanitarianism and against the United States' Theater Missile Defense (TMD) and National Missile Defense (NMD) programs. The Russian–North Korean summit captured global prime-time television and headlines when Putin revealed that the North Korean leader had pledged to eliminate his country's Taepodong missile program—a key rationale for NMD—if Western countries (meaning the United States) would provide access to rocket boosters for peaceful space research. Putin also managed to put Kim Jong Il's "satellites for missiles" issue on the agenda of the G-8 summit meeting in Japan.

Moscow's decision to help North Korea has had more to do with enhancing Russia's geopolitical capital than with money-making considerations, because Pyongyang already owes Moscow some three billion dollars for Soviet-era military and nonmilitary deliveries, a debt that it does not intend to repay. There is no guarantee whatsoever that the same story will not be repeated with the latest arms agreements. Perhaps the most revealing part of the Moscow Declaration is embodied in point five: "In order to carry out a series of bilateral plans, the Russian side confirmed its intention to use the method of *drawing financial resources from outsiders* [emphasis added] on the basis of understanding of the Korean side."[55]

As Wishnick demonstrates in chapter 5, Russia's Koreanists are always quick to point out that only Russia among the Big Four is an unequivocal supporter of Korean reunification, since the status quo gives a rising China more influence in the politics of divided Korea than would a strong nationalist and reunified Korea, especially one friendly to the United States. "One of the obstacles to the Korean peace and unification process is doubts and concerns among major powers surrounding the peninsula about the potential of a united Korea being a political and economic power," said Dmitri Rogozin, chairman of the Foreign Affairs Committee of State Duma (the Russian parliament).[56] The bottom-line logic seems simple enough: Russia would reap a huge economic reward from a successful unification that could link transport networks from Korea's Pacific ports to Russia and Europe while opening the Korean market for new Russian natural gas fields, and also from having North Korea's huge debt to Russia repaid by a unified Korea.

Although Pyongyang is increasingly active in economic contacts with Russia, economic cooperation between the two financially troubled countries flounders. Putin's new foreign policy doctrine of safeguarding Russia's economic interests and Pyongyang's damage-compensation mendicant diplomacy have often been out of sync with each other. Pyongyang still feels that it has been materially betrayed and damaged by its former mentor and asks for Russian assistance in repairing and modernizing all the industrial facilities built in North Korea by the former Soviet Union in the 1950s and 1960s. Pyongyang has been insisting on barter deals and low-interest credits that would be impossible to implement in a market economy and to which Moscow cannot agree. As shown in table 5.1, Russia-DPRK trade dropped from $2.35 billion in 1990 to $105 million in 2000, which is equivalent to only 3.7 percent of Russia-ROK trade in 2000 and only 0.34 percent of Sino-ROK trade that year. One possible solution, according to Russia's Koreanists, is to have South Korean banks and firms provide credit to the DPRK in exchange for Russian technical assistance—a solution many would consider wishful thinking, given the looming economic crisis in the South, where one *chaebol* after another is going belly up.

Still, Moscow seems excited about the geoeconomic opportunities resulting from increasing inter-Korean economic cooperation, particularly about the prospect of rail links across the DMZ, which it hopes would create a new trans-Siberian freight route linking South Korea to Europe via North Korea and the Russian Far East. The difficulty is in leveling the playing field of the highly asymmetrical Moscow-Pyongyang-Seoul economic interdependence by triangulating Russia's technical know-how and natural resources, North Korea's labor, and South Korea's capital, as well as Russia's debt to Seoul ($1.8 billion) and Pyongyang's debt to Moscow (about $3–5 billion) in a mutually complementary way.

In order for this dream of an Iron Silk Road to come true the Russian way, however, Moscow would have to overcome some major obstacles, including the huge cost (nine billion dollars); Russia's economic weakness; China's comparative and competitive advantage in connecting its railway to the inter-Korean Seoul-Sinuiju line (Kyongui Line), which would make it the gateway for cargo travel from Asia to Europe; North Korea's ongoing economic crisis and unpredictable behavior; and the politics of ideological and regional fragmentation in South Korea. Fearing that the new rail projects would diminish the role of local ports that depend on trade with South Korea, as Wishnick suggests in chapter 5, some Primorskii Krai officials are opposed to the development of a new Russian-Korean rail corridor.

Russo-DPRK regional relations provide a short-term basis for economic relations, especially through contracts for North Korean guest workers, but the expanded North Korean presence in the Russian Far East has raised new concerns about Pyongyang's involvement in nuclear smuggling, the heroin trade, and counterfeiting activities in Russia. Russian–North Korean regional cooperation will accelerate as major regional development projects such as the Tumen River project, the Kovyktinskoe gas pipeline, and the inter-Korean railway move forward, but progress will depend on the ability to attract considerable outside investment, especially from Japan but also from South Korea and China.

Kim Jong Il's scheduled state visit to Moscow in April 2001 experienced rough sailing over the issue of arms sales as aid, as North Korea demanded such arms delivery agreements as a precondition for Kim's official state visit for a second Kim-Putin summit. The accords of April 27, 2001, apparently met the preconditions well enough for Kim Jong Il's twenty-four-day, twelve-thousand-mile trek on a twenty-one-car armored train (Japanese-made) with darkened windows and gun-toting guards across Russia's vast expanse for a two-day summit in Moscow. Perhaps Kim Jong Il relished the dubious distinction of being the one and only state leader in the jet age who would spend more than three weeks on a train ride for a two-day summit, and for being the only visiting state leader who has demanded and received an honor guard that had been removed from the Lenin Mausoleum in Red Square after the collapse of the Soviet Union in 1991.

NORTH KOREA'S SURVIVAL STRATEGY

During the long Cold War years, geopolitics and ideology combined to make it possible for Pyongyang to extract maximum economic, military, and security payoffs from China and the Soviet Union and to claim that the North Korean system was a success. But the so-called *juche*-based self-reliant economy, living in essence on disguised aid from the Soviet Union and China,[57] has been revealed as a mirage in the post–Cold War era, and "our style socialism" a poor substitution ideology to cope with the deepening crisis.

One of the most telling paradoxes of North Korean foreign policy is the extent to which Pyongyang successfully managed to have its *juche* cake and eat it too. As an appealing legitimating principle, *juche* has often been turned on its head to conceal a high degree of dependence on Soviet and Chinese aid. Between 1948 and 1984, Moscow and Beijing were Pyongyang's first and second most important patrons, supplying $2.2 billion and $900 million in aid, respectively.[58] Thanks to the East-West and Sino-Soviet rivalries during the Cold War, Pyongyang was allowed to practice such concealed mendicant diplomacy. As shown in tables 1.10 and 5.1, the collapse of the Soviet Union was the most serious shock to socialist North Korea, not only for the cessation of aid and the virtual demise of concessional trade (dropping from 56.3 percent in 1990 to 5.3 percent in 2000), but also because it delivered a wrenching blow to the much-trumpeted *juche*-based national identity.

In a contradictory yet revealing manner, Pyongyang admitted as much when it attributed the failure of the Third Seven-Year Plan (1987 to 1993) to a series of adverse external shocks: the "collusion between the imperialists and counter-revolutionary forces" and the "penetration of imperialist ideology and culture" that had accelerated the demise of the Second (Socialist) World and the end of Soviet aid.[59] As much as Pyongyang may blame the economic crisis on such external shocks or on natural disaster at home, the root causes of the economic crisis are deeply systemic. The adverse external circumstances and the bad weather in 1995 and 1996 only served as triggering

Table 1.10. North Korea's Foreign Trade, 1990–2000 (U.S.$1million)

	Export	*Import*	*Total*
1990	1,333 (-)	2,437 (-)	4,170 (-)
1991	1,010 (-24.2)	1,710 (-29.8)	2,720 (-34.8)
1992	1,020 (+1.0)	1,640 (-4.1)	2,660 (-2.2)
1993	1,021 (+0.1)	1,620 (-1.2)	2,641 (-0.7)
1994	839 (-17.8)	1,269 (-21.7)	2,108 (-20.2)
1995	736 (-12.3)	1,316 (+3.7)	2,052 (-2.7)
1996	726 (-1.3)	1,250 (-5.0)	1,976 (-3.7)
1997	904 (+24.5)	1,272 (+1.8)	2,177 (+10.1)
1998	559 (-38.2)	883 (-30.6)	1,442 (-33.7)
1999	515 (-7.9)	965 (+9.3)	1,480 (+2.6)
2000	556 (+8.0)	1,413 (+46.5)	1,970 (+33.1)

Source: KOTRA, "Overview of North Korea's Foreign Trade in 2000," at www.kotra.or.kr (accessed June 15, 2001).

and exacerbating factors. The seeds of disaster were planted in the 1970s when the "Great Leader" vigorously promoted militarization, the cult of personality, and hereditary succession to the breaking point.

An inordinate amount of North Korea's state resources and expenditures has gone toward militarization. There is perhaps no other state in the world where a military-industrial-political complex exerts as much influence on the state, regime, system, and society. No other state in our time has placed its economy on such an extreme and prolonged footing of war, with a constant drain of scarce resources into military-related industries (see table 1.3). Determined not to be outperformed in the legitimation-cum-economic war, Pyongyang decided in 1972 to launch its first international shopping expeditions for capital and technology, accumulating in a few years (1972 to 1975) a trade deficit of about $1.3 billion with non-Communist countries and $700 million with Communist countries. This was the genesis of Pyongyang's debt trap.[60] Hit by the rapidly deteriorating terms of trade (the oil crisis and declining metal prices), Pyongyang defaulted on its debts in 1975, with the dual consequences of effectively cutting itself off from Western capital markets and becoming more dependent on the Soviet Union than ever before. It is common knowledge that North Korea's economic collapse in the 1990s was the inevitable result of Pyongyang's massive expenditures on military preparedness and the demise of Soviet aid and trade.

The Political Economy of System Maintenance

As shown in Marcus Noland's balanced analysis and prognosis in chapter 6, the defining and differentiating features of North Korea's external economic relations include: 1.) the extreme degree to which markets were repressed, 2.) the concentration of decision making in a single leader (the *suryong* system), 3.) a chronic trade deficit, 4.) a lack of access to international capital markets due to the 1975 debt default, and 5.) a highly unusual balance of payments profile that must be financed in highly unconventional ways. As shown in tables 1.10 and 6.1, using different sources—Korean Trade and Investment Promotion Agency (KOTRA) and International Monetary Fund (IMF)—Northeast Asia figures most prominently in North Korea's external economic relations, with China, Japan, South Korea, and Russia, in that order, accounting for more than 52 percent of Pyongyang's total global trade.

There is little doubt that extensive structural reform is required to solve the widening and deepening system crisis. Even at the level of policy pronouncements, however, the evidence is somewhat mixed and shifting. Since the adoption of the new Kim Il Sung Constitution on September 5, 1998, which marked the beginning of the Kim Jong Il era, the name of the reform game has remained the same: *kangsong taeguk* ("a strong and prosperous big state" or simply "great power"), a concept that is anything but new. The breakthrough mentality of the first *ch'ollima* ("flying horse") march of the late 1950s, which parroted Mao's Great Leap Forward, was brought back in a total mobilization campaign in the form of frenzied, Stakhanovite-style exhortations for the Second *Ch'ollima* March toward a *kangsong taeguk* as a panacea for system maintenance. The ink on the new Kim Il Sung Constitution was hardly dry when *Rodong Sinmun*, in an *ex cathedra* pronouncement of September 17, 1998, erased any reform and opening elements in the new constitution:

> We now have nothing to "reform" and "open." By "reform" and "opening" the imperialists mean a revival of capitalism. The best way of blocking the wind of "reform" and "opening" of the imperialists is to defend the socialist principle in all sectors of the economy. . . . We will never abandon the principle, but will set ourselves against all attempts to induce us to join an "integrated world."[61]

Viewed in this light, North Korean commentaries in January 2001, with references to building *kyongche kangguk* ("economic great power") as the greatest task for the party-state, represent a conceptual reorientation. While paying mandatory lip service to the revolutionary military-first policy, *kangsong taeguk* has been redefined or at least reprioritized as *kyongche kangguk*, giving top priority to power, coal and metal industries, and railway transport.[62] For better or worse, this reverses the policy priorities of agriculture, light industry, and foreign trade that Kim Il Sung enunciated in his last (1994) New Year's Message. While attacking globalization as a new form of imperialism, North Korea has also conceptually embraced the global tide in the pursuit of an information-based society and the development of a computer industry as a way of enhancing its national economic competitiveness and strength.[63] More tellingly, for the first time in the post–Kim Il Sung era, this pronouncement of the need for "new thinking" was made not in the New Year's (2001) Joint Editorial but in the January 9, 2001, issue of *Rodong Sinmun*:

> A new age demands a new ideological viewpoint and a new struggle ethos. It is impossible to advance the revolution even a step further if we should become complacent with our past achievements or be enslaved to outdated ideas and stick to the outmoded style and attitude in our work. The matter of vigorously hastening the socialist Red Flag march this year, the first year of the 21st century, to bring on breakthroughs in the building of a powerful state, is directly linked to that of effecting fundamental innovations in our ideological viewpoint, way of thinking, struggle ethos, and work attitude.[64]

However, the more critical challenge is in implementing such policy pronouncements. In addressing this question of whether North Korean leaders are capable of successfully carrying out necessary reforms, Noland carefully delineates and documents some highly unconventional ways of financing the chronic trade deficits (to the tune of almost half a billion dollars annually): missile sales (one hundred million dollars a year); continuing criminal enterprise and illicit activities in smuggling, drug trafficking, and counterfeiting (one hundred million dollars a year); and remittances from members of the pro-DPRK *Ch'ongnyon* (*Chosen Soren*) in Japan (one hundred million dollars a year). Since the mid-1990s, North Korea has also been receiving hundreds of millions of dollars annually in both bilateral and multilateral aid in various forms, with the largest contributors being the United States, South Korea, China, Japan, and the European Union. However, the lion's share of the aid amounts to in-kind transfers and cannot be used to finance the trade deficit.

Clearly, something more than these temporizing revenue-raising measures is required for economic reform and restructuring. Here Kim Jong Il finds himself in a bind. To save the *juche* system requires some system-reforming measures or even the deconstruction of important parts of the *juche* system. And yet a departure from the ideological continuity of the *juche* system that the Great Leader Kim Il Sung created, developed, and passed on to his son is viewed not as a necessity for survival but as an ultimate betrayal of the *raison d'état*. To cope with this conundrum, according to Noland (and also Manning in chapter 2), Kim Jong Il's response has been twofold: selective and controlled opening to engage in onetime attempts to earn foreign exchange through projects that would not affect system maintenance (e.g., the Rajin-Sonbong SEZ and the Mt. Kumgang tourism project), while at the same time engaging in brinksmanship to extract concessional aid from the rest of the world.

Despite North Korea's seeming determination to undertake economic reform, Noland argues that there are at least three major obstacles. First, notwithstanding the many condemnations of the perils of foreign capital as "sugarcoated poison," Chinese-style reform and opening is widely believed to be the most promising way. And yet the agriculture-led reform process we have seen in East Asian transitional economies simply may not be available to North Korea due to the very different initial conditions, which resemble East European economies or the former Soviet Union more than China or Vietnam. A second obstacle is the divided nature of the Korean peninsula and the dynastic nature of the North Korean system. To ask North Korea to follow the system-reforming trajectory is to ask it to change its national identity to be just like South Korea. As Noland puts it, "why be a third-rate South Korea when one can head south and become the real thing?" A third obstacle has to do with the many difficulties in obtaining multilateral aid from the IMF, the World Bank, and the Asian Development Bank. Pyongyang's unwillingness to meet the minimum necessary transparency standards, its placement on the U.S. list of states supporting terrorism, and Japanese opposition stemming from unresolved political issues (most notably the alleged kidnapping of some ten or eleven Japanese citizens in the 1970s and 1980s) have blocked the government's membership into these keystone international financial organizations.

Noland concludes somewhat cautiously that it remains to be seen whether the events of 2000 and 2001 represent a fundamental reorientation or purely opportunism. One possibility is that Kim Jong Il calculates that the best way to preserve the system is to constructively engage South Korea and the rest of the world, and that moving down the path of economic reform, though risky, offers the highest likelihood of ultimate success in preserving the system. Or, of course, it could be simply situation-specific tactical adaptation.

Interpreting North Korea's Military and Security Policy

In the last two chapters, Eliot Kang and Victor Cha present two competing and somewhat unconventional interpretations of North Korea's military and security policy. Despite its wide currency, as Kang argues in chapter 7, mainstream neorealism offers an excessively pessimistic and empirically deficient understanding of North Korea's security challenge. Kang suggests a different realist perspective, mercantile realism, as a more useful theoretical perspective for understanding Pyongyang's security thinking and behavior. Unlike neorealism, mercantile realism does not prematurely privilege military security at the expense of economic security. Instead, it postulates that states make security policy based on the probability of aggression, not simply the possibility of conflict. From a mercantile realist perspective, North Korea's security policy is driven not just by short-term considerations of military preparedness, but also by the long-term objective of maintaining a viable economic power base. Kang assumes a North Korea that is capable of discriminating between the possibility and the probability of war, and of devising a strategy that balances the short-term goal of military deterrence and the long-term goal of maintaining a viable economic base—the key foundation of national power. Moreover, Kang argues that North Korea will bargain, if warily and fitfully, to trade all or much of its nuclear and ballistic missile capabilities for Western economic concessions. In sharp contrast, Manning argues that in missile talks with the United States, North Korea has not shown any willingness to dismantle the already deployed missiles or to permit the sort of intrusive on-site inspection that would be necessary to make such a deal politically feasible and credible, and that North Korea seems more willing to rent its threat than to sell it.

In the last chapter, Victor Cha offers a thought-provoking prescriptive analysis of the North Korean threat. Absent more empirical and behavioral referents about the Black Box in Pyongyang, it is not possible to divine whether recent North Korean "smile diplomacy" represents a mere tactical shift or a more fundamental transformation of the regime toward reform and integration. Yet policy must be made based on some assumptions with regard to North Korean intentions. A starting premise is that the threat to the Korean peninsula peace stems not from the regime's irrationality, nor from the possibility of collapse, nor even from a second DPRK invasion and all-out war. North Korea could perceive some use of limited force as a rational and optimal choice even when there is little or no hope of victory. Hence, the danger is not that Pyongyang will commit suicide knowingly, but that it will encounter situations where belligerent lashing out is the best and only policy, the unintended consequence of which (given likely U.S. and ROK military responses) would be regime suicide or collapse.

Drawing insights from preemptive war and prospect theory, Cha advances a preventive defense rationale for engagement. For reasons having to do with the changing nature of the North Korean threat during the post–Cold War era, the appropriate policy toward the DPRK, even for hawks in Washington, Seoul, and Tokyo, remains a preventive engagement for at least three reasons. First, the policy choice is not between deterrence (containment) and no deterrence, but deterrence plus—that is, how deterrence should be combined and complemented with "isolation," "coercion," or "engagement." Second, even hawks should engage Pyongyang, not because the regime is crazy, near collapse, or misunderstood, but because such preventive engagement avoids the crystallization of conditions under which Pyongyang could calculate violence as a rational course of action even if victory were impossible. In this sense, then, engagement is a form of preventive defense—actions taken by the United States and its allies to prevent the emergence of a situation so unbearable to the DPRK that Pyongyang calculates that lashing out is rational in spite of an objective military balance unfavorable to the regime. In other words, the real danger with regard to the DPRK threat is that in spite of an unfavorable military balance, the North could still choose to initiate conflict as a wholly rational policy; that is, there is still a rational option to use force. Third, engagement remains *faute de mieux* the default policy on the Korean peninsula. Many hawks may view such defensive engagement as window-dressing for appeasing a morally reprehensible regime for lack of a clear alternative and without a responsible exit strategy. But preventive engagement actually gains a window on the degree of change in DPRK intentions while simultaneously laying the groundwork for punishment if necessary. In this sense, engagement is not in lieu of an exit strategy but comprises it.

REASSESSING PYONGYANG'S SURVIVAL STRATEGY

Let us return to some of the critical questions posed at the outset of this introductory chapter. How can we explain the paradox of the survival of the DPRK, a small and incomplete nation-state buffeted by seemingly fatal internal woes and external shocks? How has it managed to turn a threat of sanctions into blandishments from the world's sole superpower? What kind of leverage did it possess or exercise in its system-maintaining survival strategy? Is there a third way beside the stark Darwinian options of system reform or system collapse?

There is no single monocausal explanation, but a consideration of multiple and mutually interactive influences can help us answer the puzzle of Pyongyang's uncanny resilience and "the power of the weak" in the context of Northeast Asian geopolitics. Drawing theoretical insight from asymmetric conflict and negotiation theory, we may postulate that the power balance of an issue-specific relationship and the performance of the weaker state are affected by four key variables: the weak state's proximity to the strategic field of play; the availability to the stronger state of viable alternatives; the level of stakes for both states in conflict and the degree of their resolve; and the degree of control for all involved parties.[65] As a weaker state in conflict with the world's lone superpower and its allies (South Korea and Japan), North Korea has exercised and relied upon issue-specific and situation-specific power, the effectiveness and credibility of which has required resources and skills other than those of aggregate structural power. Pyongyang's proximity to the strategic field of play, its compensating brinksmanship strategy, and its high stakes, resolve, and control have all reinforced one another to make a strong actor's aggregate structural power largely irrelevant. North Korea has adopted a wide range of tactics in and out of the asymmetric conflict and negotiation processes in order to reduce the opponent's viable alternatives and weaken the opponent's resolve and control.

The geographical position of the DPRK is one of the most compelling and immutable factors in the success of Pyongyang's survival leverage strategy. Since countries can change their leaders, systems, policies, and strategies but cannot change their location, "geography or geopolitics has long been the point of departure for studies of foreign policy or world politics."[66] Surrounded by all four major powers and its southern rival, North Korea's home turf is the strategic field of play from which it exercises its brinksmanship or its collapse card. Contrary to the conventional realist wisdom, in asymmetrical negotiations the strong state does not ipso facto exert greater control than the weak state. If a small and weak state occupies territory of strategic importance to a larger and stronger state, or if the field of play is on the weak actor's home turf (as was the case in the U.S.-Panama negotiations and British-Iceland Cod Wars), the weaker state can display bargaining power disproportionate to its aggregate structural power.[67]

The ineluctable fact that North Korea is at the center of the strategic crossroads of Northeast Asia where the Big Four uneasily meet and interact has served rather well in bolstering Pyongyang's control. By dint of its proximity to what Peter Hayes called "the fuse on the nuclear powder keg in the Pacific,"[68] Pyongyang has had a head start in leveling the field of play so as to wield greater control than the United States by constantly changing the rules of entry and the rules of play in the pursuit of its preferred outcome. North Korea's manifest preference for direct bilateral negotiations with the United States is also a way of seeking the home court advantage to maximize its control in the asymmetric conflict and negotiation process.

Consider as well how Pyongyang's geographical position, combined with its 1.2 million people–strong military and its asymmetric military capabilities, provides ample fodder for its coercive leverage diplomacy with South Korea and the United States. Some 70 percent of its active force—seven hundred thousand troops, eight thousand artillery systems, and two thousand tanks—are forward deployed near the DMZ. Seoul, where one-fourth of South Korea's forty-five million people live and nearly 75 percent of the country's wealth is concentrated, is only forty kilometers (twenty-five miles) from the DMZ and thus within easy reach of North Korean jet fighters, armored vehicles, Scud missiles, and artillery guns. Within minutes, Pyongyang could turn Seoul into "a sea of fire," as it threatened to do in the heat of the nuclear crisis of mid-1994. An Allied final victory would be a Pyrrhic victory since such devastation would be crippling to South Korea.[69] Without launching such an armed invasion, Pyongyang can still exercise its "negative power" or even play its collapse card to spawn instability on the divided Korean peninsula. One of the underlying rationales for the inauguration of the Kim Dae Jung administration's "sunshine policy" was that potential implosion or explosion would put at risk South Korea's recovery from the 1997 financial crisis by discouraging foreign direct investment inflows. The financial crisis served as a wake-up call on the consequences of North Korea's prospective collapse. Hence, to deter or delay the economic effects of a North Korean hard landing as long as possible, the sunshine policy became South Korea's default policy.[70]

North Korea's geographical location is also of considerable strategic concern and importance to the Northeast Asian powers. Located at the pivot point of Northeast Asian security and at the most important strategic nexus of the Asia-Pacific region, Pyongyang is capable, by instigating hostility or instability, of entrapping any or all four great powers in a spiral of conflict escalation these governments would rather avoid. If Pyongyang's brinksmanship or Washington's sanctions escalates to war, the cost to all involved parties would be exorbitant.

Concomitant to Pyongyang's compensatory survival strategy are the limitations of America's issue-specific power to pressure Pyongyang and the lack of viable alternatives to negotiation. The twisted logic of a self-styled *juche* kingdom is that it is not as vulnerable as a normal state to public shaming and the various statecraft tools of sanctions. The viable alternatives available to the United States in the resolution of the North Korean nuclear and missile issues have remained severely limited. The credible threats of surgical military strikes and enforceable economic sanctions against Pyongyang were considered but rejected because of the Pentagon's objections, Seoul's vulnerability, China's veto threat, and even Tokyo's "reluctant realism." In effect, the United States had no alternative but to retreat by accepting North Korea's package deal proposal. Reflecting on his involvement in the emergency national security meeting of June 16, 1994, on the most serious North Korean nuclear brinkmanship crisis of his tenure as Secretary of Defense, William Perry writes about a third-way option for a negotiated deal in the face of the extremely limited alternatives available to U.S. policymakers:

> We were about to give the president a [third-way] choice between a disastrous option—allowing North Korea to get a nuclear arsenal, which we might have to face someday—and an unpalatable option, blocking this development, but thereby risking a destructive nonnuclear war.[71]

Given all the constraints on America's issue-specific power, the rise of a cost-effective foreign policy, and the collapse of a bipartisan foreign policy consensus in the 1990s, the U.S.-DPRK Agreement of October 21, 1994, could be said to be the worst deal, except that there was no better alternative.

For Beijing—and to a lesser extent for Seoul, Moscow, and Tokyo—Washington's sanctions diplomacy in mid-1994 emerged as a no-win proposition, as it would bring about the worst of two possible outcomes. It will be ineffective in controlling nuclear proliferation since it can only strengthen the determination of the North Korean leadership to go nuclear, or it will destabilize a North Korean regime that would dump many of its ill-fed, fleeing refugees on China's northeastern and Russia's far eastern provinces. Paradoxically, Pyongyang's growing difficulties and threat of collapse have increased its bargaining leverage relative to its weak aggregate structural power. The prospect of North Korean instability was the primary motivating factor in the strengthening of U.S.-Japan defense guidelines, which specifically defined the forms of military support that Japan's Self-Defense Forces may provide in the event of a North Korean contingency, and also in the strengthening of Sino-DPRK ties in recent years.[72]

Another consideration regarding leverage in asymmetrical negotiations is the matter of relative and absolute stakes and resolve. The higher the stakes for a bargaining state actor, the more it is willing to commit its resources and the greater its resolve to attain a favorable negotiation outcome. The issue of stakes may have a crucial part in explaining why the weaker North Vietnam ultimately defeated American troops during the Vietnam War fought on its home turf. Similarly, North Korea was disadvantaged against the United States in the overall correlation of forces, but there also remained a clear asymmetry in stakes and resolve favoring Pyongyang.

Of course, resolve without capability and willingness to use force is a paper tiger, and as such it cannot work well in asymmetrical negotiation. With the collapse of the Second World and Moscow-Seoul normalization came the notion that military power and threat is a fungible strategic and economic asset for regime survival. It is touted not only as the last trump card, displaying power in the fierce diplomatic and ideological standoff with imperialism, but also as a necessary and sufficient condition for the success of socialist and self-supporting economic development. It is through the combination of military power and the on-again, off-again threat, Pyongyang claims, that it has not only gained the upper hand over the imperialist offensives that seek to crush the DPRK, but has also gained economic assistance from wealthy capitalist countries out of their abiding fear of war.[73]

Despite the "new thinking" pronouncements and the omnidirectional diplomatic outreach in 2000 and 2001, there is no evidence of any change in the "military-first" orientation. On the contrary, the North Korean military continues to grow in both conventional and asymmetrical forces with increasing emphasis on the latter.[74] To abandon such military power and threat is to leave Pyongyang without the single most important lever in its asymmetric conflicts and negotiations with South Korea, the United States, and Japan. Instead, Pyongyang follows its own third way—a maxi-mini strategy, doing the minimum necessary to get the maximum possible aid from South Korea and other countries without reducing its military power or easing tensions.

North Korean nuclear and missile brinksmanship also illustrates with particular clarity that when the enactment of a national identity is blocked in one domain, it seeks to compensate in another. From Pyongyang's military-first perspective, developing asymmetrical capabilities such as ballistic missiles, special operations forces, and weapons of mass destruction (nuclear, chemical, and biological) serves as strategic sine qua non in its survival strategy as well as an equalizer in the legitimacy war and status competition with the South. It remains one of a few areas in which the DPRK commands comparative advantage in the military balance of power and status competition with the South. North Korea's humiliating defeat by its southern counterpart in the first-ever naval clash in June 1999 further emphasizes its WMD and ballistic missiles as a strategic equalizer.

In sum, Pyongyang's proximity to the strategic field of play, its high stakes, resolve, and control, its relative asymmetrical military capabilities, and its coercive leverage strategy have all combined to enable the DPRK to exercise bargaining power disproportionate to its aggregate structural power in the U.S.-DPRK asymmetric conflict and negotiations. That said, however, Kim Jong Il's pronounced commitment to survival strategy would not stand in the way of demonstrating situation-specific tactical flexibility, especially in foreign policy. Indeed, Pyongyang has pursued a great variety of coping strategies, such as brinksmanship-cum-mendicant diplomacy, overseas arms sales, appeals for humanitarian aid, and on-off joint-venture projects, to generate desperately needed foreign capital. Pyongyang has shown some adaptive, situation-specific learning as it copes with the challenges of system maintenance, but it has demonstrated no cognitive or normative learning to speak of.[75] The recent changes are all at the level of system processes, especially in foreign policy, but they remain within the primary parameters of the highly militarized fundamentalist system. Cognitive learning tends to be more difficult in closed autocratic systems than in open democratic systems; the primary parameters of closed systems are severely constrained, as the fundamentalist belief system feeds and rewards the system-maintaining status quo.[76]

FUTURE PROSPECTS

As matters stand, the theocratic system of a one-man dictatorship is not prepared for the challenges of globalization. The role of state adaptability is crucial in this respect. More than ever before in human history, the rise or fall of an effective state, even a *kangsong taeguk*, is closely keyed to the speed and extent to which the state can establish a congruence between domestic and foreign policies amid the changing trends and requirements of globalization.

In the final analysis, any successful medium- and long-term coping strategy must be systemic, involving the institutional design and implementation of measures that are consistent and congruent across different and traditionally disparate areas of policymaking and also between domestic and foreign policies. While piecemeal tactical adaptations can yield some concessions and payoffs in the short run, a series of system reform measures pursued swiftly would yield both greater benefits and, perhaps, greater dangers.

Because the interplay between North Korea and Northeast Asia is highly complex and even confusing, fraught with paradoxical expectations and consequences, there is no single or simple answer to the vexing questions of how and whether the post–Kim Il Sung system will survive and whether Kim Jong Il can rise to the challenge of moving from a system-maintaining survival strategy to a system-reforming direction without triggering a cataclysmic system collapse. What complicates our understanding of the shape of things to come in North Korea is that all the countries involved in Korean affairs have become moving targets on turbulent trajectories of their respective highly charged domestic politics, subject to competing and often contradictory pressures. As Manning suggests in chapter 2, the most that we can expect from the United States and its allies is to come up with a new comprehensive package of incentives, a "Grand Bargain" that would make it as easy as possible for Pyongyang to make the choices necessary for gradual system change, that is, for a soft landing. Despite the absence of any clear signs that such system reform has been planned in North Korea, let alone is underway, the challenge for the TCOG member states (the United States, South Korea, and Japan) is to fully test such a proposition by unambiguously presenting a Grand Bargain and a road map showing how to realize it incrementally.

NOTES

1. *Korea Times,* February 1, 2000, at www.koreatimes.co.kr.

2. Thucydides, *History of the Peloponnesian War*, trans. Rex Warner (New York: Penguin Books, 1982), 402.

3. According to the purchasing power parity (PPP) estimates of the World Bank (which are not unproblematic), China, with a 1994 GDP just under three trillion dollars, has become the second-largest economy in the world after the United States. See *Economist* (London), January 27, 1996, 102; World Bank, *World Development Report, 1996* (New York: Oxford University Press, 1996), 188.

4. Kent Calder, "The New Face of Northeast Asia," *Foreign Affairs* 80:1 (January-February 2001), 114.

5. For realist analyses along this line with some variations, see Richard K. Betts, "Wealth, Power, and Instability: East Asia and the United States after the Cold War," *International Security* 18:3 (winter 1993/1994): 34–77; Aaron L. Friedberg, "Ripe for Rivalry: Prospects for Peace in a Multipolar Asia," *International Security* 18:3 (winter 1993/1994): 5–33; Friedberg, "Will Europe's Past Be Asia's Future?" *Survival* 42:3 (autumn 2000), 147–59.

6. Samuel P. Huntington, *The Clash of Civilizations and the Remaking of World Order* (New York: Simon and Schuster, 1996), 238.

7. See Alastair Iain Johnston and Robert Ross, eds., *Engaging China: The Management of an Emerging Power* (London and New York: Routledge, 1999).

8. On power transitions, see Robert Gilpin, *War and Change in World Politics* (New York: Cambridge University Press, 1981); A. F. K. Organski, *World Politics* (New York: Knopf, 1968), chapter 14; Joshua Goldstein, *Long Cycles: Prosperity and War in the Modern Age* (New Haven: Yale University Press, 1988); George Modelski, "The Long Cycle of Global Politics and the Nation-State," *Comparative Studies in Society and History* 20 (April 1978), 214–35; William Thompson, *On Global War: Historical-Structural Approaches to World Politics* (Columbia: University of South Carolina Press, 1988); Paul Kennedy, *The Rise and Fall of the Great Powers: Economic Change and Military Conflict from 1500 to 2000* (New York: Random House, 1987); Jacek Kugler and A. F. K Organski, "The Power Transition: A Retrospective and Prospective Evaluation," in Manus I. Midlarsky, ed., *Handbook of War Studies* (Boston: Unwin Hyman, 1989), 171–94; and Charles Kupchan, *The Vulnerability of Empire* (Ithaca, NY: Cornell University Press, 1994).

9. In a RAND study headed by Charles Wolf, "military capital" is defined as and computed in terms of "the accumulated cost of new military procurement, plus spending on military research and development, minus depreciation of the previously accumulated stock of military equipment" (see Charles Wolf Jr., "Asia in 2015," *Wall Street Journal*, March 20, 1997, A16; and Charles Wolf Jr., et al., *Long-Term Economic and Military Trends, 1994–2015: The United States and Asia* [Santa Monica, CA: RAND, 1995]), 5–8.

10. William C. Wohlforth, "The Stability of a Unipolar World," *International Security* 24:1 (summer 1999), 5–41.

11. For the unipolar moment thesis, see Charles Krauthammer, "The Unipolar Moment," *Foreign Affairs* 70:1 (1991). For the alarmist and sensational account of the rise-of-China argument, see Richard Bernstein and Ross H. Monroe, *The Coming Conflict with China* (New York: Alfred A. Knopf, 1997).

12. Gerald Segal, "Does China Matter?" *Foreign Affairs* 78:5 (September-October 1999), 24–36, quote at 32.

13. The German case illustrates how national roles can change over time. German nationalism quickly withered away after World War II, whereas previous defeats (1806 and 1918) had only fueled more radical nationalism. Harold James finds an explanation in the changing international milieu—the changing international normative cycle—that molded national role expectations. See Harold James, *A German Identity, 1770–1990* (New York: Routledge Books, 1989).

14. Bruce Russett and John Oneal, *Triangulating Peace: Democracy, Interdependence, and International Organizations* (New York: Norton, 2001), 275.

15. Robert Jervis, "The Future of World Politics: Will It Resemble the Past?" *International Security* 16:3 (winter 1991/1992), 42–45.

16. David Balwin, "Power Analysis and World Politics: New Trends versus Old Tendencies," *World Politics* 31 (January 1979), 193.

17. For a startlingly candid new report from the Chinese Communist Party describing the depth and width of China's internal problems arising from economic, ethnic, and religious conflict, see Erik Eckholm, "China's Inner Circle Reveals Big Unrest," *New York Times*, June 3, 2001.

18. See Samuel S. Kim, "China as a Great Power," *Current History* 96:611 (September 1997): 246–51.

19. See "Status of Armed Conflict 1994–1997" in *The Military Balance 1997/98* (London: The International Institute for Strategic Studies, 1997).

20. See Andrew Mack, "Why Big Nations Lose Small Wars: The Politics of Asymmetric Conflict," *World Politics* 27:2 (January 1975), 175–200; John Anquilla, *Dubious Battles: Aggression, Defeat, and the International System* (Washington, D.C.: Crane and Russak, 1992); T. V. Paul, *Asymmetric Conflicts: War Initiation by Weaker Powers* (New York: Cambridge University Press, 1994); Thomas Christensen, "Posing Problems without Catching Up: China's Rise and Challenges for U.S. Security Policy," *International Security* 25:4 (spring 2001), 5–40.

21. Ivan Arreguin-Toft, "How the Weak Win Wars: A Theory of Asymmetric Conflict," *International Security* 26:1 (summer 2001), 96.

22. *Renmin Ribao* [People's Daily], September 3, 1999, 1. In a speech delivered at the conference on North Korea at Texas A&M University on April 17, 2001, John McLaughlin, deputy director of the Central Intelligence Agency (CIA), spotlighted a major intelligence failure, as made evident in a short passage from a U.S. intelligence assessment in early 1950: "an invasion of South Korea is unlikely unless North Korean forces can develop a clear-cut superiority over the increasingly efficient South Korean army." See Remarks by the Deputy Director of Central Intelligence Agency John E. McLaughlin to Texas A&M Conference, "North Korea: Engagement or Confrontation," April 17, 2001, at www.fas.org/irp/cia/product/ddci_speech_04172001.html (accessed 30 April 2001).

23. Richard Ned Lebow, *Between Peace and War: The Nature of International Crisis* (Baltimore: The Johns Hopkins University Press, 1981), 57–97.

24. Christensen, "Posing Problems without Catching Up," 13.

25. For details, see Robert Keohane, *International Institutions and State Power: Essays in International Relations Theory* (Boulder, CO: Westview Press, 1989), and Stephen D. Krasner, ed., *International Regimes* (Ithaca, NY: Cornell University Press, 1983); Celeste Wallander, Helga Haftendorm, and Robert Keohane, eds., "Introduction" in *Imperfect Unions: Security Institutions over Time and Space* (New York: Oxford University Press, 1999), 5.

26. See Jack S. Levy, "The Causes of War: A Review of Theories and Evidence," in *Behavior, Society, and Nuclear War*, vol. I, eds. Philip E. Tetlock et al., (New York: Oxford University Press, 1989), 270. See also Michael Doyle, "Liberalism and World Politics," *American Political Science Review* 80 (1986): 1151–69; Bruce Russett, *Grasping the Democratic Peace: Principles for a Post–Cold War World* (Princeton: Princeton University Press, 1993); David A. Lake, "Powerful Pacifists: Democratic States and War," *American Political Science Review* 86:1 (March 1992), 24–37; and James Lee Ray, "The Democratic Path to Peace," *Journal of Democracy* 8:2 (April 1997), 49–64.

27. For the most well-tested and well-documented study of Kantian liberalism, see Russett and Oneal, *Triangulating Peace*.

28. Friedberg, 18.

29. See the TRADP home page, at www.tumenprogramme.org.

30. For an elaboration of the theoretical and policy implications, see the October 1985 special issue of *World Politics* 38:1, especially Kenneth A. Oye, "Explaining Cooperation under Anarchy: Hypotheses and Strategies," 1–24.

31. William Bloom, *Personal Identity, National Identity, and International Relations* (New York: Cambridge University Press, 1990); Lowell Dittmer and Samuel Kim, eds., *China's Quest for National Identity* (Ithaca, NY: Cornell University Press, 1993); Peter Katenstein, ed., *The Culture of National Security: Norms and Identity in World Politics* (New York: Columbia University Press, 1996); Jill Krause and Neil Renwick, eds., *Identities in International Relations* (New York: St. Martin's Press, 1996); Yosef Lapid and Friedrich Kratochwil, eds., *The Return of Culture and Identity in IR Theory* (Boulder, CO: Lynne Rienner Publishers, 1996); Ilya Prizel, *National Identity and Foreign Policy: Nationalism and Leadership in Poland, Russia, and Ukraine* (New York: Cambridge University Press, 1998); Rodney Bruce Hall, *National Collective Identity: Social Constructs and International Systems* (New York: Columbia University Press, 1999); Alexander Wendt, *Social Theory of International Politics* (New York: Cambridge University Press, 1999); and Samuel Huntington, *The Clash of Civilizations and the Remaking of World Order* (New York: Simon and Schuster, 1996).

32. "Collective memory, by its very nature, impels actors to define themselves intersubjectively. Shaped by past struggles and shared historical accidents, collective memory is both a common discriminating experience and a 'factual' recollection of the group's past 'as it really was.'" See Consuelo Cruz, "Identity and Persuasion: How Nations Remember Their Pasts and Make Their Futures," *World Politics* 52 (April 2000), 276.

33. Dalchoong Kim and Chung-in Moon, eds., *History, Cognition, and Peace in East Asia* (Seoul: Yonsei University Press, 1997) and Barry Buzan and Gerald Segal, "Rethinking East Asian Security," *Survival* 36:2 (summer 1994), 3–21.

34. Gilbert Rozman, "Mutual Perceptions among the Great Powers in Northeast Asia," in Tsuneo Akaha, ed., *Politics and Economics in Northeast Asia: Nationalism and Regionalism in Contention* (New York: St. Martin's Press, 1999), 47.

35. George Breslauer and Philip Tetlocks, eds., *Learning in U.S. and Soviet Foreign Policy* (Boulder, CO: Westview Press, 1991).

36. For further discussion in the context of South Korea and East Asia, see Samuel S. Kim, ed., *Korea's Globalization* (New York: Cambridge University Press, 2000), and Samuel S. Kim, ed., *East Asia and Globalization* (Lanham, MD: Rowman & Littlefield Publishers, 2000).

37. Barry Buzan, "Security, the State, the 'New World Order,' and Beyond," in Ronnie D. Lipschutz, ed., *On Security* (New York: Columbia University Press, 1995), 187–211.

38. Peter Hayes, Lyuba Zarsky, and Walden Bello, *American Lake: Nuclear Peril in the Pacific* (New York: Penguin Books, 1986).

39. Samuel Huntington, "The Lonely Superpower," *Foreign Affairs* 78:2 (March-April 1999), 41.

40. For analysis by Russia's Korea experts based on their discussion with North Korean representatives, see *DPRK Report*, no. 24 (May-June 2000) and *DPRK Report*,

no. 26 (September-October 2000) at the Nautilus Institute home page, at www.nautilus.org. Interestingly enough, Han Sik Park of the University of Georgia, who has extensive connections and who regularly visits North Korea, argues that the Pyongyang summit is a continuation of "legitimacy war" by other means, not the end of it. See Han S. Park, "The Nature and Evolution of the Inter-Korean Legitimacy War," in Kyung-Ae Park and Dalchoong Kim, eds., *Korean Security Dynamics in Transition* (New York: Palgrave, 2001), 3–17.

41. Howard W. French, "Japan Now Officially Hails the Emperor and a Rising Sun," *New York Times*, August 10, 1999, A3.

42. See Calder, "The New Face of Northeast Asia," 115; Victor Cha, "The Ultimate Oxymoron: Japan's Engagement with North Korea," *North Korea's Engagement: Perspectives, Outlook, and Implications,* conference report (National Intelligence Council, Washington, D.C., CR 2001–01, May 2001), 73–85; B. C. Koh, "U.S.-Japan Security Cooperation and the Two Koreas," in Park and Kim, *Korean Security Dynamics in Transition,* 139–41.

43. See *Diplomatic Bluebook 2000* at www.mofa.go.jp/policy/other/bluebook/2000/index.html (accessed 12 June 2001).

44. Korean Central News Agency (KCNA) at www.kcna.co.jp/item/2000/200007/news07/25.htm (accessed 25 July 2000).

45. See Michael H. Armacost and Kenneth B. Pyle, "Japan and the Unification of Korea: Challenges for U.S. Policy Coordination," in Nicholas Eberstadt and Richard J. Ellings, eds., *Korea's Future and the Great Powers* (Seattle: University of Washington Press, 2001), 128.

46. Economist Intelligence Unit, *Country Report: South Korea, North Korea*, 3rd quarter, 1999, 42–43.

47. KCNA, June 1, 2000.

48. *Rodong Sinmun*, June 3, 2000.

49. You Ji, "China and North Korea: A Fragile Relationship of Strategic Convenience," *Journal of Contemporary China* 10:28 (August 2001), 391.

50. Celeste Wallander, "Wary of the West: Russian Security Policy at the Millennium," *Arms Control Today* 30:2 (March 2000), 7–12; "Russia's New Security Concept," *Arms Control Today* 30:1 (January-February 2000): 15–20; Philipp C. Bleak, "Putin Signs New Military Doctrine, Fleshing Out New Security Concept," *Arms Control Today* 30:4 (May 2000), 42.

51. Ronald Grigor, "Provisional Stabilities: The Politics of Identities in Post-Soviet Eurasia," *International Security* 24:3 (winter 1999/2000), 149.

52. Quoted in Seung-Ho Joo, "Russia and Korea: The Summit and After," paper presented at the 42nd Annual Convention of the International Studies Association, Chicago, February 20–23, 2001, 4.

53. Seung-Ho Joo, "Russia and Korea: The Summit and After," 12.

54. For an English text of the Moscow Declaration, see www.korea-np.co.jp/pk/166th_issue/2001080701.htm (accessed 10 September 2001).

55. KCNA, August 4, 2001; emphasis added.

56. Cited in *Korea Herald*, November 30, 2000 (Internet version, www.koreaherald.co.kr).

57. According to Soviet economist N. Bahanova, Soviet aid was responsible for construction of more than seventy facilities producing over one-fourth of the North Korean gross industrial output. See *Pravda*, August 6, 1990, in Foreign Broadcast Information Service (FBIS), Soviet Union, August 10, 1990, 10.

58. Eui-gak Hwang, *The Korean Economies* (Oxford: Clarendon Press, 1993), table 5.4.

59. See *Rodong Sinmun* [Workers' Daily] (Pyongyang), May 27, 1991; February 4, 1992; October 10, 1993; and March 4, 1993.

60. Byung Chul Koh, *The Foreign Policy Systems of North and South Korea* (Berkeley: University of California Press, 1984), 42–43.

61. *Rodong Sinmun*, September 17, 1998.

62. Joint New Year editorial of *Rodong Sinmun, Josoninmingun,* and *Chongnyongjonwi*, January 1, 2001.

63. See KCNA, December 20, 2000 and *Choson Sinbo,* an organ of *Chochongnyon* (pro-DPRK General Association of Korean Residents in Japan), January 14, 2001.

64. "Motun muncherul saeroun kwanchom kwa noppieso poko pulo nakacha" [Let Us See and Solve All Problems from a New Viewpoint and a New Height," editorial, *Rodong Sinmun,* January 9, 2001, 1.

65. Habeeb argues that "issue-specific structural power is the most critical component of power in asymmetrical negotiation." William Habeeb, *Power and Tactics in International Negotiation: How Weak Nations Bargain with Strong Nations* (Baltimore: Johns Hopkins University Press, 1988), 21, 130.

66. Robert A. Pastor, "The Great Powers in the Twentieth Century: From Dawn to Dusk," in Robert A. Pastor, ed., *A Century's Journey: How the Great Powers Shape the World* (New York: Basic Books, 1999), 27.

67. Ronald P. Barston, "The External Relations of Small States," in August Schou and Arne Olav Brundtland, eds., *Small States in International Relations* (Stockholm: Almqvist and Wiskell, 1971), 46; Habeeb, *Power and Tactics in International Negotiation,* 130–1.

68. Peter Hayes, *Pacific Powderkeg: American Nuclear Dilemmas in Korea* (Lexington, MA: Lexington Books, 1991), xiv.

69. A 1995 RAND Corporation study concluded that there existed a "medium likelihood" of North Korea launching an attack against South Korea out of desperation. In such a case, there would be a "high likelihood" of the use of chemical weapons by the North. *New York Times,* January 28, 1996.

70. Scott Snyder, "North Korea's Challenge of Regime Survival: Internal Problems and Implications for the Future," *Pacific Affairs* 73:4 (winter 2000/2001), 522.

71. Ashton B. Carter and William J. Perry, *Preventive Defense: A New Security Strategy for America* (Washington, D.C.: Brookings Institution Press, 1999), 123–4. A footnote for this statement explains that Ashton Carter was not present for the meeting referred to here, so Perry "tells this story himself," 123.

72. Snyder, "North Korea's Challenge of Regime Survival," 524.

73. *Rodong Sinmun*, June 1, 2000, 6.

74. Based on figures from mid-2000, the North Korean armed forces are the world's fifth largest, its ground forces are the world's third largest, and its special operations

forces are the world's largest. Some six million reserves supplement the active duty personnel. See U.S. Secretary of Defense William Cohen's "2000 Report to Congress: Military Situation on the Korean Peninsula, September 12, 2000" at www.defenselink.mil/news/Sept2000/korea09122000.html (accessed 10 December 2000).

75. For further analysis, see Samuel S. Kim, "PukMi hyopsang kwa Pukhan ui chunryak" [DPRK-U.S. Negotiations and North Korea's Strategy] in *Pukhan ui Hyopsang Chunryak kwa NamPukhan Kwangkye* [North Korea's Negotiating Strategy and South-North Relations], ed. Kwak Tae-hwan (Seoul: Institute of Far Eastern Studies, Kyungnam University, 1997), 163–86, and "North Korea and the United Nations," *International Journal of Korean Studies* 1, no. 1 (spring 1997), 77–105.

76. Charles Ziegler, *Foreign Policy and East Asia: Learning and Adaptation in the Gorbachev Era* (New York: Cambridge University Press, 1993), 166–69. See also *Wolgan Chosun* [Monthly Korea] (October 1995), 104–28 for a transcribed text of a secret tape recording of Kim Jong Il's conversations with the South Korean film director Shin Sang-ok and his actress wife, Choe Un-hui.

II

INTERACTIONS

2

United States–North Korean Relations: From Welfare to Workfare?

Robert A. Manning

The remarkable transformation in North Korean behavior toward the outside world since the June 2000 North-South Summit—from hermit kingdom to hyperactivity—has added a new layer of complexity to the situation on the peninsula—and to the dynamics of U.S.–North Korean relations. While definitive judgment on whether the political "coming out" of Kim Jong Il both at home and abroad signifies a "new," reform-oriented North Korea is premature, this chapter argues that Pyongyang's new diplomacy still fits into many traditional patterns evidenced over the past half century of North Korea's existence. U.S. relations with both Koreas—one allied, one adversarial—have reflected the structural differences and asymmetries of a global superpower, largely a preeminent maritime power in East Asia, and a continental-centered middle power as well as differences of history, culture, and geography. In the case of North Korea, relations were frozen in isolation and Cold-War enmity from the aftermath of the Korean War until 1988. Thus, this chapter focuses on the period between 1988 and 2001.

The dynamics of U.S.–North Korean relations reflect very different incentive structures driving each side's respective policies. The animating motives for the U.S. have been a mix of threat reduction, humanitarian considerations, and alliance management; for Pyongyang, achieving an opening to the United States—and all the sometimes odd twists and turns of its diplomacy—are best seen as part of a longstanding pattern of seeking to manipulate major powers' concerns to its benefit. North Korea was remarkably successful in playing China and the Soviet Union since its inception as a state. It also has viewed its dealings with the U.S. as a means to gain leverage over Seoul. It is curious that its efforts to cultivate Washington ramped up just as the Cold War was ending and Pyongyang's subsidies from Moscow were beginning to wane.

Though its posture toward the U.S. has altered in what might be called a period of engagement over the past twelve years, North Korea has had a preoccupation with the U.S. The U.S. has been perceived in Pyongyang as a major actor in the division of Korea, as having played a central role in shaping its national strategy and political mythology, and as the principal obstacle to a national strategy and foreign policy centered on enhancing Pyongyang's legitimacy (at the expense of Seoul) and achieving reunification on its terms. After World War II, and then with its intervention in the Korean War, the U.S. replaced Japan as the preeminent source of Korean division in Pyongyang's perception, and thus in North Korean mythology became the cause of Korean malaise. This theme returned in fall 2000 when North Korea strongly promoted a visit by then-President Clinton, and continued into May 2001, with Pyongyang arguing that the lack of engagement by the Bush administration was its main reason for essentially halting the renewed North-South reconciliation process begun in June 2000. (In fact, by January 20, 2001, when Bush assumed office, the North-South diplomatic process generated by the summit had come to a virtual standstill.)

This chapter assesses the dynamics of U.S.–North Korean relations in the context of both nation's' foreign policies in the post–Cold War circumstances of the 1990s. North Korean policy is judged on the basis of its behavior patterns and its objectives and intentions as discerned from its public representations, diplomatic encounters, and other substantive actions.

As the Cold War wound down, the United States loomed ever larger in North Korean strategy, becoming the focal point of Pyongyang's efforts at regime survival and the key to enhancing international legitimacy, obtaining economic aid, investment, and increased trade, as well as tactical benefits in its relations with South Korea. Where during the Cold War, the U.S. was viewed principally in adversarial terms (with intermittent hints at diplomatic openings), in this decade, Pyongyang's pattern of behavior suggests a policy designed to substitute the United States for the economic and security role previous played by the Soviet Union and China in North Korean calculus, largely by utilizing its nuclear weapons and the larger menu of threats (missiles, chemical and biological weapons, and conventional forces) as bargaining chips. This is most certainly not to argue that Pyongyang devoted enormous portions of relatively scarce resources to develop its military assets principally as bargaining chips. They serve a large role for Pyongyang, what might be termed "counter-deterrence," but its weapons of mass destruction (WMD) also serve as a prospective bargaining chip, an important incentive motivating the U.S. to diplomatically engage the DPRK.

HISTORICAL CONTEXT

Over nearly four decades after the armistice ended the Korean War, U.S.-DPRK relations were frozen in Cold-War enmity and distrust. What modest communication existed occurred principally through the Military Armistice Commission or in the form of intermittent confrontation such as the 1968 seizing of the USS *Pueblo*, intercepted on a mission in North Korean waters, and the 1976 axe murders on the demilitarized zone (DMZ). The Republic of Korea (ROK) was derided publicly by Pyongyang as little more than an extension of the United States, though privately Pyongyang's views, reflected in its dealings with Seoul, were less fanciful.[1] In the mid-1970s there was a hint of possible change, as then–Secretary of State Henry A. Kissinger raised the idea of "cross-recognition." That policy envisioned China and the USSR establishing ties with South Korea with the quid pro quo that the U.S. and Japan would then recognize North Korea.[2] To Pyongyang's chagrin, only two decades after the cross-recognition idea surfaced did anything come of it, and even then only the South Korea part of the equation was realized as a result of Roh Tae Woo's *Nordpolitik* foreign policy initiative, thus adding insult to injury.

Ironically, in the 1990s the U.S. would loom still larger in North Korean strategic calculus, but now as a potential alternate security guarantor, economic lifeline, and benefactor. This shift is a new posture borne of weakness and vulnerability. The isolation and idiosyncratic manner of the DPRK has led the American press and pundits to often portray the DPRK as crazy or unpredictable, its behavior as erratic, particularly during the apogee of the 1993 to 1994 nuclear crisis.[3] However, within its own logic, Pyongyang appears not only rational, but increasingly absolutely masterful in terms of diplomatic tactics when viewed within the internal logic system of Pyongyang's larger objective: a strategic opening to the U.S. as the lodestar of regime survival.

This slowly unfolding transformation in North Korean–U.S. relations from requited hostility, separation, and distrust to, thus far, only partially requited and still ambiguous quasi-amity reflects major policy shifts on the part of North Korea beginning in the late 1980s, in great measure forced by the end of the Cold War, the demise of the Soviet Union, and the failure of the North Korean economic model. This evolution has been playing out to a large degree in the crucible of the North Korean nuclear issue.

The dynamics behind this strategic shift in Pyongyang's basic view of the U.S. and, more broadly, in its dealings with the international community, must be understood in the historical context of North Korea's political, cultural, and economic experience, particularly the history of its relations with the Soviet Union and China. North Korea's objectives have similarly been reshaped over time, reflecting these external and internal factors. The goal of a unified Korea under Kim Il Sung, free of foreign forces on its soil—communization by force—began to look increasingly unachievable by the 1980s. Instead, the hope of some variation on a "One Nation, two systems" theme acquired more saliency as a formula for regime and state survival. In regard to the United States, it was ironically American emphasis on North Korea's nuclear weapons program that provided the avenue for a political opening.

For the U.S., North Korea remained a residue of the Cold War, but took on another dimension as a post–Cold War threat, with implications for U.S. interests in East Asia writ large, as well as for its nonproliferation policy, and even of late, according to some analysts, its larger strategic plans for constructing ballistic missile defenses. U.S. policy has been complicated by Cold-War baggage and values questions, with enormous congressional skepticism about forging a relationship with Pyongyang, indeed of North Korea even as an *interlocuteur valide*. This is reinforced by laws and legislation—on nonproliferation, on terrorism, on human rights—that serve as structural impediments to normal relations.

It is a measure of the degree to which U.S.-DPRK relations have evolved in recent years that the nuclear issue and the resulting Agreed Framework negotiated between the two states appears very different in terms of its place in the relationship in 2001 than at the time of the deal in 1994. In October 1994, and arguably until roughly late 1998, the Agreed Framework was in large measure the centerpiece U.S. policy toward North Korea. Now it is only one element, albeit still critical, in a much more textured and multifaceted relationship, including Pyongyang as a major recipient of humanitarian aid, military relations in cooperation on missing in action (MIA) issues, discussions on North Korean missiles, and in the complexity of balancing U.S.-DPRK relations so as to minimally infringe on the U.S.-ROK relationship.

THE NUCLEAR ISSUE

North Korea's nuclear program, whose origins date back at least to the 1960s, did not occur in a vacuum. North Korea's motives have almost certainly changed over time since Pyongyang first began to move into the nuclear field with scientific cadre trained in the Soviet Union in the late 1950s, and a small experimental laboratory reactor furnished by the USSR, operational in the 1960s.[4] In brief, the nuclear quest was at earlier stages probably viewed by Kim Il Sung as an instrument of both deterrence and coercion (as well as a status symbol) to serve his strategic goal of reunification by force.

Since the late 1980s, however, Pyongyang appears to have viewed its nuclear weapons program as an instrument of deterrence, an ultimate insurance policy and, in the view of at least some in its policy elite, a political bargaining chip to achieve the key goal of regime survival, one that it has employed with some success in its opening to the U.S.[5] This apparent shift in objectives is an adaptation to the new political, economic, and strategic realities resulting from the demise of the Soviet Union, qualitatively diminished ties with both the USSR and China, and the related acceleration of North Korean economic stagnation.

Beyond North Korean ideology and ambition as well as U.S. nuclear capabilities, it should also be recalled that South Korea was pursuing its own nuclear weapons program, which it halted in the late 1970s when U.S. pressure in effect forced Seoul to choose between the U.S. nuclear umbrella or strategic independence. The backdrop of South Korean nuclear ambitions, combined with U.S. military posture, provides the context for assessing the North Korean nuclear program. This security environment also underscored the importance of North Korea's relations with its two nuclear weapons–state allies, China and the Soviet Union—and of the erosion of those alliances.

It is against this backdrop, beginning in the mid-1980s, that the fortuitous chain of events building toward the nuclear crisis of the early 1990s occurred. In 1984, the Reagan administration's persuasion of Moscow to intercede with Pyongyang was a moment of maximum Soviet leverage. Apart from trade subsidies, North Korea was negotiating with the Soviets for supplying an arms modernization program, including the S-27 *Frogfoot* and M-29s, as well as four Soviet-supplied nuclear power reactors. Moscow had routinely imposed tough nonproliferation standards (e.g., return of spent fuel) on its Warsaw Pact allies. Demanding accession to the Nuclear Non-Proliferation Treaty (NPT) by North Korea as part of the nuclear reactor bargain did not require any policy shift, and it was the sort of stance by Moscow with which Pyongyang was familiar.

The DPRK had no experience in dealing with the International Atomic Energy Agency (IAEA), and prior to the 1990 Gulf War, had little reason to suspect tough pressure from the Vienna-based institution. It was the exercise of Soviet influence, the quid pro quo it demanded, that resulted in North Korea acceding to the NPT in 1985. This apparently was not a decision fully considered by Pyongyang to abide by international norms. Rather, it was an act of expedience on an issue that North Korea had little reason to expect would mushroom into a major global issue seven years later. It is unclear whether North Korea intended to comply with the IAEA full-scope safeguards requirements at all.

Incompetence on the part of the IAEA permitted North Korea extra time to reach a safeguards agreement. The IAEA sent Pyongyang the wrong set of forms to fill out. Instead of Inf-Circ/153 forms, it sent Inf-Circ/66, forms sent to non-NPT states that belong to the IAEA.[6] It was not until eighteen months later (the timeframe for member states to respond) that the IAEA became aware of its mistake, and then sent the proper forms. As a consequence, North Korea gained a de facto three-year grace period until the end of 1988 before becoming officially delinquent in meeting its IAEA obligations. These forms require a country to declare its nuclear facilities and activities to begin the process of putting in place a corresponding safeguards regime.

EVOLVING NORTH KOREAN POLICY AND "MODEST INITIATIVE"

As this diplomatic confrontation began to unfold, the Reagan administration initiated a mild thaw in its policy toward North Korea in May 1988. This nuanced shift was driven in large measure by the *Nordpolitik* initiative of Roh Tae Woo, which began to alter the diplomatic status quo in Northeast Asia as the Cold War wound down. Prior to this shift, U.S. diplomats were prohibited from even engaging in conversation with their North Korean counterparts at third country events (e.g., embassy receptions). Apart from the unrealized notion of cross-recognition and occasional nonofficial American visits, most prominently visits by then-Congressman Stephen Solarz (D-NY) in the early 1980s and several visits by evangelist Reverend Billy Graham, there had been little contact or hint of change in U.S.–North Korean relations. Stimulated by Roh Tae Woo's *Nordpolitik* openings toward the Soviet Union, China, and North Korea, the Reagan administration in its final year took what might be considered baby steps in the direction of a belated cross-recognition. It embarked on a process of political dialogue dubbed the "modest initiative" aimed at complementing Roh's *Nordpolitik.*

North Korea responded to the "modest initiative" by agreeing to open an official diplomatic channel with the U.S. in Beijing, allowing U.S. diplomats to converse informally with North Koreans in chance encounters, loosening the embargo to allow humanitarian trade, and suggesting reciprocal actions aimed at improving relations as North Korea met a laundry list of U.S. concerns. These included a renunciation of terrorism, cooperation in recovering MIA U.S. soldiers from the Korean War, addressing human rights concerns, improving North-South dialogue, and complying with Pyongyang's IAEA obligations. The administration suggested that North Korean cooperation in these areas would lead to reciprocal U.S. responses moving toward more normal relations.

This basic framework was, in essence, continued and enlarged during the Bush administration. However, the North Korean nuclear weapons program began to emerge as the centerpiece of DPRK-U.S. relations (and IAEA concern), particularly in light of the revelations about Saddam Hussein's covert nuclear weapons program in the aftermath of the Gulf War. Moreover, the entire geopolitical context of the nuclear drama was transformed. Communism began to collapse with the fall of the Berlin Wall in 1989. Another attempted family dynasty close to the Kim family (both personally and in terms of dynastic ambitions), the Ceaucescus in Romania, collapsed in December 1990, and then there was the August 1991 attempted coup in Moscow that precipitated the demise of the USSR.

North Korea's two allies, China and the USSR, began to distance themselves from Pyongyang and gravitate toward South Korea. The credibility of Pyongyang's security guarantees, let alone nuclear umbrella, was at best greatly attenuated. The Soviets put trade on a hard currency basis. Subsequently, Russian officials reinterpreted and, in effect, qualitatively downgraded their security commitment to North Korea.[7] North Korea thus faced not only new vulnerability with the loss of security guarantees, but new economic pressures as a result of withdrawn Soviet subsidies.

NUCLEAR DETERMINANT OF DPRK-U.S. TIES

The train of events that eventually led to the October 21, 1994, DPRK-U.S. Agreed Framework had its origins in the preceding years, 1989 to 1991, which generated the political crisis of 1993 and 1994. During that period, Pyongyang became seriously delinquent in meetings its IAEA obligations. This was mitigated when North Korea finally signed a safeguards agreement with the IAEA in January 1992. During this period, evidence began to surface that Pyongyang was reprocessing plutonium from its five megawatt reactor at the burgeoning Yongbyon complex where still larger reactors and a reprocessing plant the length of a football field were under construction.

Clearly, as the North Korea nuclear program became the object of heightened concern during 1990, the economic basket of concerns loomed large in North Korea's political calculus, as did a sense of military vulnerability.[8] The viability of its economy is obviously a precondition for sustaining the regime and the North Korean state. [9] Its economic decline and fears of absorption may have raised the profile of its concern about political legitimacy. It is difficult to weigh any of these closely interwoven factors separately. But Pyongyang viewed the U.S. as the keeper of the gate: neither Japan nor South Korea were likely to be very forthcoming toward the North until Washington approved. At the same time, Pyongyang had a new imperative to alter its security environment as tensions rose on the peninsula, while the reliability of its "allies" approached nonexistence.

Pyongyang saw the U.S. in the forefront on the nuclear issue, leader of the U.S.-ROK-Japan core of a global coalition, and the largest prospective threat to Pyongyang.[10] Indeed, it sought to address the entire nuclear problem through the prism of the U.S. This was most evident in 1992 through 1994, as every demand from the IAEA was met with a reply demanding some U.S. action. In any case, Kim Il Sung, in the retrospective view of several Bush administration officials, likely made a strategic decision to pursue an opening to Washington.[11]

This dimension of DPRK policy is often missed as analysts tend to focus on the tactical aspect of Pyongyang seeking to drive a wedge between Washington and Seoul. But North Korea had few other options. For all its brinkmanship and vituperative official rhetoric, Pyongyang views the U.S. in strategic terms. Though an inexact analogy, it has, in its own idiosyncratic way, embarked on a strategic shift something like Nixon's opening to China. As the Cold War began to fade, it appeared that Kim Il Sung chose to pursue a political opening to the U.S. sometime in 1990 or 1991. Some U.S. government analysts suggest this shift may have occurred as early at 1988.

Once again, the "shrimp among the whales" psychology appeared in various pieces of evidence. An opening to the U.S. could reduce the security threat Kim Il Sung feared and bring his regime greater legitimacy (opening the door to broad international economic and political engagement with it). Ultimately, Kim and his political elite hoped the U.S. might be a potential mediator or restraint factor against fears of absorption by the South. The first glimmer of potential moderation in North Korean rhetoric and political body language began to be hinted at as early as 1988, and has become increasingly evident since 1992.

From boilerplate demands for the complete and immediate withdrawal of U.S. troops from Korea—a staple of North Korean rhetoric through most of the 1980s—by late 1988 Pyongyang's rhetoric began to display a nuanced evolution. A November 7, 1988, arms control and North-South reconciliation proposal elaborated on a similar call the year before, calling for a phased reduction of U.S. troops from Korea in three stages in the context of massive North-South arms reductions to one hundred thousand, at which point the North called for U.S. forces to fully withdraw.[12] It should also be noted that since 1980, Pyongyang's public reunification proposals grew increasingly more modest, defining it in terms of a confederation of two equal, entities maintaining autonomy and their own respective social systems.[13] Sustaining the regime rather than aggrandizement was inherent in this recycled view of reunification.

In retrospect, this strategic logic was present during the tortuous diplomacy that began in 1991, though buried in the layers of hostility and distrust accumulated over the previous four decades. On top of this was a total absence of any communication, which made deciphering the DPRK's new logic highly problematic, particularly as the emphasis of U.S. policy, indeed its singular focus since 1993, was putting out the nuclear fire. Discerning this logic was further complicated by the additional factor of North-South rivalry and gamesmanship impacting on the U.S.-ROK alliance, which meant that the calculus of each U.S. action had to keep the balance in the increasingly difficult DPRK-U.S.-ROK triangle. For South Korea, the tactical aspect of Pyongyang's approach—cultivating the U.S. while marginalizing the ROK—appeared predominant. DPRK-U.S. diplomacy was, at each step of the way, constrained by South Korean concerns.

Yet this strategic logic helps explain the otherwise puzzling North Korean behavior at key decision points along the path to the Agreed Framework, particularly as the confrontation qualitatively intensified in the seventeen months prior to the October 1994 accord. Not least, this perspective also explains Kim Il Sung's dramatic response—transforming a situation on the brink of conflict to one of sweet reason overnight—when graced with an empathetic visit from former U.S. President Jimmy Carter.

THE NUCLEAR PROBLEM MOUNTS

The nuclear drama that reached its crescendo during Carter's act of freelance diplomacy in June 1994 began its first act much earlier in a political climate reflecting these parallel initiatives. North Korea's failure to conclude a safeguards agreement with the IAEA at the end of 1988 began to rouse concern in Washington as the Bush administration took office in early 1989. This concern would reach grave proportions by 1991, in no small measure because of the precedent of Iraq's complete deception of the IAEA with its covert nuclear weapons program. The Iraqi disclosures renewed global fears about nuclear proliferation and created credibility problems for the IAEA. While it is beyond the scope of this essay to recount the full diplomatic history of the nuclear issue, the aspects that illuminate North Korean motives are key to fathoming the dynamics of North Korea–U.S. relations.[14]

The net effect of this situation was intensified pressure on Pyongyang. Reflecting this concern, then–Assistant Secretary of State for East Asian and Pacific Affairs Richard H. Solomon, in a widely cited policy speech, attached a new gravity to the issue, describing the North Korean nuclear problem as "the number-one threat to Asian security."[15] This movement of the nuclear program to the center of the U.S. agenda with North Korea was the first of several key political shocks affecting Pyongyang's calculations. While this focused an unexpected spotlight on North Korea, it also may have begun to suggest to Pyongyang that the price of its nuclear weapons program was being bid up: the bigger the issue, the more it was worth. Yet despite the fact that there were no powerlines or grid connected to its Yongbyon complex, Pyongyang steadfastly maintained that it had no nuclear weapons program. Kim Il Sung himself denied the charge on more than one occasion.[16]

North Korea's standard refrain during the 1980s whenever the U.S. or South Korea raised the nuclear issue was to cite the need to remove U.S. nuclear weapons from South Korea.[17] As the nuclear confrontation intensified, North Korea systematically addressed the nuclear issue not in terms of its IAEA or NPT commitments, but solely in bilateral terms, its focus firmly fixed on the U.S. Indeed, Pyongyang cited two conditions before it would conclude a safeguards agreement with the IAEA: removal of U.S. weapons from South Korea, and a negative security assurance from the U.S.[18]

The U.S., however, continued to escalate international pressure on North Korea to cooperate with the IAEA. In July 1991, North Korea indicated a willingness to sign a safeguards agreement with the IAEA, with the expectation that it would formally sign at an IAEA general conference the following month. But North Korea reneged when the IAEA passed a resolution calling on the North to cooperate in allowing inspections.

Diplomatic encirclement limited DPRK options, painting it in a corner. However, it was not just pressure, but what Pyongyang would view as concessions or enticements that allowed a diplomatic process to begin in earnest. Unrelated but serendipitous events in Moscow opened a seminal breakthrough that created the political space for diplomatic progress: the August 1991 attempted coup and new concerns over "loose nukes" led the Bush administration to announce a unilateral withdrawal of tactical nuclear weapons worldwide on September 27, 1991, which was reciprocated by then–Soviet President Gorbachev. While this policy shift focused principally on demobilizing all tactical nuclear weapons in former Soviet republics, it affected U.S. deployments in South Korea, meeting a major North Korean concern. Then, after Gorbachev responded to Bush's action with an equally bold move, the U.S. announced it would remove all air-launched nuclear weapons deployed overseas.[19] One can only speculate on what North Korean perceptions of this U.S. unilateral move might have been. Nonetheless, one of its longstanding demands had been met.

The Bush initiative was a step in the direction of negative security assurances. It removed the frequently denounced "nuclear threat" to North Korea. Perhaps more than any other single event, the Bush nuclear initiative opened up new possibilities that quickly began to be realized. In mid-December 1991, the North and South signed a sweeping Agreement on Reconciliation, Nonaggression, and Exchange and Cooperation. Then, on December 18, Roh Tae Woo announced that there were no nuclear weapons anywhere on South Korean soil. On December 31, North and South Korea signed a joint Denuclearization Declaration in which both sides pledged they would "not test, manufacture, possess, store, deploy, or use nuclear weapons." In addition, they agreed not to "possess facilities for nuclear reprocessing and uranium enrichment." This exercise in mutual restraint went well beyond NPT and IAEA norms and requirements.

The U.S. took an additional step that addressed DPRK security concerns: canceling the major annual military exercise "Team Spirit" for 1992. Team Spirit has long been anathema to Pyongyang. It ritually denounced them as "nuclear war preparations," but its real concern was that it forced the North to mobilize its forces in countermeasures at considerable expense. After Pyongyang indicated it would soon conclude a safeguards agreement, the U.S. then took another significant step in the direction of normal relations.

On January 22, 1992, Undersecretary of State Arnold Kanter met with Kim Young Sun, a top official of the ruling Korean Worker's Party, in the highest-level contact between the two governments until 1999. That meeting laid out the broad contours of what eventually would evolve into the nuclear accord: If North Korea abandoned its nuclear weapons program and began adhering to global norms, the U.S. would move toward normal relations and welcome Pyongyang into the community of nations.

Kim pledged that North Korea would not only sign a safeguards agreement, but would also implement the bilateral inspection regime under the North-South denuclearization accord. This occurred after the U.S. indicated that the North would be permitted to inspect U.S. military bases in the South on a reciprocal basis in the context of a bilateral inspection regime. Thus, yet another DPRK demand was met. In an interesting hint of North Korea's evolving strategic views, according to former U.S. officials present at the meeting, the North Koreans suggested to Kanter that the U.S. and North Korea should form an alliance against Japan.[20]

In the wake of the Kanter meeting, North Korea did cooperate on the nuclear issue, signing an IAEA safeguards agreement on January 30. In May, IAEA Director Hans Blix visited North Korea's nuclear facilities. Subsequently, the IAEA conducted ad hoc and regular inspections of the North's nuclear facilities, including its reprocessing facility.

Nonetheless, it was clear that North Korea saw the nuclear question as its key to a wider economic and political engagement with the U.S., Japan, and the world at large. Those in Pyongyang who sought to transform its relations with the U.S. could argue that they got U.S. nuclear weapons out of Korea, Team Spirit was cancelled, and from no significant contact, they were treated to meetings with top American officials. Their behavior suggests they viewed these moves as initial good faith efforts and reciprocated. Pyongyang asked for a follow-up meeting with Kanter, which the Bush administration refused as events began a downward spiral.[21]

But Pyongyang had not yet really played its nuclear card. It saw the nuclear issue as an instrument that could be used to build relations with the U.S., but had no clear idea of what the DPRK nuclear program might be worth. IAEA pressure to clarify discrepancies in past DPRK nuclear activities began to accelerate DPRK-U.S. dangers and opportunities. The incoming Clinton administration in Washington didn't seem to know what game was being played. This perception gap—North Korea's hope of cashing in on its known nuclear program for a package of benefits versus a U.S. stress solely on proliferation, and failure to indicate the payoff for Pyongyang's nuclear weapons program—may help explain how the situation degenerated to near war in the period that followed.

THE PRESSURE COOKER

The train of events began to veer off of its promising track in the fall of 1992. International pressure on North Korea continued. In retrospect, an additional factor in the downward spiral of events appears to be the impending change of governments in Washington and Seoul: Pyongyang could wait and test two new, more liberal Presidents, Bill Clinton and Kim Young Sam, the ROK's first civilian, democratically elected President. By September, the IAEA became alarmed by the results of its laboratory analysis of the plutonium samples the DPRK had admitted reprocessing. Chemical analysis revealed that there were three separate batches produced over three years, not the one instance declared by Pyongyang: North Korea had been caught lying. By November 1992, the IAEA began to get tough, publicly accusing the DPRK of not declaring all of its facilities. U.S. intelligence made available to the IAEA indicated that two nuclear waste sites had been camouflaged and were said by Pyongyang to be off limits because they were "military bases."

The quantum leap into confrontation started in February 1993, when the IAEA took an unprecedented step, formally requesting a "special inspection." North Korea refused to permit the IAEA to visit these sites on the grounds that the 1993 Team Spirit military exercise was planned to go forward. Pyongyang also essentially accused the IAEA of illegal search and seizure because its demands were based on, "intelligence information fabricated by the

United States." In fact, U.S. intelligence had shared satellite photos with the IAEA, alerting it to what appeared to be disguised waste sites, which Pyongyang claimed were military facilities, and thus, off limits. In a letter to then–IAEA Director Hans Blix, North Korea's Nuclear Energy minister, Choi Hak Gun, said that this special inspection request was "clear evidence that you joined in the plot of a hostile country . . . which is trying to make our military sites open to disarm us and thereby strangle our socialist system."[22]

Once again, to North Korea, its relations to the IAEA were undistinguishable from its relations to the U.S., a pattern that intensified at each step along the bumpy road to the Geneva accord. At the same time, at every point along the jagged path toward the eventual outlines of an incentive structure to freeze its nuclear program, Pyongyang was careful to leave the door open, if just a tiny crack.

The combination of humiliation at the IAEA and the reinstituted Team Spirit exercise, which began on March 9, helped to precipitate the first of two benchmark acts of brinksmanship in the nuclear drama: on March 12, North Korea declared it would become the first member state to ever withdraw from the NPT. Like the subsequent watershed event—the removal of its reactor core in May 1994—it appears in hindsight to be an effort to force the U.S. to make a serious offer. That decision set the clock ticking, as it would take effect in ninety days. While the North allowed the IAEA to continue the implementation of current safeguards, it steadfastly refused IAEA requests to see the two suspected waste sites.

The Clinton administration, preoccupied with issues such as Somalia and Haiti, did not engage in any policy-level discussions with Pyongyang during its first six months in office. Pyongyang's threat managed to get the administration's attention, however, and in late April preparations for June talks began between then–Assistant Secretary of State Robert L. Gallucci and DPRK Vice Minister of Foreign Affairs Kang Sok Ju. What is striking about the joint statement and press remarks resulting from the meetings and similarly in subsequent negotiations is the remarkable difference in emphasis of the two sides.

The discrepancy between the U.S. singular focus on IAEA compliance and North Korea's steady focus on its concerns relating to the U.S. is striking. Thus, a joint statement on June 11, 1993 (twenty-four hours before the NPT withdrawal was to take effect), listed three agreed principles, beginning with "Assurances against the threat and use of force, including nuclear weapons." The other two principles included noninterference in each other's internal affairs and support for peaceful reunification. The statement added that "in this context" the two governments agreed to continue dialogue and the DPRK unilaterally suspended carrying out its NPT withdrawal.[23]

Similarly, in a second round of talks in July, a mutually agreed to DPRK press statement stressed that the U.S. "reaffirmed its commitment on assurances against the threat and use of force, including nuclear weapons."[24] But in the July talks a new blandishment emerged: both sides, said the statement, "recognize the desirability of the DPRK's intention to replace its graphite moderated reactors with light-water reactors." In addition, "as part of a final resolution of the nuclear issues," according to the statement, "the U.S. is prepared to support the introduction of LWRs [light-water reactors]."[25]

Both sides appeared to be groping toward a quid pro quo, trading the DPRK nuclear program for a still emerging package of benefits. But getting there would require a dangerous and circuitous route. To continue its negotiations with the U.S., Pyongyang would have to meet two conditions set by Washington: consultations with the IAEA and dialogue with South Korea.

This began the most dangerous period in the drama, as North Korea, apparently anxious about the detection capabilities of the nuclear watchdog agency, played a dangerous cat and mouse game with the IAEA from August 1993 until the following April, at several points not permitting the IAEA to carry out minimal safeguard activities to verify even a continuity of safeguards on its monitored program. This periodically heightened tensions to the point that by early 1994, the Clinton administration augmented its forces and sent Patriot missiles to Korea. At the same time, the administration conducted lower-level discussions with the DPRK, but would not enter into a third round of high-level talks until Pyongyang allowed the IAEA full access to its declared nuclear facilities and held talks with Seoul.

Pyongyang sought to turn the growing crisis into an opportunity. During an October 1993 visit to Pyongyang by then-Chairman of the House Subcommittee on Asian and Pacific Affairs Gary Ackerman (D-NY), the North Koreans presented a detailed "package deal" proposal to a working-level diplomat who was accompanying Ackerman. The proposal was summarily dismissed by senior U.S. officials. In November 1993, Kong Sok Ju issued a statement publicly calling for negotiating a "package solution." Then, during a visit by South Korean President Kim Young Sam in late November, the U.S. and ROK agreed on what they called a "broad and thorough" approach, using that rubric to avoid using the term "package deal." In the weeks that followed, the U.S. sought to project a conciliatory stance towards the DPRK. Nonetheless, the North Koreans refused to allow the IAEA full access to its facilities. Around this time, North-South talks broke down as a North Korean negotiator threatened Seoul would become "a sea of fire" in a conflict. North Korea had become a major political issue in the U.S., with a number of pundits calling for "preemptive strikes" against its nuclear facilities.

In this climate, North Korea pushed its brinksmanship over the edge on a second major occasion. In April 1994, Pyongyang shut off its five-megawatt reactor and informed the IAEA that it intended to refuel the reactor "at an early date." Washington had made it clear that such an escalation of the nuclear threat would mark the point of no return. Indeed, the U.S. began to push for UN security council sanctions against North Korea. Pyongyang clearly knew what its actions meant. If it refueled the reactor and reprocessed the eight thousand fuel rods from its reactor core, it could obtain enough plutonium for four to six nuclear weapons. Moreover, North Korea had said on several occasions that it would consider sanctions "an act of war."

FROM CARTER TO GENEVA

At this point, former President Jimmy Carter, who had been invited on several occasions since 1990 to visit Pyongyang, could not be dissuaded by the administration from going. While key administration officials briefed Carter, he was clearly freelancing. Despite a remarkable turn of events in which Carter created his own reality live on CNN, embarrassing President Clinton by announcing that the U.S. call for sanctions was suspended prior to an official decision, he generated a good rapport with Kim Il Sung and halted the slide toward confrontation.[26] In exchange for a freeze on North Korea's nuclear program, the U.S. agreed to a third round of talks with the DPRK in Geneva.

North Korea again succeeded in getting the administration's attention, but from its perspective it had not gotten much in tangible benefits since the 1992 meeting with Kanter. Moreover, it still did not have an answer to the one key question: If we bargain away our nuclear program, what, precisely, do we get for it? Finally, a package was to be put on the table.

In retrospect, Pyongyang appeared torn between its new imperative of cultivating the U.S. as a strategic life raft and its ideology and experience, which defined the U.S. as a mortal threat. The stridency of North Korean rhetoric and frequent disregard for U.S. admonitions about the need to meet IAEA obligations made every U.S. move toward North Korea difficult. Each small step, each meeting had to be justified, inducing extreme caution in policy managers. In 1993 to 1994 North Korea hit the front pages as a mainstream issue as commentators and legislators began suggesting preemptive strikes and accused the administration of appeasement.[27] This pressure heightened the difficulty for the administration to take any action that might be perceived as rewarding bad behavior. The Clinton administration's approach, defining the issue principally as a proliferation problem rather than a regional security or reunification problem, further complicated efforts to design a demand-centered approach to North Korea.

What is remarkable about the third round of talks is that despite the fact that Kim Il Sung suddenly died of a heart attack a day after the talks began on July 8, 1994, after a relatively brief intermission, the negotiations went forward in August and reached the outlines of a deal. An agreed statement issued on August 12, 1994, again followed the pattern of previous accords. It reaffirmed the June 1993 principles, the U.S. agreed to a package that included the replacement of North Korea's reactors with LWRs, security assurances, and the opening of diplomatic and economic relations, its three-pronged goal.

After working-level efforts fleshed out the details, the two sides reconvened in late September 1994 to craft the final language of an agreement, which was reached on October 21, 1994. Thus, despite the traumatic loss of its "Great Leader," a cult figure who had ruled North Korea since its inception in 1948, within a matter of weeks after the U.S. put a comprehensive package on the negotiating table, an accord was reached. In retrospect, it was fortuitous that Kim Il Sung had agreed to the essence of the deal before he unexpectedly died.

Moreover, the North Koreans managed to obtain a sort of promissory note from Bill Clinton to Kim Jong Il affirming U.S. responsibility for realizing the $4.5 billion LWR project. The letter, dated October 20 pledged that "in the event that this reactor project is not completed for reasons beyond the control of the DPRK, I will use the full powers of my office to provide, to the extent necessary, such a project from the United States, subject to the approval of Congress."[28] As Presidential commitments go, the letter was what is known as a nonbinding "best efforts pledge." But Pyongyang heralded the letter and the Agreed Framework as a great diplomatic achievement.[29]

At the same time, in this crisis-riven seventeen-month period, North Korean officials periodically told American visitors that in the aftermath of a peace treaty, it might not object to U.S. troops in Korea.[30] In the period following the nuclear deal, North Korean officials appeared to make this notion more explicit. As part of a campaign to replace the 1953 armistice with "a new peace mechanism," mid-level and senior officials have told Americans on several occasions that the U.S. could alter its role in Korea in the context of a new peace mechanism it seeks to negotiate with the U.S. This was reportedly repeated in June 2000, during the Kim-Kim Summit, as Kim Dae Jung claimed that Kim Jong Il was favorable to the idea of U.S. troops remaining in Korea, even after reunification.[31]

THE AGREED FRAMEWORK: POLITICAL BREAKTHROUGH?

From Pyongyang's perspective, the October 21, 1994, Agreed Framework between the U.S. and North Korea promised a framework for establishing the relationship with the U.S. it sought. It was probably viewed as attaining commitments that would prevent what to Pyongyang may have looked like a continual moving of the goalposts. In exchange for freezing, and ultimately dismantling its nuclear program and disclosing its past nuclear activities (at a later phase of implementing the agreement), the U.S. committed itself to organize a multilateral effort to provide two LWRs with about two thousand megawatts of power-generating capacity by 2003, provide five hundred thousand tons of heavy oil annually and negative security assurances, and pledge "to move towards full normalization of political and economic relations."

Section III of the Framework also commits North Korea and the U.S. to "work together for peace and security on a nuclear-free Korean Peninsula." Here, Washington "will provide formal assurances to the DPRK against the threat or use of nuclear weapons by the U.S." The accord explicitly committed both sides to "reduce barriers to trade," which to Pyongyang meant ending the trade embargo. For the U.S., it was also an admission ticket to resolving the larger nexus of issues on the Korean peninsula (e.g., military confrontation, missiles, chemical weapons, and North-South reconciliation). For Pyongyang, it was a remarkable performance: it managed to turn a threat of sanctions into blandishments from the world's single superpower. Moreover, for the DPRK, the nuclear accord likely appeared a potential bridge to a broader strategy of engagement with the U.S. and the international community.

LOOKING BACKWARD

Seven years after the nuclear accord, however, Pyongyang's expectations were only partially fulfilled. DPRK-U.S. relations thus far moved much further than many in the U.S. expected, but much less than Pyongyang had hoped. Pressure from both South Korea and a skeptical Republican Congress led to a near paralysis of U.S. policy. One important exception has been the provision of large amounts of humanitarian food aid to North Korea, as its near-famine conditions have led to shortfalls of roughly 1.5 to 2 million tons of food annually. While this sizeable food aid has been essential to the survival of millions of North Koreans, Pyongyang appears to have pocketed it, but not to have factored it in as part of the diplomatic equation with the United States. Ironically, the North's fixation on U.S. relations, putting North-South ties on the back burner has been highly counterproductive (along with its ballistic missile development and exports), limiting U.S. ability to respond to generally cooperative North Korean behavior on nuclear issues relating to the Agreed Framework and food aid.

It is worth noting the lengths to which Pyongyang felt it necessary to go to play a one-upsmanship game with Seoul in regard to the reactor project, and to try to negotiate a better deal. Difficulties in reaching an agreement between the DPRK and the Korean Peninsula Energy Development Corporation (KEDO), created to implement the agreement, led to near-crisis negotiations between the U.S. and the DPRK in June 1995. Pyongyang balked at the prospect of South Korea playing the leading role and supplying Ulchin-3 power reactors, a Korean-modified version of Westinghouse nuclear reactors. The DPRK also sought additional benefits relating to the reactors.[32]

After three weeks of difficult talks in Kuala Lumpur, agreement was announced in a joint press statement. The statement reaffirmed the Clinton letter, and specified that, "the U.S. will serve as the principal point of contact with the DPRK for the LWR project. In this regard, U.S. citizens will lead delegations and terms of KEDO as required to fulfill this role . . . a U.S. firm will serve as program coordinator."[33] In addition, North Korea got a concession in that KEDO would pay the cost of surveying and preparing the site for the reactors. But even though the reactors would be South Korean and the project managed by the Korean Electrical Power Company (KEPCO), the ROK utility, Pyongyang managed to insert the U.S. in the middle.

By the end of 1996, the principal tangible benefit received by North Korea was heavy fuel oil. The U.S. did provide eight million dollars in humanitarian food aid in 1996 as well. But the trade embargo had not been substantially loosened. Assets frozen in the U.S. were not released, nor had the U.S. opened a liaison office in Pyongyang. Provocative North Korean behavior in regard to the armistice also militated against improvements in bilateral relations.

Having successfully used its nuclear weapons program as the lever to prod Washington toward improved relations and economic assistance, Pyongyang had the remainder of its military threat as the button to push to get a response from Washington. The focal point of North Korea's effort to advance its ties to the U.S. was stepping up pressure in regard to its campaign to replace the armistice with a "new peace mechanism." But behind the campaign was mounting frustration at failure to advance diplomatic and economic relations. In late August 1995, for example, it threatened to withhold cooperation regarding MIAs from the Korean War until there was a peace treaty.[34] Nonetheless, the MIA talks went forward, as the U.S. eventually signed an accord in May 1996 paying the DPRK some two million dollars for its help.[35]

North Korea continued its efforts to wield carrots, sticks, and increasingly, tin cups, as its food crisis deepened in 1996. In February 1996, Pyongyang issued a detailed proposal for an interim peace mechanism to replace the armistice.[36] After Washington ignored its entreaty, the DPRK moved into its threat mode, as a mid-April visit to Seoul by President Clinton approached. On April 4, the DPRK announced it no longer recognized the armistice and the DMZ. It then sent armed soldiers into the DMZ for three consecutive days, creating a mini-crisis. But it failed to generate a positive response from Washington, which simply reiterated that North-South talks would be the proper venue for discussing such issues. The closest thing to a response was a joint initiative of President Clinton and Kim calling for vague four-party (U.S., ROK, China, DPRK) peace talks. The DPRK responded warily, claiming initially in an April 18 Foreign Ministry statement that it was studying the proposal. But Pyongyang persisted in seeking direct U.S.-DPRK talks as the venue for peace negotiations.

At the same time, Pyongyang dusted off its carrots, holding talks in late April with the U.S. on its missile production and export program in Berlin. The U.S. appeared to be de facto, engaging in a linkage of its own and suggesting missiles for sanctions lifting a trade-off. In June, Assistant Secretary of State for East Asian and Pacific Affairs Winston Lord said, "As we go ahead with missile talks, if they're productive, then I would imagine sanctions would come into play."[37] This linkage became a fixture of continuing U.S.-DPRK missile talks over the subsequent five years.

In sum, both North Korea and the U.S. each appeared to view the other as lagging in implementation of the vaguely worded non-nuclear aspects of the Agreed Framework. Despite language committing Pyongyang to North-South dialogue, reconciliation talks remained frozen, if not reverting to pre-1992 heated rhetoric and tension, until Pyongyang finally responded to Kim Dae Jung's overtures in spring 2000. For its part, the U.S.—in considerable measure for domestic political reasons—had not substantially eased the embargo, opened liaison offices, or more broadly taken steps to improve relations with the DPRK. Indeed, this lack of movement impacted other aspects of Pyongyang's wider engagement policy. North Korea created an ill-fated special export zone in Rajin-Sonbong in the far Northeast of the country designed to generate foreign investment, but even if the trade embargo had not largely precluded American firms from investing, there were few real world incentives to foreign investors for any significant investment to be lured there.

Though there is rather limited interest in investing in the DPRK on the part of U.S. firms, the trade embargo remained a source of frustration for the DPRK until it began to be loosened in 1999. Pyongyang's discontent reflected the mismatch in objectives: Washington viewed the Agreed Framework as principally a nonproliferation device or at least one to buy time; for Pyongyang, it was an instrument to lock the U.S. into a long-term relationship and, as it had manipulated its communist patrons during the Cold War, to maneuver the U.S. into a new political-military posture, from adversary to patron.

BEYOND THE AGREED FRAMEWORK

Well before the unexpected North Korean opening to the South, in the form of the remarkable spectacle that was the June 2000 North-South Summit, a series of developments had begun to substantially alter the U.S.–North Korean relationship. First, the reality of starvation and support for humanitarian food aid in the U.S. (food is a subsidy for U.S. farmers, providing the DPRK with something of an unintended and unacknowledged political constituency in the U.S.) added an important dimension to U.S.-DPRK relations. The widening network of contacts on food aid, Four Party Talks that occurred intermittently from 1996 to 2000, missile talks, MIA talks, and implementation of the Agreed Framework, all told, has in a sense institutionalized the relationship and created something of a web of dependency.

It must also be noted that the ascendance of Kim Dae Jung as President in February 1998 also changed the dynamics of U.S.-DPRK relations. Kim's "Sunshine policy" encouraged not just ROK engagement with the North, but also that of other outside powers, especially the U.S. Where before, when U.S. diplomacy advanced while North-South relations were stagnant, Seoul under Kim Young Sam would become very uncomfortable, thus constraining U.S.–North Korean relations. This has been transformed. Kim Dae Jung's strategy of drawing out North Korea and facilitating change turned the ROK into a cheerleader for not only U.S. involvement with North Korea but also of Japan, the European Union, and other countries. Thus, at the end of the Clinton administration, it was Kim Dae Jung strongly urging Clinton to visit Pyongyang, to cut a deal on curbing missile exports, deployments and development, and to normalize relations.

In the months just prior to Kim Dae Jung's election, however, two key developments served to call into question key assumptions underpinning U.S. policy: in August 1998, a DPRK test of a Taepodong-1 missile over Japan, and a leaked *New York Times* story about U.S. intelligence allegedly finding a secret nuclear site. These events further complicated the patterns of diplomacy. They raised the possibility of not only a secret North Korean nuclear program, but the highly inaccurate Taepodong-1 suggested a medium-range delivery system that could threaten Japan as well as U.S. bases in Japan. In the meantime, congressional concern—that four years after the Agreed Framework the security situation on the Korean peninsula was getting worse, not better—was partially ameliorated by the use of a combination of food aid and promises of removal of U.S. sanctions to produce what was at first an implicit North Korean moratorium on further missile tests, followed by an explicit moratorium in 1999.

Nonetheless, these developments forced a U.S. policy review, mandated by Congress in October 1998 legislation. Clinton appointed former Secretary of

Defense William Perry as Special Coordinator for Korea policy, who then launched a six-month review of U.S. policy. What became known as "the Perry Process" sought to address Congress' concerns about new security threats and offer North Korea a new way forward in ties with the U.S. Perry went to Pyongyang in May 1999, the highest level of contact the U.S. had at that point since the Korean War. Perry essentially offered North Korea a choice: to continue its menacing behavior, or embark on a new path of threat reduction and cooperation that would lead to a package of political and economic incentives—including normalization of relations with the U.S. and substantial aid from Japan.

The unclassified, public version of Perry's report to the President placed its emphasis on North Korean missile and nuclear programs as overriding objectives of U.S. policy. While it underscored the importance of the freeze of Pyongyang's known nuclear weapons programs, Perry's report nonetheless said that his review team "has serious concerns about possible continuing nuclear weapons-related work in the DPRK."[38] The report also stressed DPRK continuing efforts to develop "ballistic missiles of increasing range, including those potentially capable of reaching the territory of the United States." The report's assessment said that there was a state of stable deterrence on the Korean peninsula, but that deployment of nuclear weapons on ballistic missiles "might weaken deterrence." Perry recommended a "comprehensive and integrated approach that would seek complete and verifiable cessation of all testing, development, and deployment of missiles beyond three hundred kilometers (the limits of the Missile Technology Control Regime [MTCR]) as well as verifiable assurances of that the DPRK has ended its nuclear weapons program. In exchange, the U.S. and its allies would "in a step-by-step reciprocal fashion reduce pressures the DPRK perceives as threatening," and the U.S. would normalize relations.

Although the Perry report suggested that Pyongyang would reciprocate with a high level visit to Washington in the fall of 1999, the North failed to fully respond to the Perry initiative for fifteen months, when the remarkable, if deferred, visit of General Jo Myong Rok to Washington finally took place. Kim Jong Il's exquisitely bad sense of timing, in the end, left an eager Bill Clinton with insufficient time to negotiate the details of a missile deal that was to have been the centerpiece of a Clinton visit to Pyongyang.

THE SON ALSO RISES

Whatever his flaws as a strategist, a new element in the mix is Kim Jong Il's political transformation from bizarre-appearing recluse to very public figure, indeed of a serious and not unintelligent international political operator. This began with him making a visit to the Chinese embassy in Pyongyang in early 2000, then a trip to China, followed by the North-South Summit. Kim's new diplomacy began to expand with a visit in August by Russian President Putin. Pyongyang also began a diplomatic offensive to normalize ties with a host of nations in Asia and the West. After Italy took the initiative to normalize, most EU nations followed in the past year including Britain, Germany, and the Netherlands, as has the EU itself as an institution. Then, Kim's visit to Shanghai and Beijing in early 2001 on the heels of intriguing New Year's statements about the need for "New Thinking" raised fresh speculation that a North Korean version of Chinese opening and market-oriented reform might be in its formative stages.

What does all this mean for U.S.-DPRK relations? The remarkable October 2000 visit to Washington of First Vice Marshall Jo Myong Rok, as Kim Jong Il's Special Envoy, assumed great symbolic importance to the DPRK. The U.S.-DPRK Joint Communiqué that resulted from Jo's visit was a vaguely worded document the upshot of which seemed to be a desire to move toward starting "a new direction" in their relations. Importantly, the communiqué stated "that neither government would have hostile intent towards the other and confirmed the commitment of both governments to make every effort in the future to build a new relationship free from past enmity." They also agreed that then–Secretary of State Madeline Albright would visit Pyongyang (which occurred later in October 2000), and suggested that President Clinton might also visit Pyongyang. In fact, so anxious was Pyongyang that it consciously mistranslated the joint statement issued during Albright's visit to say that Clinton had committed himself to come. The Clinton administration appeared equally frantic about advancing relations with North Korea. Yet even the diplomatic niceties revealed the enduring mismatch in U.S. and DPRK objectives. During a gracious dinner hosted for General Jo at the State Department, Madeline Albright spoke of bridging gaps and forging common ground. Yet General Jo used his politely worded toast to press Pyongyang's anxieties, stating that Kim Jong Il will move toward a cooperative relationship with the U.S. "if and when the DPRK and our leadership is assured, is given the strong and concrete security assurances from the United States for the state sovereignty and the territorial integrity of the DPRK."[39]

This apparent insecurity was evident in the rush to diplomacy, with Albright's visit an extravaganza seemingly designed to reinforce Kim Jong Il's legitimacy. It was timed to coincide with a major celebration of the anniversary of the Korean Worker's Party to which Kim managed to persuade Albright to attend, and whose grotesquely unsavory aspects were overlooked by Washington in its eleventh-hour effort to make progress with North Korea.

Nonetheless, it served to further erode the image of the U.S. as the "evil empire" in the North Korean public mind. In the end, Clinton simply ran out of time to stage a presidential visit to Pyongyang, upon which North Korea appeared to put more emphasis than the missile deal.

WHITHER U.S.-DPRK TIES

Clearly, the United States remains a central factor in North Korean foreign policy, while North Korea has also become far more significant in the hierarchy of priorities in U.S. foreign and national security policy than it was prior to 1988. There is, however, an asymmetry in the significance of the relationship. For the U.S., North Korea remains principally a question of threat reduction, though one with both alliance, regional, and global implications. For Pyongyang, the U.S. appears to be a central animating force in its quest for regime survival and an incremental effort to begin to move into the post–Cold War world.

The charitable assessment is that ending confrontation with the U.S.—which would presumably lead to some arms reductions resolving the nuclear issue—curbing missile developments, and perhaps eventually conventional reductions, is viewed as a prerequisite for North Korea opening up further to the outside world, and more importantly, in terms of regime survival, launching market-oriented economic reforms to revive its moribund economy. This argument is made by senior South Korean officials who suggest that U.S.-DPRK normalization would help accelerate the North-South reconciliation process.

A less charitable argument is that, like the full panoply of new North Korean diplomacy, Pyongyang is simply altering its tactics to extract what benefits it can obtain to insure regime survival. Offering to freeze its missiles and halt exports, as well as halt new development of missiles, is a matter of playing its cards. Would Pyongyang allow the degree of transparency required to credibly verify an agreement? Few analysts would respond affirmatively. There is a troubling paradox in the logic of both U.S. and ROK diplomacy toward Pyongyang: the more benefits and inducements provided to the North, the less desperate the DPRK is. Thus, it is less likely Kim Jong Il will make difficult choices about reform (let alone reduce military assets), to gain what would be a performance-based legitimacy as in the case in China: why work when you can collect welfare?

To a risk-averse Pyongyang political elite, remaining on life support and muddling through on the kindness of strangers—however bleak the future may appear—has to date appeared a preferable option to assuming the modicum of risk to its political control and stability by opening up its economy, reducing its military capacity, and substantively advancing North-South peaceful coexistence. To date, Pyongyang has been reluctant to end any of its threats. The structure of the nuclear deal allows the North to hold on to whatever plutonium it has until the end stages of the deal, which has been passed on to the Bush administration to implement. Under the terms of the Agreed Framework, once significant portions of the first nuclear reactor are complete, North Korea must come in to compliance with its IAEA commitments before "significant nuclear components can be delivered." Under the current constructions plans, this is likely to occur in late 2004 or early 2005. Neither the IAEA nor U.S. officials display confidence that Pyongyang will fully cooperate with the IAEA to allow the necessary access to materials and records for the reconstruction of its nuclear history.

In missile talks, North Korea has not appeared willing to dismantle deployed missiles nor permit the sort of intrusive on-site inspection that would be necessary to make such a deal politically credible. Rather, it seems to want to "rent" its threat rather than sell it. Thus, it offered to freeze current deployments, much like the nuclear deal, and cease testing, development, and exports in its last talks with the Clinton administration. But the key details were not fully raised, let alone agreed to during the Clinton administration's negotiations. Among those details: the price for exports and whether the North would put some one hundred deployed Rodong missiles on the table at all, and also there was no verification or monitoring provisions discussed at all.[40]

Frustrated outgoing Clinton administration officials suggested to the press that they were actually on the verge of a missile deal—stifled by the complex and protracted process of the 2000 presidential election—and urged Bush to immediately pick up where they left off, lest the window of opportunity close.[41] Similarly, President Kim Dae Jung, anxious that his historic diplomacy was not moving forward, also urged Bush to engage North Korea in a March 2001 visit to Washington. But Bush, who praised Kim's efforts to "reach out to North Korea," said he was more skeptical of Pyongyang. The new Bush administration initially sought a break in North Korea diplomacy while it conducted a policy review of its own. This approach, in part aimed at altering preexisting patterns of U.S.–North Korean diplomacy, appeared to be vindicated when Kim Jong Il told a visiting European Union delegation in May 2001 that he would continue the missile moratorium until at least 2003, though he would continue exporting missiles. It seemed an invitation to renew missile talks.

The Bush administration's policy toward North Korea emerging from its policy review in June 2001 appeared as part of the broad evolution of U.S.

policy that began with the "modest initiative." Initial mention of interest in conventional force reductions suggested Bush would take a still more comprehensive approach than Perry. Broadly, the administration has sought new ways to implement the Agreed Framework to avoid a host of obstacles that became evident during the policy review. It also appeared to indicate a willingness to pursue missile talks—indeed it agreed to meet without any preconditions or fixed agenda with North Korea—though with a hard-headed standard for verification to which any deal would have to measure up. Some also suggest that there is a wariness on the part of the Bush administration toward the notion of continuing to keep Pyongyong on life support—even as it enhances its military capabilities—while it continues to deepen the misery of the lives of twenty-two million North Koreans. Yet prior to the July 2001 ASEAN Regional Forum meeting, Secretary of State Powell offered to meet with his North Korean counterpart with no preconditions. Similarly, after meeting with ROK President Kim Dae Jung during the October 2001 Asia-Pacific Economic Cooperation (APEC) meeting in Shanghai, President Bush reiterated the desire to initiate dialogue with North Korea "anytime, any place, with no conditions." Yet through 2001, the DPRK insisted that a precondition for opening discussions with the Bush administration was that it adopt the same policy posture as the Clinton administration. Whenever bilateral discussions between the U.S. and the DPRK resume, the flurry of optimism about North Korea in the aftermath of the June 2000 North-South Summit will be long dissipated. There was a hint of renewed diplomatic momentum, with high-level North-South talks in April 2002, and indications that Pyongyang was gearing up for dialogue with the Bush administration.

At the end of the day, it is unclear whether any policy, however perfectly designed and executed, can resolve the North Korea problem. Absent a North Korean willingness to open up and seriously reform, it will be unable to absorb substantial resource flows, nor will key donors and investors (e.g., private sector) be interested or able to politically rationalize significant resource transfers (beyond food) if Pyongyang continues to sustain its military capabilities. Unless Pyongyang is prepared to trade away its military assets, which are the foundation of the regime, it is unlikely to get the magnitude of investment and assistance necessary to refurbish its infrastructure and revive its economy.

The questions unanswered still are whether any package of economic and security incentives can motivate Pyongyang to dismantle its threatening military assets. The more basic question that this may turn on is: Does Pyongyang view the risk of the status quo and the continued degeneration of its economy and society as greater than the political risk to the regime of opening up and reforming its economy? If so, then a "Grand Bargain" might be possible. The most that one can expect from U.S. policy is the creation (along with that of the ROK and Japan) of a structure of incentives that create a political environment that makes it as easy as possible for Pyongyang to make the choices necessary for gradual change, for a "soft landing" to occur. By mid-2002, Kim Jong Il's failure to implement most things agreed to in the June 2000 summit, especially reopening the trans-Korea railway and the proposed Kaesong industrial park, remain signs that no radical systemic change (beyond at the margins) in North Korea was unfolding or even planned. It seemed that Kim Jong Il was not yet prepared to take the steps necessary for the comprehensive approach needed to succeed. Nonetheless, the wisdom of testing the intentions of North Korea, so politically opaque that its decision-making dynamics are otherwise all but unknowable, is a reasonable posture. This would be accomplished by keeping the promise of well-considered incentives on the negotiating table, and it appears the least undesirable of the menu of unpleasant choices facing both the United States and South Korea.

NOTES

This chapter was written before the author joined the U.S. Department of State and reflects solely his views, not those of the Department of State or any other government agency.

1. North Korea's vitriolic rhetoric toward the South Korean government has not disappeared. As tensions mounted in the aftermath of the September 1996 DPRK submarine intrusion into the South, Pyongyang referred to the Kim Young Sam administration as "political hooligans such as the South Korean puppets." Korean Central News Agency, Pyongyang, October 4, 1996.

2. See Henry Kissinger, *The White House Years* (Boston: Little, Brown, 1979), 1251.

3. See Charles Krauthammer, "North Korea: The World's Real Time Bomb," *Washington Post,* November 6, 1993, for a representative sample of prevalent images of North Korea and the hysterical climate surrounding the crisis.

4. See Joseph A. Yager, "Non-Proliferation and U.S. Foreign Policy," The Brookings Institution, 1980, 58, and Richard P. Cronin, "North Korea: U.S. Policy and Negotiations to Halt Its Nuclear Program, Congressional Research Service, November 18, 1994, 2. Russian official, interview with author, December 3, 1994. Exact date of acquisition is unclear, but should be viewed as part of technical aid program initially starting in the late 1950s.

5. This is not to suggest a monolithic view of North Korean decision making; some elements, particularly in the military, may still view the nuclear program as part of a reunification-by-force agenda, or may doubt the wisdom of its engagement with the U.S.

6. Former IAEA official in interview with author, November 16, 1994.

7. See *Izvestia* (Moscow), March 31, 1994, 3.

8. The first high-profile emphasis on the issue appeared in a speech on Asian Security by then–Assistant Secretary Richard H. Solomon at the University of California, San Diego, on October 11, 1990. In a passage widely cited in the press, Solomon described the North Korean nuclear problem as "The number-one threat to Asian security." U.S. Department of State *Bulletin*, Washington, D.C., November 1990.

9. See Samuel S. Kim, "North Korea in 1995," Asian Survey 36:1 (January 1996) for a brief overview of the DPRK economic crisis. For the best detailed assessment of the DPRK economy, see Marcus Noland, "The North Korean Economy," in *Joint U.S.-Korea Academic Studies*, Vol. 6, 1996, 127–78.

10. Korean Central News Agency (KCNA) November 20, 1991, in a typical sample of DPRK rhetoric cites a Foreign Ministry spokesman saying, "If the United States . . . truly intends to prevent the proliferation of nuclear weapons on the Korean Peninsula, there will arise no problem provided that it withdraws its nuclear weapons from South Korea, removes the nuclear threat to us."

11. Former senior State and Defense Department officials involved in Bush administration Korea policies in background discussions with author, November 1995, and August 1996.

12. Communiquè issued by the DPRK, published in "Dialogue with North Korea," Carnegie Endowment for International Peace, 1989, Appendix B.

13. See Appendix C, 1989 Proposal for a "Democratic Confederal Republic of Koryo," in Dialogue with North Korea," Carnegie Endowment for International Peace.

14. For a detailed account of the diplomatic history of the North Korean nuclear issue exhaustedly documented, see Mitchell Reiss, *Bridled Ambition: Why Countries Constrain Their Nuclear Abilities* (Washington, D.C.: Wilson Center Press, 1995), especially pages 231–320.

15. Richard H. Solomon, speech at University of California, San Diego, October 11, 1990.

16. The first DPRK denial that it sought nuclear weapons was in a statement carried on August 4, 1989, by KCNA. Kim Il Sung's denial in an interview with Japanese publishers was picked up by KCNA, November 11, 1991, and was also reported in a discussion with a leading Japanese politician, Kyodo News Service, September 26, 1990.

17. For a typical reference, see the July 7, 1988, communiqué. The KCNA dispatch cited above also uses the same rhetoric. As late as 1993, Pyongyang cited U.S. nuclear weapons in South Korea as an excuse for avoiding cooperation with IAEA.

18. See Don Oberdorfer and T. R. Reid, *Washington Post*, June 21, 1991.

19. See Don Oberdorfer, *Washington Post*, October 19, 1991.

20. Bush administration officials, October 14, 1995, and November 7, 1995, personal interviews.

21. Senior Bush administration officials, interview with author, November 12, 1995, June 14, 1996.

22. Annex 9 in Note by the Secretary General to the General Assembly, 12 April 1993, iii.

23. Joint statement in Department of State *Bulletin*, Washington, D.C., June 14, 1993. In separate press conferences, Kang stressed security assurances while Galucci stressed NPT and IAEA compliance.

24. DPRK press statement, and Statement by Kang Sok Ju, translated by U.S. Mission to Geneva. July 19, 1993.

25. Jointly agreed press statement, July 19, 1993, distributed by U.S. Department of State, Geneva.

26. White House official, interview with author, July 28, 1994.

27. See Reiss, "Bridled Ambition," 304. Charles Krauthammer, Peter Rodman, and others reflected this hothouse political climate.

28. Copy of letter provided by the White House. See also Samuel S. Kim, "North Korea in 1994," *Asian Survey,* Vol. 35, no. 1 (January 1995), 13–27 for discussion of the letter and the nuclear deal.

29. *Nodong Sinmun*, December 1, 1994.

30. Personal interviews with private visitors to North Korea, December 1992, October 1993, January 1994.

31. See *Washington Post,* June 18, 2001.

32. Reuters, May 30, 1995, reported that North Korea sought an additional one billion dollars in economic and technical aid in relation to the nuclear reactors.

33. Statement issued by U.S. Embassy, Kuala Lumpur, Malaysia, June 13, 1995.

34. AP dispatch from Seoul, August 28, 1995.

35. See "U.S. Pays North Korea $2 Million for Remains," *Washington Post*, May 21, 1996, A14.

36. KCNA, February 23, 1996, reported that the proposal was made in a speech by the DPRK Foreign Ministry spokesman to mark the second anniversary of its proposal for a new accord.

37. Reuter dispatch June 4, 1996. Lord made the remarks during a question session after a speech to the Asia Society in Washington.

38. See "Review of United States Policy toward North Korea: Findings and Recommendations," Dr. William J. Perry, Department of State, October 12, 1999.

39. Toasts, Department of State, October 10, 2000.

40. Senior U.S. officials, interviews with author, March 2001.

41. See Michael R. Gordon, "How Politics Sank Accord on Missiles with North Korea," *New York Times*, March 6, 2001.

3

Japanese–North Korean Relations: Going in Circles

Myonwoo Lee

Change in North Korea will likely have a major impact on both Northeast Asia in general and the Korean peninsula in particular. For every country in the region, the question of how to manage their respective policies toward North Korea is thus an important one. Japan is no exception, and indeed Tokyo has at least two special reasons to take North Korea seriously.

First, as post–Cold War editions of Tokyo's Diplomatic Bluebook indicate, North Korea is viewed by Tokyo as the last remnant of the Cold War in Asia, with the potential of disrupting and jeopardizing the current balance of power in the region as well as Japan's own security. Further, North Korea is the only country with which Japan has yet to negotiate normal diplomatic relations, leaving Japan's wartime legacy unsettled, at least at an official level. In view of these circumstances, Japan's passive stance on the issue of normalization is curious, as is the current stalemate between Tokyo and Pyongyang.

What is behind this stalemate between Japan and North Korea? Is Japan's passive or reactive style of diplomacy at fault, or have new problems arisen since the last contacts between the two countries? What are the future implications of the latest developments? This chapter attempts to explore these and related questions.

ON-AGAIN, OFF-AGAIN

The normalization talks and their preliminary meetings, stalemated after North Korea's launch of a Taepodong-I missile over Japanese territory and the incursion of an unidentified ship, reached a turning point with the visit of the Murayama delegation to North Korea in December 1999. In the preliminary meeting held before their departure, the delegation made it clear that food aid and resolution of the abduction issue would not be preconditions for normalization negotiations. In a meeting between the delegation and North Korea's Labor Party, it was agreed to reopen the normalization talks and to resume meetings between the respective Red Cross societies for discussing humanitarian issues such as food aid and the home visit of Japanese residents of North Korea. On December 19, 1999, the first preliminary meeting at the bureau chief level for restarting the normalization talks took place, and the Red Cross societies also held their first meeting. Before these meetings, the Japanese government lifted all of its sanctions, and in March 2000 it announced its decision to send one hundred thousand tons of rice aid and to hold the next round of the normalization talks.

The families of the kidnapped and their advocacy groups strongly protested against these moves. Arguing that the Japanese government does not take the kidnapping issue seriously, it announced a plan to send the petition to the members of Parliament, but the politicians responded negatively. The governing coalition decided to oppose the government's position, and many Liberal Democratic Party (LDP) politicians also protested.

Under these circumstances, the ninth round of normalization talks was held on April 5, 2000. As in the previous rounds in 1991 and 1992, "basic," "economic," "international," and "miscellaneous" problems were put on the agenda, but the two sides simply reiterated their former positions on these issues.[1] North Korea argued for its legitimacy over the Korean peninsula and demanded an apology and compensation for the Japanese colonial period, in writing, while Japan, which expressed its apprehension over the missile launch and emphasized the need to address the abduction issue, insisted on a verbal apology comparable to the 1995 Murayama statement.[2] Thus, no substantial discussion took place, except that in their joint press communiqué they agreed to hold the next round of talks, the tenth, in Tokyo in May 2000.[3]

The tenth round of talks had to be postponed, however, due to the inter-Korean summit and Japan's upper-house election, both of which were scheduled in June. The hometown visit of the sixteen Japanese wives, the third attempt of its kind, was thus postponed as well. The foreign ministers met in Bangkok in July, and they set the talks for the following month. The tenth round of normalization talks was finally held from August 21 to 24, 2000, in Kisarazu, Chiba prefecture.[4] Once again, both parties essentially repeated their previous positions. North Korea's chief delegate Jung Tae Hwa, for example, argued that the issues of settling the past—an apology and compensation by Japan—were the highest priority. Japan's Takano Kojiro, on the other hand, asserted that all the issues, including those related to abduction and missiles, must be discussed simultaneously.

There were, however, several signs of development or concessions made by each side. Japan indicated that it would be willing to adopt the same formula it had used in normalizing relations with South Korea in 1965 when it had offered South Korea "economic cooperation" aid consisting of a grant of $300 million and a loan of $200 million in lieu of "compensation." North Korea, for its part, suggested that it would not insist on "reparation" from Japan but would settle for "compensation."

Due to these developments, the joint press communiqué after the tenth round of talks was brighter and contained more specific elements. For instance, the discussion aimed sincerely toward the early establishment of a friendly relationship. Exchanges between diplomatic authorities and between nongovernmental personnel were needed for amplifying the mutual trust: the eleventh round of talks would be held in October 2000 in a third country to be agreed upon by both sides.[5] Thus, as Foreign Minister Kono Yohei put it, the tenth round was successful compared to the previous rounds.[6]

Before the eleventh round of the talks, the Japanese government, encouraged by these positive signs, took an extraordinary step. On October 19, 2000, it announced a decision to donate five hundred thousand tons of rice to North Korea through the World Food Program (WFP). What was special about this rice aid was not only its quantity, which exceeded the WFP's demand, but the decision to deliver Japanese rice rather than less expensive Thai or Chinese rice.[7] Preceding this announcement, the third group of sixteen Japanese wives had visited Japan from North Korea, from September 12 to 18, the visit that was originally scheduled at the end of June but had been postponed.

Following the positive signs of the previous talks and the Japanese efforts, the eleventh round, which was held in Beijing from October 30 to 31, 2000, could be expected to be still more productive, but it turned out to be the opposite. There was a virtual news blackout, which amplified suspicions about the results of the meetings. Even the date of the next round was sealed. It was reported that the next round of talks would be set up if both sides were ready, but this remains to be seen.[8] Although the eleventh round began cordially with North Korean thanks for Japan's rice aid and with Japan's high hopes for getting into more specific discussion on the issues, it apparently failed to produce any fruitful result.

Whatever the reason for the failure of the eleventh round of normalization talks, the main source of the delay in a follow-up meeting was the leadership changes in Japan and the United States. In Japan, Prime Minister Mori was replaced by Prime Minister Koizumi in April 2001. Koizumi is known for his conservative stance and straightforwardness, so he would not have been enthusiastic about the normalization talks. In the U.S., the Clinton administration, which had become gradually closer to North Korea, was replaced by the Bush administration, which revealed its hawkish stance against the DPRK regime during the presidential campaign. These changes in Japan and the U.S. certainly explain, in part, the long pause after the eleventh round of talks. In Japan's case, however, domestic political factors other than leadership serve better to explain the lack of progress in 2001. Political factors such as Prime Minister Mori's falling popularity, the subsequent leadership change, and the upper-house election of July have left the government little time for other matters.

The sudden change of mood surrounding the eleventh round that unexpectedly yielded no substantial results is more difficult to comprehend. One possible explanation is that the issues of "apology," "compensation," "abduction," and "missile development" are so sensitively related to nationalistic mood that the gap between the two cannot be narrowed from the outset. Though these issues are very delicate, they are not matters of life or death, as witnessed by the concessions made by both sides during the three rounds mentioned above.

Another explanation is that at the time of the eleventh round, North Korea had more room to breathe, so that an early conclusion of the talks and a following monetary inflow were no longer an urgent need. Two circumstances support this argument. First, North Korea had become more acceptable to the international society after the ninth round of talks. It was admitted, for example, into the Association of South East Asian Nations' (ASEAN) Regional Forum (ARF) in July 2000, at which time many countries began to recognize North Korea. This accelerated pace of diplomacy can be said to have reached a zenith in October 2000, before the eleventh round, when Vice Marshall Jo Myong Rok, the first deputy chairman to the DPRK National Defense Commission, visited the U.S., and when Secretary of State Albright later visited North Korea in response.

Second, there are several signs that in 2000 the North Korean economy had improved. For example, as table 3.1 shows, North Korea had experienced a positive gross domestic product (GDP) growth rate in 1999. According to one account, this recovery from the long march of negative growth rates was mainly due to aid from other countries, including Hyundai's Kumgang sightseeing fee.[9]

Table 3.2, showing the trade between Japan and North Korea from 1995 through 2000, indicates that the trade in 2000 was better than that of 1999. If we include Japan's rice aid in 2000, it is highly probable that the North Korean economy would have done better in 2000. Thus, North Korea, better off

Table 3.1. North Korea's Rate of Economic Growth (Unit: percent)

	1994	*1995*	*1996*	*1997*	*1998*	*1999*
GDP Growth Rate	-2.1	-4.1	-3.6	-6.3	-1.1	6.2
Agriculture, Forestry, Fishery	2.7	-10.4	0.5	-3.8	4.1	9.2
Manufacturing	-3.7	-5.2	-8.9	-16.8	-3.1	8.5
Building Trade	-26.9	-3.2	-11.8	-9.9	-11.4	24.3
Service	2.4	1.7	1.1	1.3	-0.5	-1.9
Government	3.3	2.8	1.8	2.2	-0.3	-4.5

Source: W. J. Jung, "Estimated Results of North Korea's GDP for 1999," 2001.1.4, www.kotra.co.kr/main/info/nk/eng/main.php3 (accessed 20 January 2001).

diplomatically and economically, may have viewed the normalization talks in a more long-term perspective.

In that nothing yet is clear about the eleventh round of talks, it is risky to condemn North Korea alone for the failure. But the process of the three rounds of talks in 2000 (the ninth, tenth, and eleventh) certainly shows that Japan had not been at all passive. In the interests of promoting the talks and getting results from them, the Japanese government contributed rice aid twice, before each of the ninth and the eleventh rounds, in spite of domestic opposition. Moreover, Prime Minister Mori made two somewhat dire attempts to speed up the normalization talks. One was a personal letter to Kim Jong Il sent through a South Korean journalist expressing Mori's desire to hold summit talks.[10] The other was the disclosure of an offer made by one of the Diet delegation members to North Korea in 1997—that Pyongyang could release the Japanese kidnap victims in a third country so that they could be

Table 3.2. Trends in North Korea's Trade to Japan (Unit: U.S.$1,000; %)

		Export	*Import*	*Total*	*Trade*
1995	Amount	339,680	254,957	594,637	84,723
	Rate	5.3	49.3	20.5	
1996	Amount	291,412	226,994	518,406	64,418
	Rate	-14.2	-11.0	-12.8	
1997	Amount	301,489	178,804	480,288	122,680
	Rate	3.5	-21.2	-7.4	
1998	Amount	219,489	175,137	394,626	44,352
	Rate	-27.2	-2.1	-17.8	
1999	Amount	202,564	147,839	350,403	54,725
	Rate	-7.7	-15.6	-11.2	
2000	Amount	256,891	206,760	463,651	50,131
	Rate	26.82	39.85	32.32	

Source: Bae Sang-bum, "North Korea's Economic Trends in FY 2000 toward Japan," 2001.7.4, www.kotra.or.kr/main/info/nk/eng/main.php3 (accessed 15 July 2001).

found as missing persons. Though this disclosure, whether intentional or unintentional, may not have been a wise choice for promoting the talks, it does reveal the enthusiasm of some parts of the Japanese government for the continuation of the talks.

If the current stalemate of the talks was caused neither by the Japanese government's passiveness nor by its notorious incrementalism, then what future course will the normalization talks between Japan and North Korea take? Before addressing this question, the next section provides a brief history of Japanese–North Korean relations in the postwar period, in order to reveal the factors that have influenced this bilateral relationship.

A TURBULENT PAST

Relations between North Korea and Japan in the postwar era have fluctuated over time, from moves toward reconciliation, to reversion, to tension. The postwar history of this bilateral relationship can thus be divided into several periods, and it will be approached here in two parts: the Cold War era and the post–Cold War era. This brief investigation will attempt to extract the changes and continuities in the relationship between the two parties and bring out implications for future prospects.

The Cold War Period, 1951 to 1990

The years before 1991 can be divided into three periods.[11] The first begins with the liberation of the Korean peninsula in 1945 and ends in 1960, when Japan and the United States renewed the U.S.-Japan Security Treaty. The first official contact between North Korea and Japan came from North Korea in 1955 in the form of a statement issued by North Korean Prime Minister Nam Il, expressing sympathy for those Japanese who had suffered under the U.S. military occupation, and stating that North Korea was willing to engage in building relationships with all countries who desired friendly relations with it. This announcement followed Kim Il Sung's comments on the possible coexistence of capitalist and socialist systems, which was an answer to the reconciliatory mood between the United States and the Soviet Union following the death of Joseph Stalin.[12]

Japan was very receptive toward these moves by North Korea. This was partly due to the characteristics at that time of the Cabinet of Hatoyama, whose conservatism pursued a foreign policy line independent from that of the United States, in contrast to his predecessor and political rival, Yoshida Shigeru. Along with his enthusiasm for normalizing relations with the Soviet

Union, Hatoyama argued for the benefits of reinstituting economic relations with North Korea.[13] In addition, the deadlocked normalization talks between South Korea and Japan due to the Kuboda incident during this period gave Japan a free hand in reaching out to North Korea.

The second period of the first stage of North Korean–Japanese relations began in 1960 with the renewal of the U.S.-Japan Security Treaty, and lasted until around 1977, when U.S. President Jimmy Carter's vow to withdraw U.S. troops from South Korea opened the way for Pyongyang to deal directly with Washington. During this period, North Korean–Japanese relations experienced numerous ups and downs.

With the renewal of the U.S.-Japan Security Treaty in 1960, the North Korean–Japanese relationship turned sour. North Korea responded by signing mutual security pacts with China and the Soviet Union in 1961 and, for the first time, it criticized Japan for renewed militarism as well as economic encroachment on South Korea.[14]

If Japan's move to strengthen its security ties with the United States was one reason for North Korean criticism, its move to conclude a normalization treaty with South Korea under the guardianship of the United States was another. At the end of 1962, North Korea issued a statement that outstanding issues between Korea and Japan should be settled after national unification. To try to settle them before unification would require North Korea's participation, and Pyongyang planned to abstain from demanding compensation for damages incurred by Japan's colonization.[15]

The severed relationship between North Korea and Japan reached another nadir when Tokyo and Washington issued the Nixon-Sato Joint Communiqué. However, this heightened tension soon waned as Washington's approach to Beijing became apparent through U.S. Secretary of State Henry Kissinger's secret visit to China and the latter's admission to the United Nations. In an interview with the editor of the *Asahi Shimbun* on September 25, 1971, Kim Il Sung remarked that even without beginning normalization talks, bilateral activity between North Korea and Japan in the areas of trade, travel, and exchanges could be promoted.[16] Kim sent a similar message one month later when Tokyo Governor Minobe visited North Korea.

Besides the changed mood in the international arena, North Korea's cautious approach to Japan was also part of its policy toward South Korea. In a series of interviews with the *Yomiuri Shimbun* in January 1972 and with *Sekai* in October 1972, Kim Il Sung stated that normal relations with Japan would automatically undermine the normalization treaty signed between South Korea and Japan.[17]

Nonetheless, Japan continued informal relations with North Korea while acknowledging the latter's two-track policy. As inter-Korean relations worsened due to the breakdown of ongoing inter-Korean talks and the Moon Se-kwang incident, exchanges of people and goods between North Korea and Japan continued. This policy was maintained until 1983, when North Korea staged a terrorist attack against South Korean government officials in Rangoon, Burma.

Japan lifted its Rangoon-related sanctions against North Korea in January 1985, ushering in the third period in pre-1991 North Korean–Japanese relations. In May 1985, a delegation from the Japan Socialist Party (JSP) visited North Korea, and in August, North Korean players entered Japan to participate in the 1985 Universiad. Under the leadership of Prime Minister Yasuhiro Nakasone, Tokyo had by this time already embarked on a positive policy toward the Korean peninsula as a way of increasing Japan's international role. In his visit to Seoul in 1984, Nakasone explained to South Korean officials Japan's positive policy toward North Korea, and at a South Korea–Japan foreign ministers' meeting later that year, the Japanese foreign minister offered three principles for preserving stability on the Korean peninsula.

Even with such positive gestures from Japan, the North Korean–Japanese relationship failed to show any dramatic development. Instead, the bilateral relationship worsened with Pyongyang's sentencing of the crew of a Japanese fishing vessel, the *Fujisan Maru*.[18] Japan responded by again imposing sanctions against North Korea, which in turn responded with its own countermeasures against Japan. Though North Korean players were allowed to participate in the Asian Table Tennis Open, Japanese government officials left their seats during the welcome ceremony.

By September 1988, however, Japanese sanctions were lifted after South Korean President Roh Tae Woo proposed reopening inter-Korean dialogue and made it clear that South Korea would not protest similar overtures to North Korea. Nonetheless, intimate contact between North Korea and Japan did not immediately follow.

The Post–Cold War Period, 1990 to 1998

The 1990 visit to North Korea of a delegation of LDP and JSP members, led by Kanemaru Shin, opened the possibility of proceeding with normalization talks. Much to Japan's surprise, Kim Il Sung made an unexpected suggestion to this effect to the Japanese delegates, whose main purpose for the trip was to secure the release of the crew of the *Fujisan Maru*.[19] This apparent change in North Korea's position should not have been a surprise, however, given the rapidly changing international environment at the time.

The collapse of the Soviet Union and the socialist bloc in Eastern Europe left North Korea as one of the last countries in the world adhering to strict communist doctrine. Moreover, South Korea's rise in international status, economic development, and relations with former socialist countries pressed North Korea to redirect its policy. In this context, Japan's signals to improve relations provided North Korea with an opportunity to overcome its various economic, political, and diplomatic crises.

After lifting sanctions against North Korea in relation to the *Fujisan Maru* incident, Japan issued an official statement on January 20, 1989, entitled "About Our Policy toward North Korea." This was soon followed in March by Prime Minister Noburo Takeshita's remarks expressing regret over Japanese colonization, indicating Japan's willingness to approach North Korea. Kim Il Sung, in a meeting with a visiting delegation of JSP legislators, responded with his own positive evaluation of Takeshita's statement.

Once set in motion, improvement in bilateral relations maintained a fast pace despite suspicion concerning North Korea's involvement in Japan's Pachinko industry and its development of nuclear weapons. Japan's National Assemblymen's League for Enhancing a Friendly Relationship with North Korea visited Pyongyang during this period, and the two countries reached a temporary agreement to cooperate in the area of fishing. The preliminary steps for Kanemaru's visit were also carried out at this time. In November 1989, the former chairman of the JSP met with a high official from North Korea in Beijing, and in March 1990 foreign ministry officials from both countries reportedly met in Paris.

Kanemaru's visit to North Korea produced a joint statement—signed by representatives from the LDP, the JSP, and the North Korea Workers' Party—consisting of eight points. First, the three parties acknowledged that Japan should apologize and pay compensation for its thirty-six-year colonization of Korea. Second, the groups recommended that normalization should be realized as soon as possible. Third, they called for establishing a satellite link and a direct telecommunications route between the two countries. Fourth, they acknowledged that Tokyo should guarantee the legal rights of North Korean residents in Japan and remove all references to North Korea in Japanese passports. Fifth, they noted that Korea comprised a single nation and that it was in the best interests of the Korean people for North and South Korea to achieve peaceful unification through dialogue. Sixth, they noted that it is necessary to abrogate all nuclear threats. Seventh, they agreed that they would recommend to their respective governments to begin official negotiations for normalization. Finally, they agreed to promote the development of bilateral cooperation.

Though Kanemaru's visit was criticized in Japan as politically excessive, it succeeded in gaining the release of the *Fujisan Maru*'s crew in October 1990 and in launching normalization talks in November. At preliminary meetings held three times through December 1990, issues were grouped into four areas for discussion: basic, economic, international, and miscellaneous.[20]

Official normalization talks were held in eight rounds. They began with a first round of meetings in Pyongyang in January 1991 and ended with the reemergence of the Lee Eun-hye issue in the eighth round in November 1992. Though the differences of opinion on the issues were apparent from the start, it was from the third round of May 1991 that differences openly emerged. At that time, Japan insisted that normalization would depend on North Korea agreeing to IAEA (International Atomic Energy Agency) inspections. In addition, Japan suggested a simultaneous entry of North and South Korea into the United Nations and asked for a confirmation of the Lee Eun-hye problem.

North Korea protested Japan's IAEA demand and criticized the Lee Eun-hye issue as a contemptible accusation. At the same time, however, North Korea suggested concluding the official diplomatic resumption process by resolving outstanding basic problems and putting aside economic and international issues for later discussion. Though Japan acknowledged this change in North Korea's position, it continued to insist on North Korea's acceptance of IAEA inspections. The gap in position was so wide that the one-day extension of the third round ended without so much as an agreement on a date for future rounds of talks.

Though confrontation over the Lee Eun-hye question and IAEA inspections continued and remained the major reason for the breakdown of the talks, these were not the only issues posing stumbling blocks to negotiation. Nonetheless, the Lee Eun-hye issue brought about an unscheduled one-day preliminary meeting before the fourth round and became the major reason that the eighth round was ended prematurely. Though Japan's insistence for IAEA inspections brought about North Korea's admission at the seventh round that it had succeeded in extracting plutonium from its nuclear reactors, Pyongyang used the impasse to end that round of talks abruptly.[21]

Japan's positions on these issues adhered to principles Tokyo had decided upon before the talks began. On January 26, 1992, Japan announced four principles for the talks: the continued peace and stability of the Korean peninsula, maintenance of friendly relations with South Korea, a genuine response to Japan's proposal for compensation for Japanese colonialism but not for postwar developments, and acceptance by North Korea of IAEA inspections.[22] Evidence suggests that these positions were taken in coordination with the United States. The *Yomiuri Shimbun* reported on October 15, 1990, that the U.S. government had handed four demands to Japan that corresponded to Japan's four principles.[23] First, Japan should get North Korea to accept IAEA inspections. Second, North Korean demands for compensation for postwar developments should not be accepted. Third, it should be agreed that compensation for colonization would not be used for military purposes.

Fourth, ongoing dialogue between North and South Korea should not be jeopardized by any normalization talks between North Korea and Japan. The Ministry of Foreign Affairs also revealed after the fifth round, in November 1991, that the United States had given Japan information on North Korea's processing facilities for nuclear materials.[24]

After normalization talks ended prematurely in November 1992, there was a long pause in contacts between North Korea and Japan for two reasons. First, in 1993 Japan experienced a major political shift when the ruling LDP lost power for the first time in 38 years and a new coalition cabinet led by Morihiro Hosogawa was formed. Second, due to heightened suspicion of North Korea's nuclear weapons development program, Pyongyang began to shift its attention toward entering into direct contact with the United States. Thus, when Japan's new foreign minister indicated his willingness to restart talks with North Korea in late 1993 and early 1994, Pyongyang was slow to reply. Instead, North Korea conducted a missile test in the East Sea (Sea of Japan) in June 1994.

Though the missile test was targeted at the ongoing negotiations between North Korea and the United States, it clearly increased Japan's apprehension and induced greater activity toward restarting the talks. The JSP decided to dispatch a second joint commission, headed by Michio Watanabe, on June 8, 1994, and the wife of former Prime Minister Takeo Miki also visited North Korea to meet with Kim Il Sung. Yet despite this series of swift moves, a visit by a delegation of Japanese politicians to North Korea could not be realized until March 1995.

There are several explanations for this delay. The first is the negative attitude of the Japanese Ministry of Foreign Affairs, which held that the timing was not right since negotiations between North Korea and the United States were still under way.[25] The second is the ongoing power struggle that was taking place within the LDP. Though the secretary general of the LDP came out in support of a visit by a delegation of Japanese politicians to North Korea, some LDP members indicated concern that such irresponsible promises as compensation for postwar developments might result.[26] However, with resolution of the nuclear issue in Geneva in late 1994 and the establishment of KEDO (Korean Peninsula Energy Development Organization) in early 1995, calls for restarting normalization talks reemerged.

On March 28, 1995, members of Japan's governing coalition (the LDP, the JSP, and the Sakigake Party) visited North Korea and issued another statement composed of four parts.[27] The first part was similar to the previous "three-party" announcement and confirmed that not only was the early resumption of normalization talks in the interests of both countries, but it also would contribute to peace in Asia.

Unlike the previous announcement, however, the second part of the "four-party" announcement simply stated the need to solve outstanding problems related to Japan's past, with no specific mention of postwar developments. The third part, on North Korea's nuclear development program, and the fourth part, on inter-Korean relations, consisted simply of the respective positions of the two sides. In the third part, Japan's Watanabe stated that North Korea should faithfully follow the Geneva Agreement negotiated with the United States, while North Korea's Kim Yong-Soon of the Korea Workers' Party declared that there was no such thing as a "South Korean-style" light-water reactor.

Even if the results of this visit were dubious, Japan thereafter showed a more positive attitude. In April 1995, Japan began to prepare for a new round of normalization talks, and the Ministry of Foreign Affairs announced that the Japanese Embassy in Beijing had already contacted North Korea to this effect. The resumption of normalization talks was delayed, however, due to North Korea's formal request for rice aid on May 26 of that year.

Negotiations over rice aid between North Korea and Japan produced disagreement over quantity and method of repayment. North Korea demanded one million tons of rice from Japan, arguing that this amount had been agreed to in the "four-party" meeting, while Japan replied that storage constraints allowed for only three hundred thousand tons.[28] To Japan's suggestion that half of any aid would be nonrepayable, North Korea insisted that all aid would be repaid in time in order to gain additional assistance. In the end, the final agreement of June 30, 1995, stated that half of the rice aid (one hundred fifty thousand tons) would be paid later but that the other half would be nonrepayable. After the first shipment, Kim Jong Il's remark that Japan's rice aid was a form of apology caused additional friction, but his subsequent letter of appreciation to Japan worked to soothe relations, and in late September negotiations over additional aid began, with Japan agreeing to supply another two hundred thousand tons of rice.

With its shipments of rice aid as momentum, Japan sought to restart normalization talks, but the two sides could not agree on the details of a resumption of negotiations. This go-slow approach was peculiar compared with the previous effort, but there are several reasons for it. The first is related to the impetus for the Watanabe delegation's visit to North Korea in 1995. Some observers suspect that this visit was not actually focused on the resumption of the talks at all, but was rather a domestically oriented maneuver to deal with excess Japanese stocks of rice.[29]

The second reason for the go-slow approach was political. In January 1996, Ryutaro Hashimoto succeeded Murayama as prime minister. Though both cabinets were supported by the same coalition of political parties, the more conservative and pro-bureaucratic Hashimoto was more cautious in pursuing talks with North Korea. In addition, Hashimoto's rivalry with LDP Secretary-General Koichi Kato contributed to the government's slow pace. Kato had supported Watanabe's visit to North Korea, and it is likely that Hashimoto thought that Kato's success in resuming normalization talks with North Korea might be a disadvantage in the upcoming LDP presidential election.

Popular Japanese resentment of North Korea's suspected abduction of Japanese citizens also contributed to Japan's restrained approach to North Korea, while South Korea's request for Japan to proceed slowly in any overtures to North Korea was yet another factor.[30] Thus, a combination of factors worked to delay the resumption of normalization talks, even though North Korea's nuclear development program had been frozen with the Geneva Agreement in 1994.

On May 21, 1997, government officials from North Korea and Japan met in Beijing to discuss resuming normalization talks. This meeting did not, however, produce any immediate, visible results. The Japanese side reportedly told the press that they would seek to resolve the easiest of several outstanding issues, namely the return of Japanese wives living in North Korea.[31] Yet although this issue was the one that North Korea could most readily agree to, opinions diverged over the number of returnees. While Japan asked for the return of all housewives of Japanese nationality—assumed to number about 1,800—North Korea insisted that only a few could be allowed to return to Japan. Thus the two-day meeting in Beijing ended with little success.

Nonetheless, the Beijing talks did serve as a stepping-stone for new talks. A preliminary meeting for resuming normalization talks was held in August 1997, followed by a nine-day visit to North Korea by a Japanese delegation to discern the predicament of Japanese wives living there. In September, the Red Cross societies of the two countries met in Beijing to schedule the eventual homecoming of these Japanese women.

With the homecoming of two groups of Japanese wives in November 1997 and early 1998, prospects for resuming normalization talks brightened. Unfortunately, the behavior of some of the Japanese wives, who returned to North Korea after a brief stay in Japan, upset many Japanese people and government officials. The public mood was further soured when Pyongyang announced that none of the Japanese citizens allegedly kidnapped and abducted to North Korea over the years were residing in North Korea.

However, the two most important reasons that development in bilateral relations was halted until late 1999 were North Korea's launch of a Taepodong-I missile over Japanese territory and the incursion of an unidentified ship, thought to be from North Korea, into Japanese territorial waters. These incidents caused the Japanese public to reappraise the North Korean threat and to lower North Korea's reputation as a potential negotiating partner.[32]

VARIABLES AND FEATURES OF NORTH KOREAN–JAPANESE RELATIONS

From this review of the history of relations between North Korea and Japan, one can distinguish several features of the bilateral relationship. First, factors both enhancing and retarding bilateral relations exist at four levels: international, regional, bilateral, and domestic. Nam Il's statements in the first period of the pre-1991 years came after the death of Stalin and the emerging reconciliatory mood between East and West, and Kim Il Sung's positive remarks on relations with Japan in the second period of the first phase followed U.S. overtures to China. Similarly, the first official normalization talks between North Korea and Japan were made possible by the end of the Cold War.

Changes in international relations have affected North Korean–Japanese relations both positively and negatively. The renewal of the U.S.-Japan Security Treaty in 1960 and the announcement of the Nixon-Sato Joint Communiqué in 1969 were the direct cause of estranged relations between North Korea and Japan. The role of the United States has been a major determining factor in shaping North Korean–Japanese relations. U.S. demands on Japan in Tokyo's normalization talks with Pyongyang clearly worked to obstruct progress in bilateral relations, even though North Korea's nuclear development program was of paramount concern for Japan.

At the regional level, North Korea's policy stance toward Japan has been intertwined with its policy toward South Korea. North Korea's initial move to reconcile relations with Japan in 1955 came about just as ongoing talks between South Korea and Japan began to stagnate. Japan's overtures toward North Korea were also carried out in consideration of South Korea. Even Shin Kanemaru felt compelled to explain to South Korea his visit to Pyongyang, while in the case of Watanabe's visit to North Korea, even before the delegation left for Pyongyang, Japan sent a delegation to Seoul to explain the visit. Indeed, one of the reasons for the delayed resumption of talks after the Watanabe visit was South Korea's request for Tokyo to keep pace with Seoul's overtures to North Korea.

At the bilateral level, the normalization process was retarded as differences of opinion on colonial-era compensation and other issues failed to subside. Continued problems in bilateral relations did not completely prevent interaction, however, and at times acted as a facilitating factor. The return of the crew of the *Fujisan Maru* and of some Japanese wives to Japan, as well as the confirmation of the case of Lee Eun-hye and other suspected abductees, provided Japan with some access to North Korea. Bilateral factors, especially popular sentiment, had more detrimental effects on further progress, however. North Korea may have been much freer in this regard, but it likely had to consider nationalist sentiment within its own ruling circle.[33]

At the domestic level, it is widely thought that internal LDP politics opened the way for both Kanemaru's and Watanabe's visits to North Korea. Prime Minister Murayama of the JSP and Secretary-General Kato of the LDP both had a stake in resuming normalization talks. These events undermined Hashimoto's own run for the presidency of the LDP and led him to proceed slowly out of concerns over handing Kato a high-profile diplomatic achievement.

These four levels of influence have varied widely in relative importance over time. International factors have been most influential in bringing about initial conditions for reorienting current bilateral relations. On the other hand, the ability of bilateral relations to proceed as reoriented by international events still depends on other factors. One of these is that resumption of bilateral relations has been very much dependent on North Korean initiatives. The first normalization talks were made possible by Kim Il Sung's unexpected offer to begin negotiations. Likewise, the initial approaches between the two began with Nam Il's remarks in the 1950s and continued with Kim Il Sung's statements in the early 1970s. This may correspond with Kent Calder's description of "reactiveness" as the main characteristic of Japanese foreign policy behavior.[34]

The more positive aspects of Japanese foreign policy behavior have come at the initiative of the country's politicians rather than its foreign policy bureaucracy. High profile political visits to North Korea have been made at the initiative of leading politicians like Kanemaru, Watanabe, and Murayama, and only with such moves has North Korea been able to respond by proposing the resumption of normalization talks. Thus domestic Japanese politics has been a major factor in bringing about changes in the North Korean–Japanese relationship. Recent progress in the normalization talks seems to be much more dependent on Japanese situations than on North Korean initiatives. This is because the Japanese government has no reason to hurry in the context of a negative public image of North Korea. Japan's foreign policy behavior may then be considered not so much "reactive" as "strategically defensive," as S. Pharr suggests.[35]

This is not to say that there has been no recent contact between the two countries. Even after the Taepodong-I missile launch, a series of contacts—distinct from the explicit accusation and the announcement of a sanction list—were attempted at the lower level. This clearly shows Japan's dilemma that it does not have many effective options other than no contact or hurried negotiations. In contrast to the prompt Japanese responses to the 1994 missile launch, however, the lack of official contact between the two countries for over a year after the Taepodong-I missile launch seems to show a lack of enthusiasm or necessity on the Japanese side.

LOOKING AHEAD

It is difficult to predict the future of North Korean–Japanese relations, given the myriad factors influencing the relationship. Based on the patterns and characteristics outlined in this chapter, however, one may consider some possible developments in the near future. The focus here must be the short term, because the long-term perspective involves too many variables. Within a reasonable short-term period, however, one may assume that the current international environment affecting North Korean–Japanese relations, including stable U.S.-Japanese relations and the U.S. stance toward North Korea, will not likely experience any sudden or drastic change.

Two contrasting dimensions need to be taken into consideration in terms of likely short-term outcomes. The first is Japan's domestic situation. Since promotion of normalization talks with North Korea has generally rested with Japanese politicians, dramatic developments in North Korean–Japanese relations are unlikely under the Koizumi cabinet. There seems to be no Japanese politician of the stature of Kanemaru or Watanabe who is influential enough to bring about substantial improvement in North Korean–Japanese relations. Even if some leading politicians, such as former Prime Minister Yasuhiro Nakasone or former Cabinet Secretary Hiromu Nonaka, were to come forward to assume such a role, Japan's precarious political situation would likely undermine any such initiative. Japanese popular sentiment toward North Korea is also a major impediment to any action. Further, as mentioned above, Prime Minister Koizumi is well known for his conservative stance and lack of experience in foreign relations, which would leave the bureaucrats (Ministry of Foreign Affairs) to handle the normalization talks. Japan can thus be expected to take only incremental steps toward improving relations with North Korea, with rapprochement left to lower-level contacts between the two governments, barring any dramatic move on the part of North Korea.

The second dimension in short-term future prospects is North Korea's domestic situation. Since finally assuming the post of party secretary in 1997, Kim Jong Il has moved to open North Korea to the outside world, albeit slightly. The inter-Korean summit in June 2000 and Kim Jong Il's following visit to Shanghai may be signs of such change. They can be understood as reflecting Kim Jong Il's need to demonstrate his leadership, not only symbolically but also materially, to a country experiencing acute economic hardship. One of the reasons that North Korea seeks to increase the pace of normalization talks with Japan is that economic recovery will require ample investment and material from outside North Korea.

Of these two contrasting dimensions, North Korea's domestic situation may be the determining factor in future bilateral relations with Japan. So far, North Korea has repeatedly taken the initiative in bringing change to the bilateral relationship. Dramatic developments in this area are unlikely, however; future relations will probably proceed incrementally and in fits and starts, as in the past. This is not only because Japan's bureaucracy will manage actual procedures, but also because the problems that most need to be addressed are time-consuming, as demonstrated in the last three rounds of the talks. In solving outstanding historical and economic issues with North Korea, Japan needs to consider carefully its relationship with South Korea, while it is unlikely that Pyongyang will easily yield on issues that involve strong nationalistic sentiments. Indeed, it took fourteen years for South Korea and Japan to normalize their relationship, and from this perspective we should wait a few more years for the materialization of a normal relationship between Japan and North Korea.

NOTES

1. The basic issues dealt with Japan's history of colonization and specifically two main questions. The first was what should constitute the baseline upon which the previous treaty was to be terminated. The second was the extent of North Korea's legal rights and sovereignty. Economic issues dealt with compensation for Japan's past colonial rule and additional compensation for postliberation suffering that included national division and the Korean War. International issues dealt with concerns over North Korea's nuclear weapon and missile development programs. Miscellaneous issues included the so-called Lee Eun-hye problem, the return of Japanese wives living in North Korea, and some others. For more information, see Masao Okonogi, *Nihon to Kitachosen: Korekara no Konen* (Japan and North Korea: Five Years from Now) (Tokyo: PHP Press, 1991).

2. *Asahi Shimbun*, April 7, 2000.

3. For the Japanese version of the press communiqué after the ninth meeting, refer to Japan's MOFA (Ministry of Foreign Affairs) site at www.mofa.go.jp/mofaj/area/n_korea/n_k/ko_press.html (accessed 20 September 2000); also see *Rodong Sinmun* (Pyongyang), April 8, 2000.

4. North Korea's Foreign Minister Paik Nam Sun's meeting with Japanese Foreign Minister Kono Yohei at the ARF meeting in Bangkok was the first encounter of the foreign ministers and the highest-level contact between the two countries. In the joint press communiqué, both sides expressed their intention to settle the past and establish new, friendly, neighborly relations, and they agreed to hold the tenth round of talks from August 21 to 25, 2000. For the communiqué, refer to Japan's MOFA Web site at

www.mofa.go.jp/mofaj/area/n_korea/n_k/kyodo.html (accessed 20 September 2000); also see *Rodong Sinmun*, July 27, 2000.

5. For the contents, refer to www.mofa.go.jp/mofaj/area/n_korea/n_k/10_kyodo.html; also see *Rodong Sinmun*, August 25, 2000.

6. Kono said that the mutual understanding was deepened and the foundations for the next meeting were prepared. *Yomiuri Shimbun*, August 25, 2000.

7. *Yomiuri Shimbun*, October 14, 2000; October 19, 2000.

8. According to one of the journalists at the Ministry of Foreign Affairs spokesman's news conference, there was a difference between the coverages of the Japanese newspaper and the North Korean newspaper. While the former reported that the setting of the date depended on the readiness of both sides, the latter argued that the next meeting would be arranged when the Japanese side was ready. The Ministry of Foreign Affairs spokesman did not answer his question on the reason for the news blackout agreement. See www.mofa.go.jp/mofaj/press/kaiken/hodokan/hodo0011.html#index (accessed 15 November 2000).

9. Jang-han Kim, "North Korea's Economy and the Prospect of Its Overseas Economic Policy in 2000," January 3, 2001, at www.kotra.co.kr/nk (accessed 20 January 2001).

10. It was reported that the letter was handed over in August 2000. *Yomiuri Shimbun*, October 3, 2000. Prime Minister Mori seemed to have seriously considered the summit. He ordered the Ministry of Foreign Affairs in August to arrange the summit (with Kim Yung-nam) for the coming United Nations millennium meeting, but it was not realized due to the cancellation of Kim's participation. *Yomiuri Shimbun*, August 26, 2000; September 6, 2000.

11. There is widespread general agreement on classifying the pre-1991 years into three periods. See Masao Okonogi, *Nihon to Kitachosen: Korekara no Konen* (Japan and North Korea: Five Years from Now) (Tokyo: PHP Press, 1991); Chong-suk Lee, "Puk-e-so bon Han-il Hyupjung kwa Cho-il Hoidam (South Korea–Japan Treaty from the Eyes of North Korea and the North Korean–Japanese Normalization Talks)," *Yuksa Bipyung* (Historical Review) 28 (1995): 57–59; Okashi Yamamoto, "Nichicho Fuseijo Kankeishi (Abnormal Relationship between Japan and North Korea)," in Sekai, ed. *Nichicho Kankei: So no Rekishi to Genzai* (The Japan–North Korea Relationship: Its History and the Present), special issue, April 1992.

12. Yamanoto, 162.

13. W. D. Lee, *Bukil Kukkyogyosup kwa Ilbon eui Daebuk Jungchek* (The North Korean–Japanese Normalization Talks and Japan's North Korea Policy) (Seoul: Seoul National University 1996), 81–4; Okonogi, 93–4.

14. Okonogi, *Nihon to Kitachosen*, 99.

15. Lee, 58–9.

16. Okonogi, 106.

17. Okonogi, 107; C. S. Lee, 64–5.

18. North Korea captured the crew of the *Fujisan Maru* in the port of Nampo in November 1983, accused them of spying, and in December 1985 sentenced them to fifteen years of labor. See Gaimusho (Japanese Ministry of Foreign Affairs), *Gaiko Seisho* (The Blue Paper) 32 (1988): 177.

19. Okonogi, 125.

20. See note 1, above.

21. *Asahi Shimbun*, May 15, 1992.

22. *Asahi Shimbun*, January 26, 1991.

23. K. W. Yang, ed., "Bukil Kukyo Jungsanghwa Gyosup: 1991–1995 (The Normalization Talks between North Korea and Japan)," in Tongilwon (National Board of Unification), *Tongil Hwangkyung kwa Tongil Kyoyuk* (The Environment and Education for Unification), 1995, 184.

24. *Asahi Shimbun*, November 26, 1991.

25. *Asahi Shimbun*, October 25, 1994.

26. Koichi Kato, "Kitachosen o sekyokuteki ni shien subekida: Kato Koichi, Jiminto Kanshicho ni kiku (We Should Help North Korea Earnestly: Interview with Kato Koichi)," *Kendai Koria*, 1995, 16–21.

27. *Asahi Shimbun*, March 31, 1995.

28. *Asahi Shimbun*, June 26, 1995.

29. For example, Hiroshi Hasegawa, "Kome Jito Kenjo no Fukaki Anto (Political Infighting for Rice Aid)," *Aera*, June 12, 1995, 19–22; Akira Tanaka, "Kitashosen Kome wa Heiwa Boke (Rice Aid toward North Korea Is Just a Disguise)," *Shokun*, 1995, 68–77; Toshimitsu Shigemura, "Gaiko o Asonda Yotou Houchotan Soudou (The Governing Parties' Delegation to North Korea to Ridicule Japan's Foreign Policy)," *Chuogoron*, June, 1995, 99–105.

30. *Asahi Shimbun*, November 6, 1995.

31. *Asahi Shimbun*, May 22, 1997.

32. Though the survey of the Japanese public on North Korea is not available, their negative sentiments about North Korea, especially after the Taepodong-I missile launch, were mentioned frequently during my interviews of 1999 and 2000 with officials and scholars in Tokyo and Niigata.

33. *Asahi Shimbun*, September 1, 1992.

34. K. Calder, "Japanese Foreign Economic Policy Formation: Explaining the Reactive State," *World Politics* 40, 4 (July 1988): 517–41.

35. S. Pharr, "Japan's Defensive Foreign Policy and the Politics of Burden Sharing," in Gerald Curtis, ed., *Japan's Foreign Policy after the Cold War: Coping with Change* (Armonk, NY: M. E. Sharpe, 1993), 235–62.

4

Chinese–North Korean Relations: Managing Asymmetrical Interdependence

Samuel S. Kim and Tai Hwan Lee

A RISING CHINA FACES THE POWER OF THE WEAK

The North Korean predicament, along with the question of how to manage it in a cost-effective way, remains one of the most important challenges confronting China's foreign relations in the post–Cold War world. For better or worse, the Democratic People's Republic of Korea (DPRK), or North Korea, is the one and only country with which the People's Republic of China (PRC) "maintains" its 1961 Cold War alliance pact—whether in name or in practice. Yet in the 1990s, especially since 1995, the possibility of implosion or explosion in North Korea seemed to have become more real than ever before. An unstable North Korea with inordinate potential to destabilize Northeast Asia through its conventional and nonconventional (asymmetrical) military capabilities and threats has extraordinary refractory ramifications for China's foreign policy in general and its two-Koreas policy in particular.

Despite some improvement in Sino–North Korean relations from 1999 to 2001, as made evident by a series of high-level political and diplomatic exchanges, including most recently President Jiang Zemin's official state visit to Pyongyang in early September 2001, there remains just beneath the surface a highly asymmetrical interdependence in all political, military, and economic issue areas. Thanks to growing enmeshment in the global system, China's concept and practice of "security" have experienced considerable expansion and diversification in the post-Mao era of reform and opening, while North Korea remains an isolated hermit kingdom, a country with seemingly fatal contradictions on the verge of explosion or implosion.

Faced with such asymmetrical interdependence realities on the ground, Beijing seeks to achieve multiple, mutually competitive goals on multiple fronts. These goals include: maintaining peace and stability on the Korean peninsula, promoting economic exchange and cooperation with South Korea, helping North Korea's regime to survive, halting the flow of North Korean refugees and South Korean Christian missionaries into Jilin Province, stopping the rise of ethnonationalism among ethnic Chinese-Koreans, enhancing China's influence in Korean affairs, preventing the formation of any anti-China coalition in East Asia, and expanding and diversifying China's foreign-policy options by viewing East Asia as the center of Chinese power and influence. More bluntly, China's foreign-policy wish list with respect to its "communist" northeast neighbor includes at least five "no's": no instability, no collapse, no nukes, no refugees or defectors, and no conflict escalation. Above all, Beijing recognizes the utility of Korea in projecting its identity as a great power; to wit, China's sheer physical size and its geopolitical and geoeconomic importance invariably make it part of the Korean solution, even as it advances its own national interests in its dealings with the three Northeast Asian powers, especially with the United States as a de facto neighbor.[1] By dint of Pyongyang's political and geographical isolation, Beijing has been serving as the gateway to Pyongyang and as an indispensable venue for North Korea's negotiations with South Korea, Japan, and the United States.

Perhaps the most useful starting point is the central challenge of Chinese foreign policy in the post–Cold War world: how to accomplish "comprehensive national strength" (*zonghe guoli*), not only as a means of accelerating China's march to great-powerdom, which Chinese of all ideological stripes believe to be their inalienable entitlement, but also as a means of compensating for growing deficits in domestic legitimation and security.[2] The image of China as a great power incorporates not only special rights and privileges and a command of formidable material power, but also corresponding special duties, responsibilities, and actions appropriate to a great power.[3] The idea that it is necessary to establish China's image as a *responsible* great power in order to deal with the various version of the "China threat theory" (*Zhonguo weixian lun*) resonates in Chinese foreign policy thinking and analysis.[4]

For the DPRK, however, the most daunting challenge is how to survive by seeking more and more aid as an external life-support system[5] without triggering a cataclysmic system collapse. The end of the Cold War, the demise of the Soviet Union, and the end of Sino-Soviet conflict and rivalry have irrevocably transformed both the context and the condition for maintaining the traditional "lips-to-teeth" strategic ties. Still, North Korea has earned a reputation as being "the power of the weak," creating and using crises to extract concessions to compensate for growing domestic failings. With continuing asymmetries of needs and expectations, Beijing's foreign policy objectives coalesce, clash, or compete with those of Pyongyang in situation-specific or path-dependent ways.

Despite the lack of consensus on China's great power status or on the feasibility and desirability of various engagement or containment strategies to manage the rise of Chinese power through balancing, bandwagoning, capitulating, or ignoring,[6] it is clear that the PRC holds greater importance in North Korea's foreign policy than the DPRK holds in Chinese foreign policy. Consider China's potential trump cards in Korean affairs: 1.) demographic weight: it is the world's most populous country (fifty-nine times the population of North Korea and nineteen times the population of the two Koreas); 2.) continental size (the world's second-largest, and forty-four times the size of the Korean peninsula) and territorial contiguity, sharing with North Korea a border some 1,416 kilometers long, across almost the entire northern stretch of the Korean peninsula; 3.) military capability that is steadily being modernized, with the world's largest armed forces (2.94 million troops in active service) and the world's third-largest nuclear weapons power after the United States and Russia; 4.) veto power in the United Nations Security Council; 5.) new economic status as the world's second-largest economy (with its 2000 gross national income at $4,966 billion, measured at purchasing-power parity);[7] and 6.) traditional Confucian cultural influence with strong historical roots.

North Korea is not, however, powerless in coping with this asymmetrical interdependence between two of the four remaining communist countries in the post–Cold War world. North Korea's geographical location is of considerable strategic importance to China's national security and is also a source of North Korea's asymmetrical power, the power of the weak. North Korea is the one and only country surrounded by the Big Four (China, Russia, Japan, and the United States) plus South Korea (Republic of Korea [ROK]). Indeed, in Chinese strategic thinking, the Korean peninsula is singled out as the "core problem" (*hexin wenti*) of Northeast Asia.[8] Chinese President Jiang Zemin has often stated that without peace and stability on the Korean peninsula there can be no genuine peace and stability in the Asia-Pacific region. Indeed, history and geography have combined to make Korea "a source of threat unless it could be controlled or neutralized, since it was a potential entry point for rival powers."[9]

Strategically located at the vortex of Northeast Asian security—indeed, the most important strategic nexus of the Asia-Pacific region—Pyongyang could, by instigating hostility or instability, potentially entrap China or all other regional powers in a spiral of conflict escalation that these governments would rather avoid. Without launching an armed invasion, Pyongyang could still exercise its "negative power" to destabilize the Korean peninsula and beyond, by using its on-again, off-again brinkmanship and the threat of its collapse. Contrary to conventional realist wisdom, in asymmetrical negotiations the stronger state does not ipso facto exert greater control than the weaker state. If a small and weak state occupies territory of strategic importance to a larger and stronger state, or if the "field of play" is on the weak state's home turf, the weaker actor can display bargaining power disproportionate to its aggregate structural power.[10] The threat of a North Korean collapse and the costs of regional spillover in the form of refugees or even armed conflict escalation have become China's strategic nightmare scenario, while simultaneously increasing Pyongyang's leverage in asymmetrical negotiations with Beijing for more aid.

This chapter proceeds from the premise that China's North Korea policy is made to order for exploring the interplay between China and the Northeast Asian powers (Russia, Japan, and the United States). This involves, on the one hand, how external factors shape Chinese international conduct and, on the other hand, how Chinese international conduct itself impacts upon the structures and processes of post–Cold War Northeast Asian regional politics. In order to capture the complex and mutating nature of Sino-DPRK relations of the post–Cold War era, three broad issue areas have been selected for analysis: political/diplomatic, military/strategic, and economic/functional. The emphasis is on the most recent developments at various systemic levels.

REPAIRING THE STRAINED RELATIONSHIP

The first step in understanding China's role in Korean affairs is to recognize that there is an uneasy, shifting balance of competing forces and identities—both conflictive and cooperative—in Beijing's post–Cold War foreign policy. China's 1992 decision to normalize relations with South Korea was the culmination of a gradual process of balancing and adjusting post-Mao foreign policy to the logic of the changing domestic, regional, and global situations. Despite habitual assaults on power politics, through its two-Koreas decision Beijing once again demonstrated its remarkable capacity to constantly redefine the international situation and adjust to changing political winds in pursuit of basic national interests. By fits and starts, the two-Koreas decision has evolved through several phases, shifting first from the familiar one-Korea policy to a one-Korea de jure/two-Koreas de facto policy, and then again to a two-Koreas de facto and de jure policy. In implementing the two-Koreas decision in the postnormalization period, Beijing has adopted a multitasking approach of emphasizing different but mutually complementary priorities in different issue areas.

Despite the inauguration of formal diplomatic relations with Seoul, Beijing has adopted a dual track approach of strengthening its traditional "special relations" with North Korea while at the same time promoting "normal state relations" with South Korea.[11] Such an equidistant two-Koreas policy has proved more easily promised than performed. In the wake of the death of Kim Il Sung in July 1994, the Sino-DPRK relationship became increasingly strained, with a growing number of Pyongyang's foreign policy interests and objectives clashing with those of Beijing. Most Chinese diplomats and scholars admit privately (and off the record) that they get along far better with their counterparts from the South than from the North. You Ji describes one aspect of the strain:

> In fact, the Chinese Ministry of Foreign Affairs regularly issues orders to the Chinese officials that they must not comment on the DPRK affairs within the presence of foreigners. This shows that China's quarrel with the DPRK is not only about reform. It is a feeling of chauvinism that has not failed to be sensed by Pyongyang and may exert profound impact on the bilateral relations in the long run.[12]

The strained relationship is also reflected in an appreciable decline in the frequency and level of mutual visits by political leaders in the post–Kim Il Sung years (1994 to 1998). For more than a decade, neither Jiang Zemin nor Kim Jong Il found it politically important or convenient to negotiate the short distance between Beijing and Pyongyang (an hour by plane) for a summit meeting.[13] In contrast, there were many summit meetings between South Korean and Chinese leaders during this period; there was even a visit to Seoul by all seven members of Politburo Standing Committee of the Chinese Communist Party, the most powerful organ of the Chinese political system.

The Kosovo war served as the proximate catalyst for setting in motion the process of repairing the strained relationship. In the wake of a rapid succession of seemingly threatening developments in the late 1990s—the new Guidelines for U.S.-Japan Defense Cooperation and the growing U.S.-Japan cooperation in the development of the theater missile defense (TMD) system, the U.S./NATO air war against Yugoslavia, and the accidental American bombing of the Chinese embassy in Belgrade—China's relations with the United States in the military and security realm have been fraught once again with worsening threat perceptions, giving rise in China to images of an America bent on global hegemony through the containment of China. For many Chinese strategic analysts, the Kosovo war would establish a dangerous precedent of bypassing the UN Security Council for American neointerventionism, of lowering the threshold for the use of force, and of replacing or trampling state sovereignty as the core principle of international relations. Worse yet, for some Chinese analysts, Kosovo served as a warning that the struggle for a multipolar world order would now last far longer than previously thought—some twenty to thirty years longer—and that America-led war disguised as humanitarian intervention might not be as remote from China's home turf as they had previously assumed.[14] Moreover, Kosovo was a turning point, according to one Chinese security analyst, causing "a shift in Chinese thinking on the matter of tolerance for U.S. forces in Asia. China now [felt] surrounded by the U.S.-Japan and U.S.-ROK alliances."[15]

By the same token, Kosovo triggered alarm in Pyongyang, filling the North Korean leadership with a sense of crisis that it, too, could become a second Yugoslavia. With the worsening external security environment, Pyongyang was now more determined to build up its military muscle.[16] Kosovo also prompted Pyongyang to feel the urgent need to restore and improve its peripheral diplomacy, especially with Beijing and Moscow.

With such shared security concerns and fears, China's Korea policy made a subtle readjustment at a time when Pyongyang was launching an unprecedented diplomatic outreach. As a result, Beijing's displeasure with its unruly socialist ally in the strategic buffer zone was largely put aside as the Chinese leadership also began to see the United States as the more clear and present threat to its own interests in Northeast Asia. In short, both Beijing and Pyongyang were sufficiently alarmed by America's military operation in Kosovo to bring back the allied relationship of strategic convenience.

Against this backdrop, Beijing's relations with North Korea began to be "renormalized," starting from the spring of 1999 via the exchange of high-profile delegations. Beijing seems to have taken the initiative in jump-starting the process of renormalization, with Chinese Foreign Minister Tang Jiaxuan's five-day visit to Pyongyang in April 1999. Two months later, in early June, a fifty-member North Korean delegation, led by Supreme People's Assembly (SPA) President Kim Yong Nam, made a high-profile state visit to China. For Pyongyang, the visit was a success not only as a turning point in the Sino–North Korean strategic partnership but also for obtaining China's promise of an additional one hundred fifty thousand tons of grain and four hundred thousand tons of coal.[17]

Kim Jong Il's choice of Beijing for his first-ever state visit, May 29 through 31, 2000, spotlights China's place in Pyongyang's diplomatic reorientation. By all signs, the China trip was catalyzed by and concerned with the proper handling of the upcoming inter-Korean Pyongyang summit, with Beijing playing the supporting role of socialist elder brother and tutor. Unlike Kim Yong Nam's state visit a year earlier, Kim Jong Il's China trip had Pyongyang publicly praising the emergent Sino-DPRK renormalization process. By achieving a "consensus of views on all the matters discussed," we are told, the Beijing summit advanced the cause of socialism and further consolidated the DPRK-China friendship—a relationship sealed in the blood of the Korean War—at a time when the international situation was becoming increasingly complicated.[18] Pyongyang also acknowledged, for the first time, significant achievements in China's socialist modernization, and that these achievements were possible only under the leadership of the Chinese Communist Party.[19]

Among all the world's major powers, China has the most to gain, at least in the short run, from the inter-Korean rapprochement process that the June 2000 Pyongyang summit reflected and effected. As Kim Jong Il's visit to Beijing a couple of weeks before the summit underscores, China was back in the center of peninsular affairs, as facilitator and cheerleader, if not honest broker. Yet the rapid pace of post-summit events and developments revealed Beijing's "crisis" (*weiji*), in the Chinese usage of the term, indicating not only danger (*weixian*), but also an opportunity (*jihui*) to be seized. Beijing welcomed the summit as a first, giant step in the inter-Korean peace process, while simultaneously worrying about any possible adverse consequences of too rapid an improvement of U.S.-DPRK relations at the expense of China's rather unique role in peninsular affairs.

As if determined to showcase its strategic balancing act, Beijing dispatched two delegations in October 2000. The first was a military delegation to Pyongyang, headed by Defense Minister Chi Haotian, to celebrate the fiftieth anniversary of its entry into the Korean War—the "War to Resist America and Aid Korea," in Beijing's lingo—and to reaffirm Sino-DPRK military ties. The second was a civilian delegation to Seoul, headed by Prime Minister Zhu Rongji, to elevate Sino-ROK relations from a "cooperative partnership" to a "full-scale cooperative partnership," pushing the United States and Japan to the sidelines. China's proactive balancing strategy may have contributed to the uncharacteristically hasty move by the Clinton administration to accelerate its normalization talks with the DPRK, stemming from American worries about losing control over the rapidly moving Korean target and concerns about China's rising role in the region.

Yet Beijing was greatly surprised and even unnerved by the extent to which Secretary of State Madeleine Albright's quasi summit meeting with Kim Jong Il overshadowed Chi Haotian's presence in the city. Such a reaction is hardly surprising, considering the rapid pace of unprecedented diplomatic events, especially the U.S.-DPRK normalization talks. The emerging inter-Korean peace process in the latter half of 2000 immediately put into play several plausible future scenarios for reshaping the regional security architecture of Northeast Asia. One possibility was that the United States might take command over the emerging reconciliation process, to the disadvantage of China's influence on peninsular affairs. Indeed, Beijing's role in Korean affairs seemed ever closely keyed to Sino-American relations, watching the development of any U.S.-DPRK warming process with a sharp realpolitik eye.

Once again we are reminded of the importance of North Korea and the Korean peninsula, not only as a strategic buffer zone but also as an important political arena for mobilizing and projecting China's national identity as a great power. In the full glow of the June 2000 inter-Korean summit, Beijing still went a long way in its official celebration of its entry to the Korean War, with a flurry of articles, programs, public events, a new official three-volume history, a major speech by President Jiang Zemin, and the dispatch of the high-powered military delegation to Pyongyang in late October 2000. This may have been not so much a public pledge to defend the DPRK at any cost or under any circumstances as it was another public demonstration and reminder of China's successful enactment, on the battlefield of the Korean War, of its national identity as a great power, defending itself against a menacing imperialist superpower and achieving a victory that put China on the world map.[20]

In the face of increasingly harsh rhetoric from the new hard-line Bush administration in Washington, Pyongyang once again shifted its geopolitical focus, turning to Beijing for guidance and support. Out of the public spotlight for more than a month, Kim Jong Il reemerged on March 22, 2001, to meet with Zeng Qinghong, a close advisor to President Jiang Zemin, to work out the details of Jiang Zemin's official state visit to Pyongyang. On March 23, China's Xinhua News Agency announced that Jiang would visit Pyongyang before the end of the year.

For the first time in eleven years, Chinese President Jiang Zemin made a three-day official visit to Pyongyang, September 3 through 5, 2001, capping the flurry of renormalizing political and diplomatic exchanges and efforts since the spring of 1999. To put Jiang's state visit in historical and comparative perspective, Mao Zedong never visited the DPRK, Zhou Enlai made two visits (1958 and 1970), Deng Xiaoping three visits (1961, 1978, and 1982), and Jiang Zemin had made one earlier visit in 1990, while Kim Il Sung had paid more than ten official and unofficial visits to China. Obviously Jiang's 2001 visit was meant to represent the formal mending of a relationship that had been troubled from 1994 to 1998 and to repay two successive visits by Kim Jong Il (one to Beijing in May 2000 and the other to Shanghai in January 2001). Once again the DPRK seems to have extracted rather substantial economic benefits, in the form of "grant-in-aid" of thirty thousand tons of diesel fuel and two hundred thousand tons of food.

Yet there was apparently far more behind-the-scenes realpolitik maneuvering than met the public eye in the Jiang-Kim summit in Pyongyang. In a sudden policy reversal on September 2, a day before Jiang's official state visit was to begin, North Korea launched a unilateral diplomatic preemptive strike, proposing that the stalled inter-Korean talks be resumed as soon as possible. The message seems loud and clear, that North Korea makes such decisions on an independent footing, not relying on China's sympathy, advice, or pressure. The Jiang-Kim summit is also notable for the absence of a joint communiqué or declaration. This may suggest China's realpolitik refusal to play with North Korea on variations of the anti-American DPRK-Russia Moscow Declaration of August 4, 2001, which had capped the Putin-Kim summit a month earlier (in regard to such issues as the ABM Treaty, the presence of U.S. troops in South Korea, antihegemony, and a multipolar world order).

NEITHER ALLIED ABANDONMENT NOR ALLIED ENTRAPMENT

For China, the single greatest challenge to smooth management of the new Beijing-Pyongyang-Seoul relationship has remained Pyongyang's security (or insecurity) behavior, which has varied from nuclear brinkmanship to missile-coercive diplomacy. Whether Beijing likes it or not, Pyongyang's nuclear/missile brinkmanship has already become an important security issue in Sino-Japanese, Sino–South Korean, and Sino-U.S. relations, as well as in the ASEAN Regional Security Forum, the International Atomic Energy Agency, and the United Nations Security Council. China's challenge, therefore, is to navigate between the Scylla of allied abandonment, with its potentials for instability or collapse in North Korea, and the Charybdis of allied entrapment, with the continuing danger of being caught in conflict escalation not of its own making.

The euphoria of 1990 to 1992—engendered by Soviet-ROK normalization, the two Koreas UN membership, the two historic Inter-Korean accords, and Sino-ROK normalization—was greatly overshadowed by the rise of the nuclear crisis in 1993 and 1994. North Korea's nuclear brinkmanship, billed in the West as the first nuclear proliferation crisis of the post–Cold War era, became an instant security challenge for Chinese foreign policy. While Seoul was more or less sidelined, the nuclear issue confronted Beijing with a new set of dangers and opportunities in the management of Sino-DPRK asymmetrical interdependence at the bilateral, regional, and global levels.

Paradoxically, it was the threat of a Chinese veto on any draft sanctions resolution in the Security Council that enabled Pyongyang to obtain what it had been seeking from the beginning: direct bilateral confrontation or negotiation with the United States. Thus began a series of high-level talks between the North Koreans and the Americans in New York and Geneva, culminating in the landmark Geneva accord—officially known as the U.S.-DPRK Agreed Framework of 21 October 1994 (hereafter AF)—thanks to former President Jimmy Carter's shuttle diplomacy in the heat of the nuclear crisis in June 1994. As if to take chief credit for the breakthrough, China highly praised

Carter's "fruitful mediation" as showing that "dialogue is better than confrontation."[21]

In a strategic game deftly played, Pyongyang used its nuclear threat to capitalize on all the uncertainties and shifting goals in Washington, Seoul, and Tokyo. The United States intelligence community judged in the mid-1990s that North Korea had produced enough weapons-grade plutonium for one nuclear bomb, possibly two, and as it soon became widely conceded that it would be virtually impossible to certify this, North Korea skillfully played a now-yes, now-no, cat-and-mouse game. Pyongyang seemed determined to refute the notion that Beijing's behind-the-scenes diplomacy had anything to do with the AF, which was quickly dubbed "the biggest diplomatic victory" by *Rodong Sinmun*: "We held the talks independently with the United States on an independent footing, not relying on someone else's sympathy or advice, and the adoption of the DPRK-U.S. Agreed Framework is a fruition of our independent foreign policy, not someone's influence."[22] The claim was that the United States had finally accepted the North Korean proposal.

In the course of Sino-ROK normalization talks, Beijing made a promise of "help" on the North Korean nuclear issue and allowed American expectations to soar unchecked with regard to its putative leverage in Pyongyang. However, the notion that Beijing was able or willing to play a decisive role in actually reshaping Pyongyang's nuclear behavior stands on shaky historical, behavioral, and normative grounds. First of all, post-Tiananmen China was afflicted with twin legitimation crises at home (the Tiananmen carnage) and abroad (the collapse of transnational communism at its epicenter). International sanctions, especially U.S.-sponsored sanctions against a socialist regime, were therefore a trigger provoking a sovereignty-based "sound and fury" response.[23]

Second, China is more committed to the immediate challenge of maintaining stability than it is to pursuing its long-term objective of nuclear disarmament on the Korean peninsula. Apart from maximizing its leverage as a balancer, the greatest danger, in Beijing's view, is from two alternative possibilities: conflict or collapse. China's junior socialist ally in the strategic buffer zone could feel so cornered that it fights back, thus triggering an armed conflict. Alternatively, economic sanctions could work so well as to produce another collapsing socialist regime on China's borders, with huge political, economic, and social consequences for Chinese domestic politics. With Chinese help, Pyongyang demonstrated to the entire world that sanctions would be accepted as a declaration of war, a no-win proposition for all the parties concerned. Indeed, the 1994 nuclear crisis on the Korean peninsula posed for the Clinton administration "a choice between a disastrous option—allowing North Korea to get a nuclear arsenal, which we might have to face someday—and an unpalatable option, blocking this development, but thereby risking a destructive non-nuclear war."[24] On the other hand, for Beijing, the realpolitik logic here seems simple enough: To abandon or rebuke Pyongyang publicly, especially during a crisis situation, is to follow the Soviet fallacy of premature allied abandonment, losing whatever leverage it may still have on the politics of divided Korea.

Third, Beijing seems to recognize the outer possibilities and limitations of its influence in reshaping Pyongyang's hypernational security thinking and behavior. From Pyongyang's vantage point, the nuclear weapons program, or at least a calculated ambiguity of its alleged nuclear weapons program, constitutes a cost-effective nuclear deterrent and a "strategic equalizer" in its competition with the South. The diminution of Russian support for the North and the de facto removal of the Russian nuclear umbrella seemed to have strengthened the determination of the North Korean leadership to go nuclear as a matter of necessity (regime survival), rather than as a matter of choice. For China, on the other hand, what remains unchanged in the post–Cold War era "is a deeply rooted hard realpolitik worldview that nuclear weapons buy both soft power (international status and influence) and hard power (military operational power)."[25] One may very well ask if nuclear weapons are necessary for China's security and status, or if China without the bomb cannot really stand up, why is the same not true for North Korea?

From Beijing's realpolitik perspective, the 1994 U.S.-DPRK Agreed Framework was seen as a window of opportunity for improving economic conditions in North Korea, for bolstering the legitimacy of the Kim Jong Il regime, and for enhancing the prospects of political stability. In addition, the Agreed Framework would go some way in alleviating the dangerous imbalance of power between the two Koreas. Thus its full implementation was regarded as essential to peace and stability on the Korean peninsula and hence vital to China's national security interests.[26] Likewise, the Kuala Lumpur Agreement of June 13, 1995, the first major post-Geneva agreement on the acceptance of South Korean models of light-water reactors (LWRs), was also seen in self-effacing terms. The quest for an equidistant neutral stand is also a manifestation of maxi-mini diplomacy—doing less to accomplish more—as is evident in China's refusal to join the Korean Peninsula Energy Development Organization (KEDO), a multinational consortium for the implementation of the AF. As China's standard refrain goes, "We can be of greater help being outside than inside the KEDO." Moreover, Taiwan's repeated offers to make financial contributions to KEDO have been blocked diplomatically by China. If Beijing wanted to stay out of North Korean nuclear harm's way in 1993 and 1994, the same cannot be said about the two-plus-two formula—the four-party peace talks formula jointly proposed by Presidents Clinton and Kim Young Sam at their summit meeting on Cheju Island, South Korea, on April 16, 1996.

With particular clarity and tenacity, Pyongyang has pursued the two-plus-zero formula in its *juche*-style (self-reliance) diplomacy. Even before the protracted U.S.-DPRK nuclear negotiations culminated in the AF, Pyongyang had put forward to the United States, in April 1994, a two-plus-zero proposal for replacing "the outdated armistice system" with "a new peace arrangement system" (i.e., a peace treaty with the United States). The two-plus-zero formula is an expression of Pyongyang's abiding unilateralism-cum-bilateralism. It is also indicative of the extent to which the United States has become the key to Pyongyang's strategy of survival. When the two-plus-zero peace formula fell on deaf ears in Washington, however, Pyongyang delivered a message to the United Nations Command on April 28, 1994, stating that the Korean People's Army had already decided to recall all remaining Military Armistice Commission (MAC) members and MAC staff personnel. At the same time Pyongyang dispatched a special envoy, Vice Foreign Minister Song Ho Gyong, to Beijing on August 30, 1994, to persuade China to do the same. After four days of talks between Song and his Chinese counterpart, Vice Foreign Minister Tang Jiaxuan, a communiqué was issued indicating that the Chinese government would pull out its forces, the Chinese People's Volunteers, from MAC, "taking into consideration the request by the DPRK and the present situation in which [North] Korea has withdrawn its delegation from MAC and that MAC has already in all actuality been paralyzed because of this development."[27] Pyongyang's withdrawal in April 1994 followed by Beijing's withdrawal in September of the same year has crippled the forty-year-old MAC.[28]

Despite initial profound reservations about the Four-Party Talks, Beijing's interest and anger was sufficiently aroused by Pyongyang's anti-Chinese behavior for China to change its mind and become an active participant. When Pyongyang was pressing hard for its unilateral two-plus-zero or a three-plus-zero formula in obvious attempts to exclude Beijing, for example, China's surprise response was that it now opposed North Korea's unilateral two-plus-zero scheme as "unrealistic, unreasonable and impossible." From Beijing's perspective, Pyongyang's formula marginalized the China factor in the security complex surrounding the Korean peninsula. As a signatory to the Korean armistice accord, Yu Shaohua, one of China's leading Koreanists, argues that Beijing has every reason and right to be a party in the Four-Party Talks designed to replace the armistice with a peace treaty or mechanism.[29]

Paradoxically, as Beijing was gearing up to play a more active role in Geneva, the Four-Party Talks were suddenly overshadowed by a series of North Korean submarine incursions into South Korean territorial waters, rising speculation about an underground nuclear construction site at Kumchang-ri, and the launching of a three-stage Taepodong-I missile over Japan on August 31, 1998. This trio of incidents on the part of North Korea dramatically illustrates how difficult it is for Beijing to keep its Korea policy on a bilateral track. To make matters worse, another trio of concerns has evolved from Beijing's perspective regarding China's own acceleration of ballistic missiles deployed against Taiwan, nuclear secrets allegedly stolen from a U.S. government laboratory, and reports of another cycle of repression against human rights and democracy activists in China since late 1998. These incidents have weakened U.S. domestic support for its policy of comprehensive engagement with China and America's "deterrence plus policy of conditional engagement" with North Korea. Meanwhile, the firing of the Taepodong-I missile has pushed Tokyo, if not Seoul, into joining America's new TMD project, with enormous military and strategic implications.

In terms of Korean security, can China really have its cake and eat it too? Is a genuine two-Korea security policy feasible despite the 1961 PRC-DPRK Treaty of Friendship, Cooperation, and Mutual Assistance? Although the present-day Sino-DPRK relationship is not as close as it once was, neither Beijing nor Pyongyang has shown any interest in modifying the treaty. Instead, the treaty is kept partly as a convenient fiction and partly as a convenient fact. Unlike the 1961 Soviet-DPRK treaty, the Sino-DPRK treaty cannot legally be revised or abrogated without prior mutual agreement (Article 7). Even though China still has a military alliance with North Korea (its one and only military alliance treaty), Beijing let it be known, if only informally at first, that it would not support Pyongyang if North Korea attacked South Korea. During Jiang Zemin's state visit to South Korea in 1995, a Chinese Foreign Ministry spokesperson stated that the alliance does not commit Chinese troops to defending North Korea.[30] On other occasions, Beijing has indicated that it would not provide support if the North launched "an unprovoked attack," or if the treaty did not require the dispatch of Chinese military forces, or China were not willing "automatically" to intervene, and so on. With such impunity, Beijing projects a strategic posture of calculated ambiguity, letting it be known to all that its treaty commitment to Pyongyang can be interpreted as Chinese leaders wish. It also seems to indicate that China does not consider the treaty to be ipso facto a hard and fast commitment and that in a crisis situation Chinese leaders may "change their minds, change their policies, or, of course, even act with reckless abandon."[31]

For at least two years, the establishment of PRC-ROK diplomatic relations had no discernible impact on PRC-DPRK military and strategic ties, as visitations of Chinese and North Korean military delegations continued unabated. In fact, during the period from August 1992 until the death of Kim Il Sung in July 1994 (i.e., during the nuclear-crisis period), mutual, high-level visits between China and North Korea accelerated greatly. From July 1994, when Kim Il Sung died, to mid-1999, however, overall military and security contacts and exchanges between the PRC and the DPRK showed a steady decline, not only in frequency but also in the level and type of military/security exchanges. Most political and military contacts and exchanges since then have been symbolic, not task-oriented, meetings on salient military and security issues.[32]

Against the backdrop of rapid deterioration of Sino-American relations in the first half of 1999, Beijing has made it known with particular vigor that despite the inauguration of formal diplomatic relations with Seoul in August 1992 and despite the "PRC-ROK Cooperative Partnership for the 21st Century," Beijing continues to maintain its traditional geostrategic ties with North Korea. In interviews with South Korean scholars and the media in late January 1999, PRC Ambassador to South Korea Wu Dawei vigorously asserted that the 1961 Sino-DPRK Treaty on Friendship, Cooperation, and Mutual Assistance is alive and well, and that there are no revision negotiations of any kind in the works. More tellingly, Ambassador Wu followed the Pyongyang party line by asserting that the Korean peninsula problem has been used as an excuse for military buildup by external powers (the United States and Japan). He also stated that China cannot concur that North Korea is not transparent at all, and hence cannot consent to a forced inspection of the suspected underground nuclear site in North Korea. On March 15, 1999, Chinese Premier Zhu Rongji flatly declared at a news conference following the conclusion of the National People's Congress that "North Korea is a sovereign state, so it is none of our business whether North Korea develops a missile or whether it researches and develops nuclear weapons."[33]

Pyongyang asserted as much in its repeated statements that if missile development is permissible for the United States, China, Russia, and Japan, then it is surely permissible for the DPRK. However tough the behind-the-scenes bargaining has been, Beijing seems determined not to criticize Pyongyang publicly. In effect, Beijing is asking Washington, Tokyo, Seoul, and Pyongyang to follow what it says—"restrainmanship"—rather than what it actually does in its own nuclear and missile development and coercive missile diplomacy. Departing from normal practice, China made a public announcement of its test-firing of a new long-range ballistic missile (Dong Feng 31), which can carry a single fifteen-hundred-pound nuclear warhead in a range of about five thousand miles and is capable of reaching the United States. Many Chinese strategic analysts reject the notion that the joint U.S.-Japan project on the TMD system serves as a protection against the North Korean threat; the U.S. Patriot missiles already deployed on South Korean soil are said to be adequate for the ROK's defense. Therefore the TMD project can only cause mistrust and suspicion in states surrounding China, thus destroying the security of Northeast Asia.[34] From Pyongyang's perspective, the U.S. NMD (National Missile Defense)/TMD plans are preprogrammed to avoid direct confrontation with Beijing and Moscow, hiding behind the excuse of North Korea as a rogue state but also reinforcing Japan's military role in East Asia, as preparations for another war in Asia.[35]

As if to demonstrate the hidden facets in the new Beijing-Moscow-Pyongyang strategic partnership, China and South Korea held their first-ever defense ministers' talks in Beijing, August 23 through 29, 1999, to coincide with the seventh anniversary of normalization between China and the ROK and as another benchmark event in the Sino-ROK relationship. For Seoul, Defense Minister Cho Sung-tae's visit was part of a diplomatic blitz aimed at winning China's support for President Kim Dae Jung's "sunshine policy." Moreover, Seoul's requests for broader Sino-ROK security cooperation also included joint PRC-ROK military exercises, a joint maritime search-and-rescue exercise, exchanges of naval port calls, the establishment of multilateral arms control and disarmament dialogue to prevent the proliferation of weapons of mass destruction, and a return visit by Chinese Defense Minister Chi Haotian. Not surprisingly, Beijing responded with the maxi-mini strategy: 1.) it accepted Seoul's invitation for Chi's return visit (which was carried out five months later in January 2000); 2.) it warned Seoul against enhancing military ties with the United States (i.e., the Ulchi Focus Lens annual U.S.-ROK joint military exercises); 3.) it preached about the danger of American hegemony (a unipolar world order) in an era of political multipolarization; and 4.) it danced away from Seoul's request for Beijing's help or response on the other issues. Beijing remains unwilling to participate with Seoul in joint exercises, even in basic areas such as search and rescue or humanitarian operations, nor in the exchange of naval port calls by each other's ships.

The publication of a new book, *Chaoxian zhan* (*Unrestricted War*), authored by Colonels Qiao Liang and Wang Xiangsui, speaks directly to China's own strategic thinking on asymmetric conflicts. For a relatively weak country like China (and perhaps North Korea) to stand up to a powerful country like the United States, we are told, it is strategically imperative to resort to such compensatory devices as terrorism, drug trafficking, environmental degradation, and computer virus propagation.[36] Coming on the heels of Kim Yong Nam's state visit in June 1999, the first-ever meetings of Chinese and South Korean defense ministers in Beijing (August 1999) may be seen as a contemporary version of China's traditional *li-yi zhi-yi* stratagem (using barbarians to control barbarians)—the divide-and-rule strategy of Western realpolitik.[37] Unlike Qing China, however, post-Mao China has considerable economic, political, and military resources to back up such a compensatory strategy. Beijing's maxi-mini equidistance strategy may be seen as a two-handed approach, propping up North Korea on geostrategic grounds while simultaneously engaging South Korea for new military exchange and cooperative partnership.

WILL NORTH KOREA BECOME A "SECOND CHINA"?

From the perspective of post-Mao reform and opening, the South Korean economy represented opportunities to be more fully exploited, whereas North Korea's economic troubles posed a burden to be lessened without damaging geopolitical ties or causing system collapse. In the wake of the 1990 Soviet-ROK normalization, China's status as, *faute de mieux,* North Korea's biggest trading partner and principal economic patron is a mixed blessing. In the process of the geopolitical and geoeconomic transformations of the early post–Cold War years, a highly asymmetric Beijing-Pyongyang-Seoul triangular economic relationship has emerged.

Some basic facts reflecting and affecting Beijing-Pyongyang-Seoul economic relations are in order. If we look at trade as a percentage of gross domestic product (GDP)—a widely used measure of a country's integration into the global economy—in 2000 this figure stood at 44 percent for China, compared to 11 percent for North Korea, 18 percent for Japan, 19 percent for India, 21 percent for the United States, and 73 percent for South Korea. Contrary to popular misconceptions shared by proponents of both engagement and containment,[38] China's economy is now two times more integrated into the global capitalist economy than that of the United States and almost four times more integrated than North Korea's! China's enmeshment in the global economy and global institutions has seen a rapid increase, with Beijing's trade/GDP ratio more than tripling from 13 percent in 1980 to 44 percent in 2000, while North Korea's trade/GDP ratio has actually declined from about 20 percent in 1990 to 11 percent in 2000.[39]

To translate these figures in terms of Sino–North Korean trade is to spotlight the extent of North Korea's autarky and economic decline in the 1990s. As shown in part in table 4.1, in 2000 North Korea's total trade with China

Table 4.1. China's Trade with North and South Korea, 1990–2000 (in U.S.$1 million)

Year	*Exports to DPRK*	*Imports from DPRK*	*Total Sino-DPRK Trade (balance)*	*Exports to ROK*	*Imports from ROK*	*Total Sino-ROK Trade (balance)*
1990	358	125	483 (+233)	2268	1553	3821 (+715)
1991	525	86	611 (+439)	3441	2371	5812 (+1070)
1992	541	155	696 (+386)	3725	4493	8218 (-768)
1993	602	297	899 (+305)	3928	5150	9078 (-1222)
1994	424	199	624 (+225)	5462	6202	11660 (-740)
1995	486	64	550 (+422)	7401	9143	17000 (-1742)
1996	497	68	565 (+429)	7219	12003	19222 (-4784)
1997	531	121	652 (+410)	9196	14929	24125 (-5733)
1998	355	57	413 (+298)	6269	14995	21264 (-8726)
1999	329	42	371 (+287)	7808	17228	25036 (-9420)
2000	451	37	488 (+414)	12798	18454	31252 (-5656)

Sources: For 1990–1992 figures, Chae-jin Lee, *China and Korea: Dynamic Relations* (Stanford: Hoover Press, 1996), 140 and 146; 1993–2000 figures are based on China's Ministry of Foreign Trade and Economic Relations data at http://www.moftec.gov.cn/moftec/official/html/statistics_data; ROK's Korean Trade Organization (KOTRA) at http://www.kotra.or.kr/main/info/nk/research/exter_19.php.3; Korea Statistical Yearbook; and China Statistical Yearbook.

(U.S.$488 million) represented 20 percent of its overall foreign trade (down from 29 percent in 1998) but only about 0.1 percent of China's global trade, while it is equivalent to only 0.15 percent of South Korea's global trade and 1.6 percent of South Korea's trade with China.

China's economic relations with the DPRK over the years is notable in several respects. First, Sino-DPRK trade seems closely keyed to and determined by turbulent political trajectories. The China percentage of total North Korean foreign trade has fluctuated greatly over the years: 1.) 25–60 percent (but the absolute value was around U.S.$100 million) in the 1950s; 2.) about 30 percent in the 1960s until 1967, after which the ratio declined to around 10 percent in the wake of the Cultural Revolution; 3.) increased to about 20 percent since 1973 (to the level of U.S.$300–600 million); and 4.) declined to the 10–20 percent range in the 1980s, although its total value had risen to U.S.$3–4 billion. In the first post–Cold War decade, the 1990s, the ratio started at 10.1 percent in 1990 but increased dramatically to around 30 percent in 1991 and stayed at this range until 1998, even as its total value began to decline from $899 million in 1993 to $371 million in 1999. Nonetheless, due to the renormalization process, Sino-DPRK trade registered a 32 percent increase in 2000 ($488 million) and a whopping 80 percent increase in the first half of 2001 ($311 million) after two years' consecutive decreases in 1998 and 1999. Despite the dramatic increases in total value, the China share declined from 29 percent in 1998 to 20 percent in 2000.[40]

The second notable aspect of Sino-DPRK economic relations is trade characterized by chronic and substantial balance-of-trade deficits for North Korea. The cumulative total of the trade balance deficits for North Korea amounted to $3.85 billion during the period 1990–2000, with total import amount from China at $5.1 billion and total export to China only $1.3 billion. North Korea's trade deficit is not likely to improve for a long time, because North Korea does not have high value products to export, and because its primary exportable commodities are losing competitiveness in the Chinese market. While China remained North Korea's largest trade partner in the 1990s in terms of total value, Beijing has allowed Pyongyang to run average annual deficits of approximately $377 million since 1995. China's role in North Korea's trade would be even larger if barter transactions and aid were factored into these figures. In contrast, South Korea's trade with China in 2000 generated a huge surplus of $5.7 billion, while North Korea's trade with China generated a trade deficit of $414 million.

At the Sixth Special Session of the United Nations General Assembly in 1974, Mao's Foreign Minister Huang Hua, as he was characterizing and criticizing the global capitalist economic system of the early 1970s, called global North-South economic relations an "interdependence between a horseman and his mount." This may remain an accurate assessment of contemporary Sino-DPRK economic relations, but it is not easy to see whether Beijing or Pyongyang is the horseman. In Tom Hart's pithy characterization, it is "a mutually grating, reluctant patron-proud mendicant relationship" in which such "cooperation" as can be observed is "chiefly in the form of Chinese grants and subsidies, plus classic protestations of traditional good neighborliness and party-to-party solidarity."[41]

There are several tactics China has employed in its behind-the-scenes diplomatic efforts. Beijing has been applying pressure on Pyongyang to lift its collapsing economy through reform and opening to the outside world. Beijing also followed Moscow's lead in demanding hard currency cash payments in trade, effective as of January 1, 1993, as another way of coaxing Pyongyang to get its act together in terms of foreign trade. It soon became clear, however, that Pyongyang would be unable or unwilling to meet such demands. Consequently China was forced to waive North Korea's debt in "friendship prices" for oil and food, becoming in the process a leading provider of humanitarian assistance and leading trade partner for North Korea through the 1990s.

Although the exact amount and terms of China's aid to North Korea remain unclear, it is generally estimated at one-quarter to one-third of China's overall foreign aid. By mid-1994, China accounted for about three-quarters of North Korea's oil and food imports.[42] Whether it intended to or not, Beijing became more deeply involved, playing a more active role and indeed a crucial role year to year in the politics of regime survival, by providing more aid in a wider variety of forms: direct government-to-government aid, subsidized cross-border trade, and private barter transactions. On May 22, 1996, then-Chinese Premier Li Peng and North Korean Vice Premier Hong Song Nam signed an agreement reportedly specifying that Beijing would provide Pyongyang with five hundred thousand tons of grain annually (half gratis and half at a "friendship price"), 1.3 million tons of petroleum, and 2.5 million tons of coal for the next five years (1996 to 2000). Moreover, Chinese food aid goes directly to the North Korean military, according to privately stated claims of nongovernmental organization (NGO) aid officials that have been corroborated by the *Chochongryun* ("Chosen Soren"), the pro-DPRK organization in Japan.[43] Beijing has also allowed limited oil subsidies to continue, despite the earlier efforts to place such transactions on a hard-currency basis. Furthermore, the Chinese government extended indirect aid by allowing private economic transactions between North Korean and Chinese companies in the border area, in spite of North Korea's mounting debt and the bankruptcy of many Chinese companies resulting from North Korean defaults on debts.

Faced with the deepening food crisis, the emergence of refugee flows, and the growing danger of system collapse in North Korea in the 1990s, especially since early 1996, Beijing and Pyongyang have become increasingly entangled in behind-the-scenes bargaining.[44] Apparently, Pyongyang invokes Taiwan in the seemingly asymmetrical negotiations in order to generate an exchange of unequal concessions by capitalizing on all the contradictions inherent in Beijing's one-China but two-Koreas policies.

Paradoxically, Pyongyang's growing dependence on Beijing for economic and political survival has also bred mutual distrust and resentment. Pyongyang has taken a sleight-of-hand approach, privately asking for more aid even as North Korean diplomats habitually deny that they have ever asked for or received any Chinese aid.[45] In every high-level meeting between the two governments, according to one Chinese scholar, the North Korean request for economic aid dominates the agenda.[46] For Beijing, a multitasking strategy is made palpably evident in its "humanitarian aid," which is designed to lessen flows of refugees to China, delay a possible North Korean collapse, and enhance China's own leverage in Pyongyang and Seoul. Since North Korea rightly perceives that China's aid is offered for its own self-interest, the aid, to Beijing's frustration, has not increased China's leverage with the DPRK.[47]

In late 1997, Beijing's patience with Pyongyang on economic issues appeared to have reached the breaking point. For example, the *Beijing Review*, which toes the party line on every international issue, published an unsigned article in which it offered an unprecedented analysis (and rebuke) of the root causes of North Korea's food crisis:

> A heavy military burden is using up much needed resources. . . . The present military expenditure of DPRK is U.S.$6 billion, bringing a huge burden to its economy. For the time being, the U.S., Japan, and Republic of Korea (ROK) are three main forces in the aid of DPRK. Due to conflicting points of view, however, many political conditions are attached to the aid process. . . . Ultimately, it's up to the [North] Korean people themselves to resolve the grain crisis. It requires spirit and will power to meet the challenge of such reforms as introducing foreign investment and opening up, while maintaining a stable political situation. And Korea needs to be flexible while carrying out diplomatic policies.[48]

The rapid growth of Sino-Korean interactions at all levels involving political, economic, educational, religious, and humanitarian (human rights) actors has also created a mixture of emerging challenges for identity politics in the complex triangle of asymmetrical interdependence. There has already emerged a Pyongyang-Beijing-Seoul triangle of human movements and frictions, involving flows of some three hundred thousand refugees from North Korea to northeast China; more than four hundred thousand Chinese middle-class tourists and about one hundred thirty-five thousand Chinese-Korean (*chosonjok*) illegal migrant workers from China to South Korea; and almost a million South Korean tourists to China in 2000.

Against this backdrop, the North Korean refugee question, hitherto much ignored but a potential time bomb for both Koreas, has brought into sharp focus Beijing's abiding concerns about a North Korean collapse leading to Korean reunification by southern absorption. Even before the eruption of the second North Korean refugee incident in late June 2001, China's "Strike Hard" campaign had already been launched at the end of May 2001. The campaign resulted in a dramatic increase in the number of humanitarian aid workers arrested and fined, and North Korean refugees forcefully repatriated. North Korea also activated in early 2001 a new corps-size garrison unit to guard its border with China and Russia, a move believed to be aimed at curbing refugee defections.[49]

The North Korean pronouncement in early January 2001 of the need for "new thinking" to adjust ideological perspectives and work ethics to promote "state competitiveness" required in the new century,[50] accompanied by Kim Jong Il's second "secret" visit to Shanghai in less than eight months (January 15 through 20, 2001) for an extensive personal inspection of "capitalism with Shanghai characteristics," prompted a flurry of wild speculation about *juche* being shanghaied and North Korea becoming a "second China." With an *ex cathedra* statement to his National Security Council, President Kim Dae Jung took the lead on this "second China" theme, declaring that Kim Jong Il's visit to Shanghai "shows that North Korea is deeply interested in the Chinese-style reform and open-door policy and that it is trying to become a second China." He is also reported to have ordered his cabinet to brace for a "considerable degree of change."[51]

However, a simple reality check may suffice to spotlight the ineluctable fact that the domestic and external conditions of post-Mao China do not apply to and are not readily reproducible in post–Kim Il Sung North Korea. It was China's fortune to have Deng Xiaoping as the paramount leader to break away from the Maoist past and to initiate reform and opening as China's "Second Revolution." In a survey of public opinion, about thirty thousand Chinese residents abroad chose Deng Xiaoping, not Mao Zedong, as the greatest Chinese leader of the twentieth century, because of his indelible contribution to liberating a large number of Chinese from absolute poverty.[52] It was North Korea's misfortune, on the other hand, to have Kim Il Sung as "the "Great Leader" (a demigod) and Kim Jong Il as the "Dear Leader," a successor whose legitimacy rests exclusively on the ideological continuity of the *juche* system that the Great Leader Kim Il Sung created, developed, and passed on to his son.

Although post-Mao China and post–Kim Il Sung North Korea remain as divided polities, the real contrast between the two cannot be more striking. For China, its rival in the legitimacy war is a little island called Taiwan with less than 0.3 percent of China's territory and less than 2 percent of China's population, posing no significant threat or challenge. For North Korea, its southern rival in the legitimacy war is a country with freshly minted national identities as a newly industrialized country (NIC), a member of the OECD (Organization for Economic Cooperation and Development), and a newly democratizing country (NDC), with a population more than twice as large, a GDP thirty times larger, and an export volume 248 times larger than North Korea's. Hence, to ask North Korea to follow the system-reforming trajectory is to ask North Korea to change its national identity to be like South Korea, or to commit ideological suicide.

There is an important difference in global geopolitical timing. Post-Mao China's reform and opening came about during the heyday of the second Cold War, when anti-Soviet China enjoyed and exercised its maximum realpolitik leverage, as was made evident by Beijing's easy entry into the International Monetary Fund (IMF) and the World Bank in May 1980. In contrast, the political, institutional, and structural obstacles standing in the way of Pyongyang's entry into the IMF, the World Bank, and the Asian Development Bank are legion.

The propitious initial social and economic conditions that enabled post-Mao reformers to launch reform in the agricultural sector to free up and channel surplus farm labor into the emerging nonstate or semiprivate light manufacturing and service sectors do not exist in heavily industrialized North Korea, which has only 30 percent of its workforce engaged in farming. Post-Mao China in 1978 and 1979 had no foreign debts to speak of, while North Korea's foreign debts are estimated at about U.S.$2.3 billion (based on 1999 dollars), with one of the highest country-risk ratings and lowest credit ratings in the world.

Unlike post-Mao China, post–Kim Il Sung North Korea does not have rich and enterprising overseas Koreans to generate the kind and amount (about 80 percent) of foreign direct investment (FDI) that post-Mao China had attracted. The closest functional equivalent of North Korean "overseas entrepreneurs" is ethnic pro-Pyongyang Koreans in Japan associated with the *Chosen Soren,* whose membership and remittances to North Korea have registered rapid and dramatic declines in recent years (from $476 million in the peak year of 1990 to about $47 million in 1997).[53] North Korea, which established the Rajin-Sonbong Free Economic and Trade Zones (FETZ) in 1991, attracted, at most, $62 million over six years, and then investments tapered off.[54] In contrast, post-Mao China found itself loaded with $1.73 billion from about twenty-eight million overseas Chinese in the initial years and now attracts some $40 billion of FDI in a single year (1999). Moreover, if North Korea undertook Chinese-style reform and opening, it would still have to compete with China, Vietnam, and other Southeast Asian countries in the global marketplace, while at the same time being handicapped by its own high wages and deficits in terms of productivity, poor infrastructure, unstable energy supply, a dismally low international credit rating, geographic and transportation isolation, ideological and bureaucratic constraints, and an uncertain future of the post–Kim Il Sung system.

Even at the level of policy pronouncements there is no evidence of a North Korean desire to follow the Dengist model of reform and opening. In six informal summit meetings between 1978 and 1991, Deng Xiaoping repeatedly urged Kim Il Sung to develop the economy through reform and opening. This only provoked Kim Il Sung's testy retort, "we opened, already," in reference to the Rajin-Sonbong Free Economic and Trade Zone.[55] In a May 1999 meeting with Chinese Ambassador Wan Yongxiang in Pyongyang, Kim Jong Il is reported to have said that he supported Chinese-style reforms. In return, he asked Beijing to respect "Korean-style socialism."[56] More recently, even in the wake of "new thinking" editorials and Kim Jong Il's Shanghai tour, one is hard pressed to find any articles on the Chinese style reform and opening in the North Korea media. Instead, *Choson Sinbo*, the official gazette of *Cho-*

chongryun, shot down any speculation about North Korea following in the footsteps of Beijing. Kim Jong Il's Shanghai tour was explained as only an examination of the economic development there, no more: "Our march in the new century focuses on pursuing the *juche* [self-reliance] idea, which we have protected in the face of hardships, instead of shifting from it."[57]

CONCLUSION

The interplay of a rising China and a declining North Korea in the changing post–Cold War world is complex and often confusing, with paradoxical expectations and consequences. On the one hand, contrary to the conventional realist wisdom and despite having more neighbors (some sixteen countries plus) and more irredentist claims than any other state, on most issues and most of the time China behaves as a largely conservative status quo power, more satisfied with its born-again national status and security than at any time since the founding of the People's Republic in 1949. On the other hand, North Korea at first glance seems like a textbook case of how most Chinese dynasties collapsed under the twin blows of *neiluan* and *waihuan* ("internal disorder" and "external calamity"). Indeed, the Democratic People's Republic of Korea has suffered a rapid succession of external shocks—the crumbling of the Berlin Wall, the end of both the Cold War and superpower rivalry, the demise of the Soviet Union and international communism, Moscow-Seoul normalization, and Beijing normalization—on top of a series of internal woes, including the death of its founder (the "eternal president" Kim Il Sung), a continuing downward spiral of production, shrinking trade, and a falling human development index. Yet North Korea has defied all the collapsist scenarios and predictions, as well as the classical realist axiom "the strong do what they have the power to do and the weak accept what they have to accept."[58]

With the demise of Sino-Soviet competition over North Korea and with Beijing and Pyongyang moving on divergent developmental trajectories, however, there emerged in the 1990s a more complex geoeconomic and geostrategic triangle involving three sets of asymmetrical mutual interests and perceptions: Beijing-Seoul, Beijing-Pyongyang, and Seoul-Pyongyang. On the first and second sides of the triangle, Beijing tried to maintain its geostrategic ties with North Korea even as it promoted new geoeconomic ties with South Korea. On the third side of the triangle, Beijing tried hard to keep out of harm's way by following a strategy of calculated ambiguity and equidistance. China has seldom put itself in the front lines of the inter-Korean conflict as either a mediator or a peacemaker for fear that it might get burned if something goes wrong.

Although Beijing's relations with North Korea began to be renormalized in recent years, this is still a fragile relationship of strategic convenience fraught with the beneath-the-surface tensions and asymmetries of mutual expectations and interests. What then explains the paradox that North Korea continues with China as its one and only formal ally even while it becomes increasingly difficult for China to deal with, if not openly hostile to, Chinese interests? Part of the answer is a matter of geography—North Korea occupying China's strategic *cordon sanitaire*. Another part of the answer has to do with North Korea's conflict behavior. Indeed, the single greatest challenge confronting Beijing is the weakness, not the strength, of post–Kim Il Sung North Korea, or perhaps more accurately the power of the weak.

In the wake of the Kosovo war, Beijing has come up with the new strategic understanding that any weakening of influence over North Korea would inevitably degrade its strategic status and interest in Northeast Asia in general and on the Korean peninsula in particular. Beijing will continue to invest the minimum necessary political and economic capital in its difficult relationship with Pyongyang in order to maximize its influence in Northeast Asian affairs. That said, however, China's multitasking two-Koreas strategy is more reactive than proactive. It is focused on the challenge of maximizing short-term gains and minimizing or avoiding short-term constraints. However, it does not appear to include a long-term strategic vision for the Korean peninsula other than to keep it as a buffer zone and to slow down the Korean reunification process as much as possible in order to maintain the two-Koreas status quo. As long as Beijing has profound concerns about the strategic orientation of a united Korea, particularly as it relates to the United States, to maintain the status quo of the two Koreas means to continue its support of the weaker DPRK no matter what the cost. The tradeoff here is that Pyongyang provides opportunity for projecting China's great-power identity. As Campbell and Reiss aptly put it, "if the road to Pyongyang runs through Beijing, Washington should expect to be charged a toll. This toll could be quite high."[59]

For its own geopolitical interests, Beijing has played a generally positive role in Korean affairs, not only by providing necessary if not sufficient (in Pyongyang's eyes) diplomatic and economic support to the DPRK, but also by making it clear to Seoul, Washington, and Tokyo that it is now in the common interest of all to promote the peaceful coexistence of the two Korean states on the peninsula rather than having to cope with the turmoil, chaos, and even massive exodus of refugees that would follow in the wake of system collapse in the North.

Paradoxically, Pyongyang's growing dependence on Beijing for its economic and political survival has served as a sure recipe for mutual distrust and resentment. Just as Mao demanded and resented Soviet aid for China's nuclear development, Kim Il Sung and now Kim Jong Il have demanded and resented Chinese aid. Indeed, Pyongyang's fundamentalism and its seeming inability to adjust or refurnish its national identity and roles to changing realities has engendered intense behind-the-scenes bargaining amidst an atmosphere of mutual distrust.

China has come to interact with the two Koreas in more ways, in more depth and complexity, and in more areas than ever before, and this leads to one obvious and somewhat paradoxical consequence. In the reshaping of the future of North Korea and the Korean peninsula, the influence of post-Tiananmen China as a rising power is arguably greater than at any time since the Korean War and also greater than any other neighboring power. However, despite all the "rise of China" hype, it remains an incomplete great power, its capacity to initiate or implement consistent policies toward the two Koreas increasingly constrained by the norms and practices of important domestic groups, Northeast Asian regional and global regimes, and the power of the United States, Japan, and Russia. Like it or not, China's two-Koreas policy cannot be contained in a state-to-state bilateral context, as an increasing number and variety of actors or interests must be taken into account. The growing complexity, density, and multilateralization has placed inordinate pressure on the Chinese foreign-policy system to develop more effective coordinating mechanisms to monitor and supervise what is really going on.

Still, there is little doubt that the future of the Northeast Asian regional order, especially on the Korean peninsula, is closely tied to the future of the People's Republic of China. Even some of the harshest critics of the rise of China thesis admit that "only on the Korean Peninsula do China's capacities seriously affect U.S. policy."[60] Although today China commands a rather unique position and influence as the only major power that maintains a good relationship with both Koreas, the future of North Korea is not for China to make or unmake. China can help or hinder North Korea in taking one system-rescuing approach instead of another, but in the end no outside power can determine North Korea's future. Only time will tell whether North Korea after Kim Il Sung can ride out its economic difficulties by means of a tenuous external life-support system, without forfeiting its *juche* identity and without a sudden crash landing.

NOTES

1. For a detailed discussion, see Samuel S. Kim, "The Making of China's Korea Policy in the Era of Reform," in David M. Lampton, ed., *The Making of Chinese Foreign and Security Policy in the Era of Reform, 1978–2000* (Stanford: Stanford University Press, 2001), 371–408.

2. For a startlingly honest new report from the Chinese Communist Party describing the depth of China's internal problems arising from economic, ethnic, and religious conflicts, see Erik Eckholm, "China's Inner Circle Reveals Big Unrest," *New York Times*, June 3, 2001.

3. For further analysis, see Samuel S. Kim, "China as a Great Power," *Current History* 96, 611 (September 1997): 246–51.

4. See Yuan Zhongze, "Pursue Extensive Peripheral Diplomacy in New Century," *Liaowang* 38 (September 17, 2001): 3–5 in FBIS-CHI-2001-0925, available for access to Columbia University Subscription (and website).

5. According to the ROK Ministry of Unification, over 20 percent of the food and over 50 percent of the fuel in North Korea comes from foreign aid. See *JoongAng Ilbo*, December 26, 2001.

6. See Alastair Iain Johnston and Robert Ross, eds. *Engaging China: The Management of an Emerging Power* (London and New York: Routledge, 1999).

7. The World Bank, *World Development Report 2002* (New York: Oxford University Press, 2001), 232.

8. Song Dexing, "Lengzhan hou DongbeiYa anquan xingshe de bianhua," [Changes in the Post–Cold War Northeast Asian Security Situation], *Xiandai guoji guanxi* [Contemporary International Relations] 9 (1998): 34–8, especially 35.

9. Robert A. Scalapino, "China and Korean Reunification: A Neighbor's Concerns," in Nicholas Eberstadt and Richard J. Ellings, eds., *Korea's Future and the Great Powers* (Seattle: University of Washington Press, 2001), 107.

10. William Habeeb, *Power and Tactics in International Negotiation: How Weak Nations Bargain with Strong Nations*. (Baltimore: Johns Hopkins University Press, 1988).

11. For a characterization of China's Korea policy along these lines, see Song, "Lengzhan hou DongbeiYa anquan xingshe de bianhua," 37.

12. You Ji, "China and North Korea: A Fragile Relationship of Strategic Convenience," *Journal of Contemporary China* 10, 28 (August 2001): 389–90.

13. Taeho Kim, "Strategic Relations between Beijing and Pyongyang: Growing Strains and Lingering Ties," in James R. Lilley and David Shambaugh, eds., *China's Military Faces the Future* (Armonk, NY: M. E. Sharpe, 1999), 306–8.

14. Yong Deng, "Chinese Perceptions of U.S. Power and Strategy," *Asian Affairs* 28, 3 (fall 2001): 151–2.

15. Quoted in Eric A. McVadon, "China's Goals and Strategies for the Korean Peninsula," in Henry D. Sokolski, ed., *Planning for a Peaceful Korea* (Carlisle, PA: Strategic Studies Institute, February 2001), 170.

16. Xinbo Wu, "Managing the Korean Issue: A Chinese Perspective," *Korea & World Affairs* 24, 1 (spring 2000), 81; Yong, 151–2.

17. Economist Intelligence Unit, *Country Report: South Korea, North Korea,* 3rd quarter, 1999, 42–43.

18. Korean Central News Agency (KCNA), June 1, 2000.

19. *Rodong Sinmun* (Workers' Daily), June 3, 2000.

20. See Erick Eckholm, "Celebrating Korea's War Even as Peace Seems Near," *New York Times,* October 26, 2000, A4.

21. *Renmin Ribao*, June 22, 1994, 6.

22. *Rodong Sinmun* (Pyongyang), December 1, 1994.

23. For a trenchant attack on U.S. "sanctions diplomacy," see *Renmin Ribao*, July 15, 1994, 6.

24. Ashton B. Carter and William J. Perry, "*Preventive Defense: A New Security Strategy for America*" (Washington, D.C.: Brookings Institution Press, 1999), 123–4.

25. Alastair Iain Johnston, "China's New 'Old Thinking': The Concept of Limited Deterrence," *International Security* 20, 5 (1995/1996): 5.

26. Banning Garrett and Bonnie Glaser, "Looking Across the Yalu: Chinese Assessments of North Korea," *Asian Survey* 35 (1995): 528–45.

27. *People's Korea* (Tokyo), September 10, 1994, 1.

28. For a more detailed discussion of this incident and its deliberation in the UN Security Council, see Samuel S. Kim, "North Korea and the United Nations," *International Journal of Korean Studies* 1, 1 (spring 1997): 78–105.

29. See Yu Shaohua, "Chaoxian Bandao Xingshi de Fazhan yu Qianjing" (The Evolving Situation and Future Prospects of the Korean Peninsula), *Guoji Wenti Yanjiu* (International Studies) 4 (1997): 12–16, especially 15.

30. *Korea Times*, www.hankooki.com/times.htm (accessed 16 November 1995).

31. Eric A. McVadon, "Chinese Military Strategy for the Korean Peninsula," in James R. Lilley and David Shambaugh, eds., *China's Military Faces the Future* (Armonk, N.Y.: M.E. Sharpe, 1999), 280.

32. Taeho Kim, "Strategic Relations Between Beijing and Pyongyang: Growing Strains amid Lingering Ties," in *China's Military Faces the Future* 306–9.

33. *ChungAng Ilbo*, www.joongang.co.kr (accessed 24 March 1999).

34. Zou Yunhua, "Zhanqu Daodan Fangyu yu Quanqiu he Diqu Anquan de Guanxi," (The Relationship between the Theatre Missile Defense and the Global and Regional Security), *Guoji wentia yanjiu* (International Studies) 1 (1998): 27–9, especially 28; see also "PRC White Paper on National Defense in 2000" in FBIS-CHI-2000-1016 (October 16, 2000).

35. *Rodong Sinmun,* February 22, 2001; March 7, 2001; and April 21, 2001.

36. Qiao Liang and Wang Xianghui, *Chaoxian Zhan* (Unlimited War) (Beijing: People's Liberation Army Cultural Press, 1999), and Peter Van Ness, "Globalization and Security in East Asia," in Samuel S. Kim, ed., *East Asia and Globalization* (Lanham, MD: Rowman & Littlefield Publishers, 2000), 255–75.

37. Samuel S. Kim, *China, the United Nations, and World Order* (Princeton: Princeton University Press, 1979), 33.

38. See Alastair Iain Johnston, "Engaging Myths: Misconceptions about China and Its Global Role," *Harvard Asia Pacific Review* (winter 1997/1998): 9–12.

39. The 2000 figures for China, Japan, India, South Korea, and the United States are based on the World Bank's *World Development Report 2002* (New York: Oxford University Press, 2001), tables 3–4, 236–9; the figures for North Korea are based on the report issued by South Korea's National Statistics Office in late December

2001 and summarized in *Korea Now* (December 29, 2001), 8; and The Economist Intelligence Unit, *Country Profile 2001: South Korea and North Korea*, at www. elu.com/schedule based on Columbia University's subscription.

40. S. H. Chang, "Current Status and Perspective of Economic Exchange between North Korea and China," Korean Trade and Investment Promotion Agency (KOTRA) at www.kotra.or.kr.

41. Tom Hart, "The PRC-DPRK Rapprochement and China's Dilemma in Korea," *Asian Perspective* 25, 3 (2001): 255–6.

42. *North Korea News* 724 (February 28, 1994): 5–6; *The Economist* (March 26, 1994), 39.

43. *Chosun Ilbo* (Seoul), July 20, 1996; Marcus Noland, *Avoiding the Apocalypse: The Future of the Two Koreas* (Washington, D.C.: Institute for International Economics, 2000), 100.

44. For further analysis, see Kim, "The Making of China's Korea Policy in the Era of Reform," 385–88.

45. In a closed executive session in New York in late May 1998 involving two high-ranking North Korean ambassadors and a dozen U.S. scholars, including this author (Samuel Kim), ambassadors categorically denied any Chinese aid, saying, "If we wanted Chinese aid, we could get one million tons of grain from China tomorrow but it would come with an unacceptably heavy price of 'dependence.'"

46. You Ji, "China and North Korea: A Fragile Relationship of Strategic Convenience," *Journal of Contemporary China* 10, 28 (August 2001): 391.

47. Scott Snyder, "North Korea's Challenge of Regime Survival: Internal Problems and Implications for the Future," *Pacific Affairs* 73, 4 (winter 2000/2001): 530.

48. "Grain Crisis Causes Hardship for DPRK People," *Beijing Review* 40, 43 (October 27–November 2, 1997): 7.

49. For further discussion and analysis, see Samuel S. Kim, "China, Japan, and Russia in Inter-Korean Relations," in Kongdan Oh and Ralph Hassigs, eds., *Korea Briefing 2000–2001: First Steps toward Reconciliation and Reunification* (Armonk, NY: M. E. Sharpe, 2002), 128–9.

50. See "21 seki nun koch'anghan chonpyon ui seki, ch'angcho ui seki ita" (The Twenty-First Century Is a Century of Great Change and Great Creation), *Rodong sinmun,* January 4, 2001, 2; "Motun muncherul saeroun kwanchom kwa noppieso poko pulo nakacha" (Let Us See and Solve All Problems from a New Viewpoint and a New Height), editorial, *Rodong Sinmun,* January 9, 2001, 1.

51. Nayan Chanda, "Kim Flirts with Chinese Reform," *Far Eastern Economic Review* (February 8, 2001), 26.

52. *Chungang Ilbo* in English, January 19, 2001, 3.

53. Shim Jae Hoon, "Disillusioned Donors," *Far Eastern Economic Review* (December 4, 1997), 28–30.

54. *ChoongAng Ilbo* (Seoul), www.joongang.co.kr (accessed 29 January 2001).

55. Economist Intelligence Unit (EIU), *Country Report: South Korea and North Korea* (1st Quarter, 1999), 40.

56. AFP, July 16, 1999 in AFP, afp@clari.net.

57. Quoted in *Korea Herald,* www.koreaherald.co.kr (accessed 12 February 2001)

58. Thucydides, *History of the Peloponnesian War*, trans. Rex Warner (New York: Penguin Books, 1982), 402.

59. Kurt M. Campbell and Mitchell B. Reiss, "Korean Changes, Asian Challenges and the U.S. Role," *Survival* 43, 1 (spring 2001): 62.

60. Gerald Segal, "Does China Matter?" *Foreign Affairs* 78, 5 (September-October 1999): 24–36; quote on 32.

5

Russian–North Korean Relations: A New Era?

Elizabeth Wishnick

In 2001, Russian–North Korean relations made front-page news, as both Russian President Vladimir Putin and the North Korean leader Kim Jong Il sought to repair their bilateral ties and adopt a more active diplomatic profile in general. Although the two leaders succeeded in reversing the downward spiral in their relations resulting from a series of domestic and international shocks—the onset of reform in Gorbachev's Russia, the collapse of the USSR, and the initial pro-Western phase in Yeltsin's foreign policy—it remains unclear what impact the improvement in Russian–North Korean relations will have on conflict resolution on the Korean peninsula. Despite Putin's energetic diplomacy in Northeast Asia, only South Korea is encouraging greater Russian involvement in future negotiations on Korean issues. North Korea remains focused on bilateral talks with the United States, and China is content to maintain its privileged position. The Sino-Russian partnership notwithstanding, the Korean issue is notable for its lack of Sino-Russian cooperation. To the contrary, China and Russia are facing off as competitors, especially in regional economic cooperation projects. The following discussion addresses the domestic, international, and regional factors that have shaped Russian–North Korean relations during the past decade.

POST-SOVIET TRANSITION AND RELATIONS BETWEEN MOSCOW AND PYONGYANG

The post-Soviet transition fundamentally altered relations between Pyongyang and Moscow. Gorbachev's major policy shifts in domestic and foreign policy served to downgrade North Korea's importance for Soviet diplomacy, and North Korean leaders became concerned about the negative impact of these changes on their country and socialism as a whole. Consequently, a mutual distancing took place by the early 1990s as a result of incompatible policies, which took Moscow and Pyongyang in opposite directions.

For Gorbachev, Soviet–North Korean relations exemplified all that was wrong with Soviet foreign policy: Moscow's relationship with Pyongyang was based on ideology to the detriment of Soviet economic interests, exacerbated U.S.-Soviet tensions in Asia, and constricted Soviet diplomatic options, especially with respect to South Korea, a potential investor in Soviet economic restructuring. Although Gorbachev's decision to engage South Korea was a major factor in the decline in Soviet–North Korean relations, by the early 1990s the more general changes Gorbachev made in Soviet foreign policy also had a far-reaching impact on relations with North Korea.

Ties with Pyongyang grew closer in the early1980s in response to Soviet-American tensions and concern about Sino-American security cooperation. In May1984, at a time when Ronald Reagan viewed the USSR as the evil empire, Kim Il Sung visited Moscow for the first time since 1967. Soviet leaders rewarded his anti-Americanism with substantial economic aid (including debt deferment, credits, power generation equipment, and assistance with technology transfers from Soviet technicians) and a major arms deal involving advanced aviation technology.[1] Military cooperation actually expanded during Gorbachev's first few years in office, despite the new leader's reformist leanings. Kim Il Sung traveled to Moscow in 1986 to reconfirm early cooperation and was not disappointed. According to the 1986 agreement, the Soviet Union agreed to deliver thirty MiG-29 fighters, as well as additional Su-25 attack aircraft, SA-3 and SA-5 surface-to-air missiles, M-2 helicopter gunships, radar equipment, and advanced nuclear power regeneration technology.[2]

By 1987, however, Gorbachev began to define his "new thinking" on foreign policy. Ideology would no longer inform foreign policy, enabling the Soviet leader to take steps to end decades of Sino-Soviet enmity and normalize relations.[3] He opened new vistas for Soviet policy in Asia by shedding dogmas about class struggle with imperialism and viewing interdependence as the main dynamic in international relations. Such changes in established tenets of Soviet foreign policy gave the Soviet leader new opportunities to engage Japan, once viewed as an appendage of U.S. anti-Sovietism in Asia, and to seek a wide range of economic partners in the region.[4] As pressures for domestic political change mounted within the Soviet Union, relations between Moscow and Pyongyang grew tense.[5]

Ties with North Korea declined precipitously after the Soviet Union decided to take gradual steps to improve relations with South Korea. As in Sino-

American relations, sports provided the first arena for expanded contact: the USSR decided to attend the September 1988 Olympics in Seoul. Although in his first major speech about Soviet Asia policy, in 1986, Gorbachev came out in support of North Korea's proposal for a nuclear-free zone in the peninsula,[6] by September 1988 the Soviet leader cautiously stated in a speech in Krasnoyarsk that Moscow would contemplate opening economic relations with South Korea.[7] Within a year, the Soviet Union and South Korea had exchanged trade representations. Just as the North Korean leadership feared, full normalization was not long in coming and took place in September 1990.[8] Pyongyang's reaction to normalization was immediate and vitriolic, portrayed in the media as "disgusting, nauseating, and unseemly."[9] Soviet media representatives, who had been increasingly critical of the North Korean regime, were forced to leave Pyongyang. Yet Gorbachev was not prepared to abandon relations with North Korea entirely. In response to the country's economic plight, the Soviet government issued a moratorium on payment for oil deliveries to North Korea. In April 1991, Moscow and Pyongyang signed an agreement providing for a limited expansion of bilateral trade, new Soviet credits for North Korea, and the repayment of its debt to the USSR in hard currency.[10]

Although Soviet weapons purchased under previous bilateral agreements continued to flow into North Korea, North Korean leaders had cause to question the USSR's commitment to the 1961 Soviet–North Korean Treaty of Friendship, Cooperation, and Mutual Assistance. Since the USSR was proving to be such an unreliable partner, Kim Il Sung sought to expand his diplomatic options by reconsidering his long-standing opposition to the entry of both Koreas into the United Nations. North Korea applied for membership in May 1991 and both Koreas were admitted as members in September.[11]

THE POLITICS OF RUSSIAN–NORTH KOREAN RELATIONS

The collapse of the USSR further exacerbated relations between Moscow and Pyongyang. North Korean leaders, who openly supported the anti-Gorbachev coup, now had to deal with a new pro-Western team in the Kremlin, which was overtly hostile to the North Korean model of socialism. In 1991 and 1992, President Boris Yeltsin and his foreign minister, Andrei Kozyrev, actively courted the United States, West European countries, and their allies, Japan and South Korea. The new Russian leadership sought their economic and political support for economic and political reform and in return was prepared to allow relations with former ideological allies such as North Korea and Cuba to wane.[12]

Although Russian critics of Yeltsin's policy toward North Korea pin the blame on Foreign Minister Andrei Kozyrev for downgrading Russia's relations with Pyongyang in the early 1990s, at the time North Korean leaders also saw the need to distance themselves from the new Russian government, which they believed could undermine their own regime. North Korean analyses faulted shock therapy for weakening the Russian state, encouraging separatism, and leading to economic and political disintegration.[13] According to a Russian Korea expert, North Korean propaganda portrayed Yeltsin's Russia as "a sort of whipping boy, a negative example of the horrors that 'deviation from socialism' brings with it."[14]

Although in January 1992 Kozyrev described the Western countries as "natural allies," by summer the Yeltsin administration began to set limits to Russia's pro-Western foreign policy and to identify its national interests on key foreign policy issues.[15] In particular, Yeltsin took steps to engage Russia's Asian neighbors. Initial hopes for a breakthrough in relations with Japan were dashed, however, due to mounting opposition in Russia to any resolution of the Kuriles Islands dispute involving the return of territory and Japan's determination to press for a return of all four islands. After abruptly canceling a planned meeting in Tokyo in the summer of 1992, Yeltsin then used his summit with Chinese leaders in Beijing in December to develop a conception of a foreign policy "balanced between East and West."[16]

Despite such statements and growing opposition in Russia to a pro-Western foreign policy, Yeltsin's Korea policy continued its one-sided emphasis on improving relations with the South, to the detriment of ties with the North. In November 1992 Moscow and Seoul normalized relations. During his visit to South Korea, Yeltsin told South Korean leaders that the Soviet–North Korean treaty existed only on paper, offered to share documents about the Korean War, and announced Russia's intention to stop its military aid program for the North.[17] Stunned by Moscow's about-face, the North Korean regime criticized these steps while trying to remind Russia's new leaders of the historic importance of relations between Moscow and Pyongyang.[18]

Recognizing the negative impact of the normalization of relations with South Korea on Russian–North Korean relations, in January 1993 Deputy Foreign Minister Georgii Kunadze traveled to Pyongyang to discuss the status of the Soviet–North Korean Treaty. Russian officials sought to reaffirm the importance of the Russian–North Korean relationship without endorsing the treaty's mutual defense clause. Ultimately, the Yeltsin government chose to prepare a new treaty instead of renewing the 1961 treaty, set to expire in September 1996.[19]

Meanwhile, Russian–South Korean political relations continued to prosper. During Korean President Kim Young Sam's June 1994 visit to Moscow, he and Yeltsin spoke of the partnership between their two countries. South Korea agreed to support Russia's membership in Asia-Pacific Economic Cooperation (APEC), while Russia pledged to uphold South Korea's bid for a rotating seat on the United Nations Security Council in 1996 and 1997.[20]

Nevertheless, in the economic sphere, Russia's new emphasis on relations with South Korea was not producing expected results. Moscow's inability to repay a $1.8 billion loan extended to the Soviet Union in 1990 obstructed economic ties.[21] A compromise reached in August 1994 involving Russian weapons transfers to Seoul as partial payment of the Soviet outstanding debt further dramatized for North Korean leaders the extent to which the new relationship between Seoul and Moscow posed a security threat to Pyongyang.[22]

Russian–North Korean economic ties declined precipitously during the early 1990s: trade plummeted from $2.35 billion in 1990 to $222 million in 1993. As part of its review of policy toward North Korea in the early 1990s, the Yeltsin administration ended transfers of military equipment and technology to Pyongyang, cultural and scientific ties were abandoned, the intergovernmental commission on economic and scientific cooperation ceased operations, and even direct flights were canceled. In response, Pyongyang refused to repay a four billion ruble loan.[23] Against this background, in September 1994 Deputy Foreign Minister Panov traveled to Pyongyang in an effort to revive flagging economic ties and explain Soviet positions on the renewal of the 1961 treaty.[24]

Table 5.1. Volume of Russian–North Korean Trade

Year	*Volume (in U.S.$1 million)*
1990	2,350
1991	365
1992	312
1993	222
1994	140
1995	100
1996	100
1997	78
1998	65
1999	100
2000	105

Sources: Data for 1990 from Xinhua, "The DPRK, Russia Add New Chapter in Annals of Friendly Cooperation," July 20, 2000, in *FBIS* (China), July 20, 2000; data for 1991–1997 from Larisa Zabrovskaya, *Rossiya i KNDR* (Vladivostok:: Dal'nauka, 1998), 67; data for 1998 from KOTRA, available at www.kotra.or.kr; data for 1999 from Prime-TASS, July 18, 2000; data for 2000 from ITAR-TASS, August 1, 2001. This table is meant to illustrate general trends in Russian–North Korean trade. Different sources at times come up with varying figures; for example, KOTRA reported fifty million dollars in Russian–North Korean trade for 1999, but the aforementioned Xinhua analysis noted more than a hundred million.

Although Kozyrev continued to pursue a pro-Western foreign policy, disillusionment with Western aid, concern about NATO expansion, efforts to reassert Moscow's influence along Russia's peripheries, and the strong showing of communists in the 1995 Russian parliamentary elections served to reinforce voices calling on President Yeltsin to move away from reflexive support for Western positions and to develop instead a foreign policy, which would promote Russia's distinctive interests as a Eurasian power. When Evgenii Primakov replaced Kozyrev in January 1996, Russian–North Korean relations began a slow mending process as the new Foreign Minister sought to restore balance in Russia's relations with North and South Koreas. The visit by Deputy Prime Minister Vitalii Ignatenko in April 1996 was the main catalyst for the improvement in relations. As the highest-level official to travel to Pyongyang since the collapse of the Soviet Union, Ignatenko demonstrated the Yeltsin administration's commitment to repairing relations with North Korea. In the aftermath of his visit, bilateral and regional economic relations were restored, political consultations resumed, and Russia provided food aid to its famine-stricken neighbor.[25] According to Igor Ivanov, who succeeded Primakov as Foreign Minister and continued his policies toward the Korean peninsula, Russia wanted "its voice to be heard in the resolution of the most explosive problem in the Asia-Pacific region . . . thanks to a balanced policy with respect to the two Koreas."[26]

Because the success of the communists in the 1995 parliamentary elections had given the North Koreans reason to believe that it would be advantageous to wait for further political change in Russia to occur that would be conducive to their interests, it would take nearly five years for an agreement on a new Russian–North Korean treaty to be reached.[27] Although Yeltsin prevailed against Russian Communist Party leader Gennadyi Zyuganov in the second round of elections in 1996, it wasn't until Putin's victory in 2000 that North Korean leadership felt satisfied that Russia had a leader with whom Pyongyang could cooperate. Indeed, North Korean commentary about the new Russian leader has been very positive, highlighting his determination to reinforce the central government's authority.[28]

The timing of Putin's election could not have been better for Kim Jong Il, who at last appeared ready to take center stage after a long period of mourning for his father's death and saw more active diplomacy as a means of addressing his country's economic and security concerns. For Putin, a higher profile on Korean issues would promote greater Russian influence over Asian affairs. In only his second month in office, the new Russian president dispatched his Foreign Minister Igor Ivanov to Pyongyang, the highest-level Russian official delegation to North Korea in a decade. A new Russian–North Korean treaty was finally signed in February 2000 during Ivanov's visit.

During the summit meeting between Putin and Kim Jong Il in July 2000 in Pyongyang, Russian–North Korean relations were fully normalized, and the two leaders signed a joint declaration outlining their shared interests.[29] In a demonstration of the new vigor in their relationship, in April 2001 Russia agreed to resume military cooperation with North Korea, although this will be limited to upgrading weapons supplied during the Soviet era.[30]

Kim Jong Il's visit to Moscow in August 2001 highlights some of the main achievements and enduring problems in Russian–North Korean relations today. This was just the third overseas trip for the reclusive North Korean leader. Unwilling to risk air travel, Kim Jong Il made the six-thousand-mile journey by train, and in the best tradition of Soviet era diplomatic visits, inconvenienced passengers all along the Trans-Siberian railroad by disrupting regular traffic. In deference to Kim, the honor guard that used to parade in front of Lenin's tomb in Moscow was reassembled for a special tribute and no press conference was scheduled at the conclusion of the two days of meetings. Such proceedings led one Russian commentator to ask: "Given its desire to become a part of the modern world, does Russia need to deal with such an historical anachronism?"[31]

To play a meaningful role in great power diplomacy, the answer is yes, but in terms of bilateral cooperation, the summit brought mixed results. On the positive side, Russian and North Korean officials agreed to connect the Trans-Siberian railroad to the North Korean rail network as a part of the inter-Korean railway plan. The Russian government also reportedly proposed building a nuclear reactor for North Korea in Primorskii Krai in an effort to resume Russia's role in energy cooperation with Pyongyang.[32]

Yet according to Article 5 of the Moscow Declaration signed by Putin and Kim Jong Il on August 4, 2001, bilateral cooperation in other areas—that is, Russian assistance for the restructuring of Soviet-built enterprises—would be contingent on the availability of "external financial resources," presumably from South Korea, China, or Japan. North Korea's inability to repay its four billion dollar debt remains an obstacle to any future Russian credits.[33] Although there was some speculation in the Russian media following the summit that Pyongyang was allowed to write off fifty million dollars of the debt by providing free labor to timber camps in the Russian Far East (discussed in the part on regional cooperation), the Russian Foreign Ministry denied the existence of any such formal arrangement.[34]

For North Korea, the elaborate visit to Russia provided a further opportunity to press for additional economic and military assistance. Despite Russia's attempt to use inter-Korean diplomacy to make a case for its greater participation in great-power talks, above all the Moscow summit gave Kim Jong Il a forum to clarify his negotiating stance vis-à-vis the United States while pointing to Russian support for North Korean positions.[35] Thus the Moscow Declaration included North Korean statements regarding the peaceful nature of their missile program (Article 2) and calling for the pressing need to withdraw American troops from the South (Article 8)—a reversal of Kim Jong Il's reported acquiescence to their continued presence in a statement the previous year at the inter-Korean summit.

THE KOREAN PENINSULA AND RUSSIA'S INTERNATIONAL ENVIRONMENT

During the Cold War era, the USSR saw North Korea as an ideological ally in an otherwise hostile Northeast Asia populated by American allies and Chinese opponents. Soviet policymakers had an interest in stability on the Korean peninsula, such that the American military presence would not be increased, and there would be no additional incentive for closer U.S.-Japanese or Sino-American strategic cooperation. In the absence of normalized relations with Seoul, the Soviet Union was supporting Pyongyang in an effort to maintain the status quo.[36] By siding with North Korea for so many years and refusing to normalize relations with Seoul until 1990, Moscow confined itself to a marginal role in conflict resolution on the Korean peninsula.[37]

Since its normalization of relations with Seoul coincided with a decline in ties with Pyongyang and economic weakness set limits to Russian–South Korean cooperation, in the post–Cold War era, Moscow has encountered additional obstacles to increasing its influence on Korean issues. Moreover, despite a growing Sino-Russian strategic partnership, Russian policymakers continually found themselves outmaneuvered by the Chinese,[38] who succeeded in achieving what Russia sought: developing a thriving economic relationship with Seoul while maintaining a solid relationship with Pyongyang. Although Russian and Chinese leaders repeatedly express their joint positions on a number of key international problems, the absence of the Korean issue from Sino-Russian bilateral documents points to underlying differences of interests and attests to the limits to their strategic partnership.[39]

Russia's marginalization on Korean issues became obvious during the nuclear crisis, brought about by Pyongyang's announcement in February 1993 that it would withdraw from the Non-Proliferation Treaty (NPT) and no longer allow International Atomic Energy Agency (IAEA) inspections of its nuclear waste processing facilities.[40] In response to mounting international concern over Pyongyang's actions, in April 1993 Russia suspended its 1991 agreement to provide North Korea with three 660-megawatt light-water reactors (LWRs) and suffered considerable financial losses as a result.[41] Construction on the four billion dollar reactor projects was nearly complete when Yeltsin decided to halt them and the North Koreans then refused to compensate the Russian firms for their previous work.[42]

After Soviet–South Korean normalization, however, the South Korean government pressed Moscow to urge North Korean officials to end their nuclear program and adhere to international antiproliferation safeguards. Sharing an interest in preventing an increasingly weakened and isolated North Korea from acquiring nuclear capability, Moscow cooperated with Seoul in efforts to prevent proliferation in North Korea.[43] Yeltsin then issued a joint statement with George Bush about the need for nonproliferation on the Korean peninsula, in which they urged North Korea to abide by its international obligations under the NPT. North Korea reacted angrily to Russia's open support for American positions on Korean nuclear issues and, in a display of tit for tat, proceeded to publicly accuse Russia of dumping nuclear waste in the Sea of Japan.[44]

Despite a record of cooperation on Korean issues with Seoul and Washington, Russia would find itself excluded from the solution to the nuclear crisis of 1993 and 1994. In March 1994 the Russian government proposed holding an international conference, bringing together North and South Korea, all of the permanent members of the UN Security Council, the UN Secretary General, and the IAEA director.[45] Yet high-level talks between the United States and North Korea diffused the situation. According to the October 1994 U.S.–North Korean Agreed Framework, the North Koreans would halt their nuclear program in exchange for access to energy technology and economic aid. The United States, Japan, and South Korea joined together to create the Korean Peninsula Energy Development Organization (KEDO), which would be in charge of assistance to North Korea. Despite Russia's involvement in North Korea's energy sector, KEDO decided to send two South Korean light-water reactors to Pyongyang at Seoul's request.[46] Building on this instance of cooperation, in April 1996 the United States and South Korea proposed holding four-way talks, including China, but not Russia.

Russia's exclusion from the four-party talks on Korea was widely criticized in policy circles in Moscow and prompted a debate about Russia's Korea policy among government officials and scholars. In June 1996 the Duma Committee on Geopolitics, headed by Alexei Mitrofanov, a communist deputy, held hearings on Russian–North Korean relations. According to Mitrofanov, Russia's policy toward North and South Korea was a failure. The reorientation of Russian policy from support for North Korea to cooperation with South Korea led to diminished ties with Pyongyang, while relations with Seoul failed to produce desired economic benefits. According to Mitrofanov, the Russian proposal to hold six-party talks was unrealistic due to negative attitudes in North and South Korea about Japanese participation. Instead, Mitrofanov proposed a policy toward North Korea that would involve restoring high-level political contacts, ending criticism of the North Korean regime, signing a new friendship treaty, developing military cooperation, and reviving economic cooperation, especially in the energy sector.[47]

By the end of the 1990s, officials and scholars on all sides of the political spectrum agreed that by downgrading relations with North Korea, Russia had lost influence in Asia. Pro-communist scholars such as Boris Zanegin sharply criticized the Yeltsin government's Korea policy.[48] Moderates like Alexei Bogaturov advocated improving relations with North Korea to diversify Russia's Asia policy and move away from a China-centered approach to Asia. Given the impasse in Russian-Japanese relations, a greater Russian role in Korean affairs would enable Moscow to assume a higher profile on Asian issues and provide new opportunities for cooperation with United States in the region.[49] According to Vladimir Li, a distinguished Korea expert at the Diplomatic Academy, scholars had been urging Russian officials to improve relations with North Korea for years, but it was not until Primakov became Foreign Minister that some progress in relations could be seen.[50]

Initially, Primakov pursued a "two-track policy" toward the Koreas. According to some analysts, there was no reason to link Russian policy toward South and North Korea since each had different goals and approaches.[51] Others noted, however, that such an approach failed to appreciate that Russia's bilateral relations with North and South Korea were interconnected. Thus Russia's lack of a broader strategy for conflict resolution on the Korean peninsula further perpetuated Moscow's marginalization on Korean issues.[52]

In response to the criticism of Yeltsin's Korea policy, Putin came into office determined to play a more active role in conflict resolution on the peninsula. After restoring high-level political cooperation with North Korea, Russian officials have tried to make use of their new access to acquaint others with Pyongyang's positions and mediate on Korean security issues. Much like Margaret Thatcher terming Gorbachev "a man we can do business with," Putin has emphasized that Kim Jong Il is well informed and only developing a missile program for peaceful purposes.[53] In the final analysis, increasing Russia's influence over Korean affairs depends only in part on Moscow's strategy.[54] The interests and actions of other involved parties also have limited Russia's participation.

From the start, Moscow expressed a preference for multilateral approaches to conflict resolution on the Korean peninsula. In his 1986 speech in Vladivostok, marking the Soviet leadership's effort to play a more active role in Asian affairs, Mikhail Gorbachev outlined a vision of Asian collective security, involving multilateral cooperation through dialogue, confidence-building measures, steps to resolve various regional conflicts, and acceptance of Soviet participation in the Asian economy.[55] Although Gorbachev envisioned the creation of a Pacific Community, it was not until the Yeltsin era that this proposal was defined in detail. Foreign Minister Andrei Kozyrev presented a concept of an Asia-Pacific security community, which would take a step-by-step approach to conflict resolution (proceeding from exchanges of information, to confidence-building measures, and then to joint measures to resolve specific conflicts). Kozyrev proposed the creation of an Asia-Pacific center for conflict prevention and a research institute on security problems.[56]

Moscow's proposals for new mechanisms of multilateral cooperation fell on deaf ears, however. By the early 1990s, several Asia-wide institutions had been formed, including APEC (1989) and the ASEAN Regional Forum (1993). The key task, as Russian leaders would come to realize, was to improve relations with major Asian powers so that Russia would be included in existing bodies. When Evgenii Primakov replaced Kozyrev as Foreign Minister, Russian multilateralism was retargeted to the former Soviet republics. Instead, Primakov hoped that through partnerships with selected states such as China and India, Russia's profile on Asian issues would be raised, and that as the international system shifted to a multipolar order, a more inclusive dialogue would develop that would take Russian interests into account.

Despite their deepening ties, Russian policymakers were unlikely to be successful in enlisting Chinese support for multilateral dialogue on Korea: China has long been opposed to multilateral security arrangements and has been quite clear in advocating bilateral diplomacy to resolve crises on the Korean peninsula.[57] When Bill Clinton and South Korean President Kim Young Sam proposed at their 1996 summit holding four-party talks including China, Chinese diplomats reportedly were uneasy about participating. It was only when North Korean officials seized on Chinese reluctance to exclude them from the talks that China insisted it belonged at the table. At the talks, which began in August 1997, Chinese diplomats used the four-party talks to advocate the need to improve bilateral relations among the parties.[58]

Russian observers note that China did little to promote Russia's inclusion or protest its exclusion.[59] Indeed, in many respects Russia and China have competing interests in the Korean peninsula. Each of the two aspires to shape developments in a direction favorable to its individual interests, but Russian and Chinese interests are far from identical on Korean issues despite their broader strategic agreement. Russian analysts are quick to point out that only Russia is an unequivocal supporter of unification, since the status quo gives a rising China more freedom of maneuver in the region than would a strong and unified Korea, especially one friendly to the U.S.[60] China has been more insistent on the need for a withdrawal of U.S. troops—one reason for increased security dialogue between Beijing and Seoul has been to give Chinese officials a forum to express their concerns about U.S. forces on the Korean peninsula.[61]

In effect, China and Russia became competitors for South Korean investment and trade, and China quickly gained the upper hand due to its greater economic stability, vast market, and greater efforts to attract foreign capital. Trade between China and South Korea expanded exponentially in the 1990s: prior to the Asian financial crisis, South Korea became China's third largest trading partner, after the United States and Japan. The Sino–South Korean trade volume reached $31.1 billion in 2000,[62] compared to the paltry $2.8 billion in Russian–South Korean trade for the same year.[63]While Russia is struggling to repay a $1.8 billion loan made by South Korea to the Soviet government, it was South Korean officials who approached Beijing about the possibility of a loan from Chinese foreign currency reserves to ease the liquidity crisis in Seoul in the early days of the Asian financial crisis.[64]

Just as Russian leaders began downgrading ties with North Korea, South Korean leaders sought to improve ties with Moscow largely to acquire additional leverage over Pyongyang. However, as Russian–North Korean relations declined, Russia lost its influence over Pyongyang, compared to Beijing, which retained an equidistant posture vis-à-vis the two Koreas. Chinese policymakers took steps to reassure North Korean leaders of Chinese friendship, even as Beijing began normalizing ties with Seoul. At the same time that Russia was sharply curtailing its economic support for the North Korean regime, Russian–North Korean political ties were lapsing, the Russian press was constantly criticizing the North Korean regime, and Chinese leaders were making an effort to demonstrate their continued economic and political support through exchanges of high-level visits and economic cooperation. China remained North Korea's principal trading partner: due to strong exports, China accounts for approximately 30 percent of North Korea's annual trade volume. China has provided more than a billion dollars in food and fuel aid annually and convinced a Hong Kong company to invest one hundred eighty million dollars to open a casino in the Rajin-Songbong Free Economic Zone (FEZ).[65]Just as China's interest in the South Korean economic model provided an additional impetus for Chinese–South Korean economic cooperation, so has North Korea's curiosity about the Chinese approach to economic reform served to enhance Pyongyang's ties with Beijing.

As a consequence, relations with Russia became less of a priority for both South and North Korea. By the end of the 1990s, North Korea appeared indifferent to a Russian role on the peninsula, preferring to pursue greater contacts with the United States.[66] Tensions in Russian–South Korean bilateral relations over a range of issues—reparations for the Soviet downing of the KAL airliner in 1983, a dispute over the ownership of some diplomatic property in Seoul, the reciprocal expulsion of diplomats on espionage charges in 1998, and Russia's decision to return North Korean migrants to China (for eventual repatriation in North Korea)—made South Korean leaders less enthusiastic about an expanded Russian role on Korean issues.

Once Kim Dae Jung was elected president in 1997, however, South Korean attitudes towards Russia began to change. The newly elected president, who himself had spent several years in Moscow as a graduate student, viewed Russia in a different light from his predecessors in the Cold War era. Much to Moscow's satisfaction, Kim's "sunshine policy" involved both a renewed interest in regional development projects, including the Russian Far East, and greater consultation with Russian officials over strategies to engage the North.

President Putin's more active diplomacy on the Korean peninsula has reinforced Kim Dae Jung's sunshine policy and demonstrated Russia's determination to be included in future discussions on Korean issues. Yet in the months leading up to President Bush's December 13, 2001, decision to withdraw from the Anti-Ballistic Missile (ABM) treaty, some of Putin's statements had more to do with Russia's opposition to American plans to deploy a national missile defense system than with a Russian strategy toward the Koreas. The Russian–North Korean summit made headlines when Putin revealed that the North Korean leader pledged to eliminate his country's Taepodong missile program—a key rationale for National Missile Defense (NMD)—if developed countries provided access to rocket boosters for peaceful space research. Putin may have read too much into the offer, which Kim Jong Il later retracted and called "a joke." Moreover, efforts to gain Kim Dae Jung's agreement to oppose NMD at their February 2001 summit meeting complicated the South Korean president's subsequent discussions with George W. Bush. At the end of their meeting, Kim and Putin signed a joint communiqué, which appeared to indicate South Korean support for the Russian position opposing American plans to develop national missile defense in violation of the ABM treaty. After several awkward attempts to dispel any notions of disagreement between Seoul and Washington and a difficult meeting with President Bush, Kim ordered a shake-up in his cabinet and replaced key officials, including the Foreign Minister and the Unification Minister.

Now that the U.S. has withdrawn from the ABM Treaty and Russia has become an active member of the anti-terrorism coalition, it remains to be seen how Putin will balance his interest in maintaining the momentum gained in Russian-American relations since the September 11 terrorist attacks with his aim to play a meaningful role on conflict resolution on the Korean peninsula. The durability of U.S.-Russian cooperation in the war against terrorism will depend on how widely the war against terrorism will be waged, as Russia is unlikely to support its extension to Iraq or other countries. North Korea, another potential target of anti-terrorism efforts, has been urging both Russia and China to moderate their support for U.S. policies, which, according to Pyongyang, could cost them "their national independence and dignity" and counteract multipolar tendencies in the international order.[67]

REGIONAL COOPERATION

Although typically analysis of Russian–North Korean relations focuses on bilateral issues or situates the relationship within the broader context of great-power relations in Northeast Asia, regional linkages between the Russian Far East and North Korea also have played a significant role in promoting political, economic, and cultural cooperation between the two countries.[68]

Because Primorskii Krai in the Russian Far East borders on North Korea, ever since the 1950s Vladivostok has served as a rendezvous point for visiting officials from Moscow and Pyongyang. Regional relations also provided an alternative channel for high-level political dialogue. From 1969 to 1987, first secretary of the Primorskii Krai communist party Viktor Lomakin, a friend of Leonid Brezhnev, developed sister-province, technical, and tourist exchanges with neighboring North Hamgyong province, where one of Kim Il Sung's relatives was party leader. Yearly exchanges of visits between the regional party leaders ensured regular dialogue on issues in Soviet–North Korean relations.[69] Vladivostok is also the home of the Pacific fleet, which established contacts with the North Korean navy in the 1970s.[70]

Regional ties between Primorskii Krai and North Korea dwindled in the late 1980s and early 1990s, mirroring trends in bilateral relations. Leadership change in Primorskii Krai disrupted the "regional channel" to North Hamgyong, and the Russia Far East, like Moscow, focused on courting trade and investment from South Korea as soon as relations were normalized. Nevertheless, Russian regional leaders realized more quickly than their Moscow counterparts that maintaining a cooperative relationship with neighboring North Korea would benefit regional development.[71] By the mid-1990s, delegations from Primorskii Krai and Khabarovskii Krai traveled to Pyongyang in an effort to revitalize relations. The recent warming trend in bilateral relations has provided additional opportunities for regional officials to expand cooperation with North Korea. In July 2000, for example, former Primorskii Krai Governor Evgenii Nazdratenko accompanied Putin on his trip to Pyongyang. As the figures below indicate, trade between the region and North Korea has been fairly stable throughout the 1990s, reflecting Pyongyang's dependence on the region's exports of food products and timber. Prospects for increasing trade will depend above all on the improvement of the economic situation in North Korea.

Table 5.2. Primurskii Krai's Trade Volume with North Korea

Year	*Volume (in U.S.$1 million)*
1992	0.69
1993	2.12
1994	3.8
1995	3.0
1996	2.1
1997	1.8
1998	3.0
1999	2.9

Sources: Data for 1992–97 from Larisa Zabrovskaya, *Rossiya i KNDR* (Vladivostok: Dal'nauka, 1998), 73. Data for 1998–99 from Primorskii Kraevoi Komitet Gosudarstvennoi Statistiki, *Primorksii Krai v 1999 godu*, (Vladivostok: Goskomstat, 2000), 188.

Khabarovskii Krai has been using North Korean labor in the timber industry as far back as 1967: approximately fifteen thousand to twenty thousand North Korean workers participate in these projects every year.[72] Beginning in the 1990s, North Korean farm workers were hired to work in the agricultural sector in Amur Oblast, Sakhalin Oblast, and Primorskii Krai.[73] Concerned that farm labor would provide a pretext for illegal immigration by Chinese farmers, regional officials prefer to hire North Korean workers, whose contracts are enforced more strictly.[74] Primorskii Krai officials had additional cause to be pleased with North Korean labor since some of the contract workers sent to the region reportedly worked for free, as partial repayment of North Korea's outstanding debt to Russia.[75]

Some small joint projects between North Korea and Primorskii Krai in seaweed processing have been progressing, but more elaborate collaboration has proved difficult to implement due to a lack of financing. In 1996, the Nakhodka Special Economic Zone (SEZ) and the Rajin-Songbong FEZ signed an agreement to explore joint activities in areas such as the forestry sector, but little has developed despite strong support from officials such as former Nakhodka SEZ director Sergei Dudnik, now a deputy in the Primorskii Krai Duma.[76]

Regional officials in the Russian Far East have reinforced their interest in expanding economic cooperation with North Korea by participating in Russia's humanitarian assistance to the country. In 1998, for example, in response to an appeal from then-Governor Nazdratenko, Primorskii Krai enterprises donated sixty tons of food to North Korea.[77]

Even as Russian–North Korean bilateral relations stagnated, North and South Korea were busy competing for influence in the Russian Far East. Competition developed over the allegiance of the Korean diaspora in the region, particularly on Sakhalin. Unlike the Russian citizens of Korean descent residing in Primorskii Krai and Khabarovskii Krai who have lived there for more than a century, the Sakhalin Koreans are former Japanese prisoners of war. Because they arrived in Russia more recently and may still have relatives in South Korea or in Japan, North Korea has been especially interested in securing their good will (and donations) and organized cultural tours of their homeland in the 1980s. As a result of these activities, in 1990 a pro–North Korea association of Sakhalin Koreans was created, the Sakhalin committee for cooperation with Korea (Pomminren). When South Korea and Russia normalized relations, however, Seoul began to take an interest in the Sakhalin Koreans, too, and enlisted Japan's financial support to fund a program to repatriate several hundred elderly Koreans in the South.[78]

Because both North and South Korea maintain diplomatic missions in several regions of the Russian Far East, including Primorskii Krai, where Pyongyang has a large consulate in Nakhodka and Seoul maintains both a consulate and Korean Trade and Investment Promotion Agency (KOTRA) office in Vladivostok, North and South Korean intelligence services periodically engage in deadly cat and mouse games. In 1996, for example, a North Korean agent assassinated a South Korean diplomat Choi Duk-kin, reportedly a member of the ROK Agency for National Security Planning. Some of the local coverage of the murder speculated that Choi may have been assassinated in retaliation for the killing of crew members of a North Korean submarine who became stranded on Southern territory.[79]

North Korean efforts to smuggle nuclear technology out of arms depots in Primorskii Krai have caused considerable concern. Because of Moscow's weakened hold over the peripheral areas such as the Russian Far East and the difficult financial conditions prevailing in many nuclear facilities in the region, control over nuclear materials, weapons, and technologies has been eroded.[80] Since the mid-1990s, North Korean agents have been caught trying to infiltrate a submarine base and attempting to buy schedules for the dismantling of nuclear submarines.[81]

As is the case with Russian-Chinese regional relations, Russia's regional relations with North Korea have added many problems to their bilateral agenda.[82] Many difficulties plague joint projects in the Russian Far East. Russian firms claim that North Korean partners frequently fail to pay for goods and services delivered. The press in Khabarovsk and Vladivostok often reports on North Korean involvement in counterfeiting and poaching. Because some of the North Koreans working on Russian contracts are not paid until they return home, they often undertake illegal second jobs. Local residents view their moonlighting positively when they work as private contractors, for example, and provide inexpensive, efficient assistance with home renovations. However, there are also have been allegations of North Koreans participating in drug trafficking in Russia. At least fourteen employees of the North Korean timber project in Khabarovsk, who turned out to be intelligence agents, were arrested for engaging in the heroin trade.[83]

The logging camps have been controversial on human rights grounds, as well. Especially in the first half of the 1990s, pro-Western officials in Moscow argued that the camps should be closed, but Khabarovsk authorities urged their continued operation due to the importance of a steady supply of cheap labor for the beleaguered timber sector.[84] After reports of workers housed in prison-like conditions and deprived of their passports, the Russian–North Korean agreement governing the timber projects was renegotiated so as to provide local officials with greater oversight and a larger share of the harvest (61.5 percent instead of 43 percent).[85]

Just as regional officials have tried to surmount problems in regional relations with China through a focus on larger ventures with major firms, so, too, have Russian officials portrayed multilateral projects in the energy and transportation sectors as the most promising vehicles for expanding regional cooperation with North Korea. One variant of the proposed gas pipeline from the Kovyktinskoe deposit in Irkutsk Oblast would run through North and South Korea en route to China. Since North Korea faces an acute energy shortage but lacks the hard currency for energy imports, Pyongyang is likely to support the trans-Korean pipeline route to benefit from transit revenues. Despite the improved political climate in inter-Korean relations, other project participants have been concerned than a trans-Korean route would provide Pyongyang with leverage over gas flows and enable it to blackmail other recipients for political purposes.[86] Apart from such political considerations, there are many outstanding questions about the project's economic viability and financing, and the pipeline's routing remains under discussion.

For the past decade, the prospects for Russian–North Korean regional cooperation have been linked to the United Nations Development Programme's (UNDP) Tumen River development project, involving Russia, North and South Korea, China, and Mongolia. In its original conception, the thirty-billion-dollar twenty-year project launched in 1991 was designed to transform the Tumen River area into a global trade, transportation, and communications gateway. The project had to be scaled back due to unrealistic expectations about foreign investment (especially from Japan, which is unwilling to invest in the Tumen River Area Development Programme [TRADP] until relations with North Korea are normalized), conflicts of interests among the participants, and instability on the Korean peninsula.[87] The UNDP now is trying to foster the development of regional trade through infrastructure development as well as to promote tourism and environmental protection in the Tumen River area.

Officials in Primorskii Krai, the Russian region bordering on the Tumen River, have not been enthusiastic supporters of TRADP due to their concern that infrastructure improvements in China, in particular, would increase competition for already scarce cargo now moving through the ports of Pos'et and Zarubino. Despite its usual reluctance to become involved in multilateral projects, China has been the strongest supporter of TRADP in an effort to achieve an outlet to the Sea of Japan by improving rail and road connections to the aforementioned ports in Primorskii Krai, as well as to Rajin and Songbong in North Korea. Chinese officials have long complained about excessive fees and duties in Russia and hope that once Rajin and Songbong can compete for cargo, shipping costs will be lowered throughout the Tumen region.[88]

Although earlier in the 1990s Primorskii Krai shippers used the ports of Rajin and Songbong, by the end of the decade they moved their cargo through Pos'et and Zarubino. When Russia and North Korea signed an investment agreement in 1996, the two countries envisaged Russian investment in the Rajin-Songbong zone. This has not materialized, as Primorskii Krai has been trying to promote investment in its southern ports,[89] now being portrayed as ideal hubs for transit trade from Northeast China and South Korea bound for Japan.

The proposal by the leaders of North and South Korea to rebuild the inter-Korean railway is being discussed now within TRADP's transportation sector. Rail traffic over the thirty-eighth parallel has not been operational since the end of World War II, when Stalin opposed an American proposal to link the two zones.[90] Russia has been active in promoting a link from the inter-Korean railway and the trans-Siberian railroad. Russia first proposed the idea to North Korean leaders during Foreign Minister Ivanov's visit to Pyongyang in February 2000 and then at the summit meeting between Putin and Kim Jong Il in June. When North Korean leaders responded positively, Putin raised the issue with Kim Dae Jung during their September 2000 meeting at the UN Millennium summit and Russia and South Korea reached an agreement in principle to connect the trans-Siberian to the inter-Korean railway.[91] In December, Russia and South Korea discussed the possibility of a connection from Pusan to Pyongyang and then to Khasan in Primorskii Krai. The nine hundred and fifty kilometer Pyongyang-Khasan line would require a two hundred fifty million dollar investment and take about two years to complete.[92] During his summit meeting with Kim Dae Jung in February 2001, Putin continued to promote a rail link from the Trans-Siberian railroad to the inter-Korean railway in an effort to encourage tripartite economic cooperation among Russia, South and North Korea.[93] Russia and South Korea established a Committee on Transportation Cooperation to continue their discussions of the proposed link between the two rail lines. Although Putin stated that his government was prepared to invest in the new railway, according to some reports, Russia is hoping to provide the technical expertise for the rail link in exchange for a reduction of the Soviet era debt to South Korea.

Once again Russia and China are squaring off as competitors: China, too, plans to connect its railway to the inter-Korean railway, via the Seoul-Sinuiju line, in hope of becoming the gateway for cargo traveling from Asia to Europe. If the trans-Siberian were connected to this line, then cargo would begin moving through Russian territory in East or West Siberia. However, if the trans-Siberian were linked to the Seoul-Wonsan line, cargo would travel a much greater distance on Russian territory, all the way from Nakhodka in Primorskii Krai, the terminus of the trans-Siberian railroad, to Europe.[94] Fearing that the new rail projects would diminish the role of local ports dependent on trade with South Korea, some Primorskii Krai officials are opposed to the development of a new Russian-Korean rail corridor.[95]

Despite all the discussion regarding the inter-Korean railway, North Korea's commitment remains unclear and the two Koreas proved unable to restore their rail connection by September 2001, as they had previously pledged. In April 2001, North Korea abandoned restoration work, but has participated in several high-level consultations with Russia about the project since August 2001.

THE ROAD AHEAD

The inter-Korean summit in June 2000 energized great power diplomacy in Northeast Asia and encouraged states like Russia, sidelined on Korean issues for much of the 1990s, to play a more active role in conflict resolution on the Korean peninsula. For Putin, the inter-Korean summit provided a new opportunity for Russia to become more engaged in seeking diplomatic solutions with both North and South Korea. Coming at a time when Kim Jong Il was finally prepared to emerge on the world stage and when Kim Dae Jong sought outside support for his sunshine policy to quell domestic critics, the Russian president's efforts were welcomed by both Koreas.

By improving relations with Russia, North Korea has gained a new intermediary in talks with the United States and South Korea. Like the European Union's diplomacy, Russia's heightened interest in Korean issues may help offset American skepticism toward the prospects for conflict resolution, but Pyongyang continues to view talks with Washington as decisive. China, despite its strategic partnership with Russia, has been pursuing a separate agenda on Korean issues, and has not provided needed support for Russia's inclusion in expanded talks. A more inclusive approach to discussion of Korean issues is likely to depend more on the normalization of North Korean–Japanese relations, which would provide a rationale for changing the format of great power diplomacy as well for as injecting funds into regional development projects.

Although Russian President Vladimir Putin burst onto the international stage with high-profile projects such as a link between the trans-Siberian railroad and the inter-Korean railway, Russia's economic weakness and its limited economic ties with South Korea, especially compared to China, will circumscribe Moscow's participation in efforts to promote cooperation on the Korean peninsula. North Korea's ongoing economic crisis also presents a major obstacle—since Moscow is no longer willing or able to subsidize Pyongyang's failing economy, economic cooperation will be difficult to achieve. Regional economic relations provide a short-term basis for cooperation, especially through contracts for North Korean guest workers, but the expanded North Korean presence in the Russian Far East has raised new concerns about Pyongyang's involvement in nuclear smuggling, heroin trade, and counterfeiting activities in Russia. Russian–North Korean regional economic cooperation will accelerate as major regional development projects such as the Tumen River project, the Kovyktinskoe gas pipeline, and the inter-Korean railway move forward, but progress will depend on the ability to attract considerable investment, especially from Japan, but also from South Korea and China.

NOTES

1. Alvin Z. Rubinstein, *Imperial Decline: Russia's Changing Role in Asia*, (Durham, NC: Duke University Press, 1997), 158.

2. Peggy Falkenheim Meyer, "Gorbachev and Post-Gorbachev Policy toward the Korean Peninsula," *Asian Survey* 32, 8 (August 1992): 758.

3. For a detailed analysis, see Elizabeth Wishnick, *Mending Fences: Moscow's China Policy from Brezhnev to Yeltsin* (Seattle: University of Washington Press, 2001), chapter 6.

4. Robert Legvold, "The Collapse of the Soviet Union and the New Asian Order," *NBR Analysis* 3, 4 (September 1992): 10.

5. Evgenii Bazhanov, "A Russian Perspective on Korean Peace and Security," *NAPSNet Policy Forum Online*, July 30, 1997, at www.nautilus.org.

6. Mikhail Gorbachev, "Rech' na torzhestvennom sobranii, posvyashchennom vrucheniyu Vladivostoku ordena Lenina" (Vladivostok speech, July 28, 1986), in M. S. Gorbachev, *Izbrannye rechi i stat'i, Tom 4,* [Collected speeches and articles, vol. 4] (Moscow: Izdatel'stvo, politicheskoi literatury, 1987), 31.

7. Mikhail Gorbachev, "Vremya deistvii, vremya prakticheskoi raboty," Vystuplenie na vstreche s predstavitelyami trudyashchikhsya Krasnoyarskogo kraya (Krasnoyarskl speech, September 16, 1986), in M. S. Gorbachev *Izbrannye rechi i stat'i, Tom 6* [Collected speeches and articles, vol. 6] (Moscow: Izdatel'stvo politicheskoi literatury, 1989), 564.

8. Rubinstein, 159; Georgi Bulichev and Dmitry Kulkin, "Russia and South Korea: Some Thoughts on the First Decade of Relations," *Far Eastern Affairs* 5 (2000): 25.

9. Eugene (Evgeniy) Bazhanov and Natasha Bazhanov, "The Evolution of Russian-Korean Relations," *Asian Survey* 34, 9 (September 1994): 792.

10. Charles E. Ziegler, *Foreign Policy and East Asia: Learning and Adaptation in the Gorbachev Era* (Cambridge: Cambridge University Press, 1993), 123.

11. Rubinstein, 159–60.

12. For a discussion of the pro-Western phase of Russia's foreign policy, see Evgenii Bazhanov, "Russia's Changing Foreign Policy," *Berichte des Bundesinstituts für ostwissenshaftliche und internationale Studien* 30 (1996): 8–9.

13. See, for example, Kim Nam-hyok, "The Latest Noteworthy Trends in Russia's Policy," *Rodong Sinmun*, November 8, 2000, in *FBIS* (East Asia), November 8, 2000, at www.fedworld.gov.

14. Goergi Bulichev, "Russia's Korea Policy: Toward a Conceptual Framework," *Far Eastern Affairs* 2 (2000): 7.

15. Herbert J. Ellison and Bruce A. Acker, "The New Russia and Asia: 1991–1995," *NBR Analysis* 7, 1 (June 1996): 14.

16. Yeltsin's press briefing, December 18, 1992, Moscow Television Network in *FBIS* (Central Eurasia), December 21, 1992, 4, at www.fedworld.gov.

17. Rubinstein, 164.

18. Bazhanov and Bazhanov, 793.

19. The treaty was renewed every five years since 1971. Rubinstein, 165.

20. Seung-Ho Joo, "Russian Policy on Korean Unification in the Post–Cold War Era," *Pacific Affairs* (spring 1996): 35.

21. South Korea had promised to extend the USSR a $3 billion loan, but only $1.47 billion was provided by the time the Soviet Union collapsed. Joo, "Russian Policy," 37. Because of accumulated interest, the total amount Russia owes South Korea now stands at $1.8 billion.

22. There are indications that the Putin government is opposed to continuing the debt-for-arms arrangement. *Yonhap*, August 17, 2001.

23. Vadim Tkachenko, "Russian-Korean Cooperation to Preserve the Peace," *Far Eastern Affairs* 2 (1999): 29.

24. Rubinstein, 168.

25. For a detailed summary of the restoration of economic and political relations between Russia and North Korea in 1996 through 2000, see Seung-Hoo Joo, "DPRK-Russian Rapprochement and Its Implications for Korean Security," *International Journal of Korean Unification Studies* 9, 1 (2000): 198–9.

26. Igor Ivanov, "La Russie et l'Asie-Pacifique," *Politique Etrangère* (February 1999): 310.

27. Tkachenko, 33.

28. "DPRK-Russia Friendship Developing in Accordance with Desire of the People of the Two Countries," Pyongyang Central Broadcasting Station, February 9, 2001, *FBIS* (East Asia), February 9, 2001, at www.fedworld.gov.

29. On Putin's diplomacy toward North Korea, see Seung-Ho Joo, "Russia and Korea: The Summit and After," unpublished paper presented to the 42nd annual convention

of the International Studies Association, Chicago, February 20 through 24, 2001, 9, 11. For the text of the declaration, see Pyongyang Korean Central News Agency (KCNA) in English, "DPRK-Russia Joint Declaration Released," *FBIS* (Central Eurasia), July 20, 2000, at www.fedworld.gov.

30. Reuters, April 28, 2001. North Korean defense officials reportedly requested five hundred million dollars in new weapons systems, including fighter aircraft and reconnaissance planes, but Moscow refused, given Pyongyang's inability to pay hard currency for the order. *Choson Ilbo* (Seoul) April 29, 2001, BBC Monitoring.

31. Aleksandr Lukin, "Zachem Moskve Pkhen'ian [Pyongyang]?" [Why Does Moscow Need Pyongyang?] *Nezavisimaya Gazeta*, August 1, 2001, at www.securities.com.

32. Agence France-Presse, August 2, 2001.

33. The full text of the Moscow declaration was published by ITAR-TASS, August 4, 2001.

34. Agence France-Presse, August 8, 2001.

35. Among the Moscow summit's highlights, an editorial in the North Korean *Nodong Sinmun* newspaper noted Putin's support for North Korea's peaceful nuclear program and understanding of Pyongyang's position on U.S. troop withdrawal as well as their joint opposition to U.S. missile defense programs. Central Broadcasting Station Pyongyang, August 22, 2001, available at www.fedworld.gov.

36. Joo, "Russian Policy," 40.

37. Georgi Bulichev and Dmitry Kulkin, "Russia and South Korea: Some Thoughts on the First Decade of Relations," *Far Eastern Affairs* 5 (2000): 26.

38. Leszek Buszynski, "Russia and Northeast Asia: Aspirations and Reality," *The Pacific Review* 13, 3 (2000): 411.

39. Vladimir Li, "Koreiskii poluostrov v mirovoi politike vtoroi poloviny XX veka," [The Korean Peninsula in the world politics of the second half of the twentieth century] in *Rossiya is Koreya v geopolitike evraziiskogo Vostoka* [Russia and Korea in the geopolitics of the Eurasian East] (Moscow: Nauchnaya kniga, 2000): 281.

40. North Korea signed the NPT in 1985.

41. Joo, "DPRK-Russian Rapprochement," 211.

42. Moscow first began assisting Pyongyang with the construction of nuclear plants in 1984, although cooperation in nuclear research was initiated in 1956. Joo, "DPRK-Russian Rapprochement," 210.

43. Joo, "DPRK-Russian Rapprochement," 211.

44. Evgeniy P. Bazhanov, "Russian Views of the Agreed Framework and Four-Party Talks," in *The North Korean Nuclear Program*, eds. James Clay Moltz and Alexandre Y. Mansourov (London: Routledge, 2000), 222–3.

45. Bazhanov, "Russian Views," 229–35.

46. Joo, "DPRK-Russian Rapprochement," 213.

47. Vasilii V. Mikheev, "Russian Policy toward [the] Korean Peninsula after Yeltsin's Reelection as President," *The Journal of East Asian Affairs* 11, 2 (summer/fall 1997): 369–72.

48. Interview with Boris Zanegin, Institute of the USA and Canada, Moscow, April 26, 1999.

49. Alexei Bogaturov, *Velikie derzhavy na tikhom okeane*, (Moscow: Institute of the USA and Canada, 1997), 297–8.

50. Author's interview with Vladimir Li, July 24, 2000, Moscow.

51. Vadim Tkachenko, "Russian-Korean Cooperation to Preserve the Peace on the Korean Peninsula," *Far Eastern Affairs* 2 (1999): 28.

52. Mikheev, 359–60.

53. Joo, "Russia and Korea," 16–17.

54. Author's interview with Russian official, Moscow, July 28, 2000.

55. Elizabeth Wishnick, "Soviet Asian Collective Security Policy from Brezhnev to Gorbachev," *Journal of Northeast Asian Studies* 7, 3 (fall 1988): 3–4.

56. Gennady Chufrin, "Asia as a Factor in Russia's International Posture," in *Russia and Asia: The Emerging Security Agenda*, ed. Gennady Chufrin (Oxford: Oxford University Press, 1999), 475–6.

57. Samuel S. Kim, "The Roles of the Major Powers," in *Patterns of Inter-Korean Relations*, eds. Bae Ho Hahn and Chae-Jin Lee (Seoul: The Sejong Institute, 1999), 233.

58. Samuel S. Kim, "The Making of China's Korea Policy in the Era of Reform," in *The Making of Chinese Foreign and Security Policy in the Era of Reform, 1978–2000*, ed. David M. Lampton (Stanford: Stanford University Press, 2001), 395.

59. Li, 280. Interview with Vladimir Li, July 24, 2000, Moscow.

60. Vadim Tkachenko, "Russian-Korean Cooperation to Maintain the Peace on the Korean Peninsula," *Far Eastern Affairs* 3 (1999): 45.

61. John B. Kotch, "Korea's Multinational Diplomacy and U.S.-Korea Relations: The Challenge of Change in the Twenty-First Century," *The Journal of East Asian Affairs* 14, 1 (spring–summer 2000): 149.

62. Korea Trade-Investment Promotion Agency, "China, Korea, and the WTO?" June 7, 2001, at www.securities.com.

63. "Problems Still Ahead to Boost ROK-Russia Economic Cooperation," *Tong-a Ilbo* (Seoul), February 27, 2001 in FBIS (East Asia), February 27, 2001, at www. fedworld.gov.

64. Beijing refused this request. See Victor D. Cha, "Engaging China: Seoul-Beijing *Détente* and Korean Security," *Survival* 41, 1 (spring 1999): 88.

65. Xiaoxiong Yi, "Dynamics of China's South Korea Policy: Assertive Nationalism, Beijing's Changing Strategic Evaluation of the United States and the Korea Factor," *Asian Perspective* 24, 1 (2000): 71–102.

66. Hong Wan Suk, *Geostrategiya Rossii i severo-vostochnaya Aziya* [Russia's geostrategy and Northeast Asia] (Moscow: Nauchnaya kniga, 1998): 137.

67. Commentary in December 8, 2001, *Minju Choson* (North Korea) cited by *Yonhap* (Seoul), December 12, 2001. Some Russian observers have criticized Putin's pro-U.S. tilt in the fall of 2001 for similar reasons. See, for example, Alexei Arbatov, "Dogovor po PRO I Terrorism," [The ABM treaty and terrorism] *Nezavismaya Gazeta*, December 26, 2001, 11.

68. Larisa Zabrovskaya, "The 1961 USSR-DPRK Treaty and Signing of a New Russia–North Korean Treaty," *Korea and World Affairs* (fall 2000): 441.

69. Larisa Zabrovskaya, "The Korean Peninsula and the Security of Russia's Primorskiy Kray," *The North Korean Nuclear Program*, 181.

70. Zabrovskaya, "The Korean Peninsula," 182.

71. James Clay Moltz, "The Renewal of Russian–North Korean Relations," in *The North Korean Nuclear Program,* 201.

72. Zabrovskaya, "The 1961 USSR-DPRK Treaty," 442.

73. Larisa Zabrovskaya, *Rossiya i KNDR: Opyt proshlogo I perspektivy budushchego*

(1990-e gody) [Russia and the DPRK: Past experience and perspectives for the future (1990s)] (Vladivostok: Dal'nauka, 1998), 73.

74. Interviews in Blagoveshchensk and Khabarovsk, October 1999.

75. Moltz, "The Renewal," 203.

76. Moltz, "The Renewal," 203.

77. Zabrovskaya, *Rossiya i KNDR*, 61.

78. Zabrovskaya, *Rossiya i KNDR*, 25–8.

79. Zabrovskaya, "The Korean Peninsula," 192.

80. James Clay Moltz, "Russian Nuclear Regionalism: Emerging Local Influences over Far Eastern Facilities," *NBR Analysis* 2, 4 (December 2000): 35.

81. Moltz, "Russian Nuclear Regionalism," 47.

82. On difficulties in Sino-Russian regional relations and their impact on the Sino-Russian bilateral relationship, see Wishnick, *Mending Fences*, chapter 9.

83. Boris Resnik, "The North Korean Heroin Trail," *Izvestia*, December 17, 1996, 5.

84. Elizabeth Wishnick, "The Environment and Development in the Russian Far East," *Issues and Studies* (Taipei) 32, 2 (February 1996): 110.

85. Moltz, "The Renewal," 203.

86. Institute of World Economy and International Relations (IMEiMO), Moscow, and The National Institute for Research Advancement (NIRA), Tokyo, "The Northeast Asia Energy and Environmental Cooperation: Russian Approach," *Russia and Northeast Asia: Economic and Security Interdependence*, Part II, (Moscow, IMEiMO, 1999), 15.

87. David Aldrich, "If You Build It, They Will Come: A Cautionary Tale about the Tumen River Development Project," *Journal of East Asian Affairs* 11, 1 (winter/spring 1997): 303.

88. Author's interviews with officials, Beijing, November 1999.

89. Zabrovskaya, *Rossiya i KNDR*, 69.

90. John Barry Kotch, "Putin, History, and the Korean Peninsula," *The Japan Times*, March 12, 2001, at www.japantimes.com.

91. *Yonhap*, September 8, 2000 in *FBIS* (East Asia), September 8, 2000, at www.fedworld.gov. Also, see Joo, "Russia and Korea," 21.

92. "Russia Offers South Korea a Shortcut to Europe," *strana.ru*, February 26, 2001.

93. O Young-Chin, "Russia Reiterates Support for ROK's DPRK Policy," *The Korea Times* (Internet version), February 27, 2001, in *FBIS* (East Asia), 27 February 2001, at www.fedworld.com.

94. Joo, "Russia and Korea," 21.

95. Irina Drobysheva, "Primorskii Krai Concerned about Russian-Korean Rail Link," *Russian Regional Investor* 3, 10 (May 23, 2001), at www.iews.org.

III

SURVIVAL STRATEGY

6

North Korea's External Economic Relations: Globalization in "Our Own Style"

Marcus Noland

For most of North Korea's history, international trade has been regarded as a necessary evil. Both the North Korean regime's *juche* ideology and the planned character of the North Korean economy are antithetical to the notions of comparative advantage and the exploitation of international trade for the purpose of increasing income and welfare; as one might expect, North Korea's economic relations with the rest of the world have been unusually brittle. The 1970s push for military modernization left the country heavily indebted relative to its meager export earnings, and the 1975 de facto default effectively cut it off from international capital markets. The economy suffered further negative shocks with the withdrawal of Soviet economic support in the mid-1980s and the subsequent collapse of the Eastern Bloc economies, which had been North Korea's largest trade partners in the early 1990s.

This deteriorating position led the regime to include foreign trade, along with agriculture and light industry, as one of its oxymoronic "three firsts" in 1994, and as the decade wore on, the regime became more solicitous of international trade and investment. Yet as opportunities for traditional barter or quasi-barter exchange with other centrally planned economies dwindled, North Korea did not expand market-based exchange with other economies. Its volume of trade declined, and as it enters the new millennium, the DPRK is an increasingly aid-dependent economy (figure 6.1).[1]

This chapter examines North Korea's external economic relations. It begins with an overview of its trade, financial, and aid relations, and concludes with a discussion of North Korea's current reform efforts. To preview the conclusions, it is clear that North Korea is attempting to revitalize its external economic relations. It is less clear just how far the regime is willing to go to

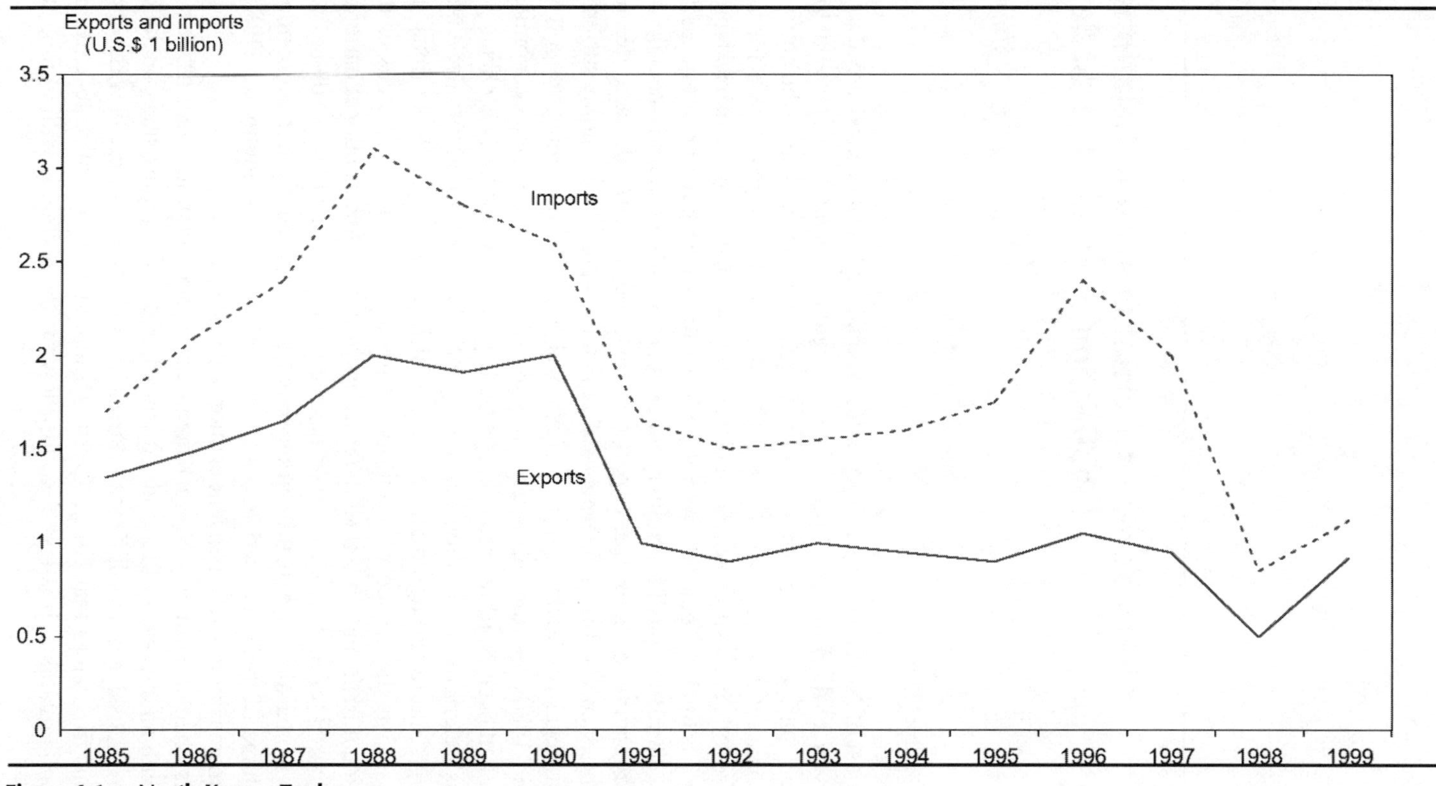

Figure 6.1. North Korean Trade.
***Sources*: Bank of Korea, KOTRA, IMF, Ministry of Unification**

accomplish this, nor for that matter is it clear what the ultimate aims of the North Korean regime are. If economic reform were successful, would the gains from reform be used to address the pressing material needs of the North Korean people, or would the fruits of change be put to some other purpose?

INTERNATIONAL TRADE

A variety of party and state organs handle trade policy matters. The governmental units were reorganized in the August 1998 constitutional revision into a ministry of trade. Historically, trade was funneled through a few large trading firms. This system was partially decentralized in 1984, and now roughly a hundred trading firms are reportedly in operation. In theory, North Korea maintains a system of multiple currencies and exchange rates. In reality, although domestic currency is still used as a vehicle for small transactions, it does not appear to be used as a store of value or even a medium of exchange for larger transactions, and the economy appears to be effectively dollarized.

The North Korean government does not normally release international trade data. In principle, "mirror statistics" reported by North Korea's trade and investment partners can be used to deduce North Korea's external transactions. This data is subject to considerable uncertainty: the figures reported here are based on partner country submissions to the International Monetary Fund (IMF) and the World Trade Organization (WTO), supplemented with data from the South Korean National Unification Board (NUB) in the cases of countries that do not report the commodity structure of their trade with North Korea to the international organizations. Per standard accounting conventions, in-kind aid contributions are omitted from these data.[2] Countries do not report barter or countertrade transactions; to the extent that North Korea has been able to successfully conclude barter deals, this trade will also be missing from the statistics. Figure 6.1 displays the time path of aggregate imports and exports. The data show that imports have consistently exceeded exports and that, after peaking in the late 1980s, trade has fallen substantially in the 1990s, though there appears to have been some rebound in recorded trade in 1999, largely due to an expansion of processing-on-commission (POC) trade with South Korea.[3] POC trade increased considerably in 2000.[4]

As can be seen in table 6.1, China is by far and away North Korea's main trade partner. It has allowed the North Koreans to run annual bilateral deficits of approximately one-half billion dollars since 1995. Indeed, China's prominence in North Korea's trade would be even larger if barter transactions and aid were counted in these figures. If North Korea's trade with China is

Table 6.1. North Korean Trading Partners, 1999 (in U.S.$1 million)

Partner Country	*North Korean Exports* [a]	*North Korean Imports* [b]	*Net Exports*
China			
Raw	93	391	
Corrected	84	430	-346
Japan			
Raw	200	147	
Corrected	180	162	18
South Korea[c]			
Raw	121	68[d]	
Corrected	121	75	46
Russia			
Raw	7	49	
Corrected	6	54	-48
Germany			
Raw	24	33	
Corrected	22	36	-15
Global Total			
Raw	922	1193	
Corrected	830	1312	-483

Sources: IMF, *Direction of Trade Statistics*; National Unification Board.

[a] IMF, Direction of Trade Statistics export data (of partner country) adjusted for "missing" transportation and insurance costs.

[b] IMF, Direction of Trade Statistics import data (of partner country) adjusted for transportation and insurance charges.

[c] North-South Korea trade data from South Korean National Unification Board (NUB). NUB data based on a customs clearance.

[d] Unilateral aid is subtracted from exports to North Korea. Corrected, aid-inclusive exports to North Korea come to U.S.$233 million in 1999.

regarded as politically determined, it is financing more than half of the North Korean deficit. Following China, North Korea's largest trade partners are Japan, South Korea, Russia, and Germany.[5]

The commodity composition of trade for 1997 (the most recent year available) is reported in table 6.2. Again, interpretation is problematic. The data reported in table 6.2 by commodity do not match the 1997 data (not shown) reported by partner. Some countries may report overall trade with the DPRK but not its commodity composition, so the part of the sample underlying the trade by partner figures are omitted from table 6.2. For example, it is unclear how arms sales are counted (if at all) in these figures. These products could be misclassified (i.e., a missile could be listed as "fabricated metals product" or put in the miscellaneous "non-identified products" category) or simply unreported. With these caveats in mind, the data in table 6.2 indicate that natural resource products and light manufactures dominate North Korea's exports. On the import side, cereals, petroleum, and industrial intermediates are the largest import categories.

Table 6.2a. North Korean Exports by Largest Commodity Groups, 1997

Industry (SITC-4 classification)	*Exports (in U.S.$1 million)*	*Share (percentage)*
Gold, non-monetary	161.22	15.1
Parts of telecommunications and sound apparatus	58.73	5.5
Other outer garments of textile fabrics	54.86	5.1
Crustaceans and mollusks, fresh, chilled, frozen, etc.	49.72	4.7
Hay and fodder, green or dry 47.48 4.5		
Gramophone records and similar sound recordings	47.44	4.4
Machines and appliances for specialized particular industries	38.81	3.6
Overcoats and other coats, men's	36.24	3.4
Thermionic, cold and photo-cathode valves, tubes, parts	34.56	3.2
Other fresh or chilled vegetables	25.72	2.4
Total, all commodities	1066.18	

Table 6.2b. North Korean Imports by Largest Commodity Groups, 1997

Industry (SITC-4 classification)	*Exports (in U.S.$1 million)*	*Share (percentage)*
Maize (corn), unmilled	96.43	7.7
Petroleum oils and crude oils obtained from bituminous minerals	65.49	5.2
Meal and flour of wheat and flour of meslin	65.47	5.2
Res: Petroleum products, refined	53.80	4.3
Iron ore and concentrates, not agglomerated	53.06	4.2
Rice semi-milld or wholly milled, broken rice	47.55	3.8
Passenger motor cars, for transport of passengers and goods	38.93	3.1
Mineral or chemical fertilizers, nitrogenous	33.21	2.6
Fabrics, woven, containing 85 percent of wool/fine animal hair	26.55	2.1
Fabrics, woven of continuous synthetic textile materials	26.35	2.1
Total, all commodities	1259.13	

Source: Statistics Canada, *World Trade Analyzer* (1980-1997)

OTHER EXTERNAL TRANSACTIONS

Data on North Korea's accumulated foreign debt and its debt/export ratio are displayed in figure 6.2. North Korea's debt is modest in absolute terms ($7.6 billion in 1994), and the vast majority of this figure ($6.2 billion) is long-term debt owed to former centrally planned economies (CPEs). (The South Korean National Intelligence Service valued this at $11.9 billion at the end of 1997,

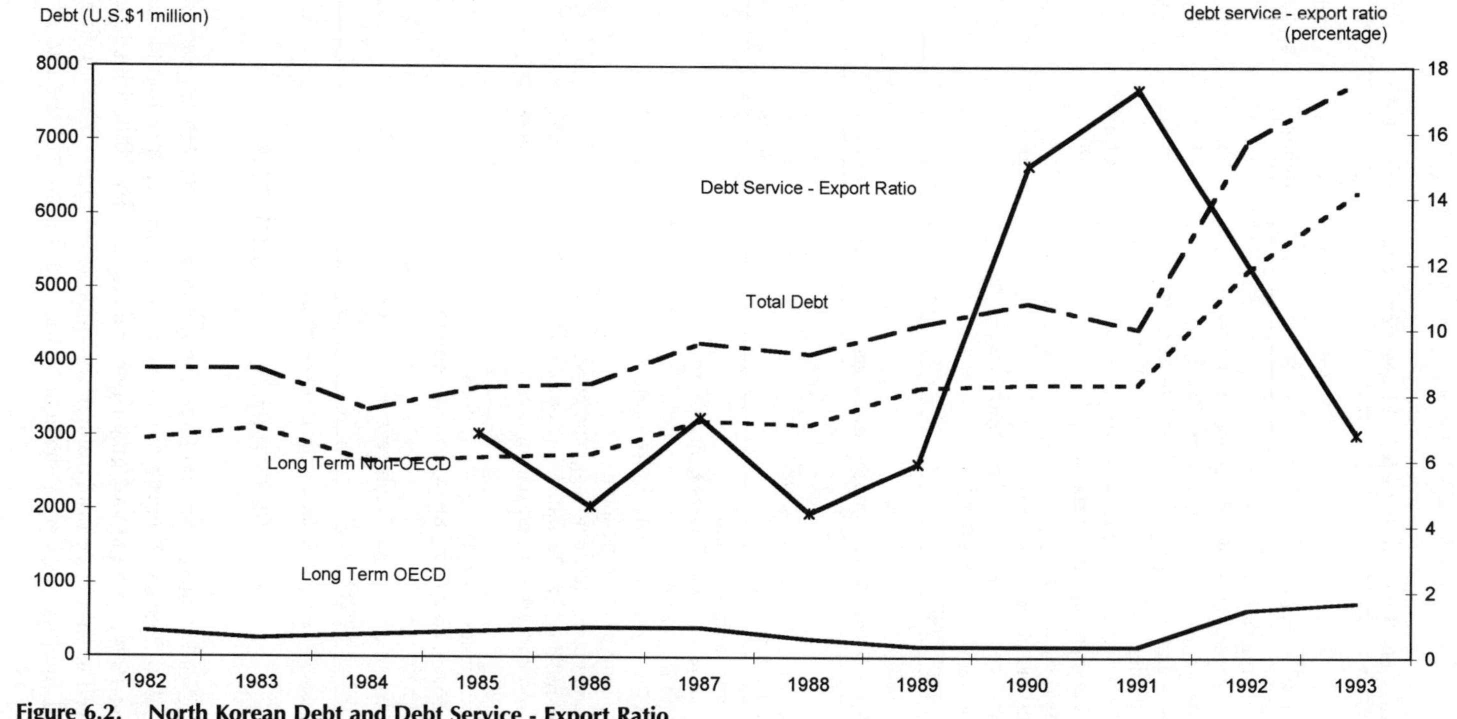

Figure 6.2. North Korean Debt and Debt Service - Export Ratio.
***Sources*: OECD**

with $7.35 billion owed to former CPEs and $4.55 billion owed to Western countries.) It is questionable how much, if any, of the ruble-denominated debt will ever be repaid. Approximately $650 million is long-term debt owed to Organization for Economic Cooperation and Development (OECD) countries. This figure has been relatively constant, reflecting the unwillingness of Western banks, governments, and multilateral institutions to increase their long-run exposure in North Korea. (The North Koreans reportedly owe another $2 billion in arrears to Western banks.) The remainder ($1 billion) consists of short-run loans that are generally rolled over. Given that in reality North Korea has defaulted on most of its long-term debt, its reservice payments are modest ($70 million) except for a spike in repayments during the period 1990 and 1991. Compared to other CPEs, North Korea's debt-to-exports ratio (including the ruble-denominated debt) is quite high (770.6 percent). However, the debt service to exports ratio is low (6.9 percent) since North Korea has essentially stopped paying its debt and no longer has access to long-term capital markets.

A thin secondary market exists for North Korean debt that seems to move mainly on speculation and rumor. Although there was some run-up in the market prior to the June 2000 summit, prices for this "exotic" paper have drifted downward to around twenty cents on the dollar since then.

Given North Korea's lack of access to conventional channels of international finance, the question naturally arises: How has it financed the chronic trade deficits? One possibility is arms exports. North Korea sells small arms, training and consulting, and praetorian guard services.[6] In the 1980s, it emerged as a significant player in the global arms market, with the U.S. Arms Control and Disarmament Agency (ACDA) putting exports at more than one-half billion dollars at times, accounting for more than one quarter of North Korea's exports (see figure 6.3). Having been linked to nearly every major exporter of oil, North Korea reputedly maintains the world's third largest store of chemical weapons and is alleged to have biological weapons including the smallpox virus. What has really attracted attention, however, has been its missile program.

The North Koreans produce a range of missiles. Single-stage missiles include the medium-range Scud-B, Scud-C, and Scud-D (a.k.a. Rodong), while long-range multistage missiles include the Taepodong-I (tested in August 1998), the yet untested Taepodong-II, and the Taepodong-III, which is still in development. The Rodongs have a range of 1000 kilometers with a 1000 kilogram nuclear or chemical warhead putting them within striking range of both South Korea and Japan, while the Taepodong-I is thought capable of hitting Guam and parts of Alaska. While the Rodongs are thought to have problems with their engines and guidance systems limiting their military usefulness, properly armed they could nevertheless present a significant deterrent to potential adversaries.

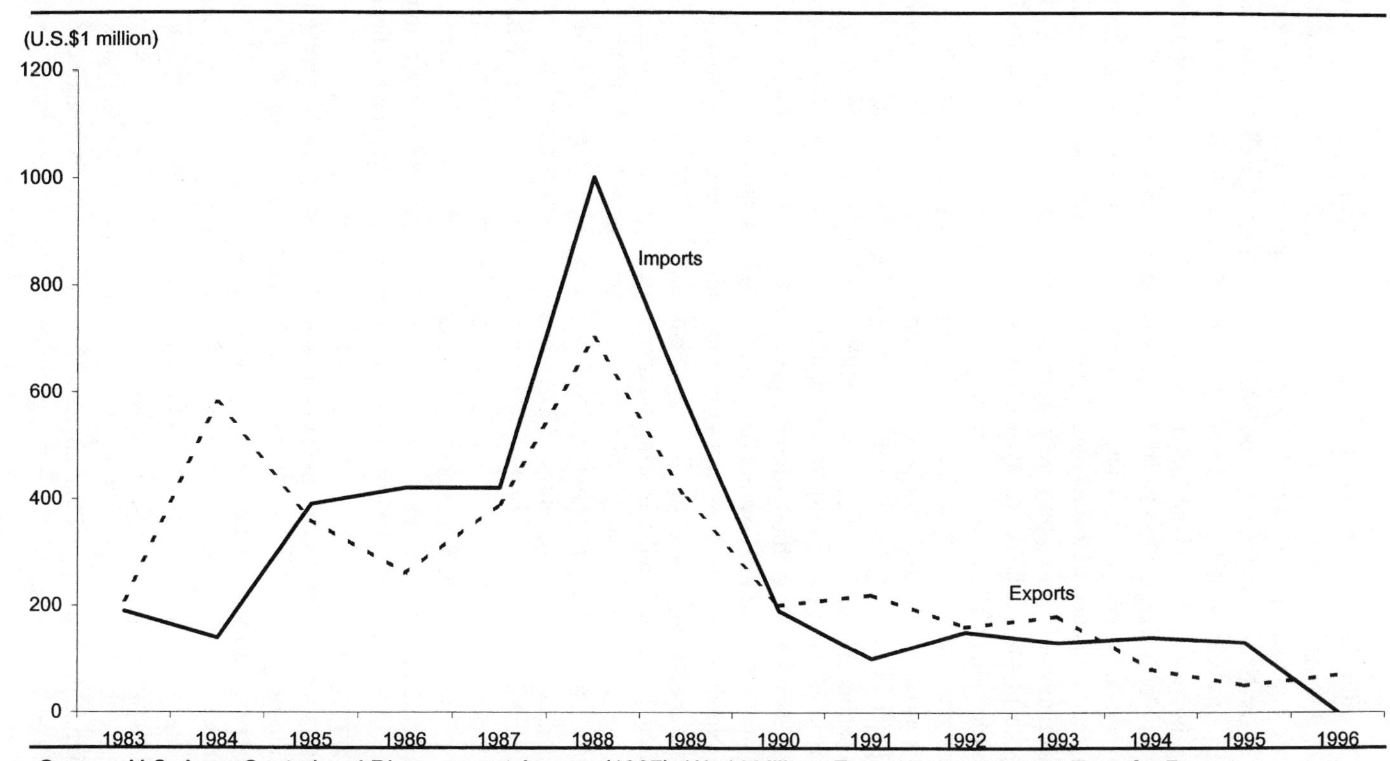

Source: U.S. Arms Control and Disarmament Agency (1997), *World Military Expenditure and Arms Transfer Report.*

Figure 6.3. North Korean Arms Trade.

Sources*: U.S. Arms Control and Disarmament Agency (1997), *World Military Expenditure and Arms Transfer Report.

On June 16, 1998 the North Koreans admitted what the world had long suspected: that North Korea exports missiles. Most observers believe that these exports began in the 1980s. Over the years, Iran and Syria have been among Pyongyang's most important customers, though the North Koreans are also alleged to have had dealings with Iraq, Libya, Nigeria, Pakistan, and Egypt.

Total revenues from missile sales are subject to dispute, with the conventional wisdom putting missile exports at around one hundred million dollars per year. The October 1999 moratorium on long-range missile testing reached in negotiations with the U.S. presumably limits North Korea's ability to develop and market the Taepodong series. The data reported by the ACDA does not support the idea that clandestine arms sales are sufficient to cover the trade gap (figure 6.1, table 6.1). Nevertheless, the fact that the military maintains its own trading channels outside the central plan is potentially of enormous policy importance; to the extent that the proceeds from arms sales are going directly to the military, the military may have a purely pecuniary incentive to continue selling arms, even if other parts of the government would like to restrict sales for broader foreign policy reasons.

One commentator likened the South Korean economy under the Chun government to a continuing criminal enterprise.[7] In contradistinction, the Kim Jong Il regime *is* a continuing criminal enterprise, and illicit activities—smuggling, drug trafficking, and counterfeiting, for example—offer another possibility for financing the trade gap. During the 1990s, North Koreans, mostly diplomats, were arrested for smuggling to evade border taxes (cigarettes, alcohol, gold), and smuggling counterfeit goods (cigarettes and CDs), endangered species, ivory, and military equipment in countries as diverse as Sweden, Finland, Estonia, Russia, Germany, Egypt, China, Nepal, Cameroon, Guinea, Kenya, Zambia, Thailand, and Cambodia. Official North Korean involvement in ivory trafficking has been so extensive that in 1999 the secretariat of the Convention on the International Trade in Endangered Species (CITES) actually sent a *demarche* to the North Korean embassy in Switzerland. The big money is in drug trafficking, though.

North Korea has been involved in at least thirty drug trafficking incidents internationally, many involving diplomats.[8] These mainly appear to take the form of North Koreans attempting to distribute drugs produced for export in North Korea, or North Koreans using diplomatic immunity as an advantage in distributing drugs produced by non-Korean criminal cartels. North Korea is believed to have begun refining opiates for export in the mid-1980s, with peak production of fifty tons of raw opium occurring in 1994. Poppy cultivation was adversely affected by bad weather and shortages of fertilizers and insecticides, however, and the North Koreans have shifted toward the production of methamphetamine in more recent years. North Korean pharmaceutical labs reportedly have the capacity to process a hundred tons of opium a year. Methamphetamine production is relatively simple, and capacity virtually limitless, constrained only by the ability to finance intermediate inputs.[9] A conservative estimate of North Korean revenues from drug trafficking is $71 million annually, with $59 million coming from opiates and $12 million from amphetamines, suggesting that net exports of drugs are probably of the same order of magnitude as arms.[10] If the estimates of the State Department's Bureau of Narcotics Control are correct, North Korea would have the world's third highest opium poppy acreage (trailing Afghanistan and Burma by a considerable margin). However, drugs would account for a lower share of exports in North Korea than in Colombia, Afghanistan, or Burma.

Counterfeiting is a third illicit source of potential revenue. Given the considerable expertise of North Korean counterfeiters, the move to new U.S. currency designs were reportedly undertaken in part to discourage their activities. High-profile counterfeiting busts have occurred in Macau, Cambodia, and Russia. South Korean intelligence estimates put counterfeiting revenues at fifteen million dollars a year; U.S. officials regard this estimate as high.[11]

North Korea receives official aid in the form of bilateral assistance, humanitarian assistance through UN agencies (principally the World Food Program), Korean Peninsula Energy Development Organization (KEDO), and other channels from more than twenty countries, as documented in table 6.3. These figures indicate that North Korea has been receiving aid flows in the hundreds of millions of dollars annually, roughly two-thirds as large as aggregate exports, with the largest contributors typically being the U.S., South Korea, China, Japan, and the EU. However significant as the aid inflows listed in table 6.3 might be for the North Korean economy, in principle they cannot be used to finance the trade deficit.[12] The previously calculated trade deficit is defined with respect to market transactions on commercial terms. In balance-of-payments terms, the lion's share of these aid flows amount to in-kind transfers. So, for example, the food aid listed in table 6.3 is distinct from, and in addition to, the commercial imports listed in tables 6.1 and 6.2.

Another possibility is that the trade deficits have been implicitly financed by China, which has permitted North Korea to accumulate large arrears in its trade account. A final possibility is that these deficits have been financed with remittances from Japan, which are sometimes reported to be in the billions of dollars. However, research by Eberstadt,[13] Noland,[14] and Noland[15] suggest that the actual values are probably far smaller, most likely less than a hundred million dollars annually, or roughly the same magnitude of the estimates of missile and drug revenues.[16] It has also been alleged that Pyongyang demands large sums (fifty to one hundred thousand) for Koreans in the diaspora to visit relatives in North Korea.

Table 6.3. Aid Balance Sheet for North Korea (in U.S.$1 million)

Donor Country	*1999*	*2000*[a]
Australia	3.411	4.505
UN Agencies	2.279	3.905
Other Humanitarian Aid	-	-
KEDO	1.295	0.600
Austria	0.010	-
UN Agencies	-	-
Other Humanitarian Aid	0.010	-
KEDO	-	-
Canada	0.161	0.665
UN Agencies	-	-
Other Humanitarian Aid	-	-
KEDO	0.161	0.665
Chile	-	0.020
UN Agencies	-	-
Other Humanitarian Aid	-	-
KEDO	-	0.020
Denmark	0.557	1.511
UN Agencies	0.557	1.511
Other Humanitarian Aid	-	-
KEDO	-	-
European Union	0.338	-
UN Agencies	-	-
Other Humanitarian Aid	0.338	-
KEDO	-	-
Finland	0.814	0.883
UN Agencies	0.722	0.807
Other Humanitarian Aid	-	-
KEDO	0.092	0.075
Germany	0.638	-
UN Agencies	0.200	-
Other Humanitarian Aid	0.438	-
KEDO	-	-
Ireland	0.266	-
UN Agencies	0.266	-
Other Humanitarian Aid	-	-
KEDO	-	-
Italy	1.821	0.924
UN Agencies	-	0.924
Other Humanitarian Aid	-	-
KEDO	1.821	-
Japan	1000.433	219.414
UN Agencies	-	35.226
Other Humanitarian Aid	-	90.000[b]
KEDO	-	94.188
Mexico	0.100	-
UN Agencies	-	-
Other Humanitarian Aid	-	-
KEDO	0.100	-
Netherlands	0.237	0.100
UN Agencies	-	0.100
Other Humanitarian Aid	0.237	-
KEDO	-	-

Table 6.3. Aid Balance Sheet for North Korea (in U.S.$1 million) (*continued*)

Donor Country	*1999*	*2000*[a]
New Zealand	0.261	-
UN Agencies	-	-
Other Humanitarian Aid	-	-
KEDO	0.261	-
Norway	0.816	2.139
UN Agencies	0.816	1.889
Other Humanitarian Aid	-	-
KEDO	-	0.250
Oman	-	0.050
UN Agencies	-	-
Other Humanitarian Aid	-	-
KEDO	-	0.050
Others, not classified[c]	19.056	22.543
UN Agencies	3.486	8.288
Other Humanitarian Aid	-	-
KEDO	15.570	14.255
Peru	-	0.100
UN Agencies	-	-
Other Humanitarian Aid	-	-
KEDO	-	0.100
Philippines	0.001	-
UN Agencies	0.001	-
Other Humanitarian Aid	-	-
KEDO	-	-
Singapore	0.400	0.300
UN Agencies	-	-
Other Humanitarian Aid	-	-
KEDO	0.400	0.300
South Korea[d]	50.500	339.209
UN Agencies	-	-
Other Humanitarian Aid	47.000	114.000[e]
KEDO	3.500	225.209
Sweden	4.404	2.935
UN Agencies	3.831	2.935
Other Humanitarian Aid	0.573	-
KEDO	-	-
Switzerland	-	0.951
UN Agencies	-	0.951
Other Humanitarian Aid	-	-
KEDO	-	-
United States	204.488	33.055
UN Agencies	39.388	18.055
Other Humanitarian Aid	100.000	-
KEDO	65.100	15.000
TOTAL	4785.111	404.095

Sources: KEDO, UN Office for the Coordination of Humanitarian Aid, National Unification Bulletin, AP.

[a] Includes KEDO contributions through July 2000.

[b] Represents 500,000 MT of grain, pledged in 2000.

[c] Includes contributions to KEDO by EAEC (European Atomic Energy Community).

[d] All South Korean contibutions to KEDO accounted as $3.5 billion in 1999 as part of multi-year commitments.

[e] Includes in-kind aid (600,000 MT of grain and 300,000 MT of fertilizer in 2000) by the ROK government, as well as medical supplies and other donations by private organizations.

In summary, North Korea maintains a highly unusual balance of payments profile. Trade volumes are very small, with annual recorded exports less than a billion dollars. The country runs a chronic trade deficit, but without access to conventional financing, must finance the deficit in unconventional ways. Aid and revenues from illicit activities together are roughly equal to the value of recorded exports. Yet the trade volumes are so small that a modest improvement in export performance would permit the North Koreans to forego aid and illicit activities without suffering a balance of payments squeeze—should the regime decide to pursue this course of action.

PROSPECTS FOR OPENING

The year 2000 witnessed considerable diplomatic activity on the part of North Korea, culminating in the June 2000 North-South summit. The April 2000 North-South summit announcement stunned the world. The timing, coming three days before South Korean national assembly elections in which Kim Dae Jung's party trailed in the polls, raised questions about whether this rapprochement was genuine, or whether it might be no more than a tactical move on the part of the North Koreans timed to extract maximal concessions out of an electorally weak Kim Dae Jung and to buy some insurance against a harder-line U.S. administration possibly taking office in January 2001. Skepticism was fed by North Korea's history of extorting resources from foreigners to secure its participation in diplomatic activities, and South Korea's own history of "checkbook diplomacy," most notably in the process of normalizing relations with the USSR. Given the Berlin Declaration and Kim Dae Jung's willingness to directly underwrite the economic rehabilitation of the North, many continue to speculate as to what President Kim may have promised the North in order to secure the preelection summit announcement.

In this light, the first question then is whether the North Koreans are serious about pursuing at a minimum economic reform, or whether the diplomatic activity of the past year amounts to an elaborate *feint*, undertaken to diversify the North Korean's aid donor base. The evidence on this point is mixed. One bit of evidence can be adduced from North Korean statements. For the past decade, the North Koreans in general (and specifically in writings or statements attributed to Kim Jong Il) have been absolutely scathing in their denunciations of the reforms undertaken in Eastern Europe and the former Soviet Union. Foreign influences have been likened to "germs," "mosquitoes," and other vermin to be kept at bay. "Reform" has been described as "honey-coated poison" and "opening" as "a Trojan horse tasked with destabilizing socialism."[17]

In 1994, the North Koreans went so far as to call the Chinese "traitors to the socialist cause" until their own worsening situation and growing dependence on China made it prudent to tone down the rhetoric. During Supreme People's Assembly, leader Kim Yong Nam's visit to Beijing in 1999, the two countries adopted an "I'm OK, you're OK" formulation in which they agreed to pursue socialism according to their respective national characteristics.

The language used during Kim Jong Il's May 2000 presummit visit to Beijing was very different, however. In remarks widely broadcast in China and reported in the international press, Kim noted the "great achievements of opening up the country" by Chinese reformer Deng Xiaoping and announced that North Korea "supports the reform policy pursued by the Chinese side." These comments suggested a new receptiveness to economic reform on the part of the North Koreans, and open up the possibility of Chinese adopting their natural role as mentors in this regard.[18] Kim's remarks were not reported in the vernacular press however, and the week after his return, North Korean television rebroadcasted the "opening" as a "Trojan horse tasked with destabilizing socialism" editorial, which some have interpreted as indicating that Kim's Beijing remarks were insincere or made under economic duress. As subsequent events have demonstrated, this evaluation may have been too harsh. It was probably naïve to project onto Kim Jong Il the belief that a firewall can be maintained between statements widely broadcast in China and elsewhere and what reaches the North Korean elite. Indeed, a mild version of Kim's remarks on China were published in English by the official Korea Central News Agency on June 1, 2000. Moreover, politically it is hard to imagine that Kim could travel to foreign soil, and then, in effect, announce that the previous fifty years of economic policy (undertaken by his deified father) was flawed. Rather, it is more likely that North Koreans are searching for a face-saving way to introduce these ideas into domestic discourse.

In fact, North Korean commentaries beginning with the joint New Year's Day editorial of the newspapers of the Korean Workers' Party (KWP), the Korean People's Army (KPA), and the Kimilsungist Socialist Youth League began signaling a possible policy shift with repeated references to the need for "new thinking" to address current problems. This was followed by the January 4, 2001, publication of remarks attributed to Kim Jong Il emphasizing the need for new thinking in the new millennium.

This possibility of policy reform received another boost with Kim Jong Il's January 2001 return trip to China in which he visited economic venues such as the Shanghai stock exchange and a semiconductor factory. Some have interpreted these visits, in which Kim was accompanied by senior military figures, as an attempt to demonstrate to his reputedly recalcitrant military establishment the possibility of pursuing economic reform while maintaining political control and military strength. And unlike the previous May 2000 visit to China, the 2001 visit received extensive coverage in the vernacular press, perhaps signaling the expansion of the bounds of permissible internal discussion of economic issues.

A second piece of evidence can be inferred from what the North Koreans have signed. In November 2000, they signed four documents on economic cooperation with the South. These agreements, establishing rules for taxation, investment guarantees, means of direct financial transactions, and settlement of trade disputes, create the legal framework for southern investment in the North. As such, they could be quite important in terms of facilitating investment by South Korean small- and medium-sized enterprises.

A final piece of evidence can be adduced from North Korean actions. The most prominent example of North-South economic cooperation has been the contract that Hyundai signed with Pyongyang. Although the Mount Kumgang tourism project understandably has attracted the most attention, the provision for Hyundai to construct an industrial park may have more economic significance in the long-run by encouraging investment by small- and medium-sized firms. Establishment of the industrial park has been delayed by a dispute over the proposed location. Kim Jong Il reportedly has expressed a preference for Shinuiju over the Haeju district, despite the latter's greater attractiveness as an economic hub. Some have argued that the choice between Haeju and Shinuiju will signal whether economics or politics are driving policy.[19] The announcement in August 2000 that the facility would be located at Kaesong would seem to suggest that economic rationality is beginning to assert some predominance over political symbolism. The North and South have since entered into agreements to construct transportation links between the South and the future industrial park, though little actual progress on the ground has been made to date. The possibility of a second Hyundai-developed special economic zone (SEZ), located at Tongchon on the east coast near Mount Kumgang, has also been reported.

These projects may ultimately turn out far differently than initially planned: Hyundai has reportedly lost four hundred million dollars on the Mount Kumgang project, and the group's centrality to the engagement process (and indeed its future financial viability) is in some doubt.[20] In December 2000 it was unable to make its twleve million dollar monthly payment, and in March 2001 appealed directly to the South Korean government for direct subsidy for the project. Given the degree of South Korean government commitment to the process of economic engagement, it is likely that these projects will continue, at least through the Kim Dae Jung presidency, with or without Hyundai. It may well be that the government of South Korea has a legitimate national interest in promoting economic integration with the

North. This could be done in a more efficient and transparent manner through the tax system in comparison to the current opaque and ad hoc approach. The rumored response—having Samsung, South Korea's one legitimately financially healthy *chaebol*, assume the Mount Kumgang project on its original terms should Hyundai be unable to carry it out—would be the worst of all possible solutions.

Assuming that the North Koreans have made the decision to undertake economic reform, the issue then is whether they are capable of successfully managing reform. In this regard they face significant obstacles, and have one tremendous advantage.

There is now an extensive corpus of evidence on the experiences of socialist economies making the transition from the plan to the market. What stands out is importance of idiosyncratic factors in determining relative success. To the extent that there are systematic determinants of success, the experiences of other CPEs indicate that there are three reasonably robust indicators of likely success in transition: the degree of macroeconomic stability at the time that reform is initiated, the existence of a functioning pre-socialist commercial legal system, and the existence of a large, labor-intensive agricultural sector.[21]

In the case of North Korea, there is some uncertainty surrounding each of these issues. Little is known about the current degree of macroeconomic stability, though the effective dollarization of the economy is not an auspicious sign in this regard. As for its pre-socialist commercial legal system, some argue that the commercial institutions of the Japanese colonial period, while not as advanced as those in pre-socialist Czechoslovakia or Hungary, might form an acceptable foundation for the construction of market institutions. Perhaps the issue of the agricultural sector is both the most straightforward and the source of the greatest misconception.

In Asia, one hears too often the following syllogism. There are two ways of reforming centrally planned economies: the unsuccessful European big bang approach, and the successful Asian gradual approach. North Korea is an Asian country, ergo it will adopt the successful Asian gradual approach and begin growing 10 percent annually upon commencement of reforms. This view is mistaken, conflating the issues of speed of transition and initial conditions.

There are two large Asian countries that have experienced relatively successful transitions from central planning to the market, namely China and Vietnam. As shown in table 6.4, both China and Vietnam had more than 70 percent of their labor forces in the agricultural sector when they began their reform processes, and the relative success of their reforms was strongly affected by the existence of this large pool of extremely low productivity labor

Table 6.4. Percentage Distribution of Labor Force at Time of Reform

		Sector		
Country	*Year*	*Agriculture*	*Industry*	*Service*
Czech Republic	1989	11	39	50
Slovakia	1989	15	34	51
Poland	1989	7	37	56
Hungary	1990	15	36	49
Soviet Union	1990	19	38	43
Ukraine	1990	20	40	40
Belarus	1990	20	42	38
Romania	1990	28	38	34
Bulgaria	1989	19	47	34
North Korea	1993	33	37	30
China	1979	71	15	14
Vietnam	1989	71	12	17

Source: Noland (2000), table 3.7.

in the agricultural sector. The authorities could liberalize agriculture, generating a relatively rapid supply response, and then release surplus labor from the agriculture sector into the nascent nonstate-owned light manufacturing sector. (In theory, one could then tax the light manufacturing sector to generate financial resources for the restructuring of the old state-owned heavy industry sector.)

This agriculture-led reform process may simply not be available to North Korea due to its very different initial conditions. Economically, North Korea more closely resembles some countries of Eastern Europe or the former Soviet Union than China or Vietnam. Vexing issues such as the restructuring of state-owned industrial enterprises, which no country has handled very well, may play a much more central role in North Korea's transition than they have in the experience of China or Vietnam.

A second obstacle is political. Again, consider the cases of Vietnam and China. In the case of Vietnam, North Vietnam, and its Vietcong allies defeated South Vietnam in a civil war and unified the country. The government in Hanoi became the sole arbitrator of what it meant to be Vietnamese. When the reform policy of *doi moi* was undertaken in the late 1980s, the ideologues in Hanoi could come up with justifications of why the new policy was really what Uncle Ho had in mind. Similarly, while China confronts the rump of Taiwan, perhaps until the March 2000 defeat of the Kuomintang candidate for the presidency, no one seriously believed that the government in Taipei presented an ideological threat to Beijing. When Deng Xiaoping spearheaded the Chinese reforms in the late 1970s, the ideologues in Beijing were free to come up with slogans rationalizing the new policy.

The divided nature of the Korean peninsula presents prospective North Korean reformers with a very different ideological challenge. Reforms that bring North Korean society closer to South Korea could undermine the whole ideological justification for the regime—why be a third-rate South Korean when one can head south and become the real thing? The dynastic nature of the North Korean regime makes this political task harder still, as the son will, in effect, have to disavow the policies of the father.[22]

Balanced against these challenges is one great advantage that other transitional economies have not had—namely the existence of a benefactor in the form of South Korea.

GLOBALIZATION IN OUR OWN STYLE

International cooperation could be expected to yield economic benefits to North Korea in the form of enhanced trade and investment, assistance from multilateral development banks, and settlement of postcolonial claims against Japan. At the same time, to obtain these benefits, North Korea presumably would have to forego its current revenues from exportation of medium-range missiles and weapons of mass destruction (WMD), drug trafficking, and counterfeiting. Furthermore, North Korea would have to settle private claims arising from past international loan defaults were it to reenter international capital markets. Such a deal could well involve the alteration or renegotiation of the Agreed Framework upon which much of North Korea's economic interaction with the rest of the world is conditioned.

Fundamental reform of the North Korean economy would have two profound effects: first, there would be a significant increase in exposure to international trade and investment (much of this with South Korea and Japan, two countries with which North Korea maintains problematic relations), and second, changes in the composition of output could be tremendous, involving literally millions of workers changing employment.[23] Both developments could be expected to have enormous political implications, or alternatively, these implications could be thought to present significant, perhaps insurmountable, obstacles to reform under the current regime.

Nevertheless, it is possible that North Korea could attempt a less ambitious reorientation of its economic policies and practices supported by help from abroad. The North Korean economy desperately needs two things to meet the minimum survival requirements of its population: food and energy. It may well be that the country obtains enough income through production or aid to attain the minimum survival basket, but chooses not to do so (i.e., the regime has a strong preference for guns over butter). Taking these preferences as given, how much additional income would the country need to hit the minimum survival basket? Under current conditions, North Korea runs a structural food deficit of around two million tons. The cost of closing this gap through commercial imports would be on the order of several hundred million dollars, depending on prevailing global prices. For the last five years, this gap has mainly been closed through the provision of international assistance. This reflects both North Korean political interests—why pay for something that can be obtained for free?—and the political interests of Western governments, most prominently that of the United States, which face less domestic resistance to providing in-kind "humanitarian relief" to North Korea than straight aid to the Kim Jong Il regime.

In addition to food, North Korea needs energy. It is reliant on imported oil to generate fuels and fertilizer for use in transportation and agriculture. Electricity is mainly generated using coal and hydropower. Generation has been hampered by difficulties in extracting increasingly inaccessible and low quality domestic coal reserves. Beyond this problem, the power grid (largely underground for security purposes) is said to suffer from extraordinarily large transmission losses. The 1994 Agreed Framework between North Korea and the United States provides for the construction of two light-water reactors (LWRs) and the provision of oil in the interim. The problem is that this is essentially a diplomatic agreement over North Korea's nuclear program, and does not really address the true needs of the North Korean economy. From an economic standpoint, it would be better to renegotiate the Agreed Framework, scrapping the costly light-water reactors, and instead building more cost-effective electrical generating systems, refurbishing the existing electrical grid, and building the necessary infrastructure that would allow North Korea to export electricity to South Korea and China, and thereby earn foreign exchange.[24] Indeed, North Korea appears to have recognized this, and rather than waiting a decade or more for the LWRs to be operational, has requested that South Korea supply it with electricity directly.[25] Presumably, this electricity, if forthcoming, would be linked to the North's obligation under the Agreed Framework to submit to International Atomic Energy Agency (IAEA) inspections.

If suitable electricity supplies were available, either through the Agreed Framework or some other scheme, the actual cost of purchasing the estimated shortfalls in grain and energy inputs, as well as desperately needed supplies of fertilizers, pharmaceuticals, and the like, might not be very large, less than a billion dollars.[26] Assuming that a sustainable modus operandi for the Mount Kumgang project can be arranged, the original terms of the tourism deal guarantee North Korea nearly one hundred fifty million dollars annually over the relevant time period. This is a minimum. North Korea receives a payment per visitor. If Hyundai (or its successor) were to fill all the berths on its ships, North Korea would stand to net approximately four hundred fifty million per year—enough to cover its grain deficit on commercial terms.[27] Moreover, other South Korean firms have expressed interest in similar tourist ventures. If North Koreans went through with the other projects in the Hyundai agreement, including the establishment of an industrial park at Kaesong, they could generate additional revenue.

These figures refer to recurrent flow expenditures. In addition, there are one-time needs to rehabilitate the North Korean infrastructure, and a variety of organizations have come up with estimates of what this might entail. To use a Seoul metaphor, to a certain extent it depends on whether one takes the black (expensive) taxi or the silver (cheap) one. For example, Williams, Hayes, and Von Hippel estimate that a rural energy rehabilitation program would cost about two to three billion dollars over five years.[28] Their estimated price tag for a more comprehensive economy-wide program is twenty to fifty billion dollars over twenty years. The Construction and Economic Research Institute of Korea, a think tank affiliated with the Ministry of Construction, has estimated that the North Korean infrastructure is at around South Korea's 1975 level, and that it would cost more than six billion dollars to bring it up to South Korea's 1990 level. Hong estimates that transfers on the order of 2 to 4 percent of South Korean gross domestic product (GDP) would be needed for an extended period of time to raise the level of North Korea's infrastructure to South Korea's 1980 level.[29]

For two billion dollars annually, one could undertake a fairly bare-bones reconstruction program in North Korea that would generate rising living standards and possibly reduce discontent and contribute to political stability, though one should be careful about making too hasty a linkage between material prosperity and political stability. Around half of this would be for recurrent flow consumption expenditures, and around half would be for industrial and infrastructural investments that could be self-financed through export revenues. Most of this trade would be with South Korea and Japan, with China and the U.S. playing smaller roles—even with the U.S. partially lifting its embargo against North Korea in June 2000.[30] Thus the necessary recurrent external financing needs would be around a billion dollars annually.

Where could this money come from? The government of South Korea has set up a special development fund, but the resources are far too small to meet the North's rehabilitation needs. Instead, the single biggest potential source of additional financing would be the resolution of North Korea's postcolonial claims against Japan. This issue was raised by former U.S. Secretary of Defense William Perry during his visit to Pyongyang in 1999. The Japanese government paid the South Korean government eight hundred million dollars in compensation for colonial and wartime activities at the time of normalization of diplomatic relations in 1965, with three hundred million in the form of grants, two hundred million in development assistance loans, and three hundred million in commercial credits. The North Korean government expects similar compensation. Adjusting the South Korean payment for differences in population, accrued interest, inflation, and appreciation of the yen since 1965, one obtains a figure in excess of twenty billion dollars.[31] An additional issue raised by the North Koreans that was not included in the South Korean package is compensation for "comfort women" who were pressed into sexual slavery during the Second World War. Reputedly, settlement figures on the order of five to eight billion dollars have been discussed within the Japanese government. In comparison, Yi Chong Hyok, Vice Chairman of the Korea Asia-Pacific Peace Committee, a KWP organization, in remarks before a Washington audience in 1996 indicated that ten billion dollars would be the minimum bound for compensation. Japan will certainly argue that its food aid and its one billion dollar contribution to KEDO should be counted against this charge. Some have speculated that Japan will even try to claim credit for the costs of recapitalizing bankrupt *Chochongryun*-controlled financial institutions in Japan. In any event, such sums, properly deployed, could go a long way in restoring North Korea creditworthiness and financing economic modernization.

If North Korea were to accept the Perry review's terms of engagement, another carrot that the U.S., Japan, and South Korea could hold out would be membership in the international financial organizations and the prospect of multilateral economic assistance. Pyongyang has periodically expressed interest in joining the IMF, World Bank, and Asian Development Bank (ADB), and formally applied to join the ADB in August 2000. Membership talks have never made much progress, however, for they were snagged on North Korea's unwillingness to permit the kind of access to economic data and information required for membership in these organizations, its position on the U.S. list of states supporting terrorism, and Japanese opposition relating to unresolved political issues, most notably the alleged kidnapping of Japanese citizens.[32] North Korea was invited to the 2000 joint annual meetings of the World Bank and IMF, but declined attending. The World Bank and IMF again signaled their willingness to engage North Korea during separate March 2001 visits to Washington by DPRK foreign ministry officials and South Korean President Kim Dae Jung.

Under normal circumstances, if North Korea were to join these organizations, in the absence of considerable reorientation in domestic economic policies, it would be unlikely that the multilateral development banks would make significant loans. However, given the political importance of North Korea to the U.S. and Japan (influential shareholders in the World Bank, and the dominant shareholders in the ADB), one would expect that North Korea might receive favorable treatment.[33] Technical advice and assistance would really be more important than direct lending activities, which would ultimately only complement the activities of private investors. Working from the case of Vietnam (another Asian transitional economy where the government undertook rapid economic reforms) and scaling down the multilateral development banks' lending program for the smaller size of the North Korean population, one obtains lending on a scale of one hundred fifty to two hundred million dollars annually. Not trivial, but not enough to finance even a barebones recovery program. More money might be available if the U.S., Japan, South Korea and others set up a special fund for North Korea at the World Bank or ADB.[34] Such a fund might be a particularly useful way of politically laundering Japanese reparations. It is possible that under some circumstances North Korea could obtain international financial institution loans even if it were not a member.[35] For example, the World Bank maintains a special program for peace and sustainable development in the Middle East through which it makes loans in the areas controlled by the Palestinian Authority. It also has adopted a policy that allows it to assist countries that are emerging from crises even though they are not members in good standing of the Bank. This policy was adopted after the Bank was precluded from lending to Cambodia because of a debt arrearage problem. The key attributes in these cases appear to be a cooperative recipient government and strong support from major Bank shareholders. Bank staff has also expressed the view privately that an independent, poor North Korea would probably be able to access more lending than a unified middle-income Korea. In any event, the settlement of postcolonial claims with Japan would dwarf anything North Korea could expect from the multilateral development banks.

These developments might be thought of as the necessary, though not sufficient, conditions for consensual unification. Even if they were to occur, they would only get the two Koreas part way down the road. Moreover, these developments do not necessarily imply progress toward consensual unification. North Korea could adopt the minimalist reform program and reject unification overtures from the South. Indeed, while implementing such a program, the North might feel compelled to limit discussion of unification precisely to prevent system overload and a loss of control.

POLICY IMPLICATIONS

Like other CPEs, North Korea initially achieved some success in mobilizing resources for development. Its uniqueness lay in the extreme degree to which markets were repressed and decision making was invested in a single individual, Kim Il Sung. Like other CPEs, it began to stagnate when opportunities for "extensive" development had largely been exhausted and "intensive" development and technological dynamism were required instead.

Kim's response in the 1970s was to try to circumvent this conundrum by borrowing capital and technology from abroad. This tactic failed, however, and North Korea defaulted on its debts, leaving it highly dependent on the Soviet Union. Given its lack of alternatives, the decline in relations with the Soviets and the Soviet Union's eventual collapse were blows from which the North Korean economy has never recovered.

The regime found itself in a terrible bind—its economy was failing, its primary patron was no more, and it feared that economic reform would mean the end of the regime as had been the case in Eastern Europe. The regime's response was essentially two-fold: engage in on-off attempts to earn foreign exchange through projects that would not affect the systemic organization of the economy (the Rajin-Sonbong SEZ and the Mount Kumgang tourism project), while at the same time engaging in brinkmanship to extract resources from the rest of the world.

Whether the events of 2000 and 2001 mark a fundamental reorientation of North Korean policy is a critical issue. It could be that the Kim Jong Il regime has made the calculation that the best way to preserve their own power and perquisites within the North Korean system is to constructively engage South Korea and the rest of the world, and that moving down the path of economic reform, though risky, presents them with the highest likelihood of ultimate success in preserving themselves within their system. Or, it could be purely opportunistic.

How can we tell? Despite the reported stabilization of the economy (or even its revival), and enhanced revenues from the Hyundai deal, North Korea has increased its reliance on international food assistance. The share of food imported into North Korea has risen from nil in 1994 to more than 80 percent today. In other words, concessional assistance has almost completely crowded out imports on commercial terms. Food is fungible and food aid acts as implicit balance of payments support—funds that would have otherwise been expended on food can be spent on other items. The issue is then the preferences of the regime, and in the case of North Korea, there is reason for unease.[36]

So what are the policy implications of this? From the standpoint of South Korea, Kim Dae Jung is fundamentally correct that the focus of policy should be aimed at supporting the constructive transformation of the North. Militarily, North Korea already holds Seoul hostage with its forward-deployed artillery. The South Koreans might as well engage North Korea in an attempt to reduce tensions and ultimately achieve reconciliation and unification, because the marginal increase in North Korea's threat capability that might be achieved through economic reform is relatively small. The South Koreans are already over that Rubicon.

Therefore, the goal of South Korea should be to domesticate North Korea, pursuing a two-track strategy of trying to defang it militarily while at the same time rehabilitating its economy. The problem from the standpoint of South Korea is the impact that increased integration with North Korea could have on the South Korean economy. The financial crisis has at least temporarily reversed a twenty-year trend toward reduced direct state involvement in the South Korean economy. As a consequence of its increased presence in the financial sector and other, more indirect levers on power, the South Korean state has a bigger influence on strategic decisions by the *chaebol* than it did on the eve of the crisis. The difficulty is that despite the good intentions of the South Korean government, politics and economics are inseparable in the North—even in theory. Any significant interchange with the North will be highly politicized. The South Korean government inevitably will be tempted to directly intervene in the economy to promote its foreign policy goals.

In this light, South Korea should promote two goals in its dealings with the North: transparency and the transformation of the North Korean system. With regard to the first goal, economic integration between the North and South may convey positive externalities to South Korea and the social rate of return on South Korean investment in the North may exceed the private rate of return on such investment. As a consequence, there is a public policy justification for encouraging investment in the North. It would be better though, to introduce broad tax incentives for investment in the North than use the state's influence over the financial system to encourage such investment on an ad hoc basis. The notion behind a tax-based policy would be to divorce the overarching societal goal of investment in the North from state influence on particular investment decisions. The advantage of such an approach is that it would preserve the microeconomic efficiency of private firms selecting among potential investment projects on the basis of expected rates of return, while taking the broader social imperative to encourage such investment into account.

With respect to the second goal, one can imagine a hierarchy of modalities of engagement. The worst would be projects such as the Mount Kumgang project, which can literally and figuratively be fenced off from the rest of the North Korean economy and society and offer little prospect of structural transformation. Given the historical enmity and distrust between the North and the South, the Mount Kumgang project may have been a necessary first step to build confidence and trust. But having successfully made that step, future projects should be evaluated with a more critical eye.

Marginally preferable to the Mount Kumgang project would be mining concessions or SEZs in remote areas such as Rajin-Sonbong. These are classic enclave economies with little prospect for spillover into the broader society.

Industrial parks, bonded warehouses, and other preferential investment zones in urban areas would be preferable, and free investment by South Korean firms throughout the country would be the best of all. The latter would not only maximize the contact between North and South Koreans (and thus demonstration or educational effects with respect to the operation of a market economy), it would create competition between local authorities to attract investment.

The point is that North Korea faces a fundamentally supportive international environment. South Korea, Japan, China, and even the U.S. want to see a less belligerent North Korea survive until a consensual process of reconciliation and unification can take place on the Korean peninsula. The three questions are whether North Korea is willing to change, whether it is capable of successfully managing change, and to what purposes would it apply the fruits of change. I am hopeful on the first question, skeptical on the second, and wary about the third. I believe that the most likely outcome is a kind of muddling through in which the regime makes a series of ad hoc adjustments while supported by external powers that would prefer to see a less belligerent North Korea muddle along to the risks of instability or collapse. The outcome could well be what I have described elsewhere as "apparatchik capitalism," in which the political elite would use their control over state power to channel the lion's share of rents generated by a partially marketized and nontransparent economy to themselves.[37]

NOTES

I would like to thank Samuel Kim for helpful comments on an earlier draft of this chapter, and Derek Bruzewicz for assiduous research assistance.

1. See Marcus Noland, *Avoiding the Apocalypse: The Future of the Two Koreas* (Washington, D.C.: Institute for International Economics, 2000). It would be interesting to compare the responses of North Korea and Vietnam to the common shock of the withdrawal of Soviet aid and the collapse of the USSR. My supposition is that the Vietnamese were able to far more effectively reform their more agriculturally based economy and boost exports to ease the balance of payments constraint, while, in the absence of greater export orientation, the North Koreans were forced to reduce the level of domestic activity. Unfortunately the extreme uncertainty surrounding the North Korean balance of payments position (largely because of the issue of nonreported trade remittances addressed later in this chapter) effectively precludes quantitative inquiry along

this line. However, Nicholas Eberstadt, "Prospects for U.S.-DPRK Economic Relations," *Korea and World Affairs* 21, 4 (winter 1997), calculates that between 1989 and 1995, the Vietnamese nearly tripled their exports (largely by liberalizing the price of rice, their major exportable, thus encouraging increased output), while North Korean exports fell by half.

2. For example, in reporting inter-Korean trade, South Korean organizations have at times misclassified KEDO contributions, in particular KEDO oil shipments, as South Korean exports to North Korea.

3. The prevalence of processing on commission trade, in which intermediate inputs are shipped through China for assembly into finished products, raise the possibility of significant double-counting of North Korea's trade with China and South Korea.

4. See www.kotra.or.kr/main/info/nk/eng/main.php3 (accessed March 23, 2001).

5. Noticeably absent from this list is the U.S., which effectively maintains an embargo against North Korea despite minor relaxation of restrictions in 1995 and 1999. However, while not engaging in much trade, the U.S. has been a major provider of assistance in the form of food, KEDO payments, and payments for the remains of U.S. soldiers missing from the Korean War. Indeed, North Korea is now the largest U.S. aid recipient in Asia.

6. For example, North Korean troops have reportedly fought on the government side in the Congolese civil war in exchange for uranium and other mineral concessions.

7. See Mark Clifford, *Troubled Tiger* (revised version) (Singapore: Butterworth-Heinemann Asia, 1997).

8. See Raphael Perl, *North Korean Drug Trafficking: Allegations and Issues in Congress* (Congressional Research Service, March 9, 1999), processed.

9. In both cases, there are more benign explanations. North Koreans use opium to make morphine for military uses as well as for use as a traditional medicine. Given shortages of imported medicines and pharmaceuticals, opium may increasingly be used as a pain reliever in the North. Likewise, methamphetamines were originally developed for military uses, and some share of production may be devoted to officially sanctioned domestic usage.

10. See Perl, *North Korean Drug Trafficking*. In 1999, the South Korean Ministry of Foreign Affairs and Trade estimated revenues from all illegal activities (not including arms sales) at one hundred million dollars.

11. Perl, *North Korean Drug Trafficking*.

12. In theory, these aid flows could be used to finance the North Korean trade deficit if the North Koreans resold the aid shipments on world markets, and in the past there have been allegations of "calorie arbitrage" in which the North Koreans reputedly resold high value food aid for lower quality foodstuffs on world markets.

13. See Nicholas Eberstadt, "How Much Money Goes from Japan to North Korea?" *Asia Survey* 36, 5 (May 1996).

14. See Marcus Noland, "The External Economic Relations of North Korea and Prospects for Reform," in *North Korean Foreign Relations*, ed. by Samuel S. Kim (Hong Kong: Oxford University Press, 1998).

15. See Noland, *Avoiding the Apocalypse*.

16. Alternatively, remittances could be much larger, as is often reported in the press, but in this case a corresponding magnitude of expenditures are missing, or North Korea is running a balance of payments surplus and exporting capital to the rest of the world (despite experiencing a famine). A critical issue is the extent to which the Chinese have been implicitly providing aid by permitting the North Koreans to build up arrears on their imports. Under the assumption that the Chinese simply barter their exports for whatever imports North Korea can provide and allow the difference to be built up in arrears, the remittances necessary to finance imports would be less than one hundred million, which is far lower than commonly thought. However, to the extent that the Chinese are successful in extracting hard currency payments from the North Koreans, they could be soaking up whatever remittances the *Chochongryun* can provide.

17. See Noland, *Avoiding the Apocalypse*, for specific references to these formulations.

18. In a similar vein, during U.S. Secretary of State Madeleine Albright's October 2000 visit to Pyongyang, Kim expressed interest in the "Swedish model." During his second visit to China, he also reportedly expressed interest in the policies of Park Chung Hee.

19. See Chung-in Moon, "Korea and Asian Security in the Twenty-First Century," *Asian Voices: Promoting Dialogue between the U.S. and Asia* (Washington, D.C.: Sasakawa Peace Foundation USA, 2000.)

20. Hyundai narrowly averted bankruptcy in November 2000 when state-dominated banks extended it emergency loans. Hyundai is one of the prime contractors on the KEDO project, and the industrial park at Kaesong could play an important role in inter-Korean economic integration. The fear, of course, is that the South Korean government will be tempted to reward Hyundai or other firms that do its bidding in the North with preferential treatment. It should be noted that while Hyundai has been losing money in the North, this has not been the principal financial drain on the group.

21. See Noland, *Avoiding the Apocalypse*, especially chapter 7 for an extensive discussion of these issues and references to the relevant literature.

22. The dynastic aspect of the regime could convey certain short-run advantages, however. Presumably, Kim Jong Il will claim that in private conversations Kim Il Sung expressed views conveniently consistent with whatever policy Kim *fils* wishes to pursue.

23. On the first point, see Noland, *Avoiding the Apocalypse*. For detailed analyses pertaining to the second point, see Marcus Noland, Sherman Robinson, and Monica Scatasta, "Modeling North Korean Economic Reform," *Journal of Asian Economics* 8, 1 (1997): 15–38. Also see, Marcus Noland, Sherman Robinson, and Tao Wang, "Rigorous Speculation: The Collapse and Revival of the North Korean Economy," *World Development* 28, 10 (2000): 1767–87.

24. See, David Von Hippel and Peter Hayes, "DPRK Energy Sector: Current Status and Scenarios for 2000 and 2005," in *Economic Integration of the Korean Peninsula,* ed. Marcus Noland (special report 10, Washington, D.C.: Institute for International Economics, 1998).

25. The irony of this would be striking: In May 1948, at the time of the partition, North Korea cut off electricity supplies to the South.

26. See R. Anthony Michell, "The Current North Korean Economy," in *Economic Integration of the Korean Peninsula,* ed. Marcus Noland (Washington, D.C.: Institute for International Economics, 1998).

27. North Korea and Hyundai have been in conflict over Hyundai's desire to significantly increase the number of tourists that it brings to Mount Kumgang by including large numbers of non-Koreans. In September 2000 the two sides agreed to begin permitting a limited number of Japanese to take part in Hyundai's tours, which would have obvious implications for the bottom line of Hyundai or its successor.

28. See James H. Williams, Peter Hayes, and David Von Hippel, "Fuel and Famine: North Korea's Rural Energy Crisis," paper presented to the Pentagon Study, group on Japan and Northeast Asia, Washington, D.C. October 22, 1999.

29. See Soon-jick Hong, "North Korea's Infrastructure Conditions and Strategies for Investment," VIP Report (Hyundai Research Institute, July 2000).

30. This assumes that liberalization in the North was on a nonpreferential basis. As shown in Marcus Noland, Sherman Robinson, and LiGang Liu, "The Economics of Korean Unification," *Journal of Policy Reform* 3 (1999): 255–99 and Marcus Noland, Sherman Robinson, and Tao Wang, "Modeling Korean Unification," *Journal of Comparative Economics* 28, 2 (2000): 400–21, the formation of a customs union between North Korea and South Korea would have a big impact on the North while it would have a trivial impact on the South. The customs union would represent a major trade liberalization on the part of the North, while the North's economy would be too small to have much of an impact on the South's economy. (Think of the impact of NAFTA on the U.S. or the accession of a small central European economy on the EU.) This story—big impact on the North, small impact on the South—would change considerably if integration were to come through collapse, as discussed in Noland, *Avoiding the Apocalypse*.

31. See Mark E. Manyin, "North Korea–Japan Relations: The Normalization Talks and the Compensation/Reparations Issues," CRS Report for Congress, Washington, D.C.: Congressional Research Service, April 21, 2002, for alternative estimates and additional discussion of compensation issues.

32. Under U.S. law, U.S. executive directors at the development banks could not vote in favor of extending loans to North Korea until it was removed from the list of countries engaging in state-sponsored terrorism. At the ADB annual meeting in May 2000, U.S. Treasury official Ted Truman reportedly stated that "our position on membership is unchanged. Both because our own legislation requires us to do so [and] because North Korea is an international terrorist state. . . . [A]s long as that situation prevails and the North Korean regime is one which is fundamentally incompatible with the principles of institutions such as the ADB, we would oppose membership." (Agence France Press, May 7, 2000).

33. World Bank President James Wolfensohn already signaled as much, writing in a July 2000 letter to South Korean President Kim Dae Jung, "We at the World Bank stand ready to support inter-Korean economic cooperation. We hope to assist in the development of North Korea, within our capacity and mandate, whenever the North Korean authorities are ready to work with us."

34. The ideas of a Northeast Asia fund or a Northeast Asia Development Bank have also been mooted.

35. An April 2000 statement to this effect by the IMF resident representative in Seoul, David T. Coe, was immediately denounced by Representative James Saxton (R-NJ).

36. According to the 1999 Ministry of Defense, *White Paper* (Seoul: Ministry of Defense, 1999), South Korean National Defense White Paper, North Korea increased its reserves of chemical weapons, boosted KPA manpower by ten thousand troops, created a missile division, and added ten submarines to its fleet. In August 1999 it was revealed that North Korea had purchased roughly forty aging MiG-21 fighters and eight military helicopters from Kazakhstan. It was subsequently reported that North Korea was trying to obtain more advanced MiG-29 and SU-30 fighters as well. In September 1999 a classified U.S. Air Force report allegedly describing continued North Korean work on its Taepodong missile was leaked to the press. In October, in testimony before the Senate Armed Forces Committee, General Thomas Schwartz, the newly appointed commander-designate of U.S. Forces Korea, stated that North Korea had accelerated its arms buildup and was forward-deploying artillery and rocket-launchers in underground facilities. In March 2000 Admiral Dennis Blair, Commander-in-Chief U.S. Pacific Forces, indicated that North Korean military exercises during the winter of 1999 and 2000 had been the most extensive in recent years. Other U.S. military sources indicate that the 2000 summer exercise cycle, too, was the most extensive in years. In the 2000 Ministry of Defense, *White Paper* (Seoul: Ministry of Defense, 2000), the South Korean National Defense ministry indicated that North Korea had deployed five hundred short-range missiles and other artillery near the border with South Korea. For its part, North Korean official statements have been replete with references to it's "military-first" policy.

37. See Noland, *Avoiding the Apocalypse*, especially chapter 9 for further elaboration on this theme and a comparison to the Romanian case.

7

North Korea's Security Policy: Swords into Plowshares?

C. S. Eliot Kang

Tzu-kung asked about government. [Confucius] said: "Enough food, enough weapons, and the confidence of the people." Tzu-kung said: "Suppose you definitely had no alternative but to give up one of these three, which would you relinquish first?" The Master said: "Weapons."

—*Analects* (12.7)[1]

We should adhere to the party's economic policy and create new turning points in this year's socialist economy building. By doing so, we can brilliantly realize the respected and beloved general's intention to decisively upgrade our people's daily lives. We should exert the greatest efforts on economy building to increase agricultural production, which is to smoothly resolve the issue of our people's eating lives [sic]. We should create great achievements in economy building in order to produce consumption goods, necessary for people's daily lives, on a large scale.

—*Rodong Sinmun* editorial, January 16, 2001[2]

Despite being racked and ravaged by famine and draught, North Korea can claim spectacular security policy successes in recent years. Most notably, in 1994, a destitute North Korea went eyeball-to-eyeball with the world's greatest military and economic power and emerged without a scratch. In June 2000, North Korea was able to broadcast all over the world the images of the beaming faces of first South Korean President Kim Dae Jung and later U.S. Secretary of State Madeline Albright toasting Chairman Kim Jong Il in Pyongyang. Though not as photogenic, North Korea's tide-like normalization diplomacy with Japan, with its promise of a huge economic windfall for Pyongyang, made new advances as well. These achievements are largely the result of North Korea's *apparent* willingness to trade its nuclear and ballistic missile capabilities for economic resources from the United States, South Korea, and Japan. Will North Korea really bargain away its military trump cards for economic engagement with the West?

Although Seoul's "sunshine policy" and Tokyo's normalization diplomacy are premised on an affirmative answer to the question posed, strong skepticism persists among many security analysts about North Korea's willingness to follow through with the exchange. Indeed, the foreign policy principals of the current U.S. administration, including President George W. Bush himself, have expressed doubts about North Korea's intentions and questioned the wisdom of continuing the "Perry Process" of engagement begun by the Clinton administration.[3] Whether acknowledged or not, these reservations are framed or reinforced by a neorealist conception of security that pervades the conventional thinking about post–Cold War East Asia.

Although under continuing attacks from liberal institutionalism and constructivism in the academy, neorealism still retains its position as the leading, if not dominant, analytical framework among international security specialists, particularly those specializing in East Asia. Standard neorealism[4] would predict that North Korea, a garrison state par excellence, will not bargain away its nuclear and ballistic missile capabilities.[5] Swayed by the neorealist logic, many Western analysts and officials doubt that North Koreans would give up something that has provided them with asymmetrical bargaining power against those possessing far greater aggregate power.

Some suspect that North Korea is bargaining deceitfully and using time and resources provided by the United States, South Korea, and Japan to strengthen its military capabilities.[6] This suspicion leads them to oppose engagement with North Korea, predicting that North Korea will emerge more dangerous from "appeasement."[7] Others who believe that North Korea is predatory by nature, unwilling to give up the dream of unifying Korea on its terms, join them in calling for containment of North Korea.[8] No analyst, however, is calling for a preemptive war against North Korea, an extreme—but some would argue, logical—policy conclusion of neorealist thinking.[9]

Despite its currency, neorealism presents an excessively deterministic understanding of North Korean security policy. I offer a different realist perspective—"mercantile realism"[10]—as a more useful tool for analyzing North Korea's security policy.[11] This essay does not present a case study that "tests" a theory in a strict sense, but I evaluate mercantile realism for its utility as an "instrumental theory." I present it as a corrective to the neorealist perspective on Pyongyang's behavior that many security analysts and policymakers implicitly or explicitly hold. To whatever extent that academic theories influence policymakers, the neorealist answer to the question posed calls for policies that could turn the overly gloomy neorealist prognosis into a self-fulfilling prophecy. My approach provides a systemic/materialist basis for expecting a range of North Korean behavior that does not preclude a more optimistic answer to the question posed.[12]

Mercantile realism does not privilege military security at the expense of economic capacity in a manner of neorealism.[13] Further, it holds that states make security policy based on *probability* of aggression, not simply *possibility* of conflict.[14] Mercantile realism views North Korea's security policy as being subject to not just short-term consideration for military preparedness but to long-term objective of maintaining a viable economic power base.

If the mercantile realist logic holds true in the North Korean case, the possibility exists that North Korea will bargain, if warily and fitfully, to trade much of its nuclear and ballistic missile capabilities for Western economic engagement.[15] If North Korea believes that the current probability of conflict on the Korean peninsula is *tolerably* low, while its long-term economic power base would be made more secure by the swap, North Korea should go ahead with the exchange in good faith. Of course, mercantile realism cannot predict with certainty that North Korea will make the swap, but its modality captures the contingent possibility of the exchange, depending on the North Korean calculus of war. The policy implication for the United States, South Korea, and Japan is then that they should engage North Korea in order to build security and confidence. However, this engagement policy must be framed by a clear-eyed strategic understanding that North Korea's motive for opening up to the West is the expectation that engagement will strengthen its economic base, a key element of its national power.

ANALYTICAL FRAMEWORK

I employ a systemic/materialist framework to analyzing North Korea's security policy, and this choice is deliberate given the state of North Korean security studies. Ideational factors and individual decision-makers impact the production of security policy, particularly in a country as ideological and autocratic as North Korea. Nonetheless, my approach is not only more parsimonious than those emphasizing North Korean culture, ideology, history, or identity, but it is a necessary response to the following two related problems: First, North Korea remains "the blackest of black boxes;" second, the debate about North Korean security policy is ideologically charged.[16]

According to Walter Mondale, "Anyone who tells you that they are an expert on North Korea is either a liar or a fool."[17] Perhaps the former vice president is unfair, but there is some truth to his judgement to the extent that not much is known about North Korea. For years, Western security analysts have guessed the motive and logic behind North Korean actions and pronouncements. Even compared to Kremlinology of the Soviet era, the study of North Korea's security policy is complicated by a lack of reliable information, as well as an abundance of disinformation about North Korea.

Without credible data, it is anyone's guess what the real strategy and goals of the North Korean government are, and any unit-level analysis of North Korea's security policy serves as a kind of Rorschach test of the analyst's own policy preference. Based on their own preconceptions about North Korea, the contending analysts fill the information void with conjectures extrapolated from a few pieces of evidence that support their policy positions.

Those inclined to stress containment as the preferred policy focus on whatever evidence there is of North Korean truculence and Pyongyang's desire for reunification, even if that entails a suicidal war with South Korea.[18] They paint a picture of North Korea as an atavistic Stalinist dictatorship bent on aggression.[19] Those inclined to stress engagement or crisis avoidance focus on North Korea's willingness to bargain and the possibility of North Korea lashing out if pushed to the wall.[20] They paint a picture of North Korea as a misunderstood relic of the Cold War that needs to be brought in from the cold, lest it implodes from deprivation or lashes out in desperation.[21]

A more serious problem for the scholarship on North Korea is that the lack of data has fostered many speculative but little cumulative theoretical works. To the extent that theories are employed to analyze North Korean security policy, they tend to be instrumental variants of neorealism that its critics argue failed to predict the collapse of the Soviet Union and the end of the Cold War.

The widespread criticism of neorealism is understandable, but there are good reasons why structural realist approaches of various sorts continue to be hegemonic in security studies and why they still have utility in examining North Korean security behavior.[22] As a research program, no other rival outranks structural realism's ability to specify causality and operationalize variables for empirical testing. Structural realism's clarity and ease of employment make it "user-friendly," though even many realists find the neorealist variant deficient empirically.[23]

My approach to North Korea's security policy, "mercantile realism," is as systemic and materialist as the neorealist variety. As a structural realist analysis, it takes for given that North Korea is concerned with survival and acts calculatingly to preserve and, if possible, enhance its security and power. However, unlike neorealists, I assume a North Korea that is capable of discriminating between the *possibility* and the *probability* of war and devising a strategy that balances the short-term goal of military deterrence and the long-term goal of maintaining a viable economic base, arguably the foundation of national power.

For neorealists, states are obsessed with identifying dangers to their survival and counteracting them. States balance power, either internally by arms racing or externally by forging military alliances. They consider military preparedness as the only true assurance against potential enemies. From this perspective, it is not surprising that North Korea has increased its military readiness and accelerated its weapons of mass destruction (WMD) programs in the post–Cold War era because North Korea has lost its ability to externally balance the growing power of South Korea and its allies.[24] Judging by its paranoid and bellicose rhetoric and obsessive military preparedness, North Korea appears to be the very model of a neorealist state.

However, neorealism has had problems dealing with the realities of the post–Cold War world, most notably, the behavior of Japan and Germany. If states in fact balance power and operate by the worst-case assumption undergirding neorealism, as Kenneth Waltz and John Mearsheimer predict, Japan and Germany should be rearming to their full potential and acquiring nuclear weapons to balance the United States, the sole military superpower in the current world system.[25]

Constructivists and liberal institutionalists have been critical of neorealism's failings, but other realists have also questioned neorealism's core assumptions. For example, Stephen M. Walt finds that states actually balance "threat," not "power."[26] And, as Stephen Brooks contends, states do not always act according to the worst-case assumption.[27] States respond to external threat only when the threat is not just a matter of possibility but when the threat becomes more likely to be real.[28]

The assumption that states make security policy decisions on the probability of conflict, as opposed to the possibility of conflict, fits better with reality. States in the real world often have the discretion to look beyond their immediate military security and perform cost-benefit calculations about the long-term consequences of their actions. This view is consistent with the "bandwagoning" behavior of Japan and Germany in the post–Cold War era and evidence presented by liberals that democracies do not war against other democracies.[29] It is also consistent with the constructivist observation that shared understandings, norms, and identity influence the likelihood of interstate war.[30]

It is also more "real" in that it conforms to the everyday reality that states trade off a degree of military readiness if the potential net gain in economic capacity is substantial relative to the probability of military defeat. Neorealists unduly prioritize security at the expense of power, which derives from military as well as economic resources.[31] I am not arguing that the emphasis should be on economic capacity and not on military preparedness: What is important is the tradeoff between the two. As Brooks argues, a state may decide to trade off some degree of military readiness when the potential economic gains that enhance its long-term power base are significant compared to the likelihood of military defeat. The Soviet Union under Mikhail Gorbachev attempting to engage the West is a dramatic example of this calculation in practice. Could North Korea turn out to be another?

To be sure, military readiness and economic capacity are not always incompatible. However, in the long run, there is a tradeoff between guns and butter.[32] All things being equal, this tradeoff should be most acute in nonmarket economies, such as the defunct Soviet Union and North Korea, where price signals do not operate. It should also be the case with economically constrained states, again, such as the old Soviet Union and North Korea, where investment capital is scarce. In contrast, wealthy capitalist countries of the Organization for Economic Cooperation and Development (OECD), such as the United States, South Korea, and Japan, do not have to worry about this tradeoff *as much* because there may be market-conforming synergies or positive externalities associated with defense preparedness.

A MERCANTILE REALIST ACCOUNT OF NORTH KOREAN SECURITY POLICY

How does mercantile realism's account of post–Cold War North Korean security policy differ from the neorealist one? First, let us examine what a neorealist would say about North Korean security policy.

A neorealist would argue that the end of the Cold War left North Korea with no choice but to internally counteract the sharp deterioration of the external balance of power.[33] North Korea's nuclear and ballistic missiles programs as well as its steady buildup of conventional military capabilities are the inevitable results of this compensating act. Some analysts might add that North Korea's economic collapse is also a logical outcome of internal balancing and has forced Pyongyang to engage in the risky enterprise of trying to extort economic aid from the United States, South Korea, and Japan.

Indeed, analysts looking through a neorealist lens would argue that the chance of North Korea giving up its nuclear weapons and ballistic missiles capabilities is small.[34] Also small is the likelihood of North Korea giving up its brinkmanship diplomacy and use of anti-state terrorism.[35] The United States, South Korea, and Japan then would have to contend with a high probability that North Korea is not really trying to trade its nuclear and ballistic missiles capabilities for economic assistance but only trying to buy time and acquire resources to perfect its WMD capabilities.

Although there are similarities to the neorealist account on certain points, mercantile realism's explanation of North Korea's post–Cold War security policy would focus on North Korea's assessment of the tradeoffs between immediate security and economic power. A mercantile realist account might begin with the collapse of the Soviet Union when North Korea was faced with not only the loss of a superpower ally but the loss of economic subsidies and access to Eastern European "markets." In order to compensate for this calamity, mercantile realism would argue that North Korea channeled its dwindling resources to it nascent nuclear energy and ballistic missiles programs that have not just a military justification but an economic rationale. Indeed, some contend that the North Korean nuclear program is not just a weapons program but an energy program intended to give North Korea long-term, autonomous power-generation capability.[36] Also, North Korea's ballistic missiles program is a vital cash cow for Pyongyang, generating badly needed income from the sale of missile parts and technology to countries such as Iran, Syria, Iraq, and Libya.[37]

At the same time, taking advantage of conciliatory overtures by the United States, South Korea, and Japan during the late 1980s and the early 1990s, North Korea tried to obtain economic resources from the West in exchange for engaging in confidence and security-building measures.[38] When these resources were slow in coming, Pyongyang abandoned the confidence and security-building process, only to collide with the United States over its expanding WMD capabilities. However, by adroitly mixing threats and accommodations, North Korea has been able to play its nuclear and ballistic missile cards to extract significant economic resources from the United States, South Korea, and Japan. Given the proven leverage of these cards in obtaining "goodies" such as the Agreed Framework, it is possible that North Korea would continue to bargain with the West, ultimately exchanging a significant portion of its nuclear and ballistic missiles resources for sufficient economic resources to rehabilitate its dilapidated economy.

A convinced neorealist would no doubt reject this interpretation, though not all aspects of the account. The fact that North Korea's economic collapse in the 1990s is in large part the result of Pyongyang's massive expenditure on military preparedness is common knowledge and indisputable.[39] No one would question that North Korea has been facing a stark tradeoff between short-term military security and long-term economic survival. Hence, the contention that North Korea has had every reason to revitalize its economic capacity should not be controversial. However, the assertion that North Korea's perception of the probability of South Korea or the United States or

Japan or all or any combination of them attacking North Korea has been tolerably low for Pyongyang to bargain away its military assets will meet strong neorealist skepticism. Nonetheless, despite North Korea's vitriolic propaganda to the contrary, evidence is there to support the contention.

PYONGYANG'S THREAT PERCEPTION

It must be kept in mind that, as the Cold War was coming to an end, North Korea was the recipient of conciliatory gestures from the United States and South Korea. It may come as a surprise to some, but it was Ronald Reagan's White House, not Bill Clinton's, that first probed for opening with North Korea. With the winding down of the Cold War and strategic transformation taking place throughout the world, the Reagan administration recognized that Pyongyang's increasing isolation was a dangerous destabilizing factor in Northeast Asia and launched what was termed a "modest initiative" to start a dialogue with North Korea. President Reagan authorized the State Department in the fall of 1988 to hold substantive discussion with North Korean representatives in neutral settings and allow nongovernmental visits from North Koreans in the areas of academics, culture, sports, and few others. His administration also ended the almost total ban on commercial and financial transactions with North Korea by allowing certain exports on a case-by-case basis.[40]

President George H. W. Bush continued the carefully calibrated diplomatic probe and, during his administration, a high-level official meeting between the United States and North Korea took place when Undersecretary of State Arnold Kanter met Korean Worker's Party (KWP) Secretary Kim Yong Sun in January of 1992. This meeting was in support of an earlier diplomatic initiative launched by South Korean President Roh Tae Woo to ease tensions and promote peace and stability on the Korean peninsula.

The South Korean initiative resulted in the North-South Agreement on Reconciliation, Nonaggression, Exchanges, and Cooperation and the Declaration on the Denuclearization of the Korean Peninsula. The former called for the establishment of four joint commissions to facilitate reconciliation and nonaggression between Pyongyang and Seoul whereas the latter forbade both sides to test, manufacture, produce, receive, possess, store, deploy, or use nuclear weapons and prohibited the possession of nuclear reprocessing and uranium enrichment facilities. The denuclearization declaration also called for the establishment of a procedure for inter-Korean inspection.

However, central to the success of the South Korean overture was the American withdrawal of the forward deployed tactical and theater nuclear weapons in South Korea in late 1991. Also critical was the concomitant issuance of a "negative security guarantee" in the form of a general policy announcement that the United States would not use nuclear weapons against a non-nuclear power unless that country attacked the United States or an American ally and received support from a nuclear power.

These moves by Washington no doubt lowered the risk assessment of war by the North Koreans. They must have helped in persuading Pyongyang to sign the two inter-Korean agreements in December 1991 and, ultimately, a nuclear safeguards agreement with the International Atomic Energy Agency (IAEA) as it had pledged to do in 1985 when acceding to the Nuclear Non-Proliferation Treaty (NPT). In turn, this allowed for IAEA inspections of North Korean nuclear facilities to commence in the spring of 1992.

Of course, for whatever reasons only the North Korean leadership knows for sure, Pyongyang withdrew from the engagement process that resulted in the two agreements and threatened to pull out from the NPT, ultimately leading to a dangerous standoff with the United States. Perhaps North Korea became impatient with the slow pace and meager economic results of engagement; or perhaps it intentionally decided to extort, using nuclear and ballistic missile capabilities, Western economic assistance that was not materializing fast enough for Pyongyang's liking.

Whatever may be the case, the point is this: Though deprived of the Soviet nuclear umbrella and experiencing a rapid economic decline that was adversely impacting its military readiness, North Korea was receiving from the United States and South Korea signals that they had no intention of challenging the status quo on the Korean peninsula.[41] Although there is no way of knowing for sure what Pyongyang is thinking, even if North Korean leaders avail themselves to interviews, there are indications that North Korea has felt safe enough for some time to swap its nuclear and long-range ballistic missile capabilities for Western economic resources. In fact, Pyongyang recently has given tantalizing signals that may indicate that it is beginning to think seriously about making fundamental economic reforms. The success of these reforms would depend on a massive injection of Western capital, which would be made available only if North Korea effectively de-fangs its nuclear and ballistic missiles programs.

RATTLING FOR DOLLARS

Leon V. Sigal's controversial but well-documented account of the North Korean–U.S. nuclear diplomacy leading to the Agreed Framework is consistent with the mercantile realist explanation sketched above.[42] His criticism of

Washington and Seoul's role in the nuclear diplomacy with Pyongyang may be overdrawn, but he builds a detailed case that North Korea has demonstrated its willingness to exchange weapons for economic assistance with the United States, if not so much with South Korea, at least initially.

Sigal insists that North Korea is not hell-bent on acquiring nuclear weapons. He reasons:

> A country determined to make [nuclear] bombs would want to unload spent fuel rods from its nuclear reactor as soon as possible and reprocess them, extracting the plutonium from the rest of the nuclear waste. Yet North Korea has done no reprocessing since 1991. It also delayed discharging spent fuel, at least from the spring of 1993, when the IAEA expected the reactor to be refueled, until May 1994. While it resisted full international inspections, it did permit IAEA inspectors to verify that it was not removing spent fuel from the reactor or reprocessing to give up nuclear-arming in return for American security assurances and political and economic benefits.[43]

Sigal's interpretation is not unproblematic, and there are other possible reasons why North Korea behaved as it did at specific junctures. For example, one critic of Sigal's account cites the Chinese pressure on North Korea could explain why Pyongyang stopped reprocessing in 1991.[44] Or the steady warnings issued by Washington, and later Seoul, could explain its restraint. However, there would not be a clear and definitive neorealist explanation of the nuclear diplomacy as it actually turned out, with North Korea "capping" its nuclear program for the promise of Western engagement. Some neorealists might have predicted at the height of the crisis that North Korea would lash out against the United States and South Korea and possibly even against Japan instead of making a deal. Mercantile realism would have predicted, as one of the most likely possibilities, a calculating Pyongyang regime trying to make a deal with Washington, Seoul, and Tokyo in order to engineer a "soft landing" and rebuild its economic power base.

The missile diplomacy between North Korea and the United States is also consistent with the mercantile realist view of North Korean security policy.[45] Since the early 1990s, North Korea has made it clear that it wishes to trade some aspects of its ballistic missile program for cash. Israel was the first to respond to signals coming out of Pyongyang when it offered North Korea economic assistance in exchange for Pyongyang not selling missiles and missile parts to states hostile to Israel. The deal would have been struck were it not for the pressure the United States put on Israel to forget the deal.

The United States, however, started its own missile diplomacy with North Korea in 1996, two years after the Agreed Framework was signed. Though the story of this negotiation has lacked the drama of the nuclear diplomacy, it had a moment of high anxiety when North Korea test-fired a Taepodong-I missile, which reached the stratosphere over the Japanese home islands in August 1998. Although the missile diplomacy has not yet led to a KEDO-style[46] fix, the Taepodong launch has refocused Washington and Tokyo's attention on Pyongyang's long-standing willingness to trade its missile capabilities for economic compensation.

Before time ran out on the Clinton administration, Washington and Pyongyang were negotiating an understanding that would limit all North Korean missile systems, including the Taepodong missile.[47] Some argue, perhaps too sanguinely, that, were it not for the long and awkward transition between the Clinton and Bush administrations because of the political problems stemming from the close presidential election of 2000, the United States and North Korea could have resolved the missile issue. They argue that this resolution then could have led to normalized relations between Washington and Pyongyang.[48] Although a number of issues remained unresolved, particularly regarding the all crucial compensation and verification agreements, one government official reportedly said, "We got further than we thought was possible on the missile issue."[49] Supposedly, the North Korean government was prepared to pledge not to produce, test, or deploy long-range ballistic missiles and also offered to cease the sale of missiles, and missile components, technology, and know-how to other countries.

PREPARING FOR THE GRAND BARGAIN?

Indeed, in early 2001, North Korea sent out tantalizing signals that may indicate that it is serious about economic reforms entailing a "grand bargain" with the West. To be sure, these signals have not convinced those in Washington, Seoul, and Tokyo who have been most critical about North Korea's propensity for extorting aid by engaging in brinkmanship.[50] Nonetheless, Kim Jong Il has said things and acted in such a manner to give the appearance that a major transformation may be coming in North Korea's strategy of dealing with its economic collapse and security dilemma.

The most notable indicator is Kim Jong Il's visit to China in mid-January 2001. As the Bush administration was being installed in Washington, Kim spent five days in Shanghai, taking in the scope and depth of China's advancement since China opened itself up economically to the West. Accompanied by Zhu Rongji, the pragmatic prime minister of China, Kim toured joint-venture operations of General Motors, a Japanese semiconductor plant, the Shanghai stock exchange, the Pudong high-technology park, and other enterprises.

Later in a meeting with President Jiang Zemin, Kim Jong Il endorsed the market-oriented policies that China adopted in the last twenty years. According to a Chinese foreign ministry spokesman, "Mr. Kim stressed that the big changes that have taken place in China, and Shanghai in particular, since China began its reform and opening-up have proved that the policies pursued by the Chinese Communist Party and people are correct."[51] It should be noted that, during Kim's last visit to Shanghai in 1983, he condemned Deng Xiaoping's fledgling market-oriented reform as a dangerous departure from socialist doctrine.

Perhaps even more telling is the fact that senior military aides—including the KPA chief of staff, Kim Yong Jun—accompanied Kim Jong Il in his Shanghai trip. Some speculate that one of the goals of the Shanghai visit, especially to the Pudong high-technology park, was to impress upon the North Korean military the importance of economic reform.[52] Even without prodding, it is possible that the North Korean military is beginning to see the connection between military modernization and economic reform. For example, before meeting President Clinton in October 2000, Marshal Jo Myong Rok, the First Vice Chairman of the North Korean Defense Commission and the highest-level North Korean official to visit the United States, toured Lucent Technologies and other high-technology concerns in Silicon Valley.[53]

Furthermore, Radio Pyongyang, a news outlet accessible to ordinary North Koreans, gave a detailed report of Kim Jong Il's Shanghai visit.[54] It gave account of Kim's purported amazement at the "cataclysmic change" in modern Shanghai. While the report did not mention anything about the need for fundamental reform, it may be another step in preparing the North Korean people for more drastic economic changes to come.

Since 1998, the North Korean media have been saying much about building a "kangsong taeguk [powerful and prosperous state]" where being a "kyongche taeguk [economic superpower]" is a crucial element.[55] To be sure, the 1999 New Year's Joint Editorial gave no indication of any fundamental economic reform: The "military-first" rhetoric still prevailed, requiring the people to "tighten their belts."[56] However, the tone of this year's joint editorial was quite different.

In fact, in a series of editorials in January 2001, North Korean media began to give new emphasis to the economy. For example, on January 4, *Rodong Sinmun* blasted "the old backward way of thinking" among party cadres. It said, "In the new millennium when we require new measurements to approach our problems, we need to resort to new ways of thinking to solve them."[57] And a January 16 editorial said, in effect, the way to fulfill the "military-first" policy was now through building economic strength.[58]

In these editorials, the North Korean media records Kim Jong Il as using terms such as "saesidaeui yogu [the demand of a new age]," "ilsin [renovation]," "kyolchongjok chonhwan [a decisive change]," and "saeroun hyoksin [new innovation]." Political slogans such as "the March of the Red Banner of Socialism" and "the military-first revolutionary line" have not disappeared, but these editorials perhaps sound a new note that signals North Korea is now serious about rehabilitating the economy and improving relations with the West.[59]

When taken with the fact that, since the landmark June 2000 inter-Korean summit, the North Koreans have signed some practical agreements on economic cooperation with South Korea, these words may not be completely empty.[60] Of course, it is hard to imagine what Kim Jong Il might have meant when he remarked to visiting Secretary of State Albright that he is interested in the "Swedish model." Nonetheless, these agreements have led to some concrete steps, the most significant of these being the contract that Pyongyang signed with Hyundai to construct an industrial park that would encourage investment by small- and medium-sized Western firms.

Of course, the modus operandi of the North Koreans being what it is, the establishment of the industrial park has been delayed by a dispute over the proposed location: the North Koreans have a preference for Shinuiju over the Haeju district, despite the latter's greater business logic. However, as Marcus Noland notes in chapter 6, the announcement in August 2000 that the facility would be located at Kaesong would seem to suggest that economic rationality is beginning to take precedence over other calculations.

CONCLUSION

Skeptics might argue that a leap of faith is required to accept that Pyongyang's perception of threat from Washington and Seoul has been low enough for North Korea to risk exchanging its nuclear and ballistic missiles capabilities for Western resources needed for a major economic reform. This may be so, but the leap is no longer than the neorealist one that North Korea bases its security policy on the worst-case scenario and gives no regard to the economy.

To the extent that North Korea has dithered about engaging the West, the hesitation appears to be largely a function of the North Korean leadership's concern about internal security. No doubt, North Korean elites worry that economic engagement, if not carefully managed, could unleash internal disturbances capable of undermining the regime. Nonetheless, a Chinese-type of opening to the West appears to have much attraction for the North Korean leadership, and Kim Jong Il's Shanghai tour in early 2001 may portend a more decisive step toward reform and engagement.

Of course, as noted earlier, the current administration in Washington, now on a war footing, is much more skeptical than its predecessor as well as the Kim Dae Jung administration about North Korea's intentions.[61] In fact, the belief that North Korea is untrustworthy is a central justification for President George W. Bush's National Missile Defense (NMD) initiative. A hostile and aggressive Washington would obviously change Pyongyang's security calculation. Nonetheless, even as it is dealing with a world remade by the events of September 11, 2001, the Bush administration appears to be taking up the engagement policy where the Clinton administration left it. In early June 2001, after a six-month policy review, the administration announced that it is ready to resume negotiations with Pyongyang on a broad range of issues, including WMD and their delivery systems, as well as conventional weapons. The "war on terrorism" appears not to have changed this policy stance.

No doubt the Bush administration, now battle-tested in Afghanistan and its "threat credibility" very high, will be more demanding and exacting than the Clinton administration in its negotiations with North Korea. However, it is unlikely that President Bush will abandon the engagement policy that has its beginnings in President Reagan's and his father's administrations.[62] As with their predecessors, President Bush and his advisers no doubt will try to preserve the status quo in Northeast Asia by continuing to guarantee the security of a Cold War ally, Japan, and reassure a Cold War adversary, China, through a multifaceted engagement policy. This is consistent with a grand strategy that seeks the maintenance of America's primacy in the post–Cold War international system.[63] In light of this strategy, as well as the need to maintain an international "coalition against terrorism," it makes sense that the United States should show restraint in dealing with North Korea. The restraint signals to Tokyo that Washington is being sensitive to the Japanese fear of being dragged into a confrontation with Pyongyang and comforts Beijing that it is unnecessary to balance against the United States.[64]

Of course, North Korea may play hard to get, particularly with the United States preoccupied with the war on terrorism. Furthermore, it may not be willing to give up every scrap of its nuclear weapons and ballistic missile resources. In fact, it may attempt to hide enough residual capacity to keep the world wondering about a handful of secreted bombs and rockets. It may also try to compensate for the lost or diminished deterrent value of the nuclear and ballistic missile programs by building more chemical and biological weapons and increasing the material resources and readiness of its conventional forces. However, as long as it feels that the long-term economic benefit outweighs the short-term military risk, it should give up most, if not all, nuclear and ballistic missile capabilities as well as other WMD resources if pressed to bargain.

If the modality of mercantile realism is applicable to North Korean security behavior, then, the logical policy course for the United States, South Korea, and Japan is more engagement, assuming that *peace* and *stability* on the Korean peninsula are the overriding goals. The mercantile realist logic supports those officials and analysts, for their own varied reasons, who want to make a "grand bargain" with North Korea.[65]

Engagement means, however, strengthening North Korea's long-term economic capacity. After all, North Korea's motive for the exchange is the expectation that Western economic engagement will strengthen its economic base, a key element of its national power. Consequently, Korea may not be reunified anytime soon if that is still the goal of any interested party, including the two Koreas. Worse, from a humanitarian point of view, North Korea would likely remain an Orwellian nightmare that disturbs the West's conscience.

From a realist point of view, the most troublesome possibility for the United States, South Korea, and Japan is that engagement could lead to a revitalized adversary with a strong enough economy that rekindles the dream of reunifying Korea under Kimilsungism. Some analysts suggest that North Korea's economic recovery through engagement could bring the country into a responsible and interdependent relationship with the West.[66] Indeed, creating that kind of "interdependence" should be the prudent goal of the United States, South Korea, and Japan. Nonetheless, the danger exists that North Korea could successfully pull off a Chinese-style reform that preserves the hardliners and strengthens the military industrial base of the KPA. In fact, mercantile realism would predict this outcome as a distinct possibility given the logic of the theory.

A limited "regime maintenance" type of engagement, which appears to be Pyongyang's preferred choice, is less risky for Washington, Seoul, and Tokyo. In this course of action, North Korea gives up the most dangerous elements of its nuclear and ballistic missiles program for enough economic resources from the West to make survival possible for the North Korean leadership. However, in this kind of limited opening, not only the continuing survival of a Stalinist regime pricks the conscience of those in the West but also the specter of undernourished, if no longer starving, children of the hermit kingdom.

NOTES

1. Arthur Waley, *The Analects of Confucius* (London: Allen and Unwin, 1938).
2. "Let Us Accelerate the General Onward March for Building an Economic Power," *Rodong Sinmun*, January 16, 2001, in *FBIS*, January 16, 2001.
3. Elaine Sciolino, "Colin L. Powell: Ultimate Insider with Star Power," *New York Times*, January 16, 2001; Boo Hyung-Kwon, "Ripple of Armitage's Comment on

'Sunshine Policy,'" *Tong-a Ilbo*, January 29, 2001; Howard W. French, "Signs of Uneasiness in Seoul over Change at White House," *New York Times*, February 19, 2001; and David E. Sanger, "Bush Tells Seoul Talks with North Won't Resume Now," *New York Times*, March 8, 2001.

4. By "standard neorealism" I mean the neorealism of Kenneth N. Waltz in *Theory of International Politics* (New York: Random House, 1979) and those who closely adhere to his formulation of realism; for example, John Mearsheimer, "Back to the Future: Instability in Europe after the Cold War," *International Security* 15, 1 (summer 1990): 5–56.

5. See Waltz's predictions about nuclear weapons proliferation in his article, "The Emerging Structure of International Politics," *International Security* 18, 2 (fall 1993): 44–79.

6. Arguing that the United States should force North Korea to choose between cooperation and hostility, Robert A. Manning states that time has allowed North Korea "to develop new longer-range ballistic missiles, and thus the capacity for nuclear blackmail." See "The Enigma of the North," *The Wilson Quarterly* 23, 3 (summer 1999): 76.

7. William J. Taylor Jr., argues, "Engaging North Korea is akin to hugging a rattlesnake." See his chapter, "The Korean Peninsula at the Crossroads: Which Way?" in Wonmo Dong, ed., *The Two Koreas and the United States: Issues of Peace, Security, and Economic Cooperation* (Armonk, NY: M. E. Sharp, 2000), 225.

8. For example, Norman D. Levin, "Feel Their Pain (If You Like), But Watch Their Actions," *Survival* 38, 4 (winter 1996/1997): 41.

9. Henry Sokolski, a former deputy assistant secretary of defense during the Reagan and Bush administrations, stated before the House Armed Services Committee on March 24, 1994, that "the only sure way to defuse the North Korean strategic threat is to *defuse* the regime." Cited by Leon V. Sigal, *Disarming Strangers: Nuclear Diplomacy with North Korea* (Princeton, NJ: Princeton University Press, 1998), 240.

10. By "mercantile realism" I mean a strain of realist logic following Robert Gilpin in *War and Change in World Politics* (Cambridge: Cambridge University Press, 1981). Whereas Waltzian realism views the pursuit of power as secondary to that of security, Gilpin's realism regards rational states as ultimately seeking to increase the economic resources under their control, subject to the constraints of providing for short-term military security. See also Eric Heginbotham and Richard Samuels, "Mercantile Realism and Japanese Foreign Policy," *International Security* 22, 4 (spring 1998): 171–203. They argue that Japan's security policy is organized around the goal of advancing its techno-economic position. Calling their theoretical approach "mercantile realism," Heginbotham and Samuels seek to explain the "Japanese anomaly" in the neorealist view of the world.

11. It is important to note that there is no single theory of realism. Realism is a research program with different strands of thoughts. For a thorough discussion of the diversity of theorizing that exist in realism, see Stephen G. Brooks, "Dueling Realisms," *International Organizations* 51, 3 (summer 1997): 445–77; also Daniel Deudney, "Dividing Realism: Structural Realism versus Security Materialism on Nuclear Security and Proliferation," *Security Studies* 2, 3/4 (spring/summer 1993): 7–36.

12. As it will be discussed later, although constructivism offers an alternative unit-level perspective, the lack of reliable data about North Korea severely limits its usefulness in analyzing North Korean security. And for obvious reasons, liberal institutionalism offers even less utility.

13. What is crucial is not so much the hierarchy of objectives between security and economic power but "the mix and the trade-offs of objectives." Gilpin, *War and Change in World Politics*, 22.

14. Brooks argues that this distinction between "probability" and "possibility" distinguishes Gilpin's realism from standard neorealism and also "defensive realism" from "aggressive realism."

15. From the perspective of the United States, South Korea, and Japan, what is important is eliminating "significant" North Korean nuclear weapons capability. I agree with former congressman Stephen Solarz who argues, "A single North Korean bomb will not threaten global stability. Many North Korean bombs will." Stephen J. Solarz, "Next of Kim," *The New Republic*, August 8, 1994, 27. See also the argument for abiding North Korea "going just a little nuclear" in Michael J. Mazarr, "Going Just a Little Nuclear," *International Security* 20, 2 (fall 1995): 92–122.

16. For a contrasting strategy, see Samuel S. Kim, "In Search of a Theory of North Korean Foreign Policy," in Samuel S. Kim, ed., *North Korean Foreign Relations in the Post–Cold War Era* (Oxford: Oxford University Press, 1998), 3–26. Kim calls for a greater focus on ideational and cultural variables in analyzing North Korea's foreign policy behavior.

17. Quoted by Marcus Noland in "The Economic Situation in North Korea," Dong, ed., *The Two Koreas and the United States,* 19.

18. Sang Hoon Park, "North Korea and the Challenge to the U.S.-South Korean Alliance," *Survival* 36, 2 (summer 1994).

19. In addition to Taylor's "The Korean Peninsula at the Crossroads" and Levin's "Feel Their Pain (If You Like), But Watch Their Actions," see Chuck Downs, *Over the Line: North Korea's Negotiating Strategy* (Washington, D.C.: The AEI Press, 1999); Fred C. Ikle, "U.S. Folly May Start Another Korean War," *Wall Street Journal*, October 12, 1998; Karen E. House, "Let North Korea Collapse," *Wall Street Journal*, February 21, 1997; and Nicholas Eberstadt, "Hastening Korean Unification," *Foreign Affairs* 72, 2 (March-April 1997): 77–92.

20. For example, Victor D. Cha, "Is There Still a Rational North Korean Option for War?" *Security Dialogue* 29, 4(1998): 477–90. Cha criticizes those who characterize North Korea as irrational; nonetheless, he makes the argument that, to avoid being devoured by the South, the North might launch a "preventive war." In my view, even a preventive war (as specified by Cha) would be *ipso facto* irrational given the virtual certainty of North Korea's defeat. Why would North Korea choose swift and certain annihilation over the *possibility* of military defeat? Cha argues that North Korea could succumb to the "double-or-nothing" logic of a losing gambler, but how rational is a "double-or-nothing" gambit given the certainty of loss?

21. See Denny Roy, "North Korea as an Alienated State," *Survival* 38, 4 (winter 1996/1997): 22–36 and Selig S. Harrison, "Time to Leave Korea?" *Foreign Affairs* 80, 2 (March-April 2001): 62–78. See also, Leon V. Sigal, "Who Is Fighting Peace in

Korea? An Undiplomatic History," *World Policy Journal* 14, 2 (summer 1997): 44–58 and Bruce Cumings, "Toward a Comprehensive Settlement of the Korea Problem," *Current History* 98, 632 (December 1999): 403–8.

22. Attacks against contemporary realism tend to ignore its diversity. As pointed out earlier, there are many strains of structural realism besides Waltzian neorealism.

23. For example, finding unrealistic the neorealist assumption about the central role that the distribution of military capabilities have on international relations, one group of realists has emphasized the impact that technology can have on conflict. See George Quester, *Offense and Defense in the International System* (New York: John Wiley and Sons, 1977); more recently, Charles Glaser, "Realists as Optimists: Cooperation as Self-Help," *International Security* 19, 3 (winter 1994/1995): 50–90. Another group emphasizes geography. For example, Robert S. Ross, "The Geography of the Peace: East Asia in the Twenty-First Century," *International Security* 23, 4 (spring 1999): 81–118.

24. For this line of reasoning, see David Kang, "Rethinking North Korea," *Asian Survey* 35, 3 (March 1995): 253–67.

25. Waltz, "The Emerging Structure of International Politics" and Mearsheimer, "Back to the Future."

26. Stephen M. Walt, *The Origins of Alliance* (Ithaca, NY: Cornell University Press, 1987) and "Alliance Formation and the Balance of World Power," *International Security* 9, 4 (spring 1985): 208–47.

27. Brooks, "Dueling Realisms."

28. In criticizing the worst-case assumption of neorealism, Brooks point out "although neorealists are leading critics of classical realist explanations of international behavior predicated on particular conception of human nature, the internal coherence of the neorealist framework itself depends fundamentally on the psychological assumption that actors are characteristically highly fearful." Brooks, "Dueling Realisms," 449.

29. On "democratic peace," see Bruce Russett, *Grasping the Democratic Peace: Principles for a Post–Cold War World* (Princeton: Princeton University Press, 1993).

30. Alexander Wendt, "Anarchy Is What States Make of It: The Social Construction of Power Politics," *International Organization* 46, 2 (spring 1992): 391–425. Specifically on Germany and Japan, see Thomas U. Berger, "Unsheathing the Sword? Germany and Japan's Fractured Political-Military Cultures and the Problem of Burden Sharing," *World Affairs* 158 (spring 1996): 174–91.

31. Brooks argues that broadening the concept of security to include economic factors simply cannot be accomplished within the neorealist framework because that would require dismantling the underlying assumptions (e.g., worst-case focus) that provide neorealism with its internal coherence. Brooks, "Dueling Realisms," 453.

32. In addition to Gilpin's *War and Change in World Politics*, see also Paul Kennedy *Rise and Fall of the Great Powers: Economic Change and Military Conflict from 1500 to 2000* (New York: Random House, 1987).

33. See David Kang's "North Korea: Deterrence through Danger," in Muthiah Alagapa, *Asian Security Practice: Material and Ideational Influences* (Stanford, CA: Stanford University Press, 1998), 234–63. Tracing North Korea's security behavior

from its founding, Kang argues that Pyongyang has acted rationally and its security policy is consistent with the predictions of neorealism. He contends that North Korea is currently practicing deterrence through "danger" (engaging in state-sponsored terrorism and making threats) against increasingly powerful South Korea. See also his earlier work, "Rethinking North Korea."

34. Andrew Mack also argues that North Korea is unlikely to give up nuclear arming, as "states are taken more seriously as players in the world of geopolitics when they are nuclear-armed." See his "The Nuclear Crisis on the Korean Peninsula," *Asian Survey* 33, 4 (April 1993): 343.

35. D. Kang, "North Korea: Deterrence through Danger," 262-3.

36. For example, Vladimir D. Andrianov writes, "It is important to note that the lack of sufficient domestic energy sources and the heavy dependence on energy imports predetermine the importance of the development of the atomic energy sector in North Korea." See his "Economic Aspects of the North Korean Nuclear Program," in James Clay Moltz and Alexandre Y. Mansourov, eds., *The North Korean Nuclear Program: Security, Strategy, and New Perspectives from Russia* (New York and London, Routledge, 2000), 41–50.

37. Scott Snyder, "Pyongyang's Pressure," *The Washington Quarterly* 23, 3 (summer 2000): 163.

38. I am referring to basically two things: first, Ronald Reagan's "modest initiative" to start a dialogue with North Korea, a process that George H. W. Bush continued during his presidency; second, South Korean President Roh Tae Woo's diplomatic initiative that led to the signing of in the Agreement on Reconciliation, Nonaggression, Exchanges, and Cooperation and the Declaration on the Denuclearization of the Korean Peninsula. However, also relevant is the attempt by Prime Minister Kaifu Toshiki, guided by Kanemaru Shin, to begin normalization talks between Japan and North Korea in early 1991.

39. For a balanced analysis of and prognosis for the North Korean economy, see Marcus Noland, "Why North Korea Will Muddle Through," *Foreign Affairs* 76, 4: 105–18. See also his "The Economic Situation in North Korea" and chapter 6.

40. Testimony of Mark Minton, Director of the Office of Korean Affairs, before the Senate Foreign Relations Committee, Subcommittee on East Asian and Pacific Affairs, Washington, D.C., September 12, 1996.

41. Some analysts such as Michael Mazarr and Leon Sigal would argue that Seoul and Washington's decision to resume a postponed massive military exercise, "Team Spirit," in 1993 constituted a war threat to Pyongyang. However, the *resumption* was a response to the slowness of North Korea in carrying out the provisions of the inter-Korean nuclear agreement. The fact is, the exercise was carried out every year since 1986 until President Bush canceled it in 1992 as a confidence-building measure. See Mazarr, "Going Just a Little Nuclear," 112, and Sigal, *Disarming Strangers*, 46–50.

42. See Mazarr, "Going Just a Little Nuclear," 112, and Sigal, *Disarming Strangers*.

43. Sigal, *Disarming Strangers*, 6.

44. See Daniel Drezner's skeptical book review of Sigal's *Disarming Strangers* in *American Political Science Review* 92, 3: 757–8.

45. Sigal's interpretation of North Korea's missile diplomacy can be found in "Negotiating an End to North Korea's Missile-Making," *Arms Control Today* 30, 5 (June 2000): 3–7. His analysis of the missile diplomacy parallels his explanation of the nuclear diplomacy.

46. KEDO stands for Korean Peninsula Energy Development Organization. Its executive board members include the United States, South Korea, Japan, and the EU. The Agreed Framework calls for KEDO to supply North Korea with two one thousand megawatt proliferation-resistant light-water reactors (costing about $4.5 billion and to be financed by South Korea and Japan) and five hundred thousand tons of heavy fuel oil per year until the completion of the first reactor. In return, North Korea agreed to close down its existing reactor at Yongbyon. There is much speculation among policy analysts whether a similar swap agreement could be reached with the North Koreans on the missile issue.

47. See Joel Wit, "The United States and North Korea," *Brookings Policy Brief* 74, March 2001, 6.

48. Author's interviews with former Clinton administration officials. Washington, D.C., March 2001.

49. Michael R. Gordon, "How Politics Sank Accord on Missiles with North Korea," *New York Times*, March 6, 2001.

50. Referring to Kim Jong Il's January 2001 visit to Shanghai where he praised China's brand of market-oriented economic strategy, Nicholas Eberstadt cautions that the visit "may be part of the dance that the North Korean side calculates it needs to do in order to receive aid [from China]." Quoted in Nayan Chanda, "Kim Flirts with Chinese Reform," *Far Eastern Economic Review*, February 8, 2001.

51. Erik Eckholm, "North Korean Placed Focus on Business in China Visit," *New York Times*, January 21, 2001.

52. For example, Aidan Foster-Carter, "Great Thespian: Kim Jong-il's Political Theater," *Asia Times Online*, January 26, 2001, at www.atimes.com/koreas/CA26Dg01.html (accessed February 10, 2001).

53. *Chosun Ilbo*, October 9, 2000.

54. Foster-Carter, "Great Thespian."

55. *Rodong Sinmun*, August 22, 1998.

56. "Let Us Glorify This Year as a Great Year That Will Become a Turning Point in Building a Powerful State," New Year's Joint Editorial read on Korean Central Broadcasting Station, January 1, 1999, in *FBIS*, January 3, 1999.

57. *Rodong Sinmun*, January 4, 2001.

58. Chanda, "Kim Flirts with Chinese Reform."

59. See Yu Yong-ku, "Kim Chong-il's Remarks" *Seoul Chungang Ilbo*, January 15, 2001, in *FBIS*, January 15, 2001.

60. The agreements established the legal framework for South Korean investment in North Korea.

61. As they were coming into office, the foreign policy principals of the new Bush administration talked tough about North Korea. For example, Secretary of State Colin Powell during his confirmation hearing indicated that the administration would seek

strict reciprocity from North Korea. See *Chosun Ilbo*, January 18, 2001. See also Sciolino, "Colin L. Powell."

62. Apparently, during the Bush administration's North Korea policy review process, former President George H. W. Bush sent to the president through his aides a memo forcefully arguing the need to reopen negotiations with North Korea. See Jane Perlez, "Fatherly Advice to the President on North Korea," *New York Times*, June 10, 2001.

63. No U.S. administration has ever stated the goal of preventing other states from challenging the United States. However, the strategy of maintaining American primacy was clearly evident in the draft version of Defense Planning Guidance (DPG), which was leaked to the press in 1992. Zalmay Khalilzad, the Assistant Undersecretary of Defense for Policy Planning when DPG was written, has stated that the United States would not want Germany and Japan to be able to conduct expeditionary wars. See his "Losing the Moment? The United States and the World after the Cold War" in Brad Roberts, ed., *Order and Disorder after the Cold War* (Cambridge, MA: The MIT Press, 1995), 57–77. See also the assessment of Barry R. Posen and Andrew L. Ross, "Competing Visions for U.S. Grand Strategy," *International Security* 21, 3 (winter 1996-1997): 44–50 and Michael Mastanduno, "Preserving the Unipolar Moment: Realist Theories and U.S. Grand Strategy after the Cold War," *International Security* 21, 4 (spring 1997): 49–88, especially 51.

64. The elaboration of this argument is found in C. S. Eliot Kang, "North Korea and the U.S. Grand Strategy," *Comparative Strategy* 20, 1: 25–43.

65. For example, Robert A. Manning, "The United States and the Endgame in Korea: Assessment, Scenarios, and Implications," *Asian Survey* 37, 7 (July 1997): 597–608.

66. Kongdan Oh and Ralph Hassig, "North Korea between Collapse and Reform," *Asian Survey* 39, 2 (March-April 1999): 288.

8

Assessing the North Korean Threat: The Logic of Preemption, Prevention, and Engagement

Victor D. Cha

Viewed through the lens of Korean security, the terrorist attacks of September 11, 2001, did little to make the enigmatic nature of the Democratic Peoples' Republic of Korea (DPRK or North Korea) any more intelligible. The United States focused with laser-beam intensity on the war against terrorism as the premier national security problem, shifting its attention away from "rogue regimes" like the DPRK. While this reprieve from scrutiny might have been taken as an opportunity, Pyongyang's statements of condolence for the victims but lack of any significant proactive support for the anti-terror campaign validated neither the skeptics nor supporters' claims about the significance of the DPRK's recent opening. Indeed, September 11 only reinforced the unresolved debates that raged about the regime's desires and intentions in the eighteen months preceding the terrorist attacks. The DPRK's diplomatic offensive in 2000 and 2001, starting with the normalization of relations with a number of European countries, followed by the June 2000 inter-Korean summit, DPRK special envoy General Jo Myong Nnok's visit to Washington (August 2000), and Secretary Albright's trip to Pyongyang (October 2000), raised more questions about this opaque regime than it answered.[1] Was the DPRK truly in reform mode after a long period of uncertainty dating back to Kim Il Sung's death in 1994? Did recent events suggest a "new" Kim Jong Il who had been fundamentally misunderstood by the outside world? Was the path of engagement undertaken by the United States, the Republic of Korea (ROK or South Korea), and Japan since 1993 validated by these apparent changes? Finally (and most importantly), what, if any, is the larger theory of influence behind American engagement with the DPRK?

Policy makers in Washington, Seoul, and Tokyo still wrestle over these questions and dichotomous images of North Korea. At the core of these debates are differing assessments of whether the conditions for effective engagement are present in the DPRK case. Although the Bush administration intends to resume dialogue with North Korea, there is a healthy dose of skepticism, expressed at the highest levels, about the ultimate success of this process. According to this view, one needs to distinguish between tactics and intentions in assessing recent DPRK behavior. There is no denying that Pyongyang's opening contacts with the outside world reflect a change in diplomatic tactics for the purpose of gaining the food and economic aid necessary to keep the debilitated regime afloat. However, there is nothing in DPRK behavior (e.g., drawdowns in its threatening military posture) thus far consonant with or indicative of a deeper and more fundamental change in the nature of the regime and its intentions. Hence engagement is at best ill-advised and at worst dangerous as it will revive a regime still bent on overturning the status quo on the peninsula.

By contrast, those in Seoul favoring engagement agree that recent DPRK behavior represents tactical changes for the purpose of regime survival, but they believe that such behavior in fact reflects a fundamental change in Pyongyang's intentions (with further concessions by the North awaiting larger carrots from the West). Those less willing to accept the "true believer" propositions still welcome the mere tactical changes in DPRK behavior because these changes, in conjunction with engagement, are seen to eventually result in a positive and peaceful transformation of the regime's character and its intentions.

The dilemma regarding North Korea for the United States and its allies in Seoul and Tokyo is clear: Absent more empirical evidence, this debate about true change in the DPRK's intentions remains unresolved. Nevertheless policy—which is presumably based on some assessment of the regime's intentions—must still be made. "True believers" willing to advocate engagement without concrete evidence are criticized of entering the realm of "theology." Those hardcore skeptics opposed to engagement are criticized for not giving diplomacy a chance. Moreover, the stakes of this policy choice are high, involving nuclear and missile proliferation and the potential for renewed conflict on the peninsula.

This chapter addresses this policy dilemma. It agrees with the skeptics that policy makers would be ill-advised at present to posit major change in DPRK intentions. Absent changes in the military situation on the ground that go beyond the "smile summitry" and political atmospherics of 2000 and 2001, and given the history of DPRK revisionist intentions on the peninsula, it is difficult to assume that the recent tactical warming by Pyongyang carries deeper meaning. However, such skepticism does not preclude engagement as the chosen policy by the United States and its allies. On the contrary, for reasons having to do with the changing nature of the DPRK threat since the end of the Cold War, I argue that the appropriate policy on North Korea—even for "hawks" in Washington, Seoul, and Tokyo—remains engagement.

Three conceptual points substantiate this argument. First, deterrence and robust defense capabilities (i.e., containment) remain the cornerstone of U.S.-ROK-Japan security on the Korean peninsula, and these will remain integral to any new policy vis-à-vis the DPRK. The policy choice is therefore not between containment and some other policy, but how this military capability should be complemented diplomatically. In other words, should the policy be containment-plus-diplomatic isolation (i.e., benign neglect), containment-plus-coercion, or containment-plus-engagement?

Second, there is a hawk rationale for engagement. The three primary "theories" put forward by advocates of engagement have no credibility with hardliners. These are the "insecurity spiral" argument, which basically says we should engage Pyongyang because it is misunderstood; the "collapse" argument, which sees engagement as preventing regime entropy; and the "irrationality" argument, which calls for engagement to create predictability in DPRK behavior.[2] Hawks reject all rationales because: 1.) they do not believe that rogue regimes are reformable (which is the presumed outcome of engagement advocates); 2.) they chafe at the notion of supporting such a morally reprehensible regime; and 3.) engagement (or appeasement) creates moral hazard incentives for other regimes to "act crazy."

This chapter incorporates insight from preemptive war and prospect theory to deduce a preventive defense rationale for engagement.[3] In short, hawks should engage Pyongyang not because the regime is crazy, near collapse, or misunderstood, but because engagement avoids the crystallization of conditions under which Pyongyang could calculate war as a "rational" course of action even if victory were impossible.[4] In other words, the real danger with regard to the DPRK threat is that in spite of an objective military balance unfavorable to the regime, the North could still choose to initiate conflict as a wholly rational policy—that is, that there is still a "rational" option to use force. In this sense, engagement is a form of preventive defense—actions taken by the United States and its allies to prevent the emergence of potentially dangerous and conflictual situations.[5]

Third, engagement remains the "default" policy on the peninsula. Many hardliners may view the preventive defense rationale for engaging the DPRK as merely window-dressing for appeasement. They would argue that we are rewarding this rogue regime for its bad behavior; moreover, engagement-advocates are pursuing this policy for lack of a clear alternative, and without a responsible "exit" strategy. This chapter makes a number of sub-arguments as to why engagement, while gaining a window on the degree of change in

DPRK intentions, is also simultaneously laying the groundwork for punishment if necessary.[6] In this sense, engagement is not in lieu of, but comprises the exit strategy. In short, regardless of whether one is a "hawk" or "dove" on North Korea, the optimal policy is engagement.[7]

THE NATURE OF THE DPRK THREAT

The conventionally argued threats to peace on the Korean peninsula have been the "irrationality" of the DPRK and the potential for regime collapse. The former dimension largely derives from the opacity of the regime and the perceived recklessness and unpredictability of the leadership. In short, North Korea has done "crazy" things in the past, and despite its weakened state, it still possesses the wherewithal (i.e., forward deployed forces, heavy artillery, long-range missiles, and nuclear-biological-chemical [NBC] potential) to do terrible things again. The latter dimension held sway particularly in the early 1990s when the DPRK started to register negative economic growth and revealed the extent of its chronic food and energy shortages. These conditions coupled with the uncertain political transition after the death of Kim Il Sung (1994) raised serious concerns about a Romania-type collapse of the regime, sending ripples of instability throughout the region.[8] However, as regional and military experts have argued, a premeditated all-out assault by North Korea seems unlikely.[9] The American security guarantee to the ROK is not in doubt; Beijing and Moscow do not support aggression by Pyongyang; moreover, the military balance on the peninsula favors the combined U.S.-ROK forces in terms of quality and firepower. In short, the conditions that prompted Kim Il Sung to exploit windows of vulnerability in June 1950 are now tightly shut. A renewal of hostilities would no doubt be bloody; however, in the end it would amount to a U.S.-ROK war-winning exercise that would result in the extinction of the North Korean state.

Regarding the regime collapse scenario, the DPRK survived despite the many premature eulogies written about the regime in the early 1990s, and has "muddled through" largely because no party, including South Korea, wanted to deal with its collapse and expensive absorption. Food aid from China and international relief agencies, and interim fuel sources from the United States kept the regime on "life-support" in a crippled but less ominous state.[10]

The logic of both of these counterarguments to the conventional wisdom are powerful and persuasive. Implicit is the view that North Korean behavior still adheres to a basic sanity in terms of state survival; North Korea is indeed not "crazy," and U.S.-ROK efforts to convey deterrent threats are understood in Pyongyang. The regime collapse scenario, while certainly plausible, lacks the internal and external conditions that would assign it a high probability. Moreover, such a scenario still leaves unanswered the question of what circumstances or actions by Pyongyang might trigger such an event.

I argue that the threat to Korean peace stems neither from the regime's irrationality, collapse, nor even a second DPRK invasion and all-out war. Instead, North Korea could perceive some use of limited force as a rational and optimal choice even when there is little or no hope of victory. The danger is not that the North will commit suicide knowingly, but that it will encounter situations where belligerent "lashing out" is the best and only policy—the unintended consequence of which (given likely U.S. and ROK military responses) is suicide or collapse.

The logic of preemption and prevention suggest conditions under which the recourse to hostility can be a rational act even if objective factors weigh against victory.[11] Preemption occurs when a state perceives aggression by another as imminent and acts first to forestall the impending attack. Preventive action occurs when a state is motivated to attack first, or otherwise suffer increasing inferiority in capabilities vis-à-vis the opponent over time. While preemptive and preventive motivations represent two discrete paths to conflict,[12] they are similar in a number of respects. First, they are motivated by fear more than aggression. Belligerent actions are undertaken largely as a result of closing windows of opportunity or expanding windows of vulnerability brought on by relative power shifts.[13] Second, both are acts of anticipation. The decision to preempt or prevent hinges as much on misperception and images of the adversary as on the objective military situation. Third, both types of belligerency stem from a fundamental dissatisfaction with the status quo. States do an expected-utility calculation in which the costs of the current situation are higher than the costs of change. In the preemptive situation, maintaining the status quo means being the victim of imminent aggression. In the preventive situation, maintaining the status quo means certain inferiority and defeat in the future. In both cases, the expected costs of peace are higher than the potential costs of conflict. Winston Churchill once assessed Japan's 1941 decision to attack at Pearl Harbor as one that "could not be reconciled with reason. . . . But governments and peoples do not always take rational decisions. Sometimes they take mad decisions."[14] However, if any situation is better than the current one, states can rationally choose to fight even when there is little hope of victory.[15]

There is no denying that the North–South Korea summit in June 2000, U.S.-DPRK dialogue during the Clinton administration at the end of 2000, and the improved DPRK–European Union relationship in 2001 have temporarily moved the peninsula beyond the decades of confrontation that defined it. However, as this cooperative phase waned at the end of 2001 and the United

States shifted it primary focus to the war against terrorism, it is not difficult to imagine North Korea succumbing to this preemptive logic of striking first. While fears of an imminent South Korean attack are not a salient preemptive/preventive motivation for Pyongyang today,[16] the yawning deficit in capabilities vis-à-vis the South undoubtedly raises anticipatory fears of extinction-through-absorption. Throughout the first three decades of the Cold War, the two regimes faced off as relative equals with each buttressed by security guarantees from its great-power patrons. From the early 1960s to 1970s, North Korean gross national product (GNP) per capita and conventional military capabilities rivaled if not surpassed that of its southern counterpart.[17] This relative equality enabled each regime to privilege its particular vision of unification, which essentially meant domination of one over the other. Parity also entitled each to legitimize any dialogue with the other as a step toward this ultimate goal of hegemonic unification.

By the 1990s, however, what emerged was an enormous and insurmountable gap between the two countries. Annual 8 percent growth in the ROK (before the financial crisis) versus successive years of 2 through 3 percent negative growth in the North resulted in a four hundred billion dollar southern gross domestic product (GDP) fifteen to twenty times that of the DPRK. Although Pyongyang clings to *juche* (self-reliance) and visions of hegemonic unification, even staunch ideologues like Hwang Jang Yop admitted after defecting in 1997 that a Communist revolution in the South is no longer a viable DPRK objective.[18] In a similar vein, a low-key but very significant event at the September 1998 session of the Supreme People's Assembly (1st session, 10th term) was abolition of the Unification Committee.[19] Propaganda emanating out of Pyongyang under Kim Jong Il, while still promoting strict adherence to "revolutionary traditions," increasingly admits that "existing theories" may not be sufficient to deal with new problems and developments. Russian observers note that among the core principles that have made up the *juche* ideology, emphasis has shifted over the past year from universal "communization" to "self-dependency" as the ultimate revolutionary goal.[20] Moreover, in moments of candor, DPRK propaganda itself acknowledges how national goals have changed. An editorial in the government-run newspaper *Rodong Sinmun* stated bluntly, "The masses' independent demands grow higher ceaselessly with the times as the revolution develops. . . . Should the regime fail to strengthen and develop fast enough to meet the masses' incessantly growing independent demands, the people would turn their back on it and eventually it would collapse."[21] As one expert noted, "[t]hirty years ago a very different verdict on the national strategies of the two Koreas might have been rendered. . . . [T]he North Korean goal of enforcing a Socialist unification upon the South was no mere pipedream."[22] Now, Pyongyang's end game has changed from one of hegemonic unification to basic survival, avoiding collapse, and avoiding dominance by the South, precisely the type of fears behind a preventive lashing-out type action.

THE ABSENCE OF MITIGATING FACTORS

Many of the theoretical factors that mitigate the motivations for striking first are absent in the North. For example, if a state operates with longtime horizons (viewing as temporary a disadvantageous position vis-à-vis the adversary), it can reduce the urgency to act. Internal military buildups or power accretion through new external alliances also reduces the need to deal with widening windows of vulnerability through preemption/prevention. However, the collapse of the USSR has invalidated any Marxist-Leninist notions that, with patience, socialist regimes would eventually witness capitalist countries collapsing over their own contradictions. Power accretion through alliances or internal balancing is not feasible for Pyongyang, given the effective security and economic abandonment by Moscow and Beijing in 1990 and 1992. The North has also been relatively unsuccessful in attempts to drive a wedge in ROK relations with the United States and Japan over the nuclear issue or a peace process on the peninsula. The absence of China and Russia as allies also removes impediments to North Korean contemplation of preventive/preemptive action. The unwritten purpose of alliances on both sides of the demilitarized zone (DMZ) during the Cold War was to restrain the two combatants from entrapping the superpowers into another war as much as supporting them.[23] Such constraints are effectively gone; as one Chinese official observed, "The North Koreans don't listen to us . . . they don't listen to anyone."[24]

The prolonged economic crisis afflicting the ROK economy may marginally raise the North's hopes that it can muddle through; however, any aspirations of closing the gap with the South have been thoroughly erased, the financial downturn notwithstanding. If anything, the aggregate effects of negative economic growth, yearly food shortfalls, energy shortages, and an increasingly confident and militarily growing South Korea have shortened rather than lengthened the North's time horizon.[25] Despite the economic crisis, North Korea's August 1998 provocative missile test, and questions about the Agreed Framework's viability during the Bush transition, the ROK has maintained commitments to be the primary financial backer of light-water reactors for North Korea; it is also the only source of large-scale support to remedy the North's agricultural deficiencies and chronic food shortages. The current atmosphere of rapprochement between the two Koreas may somewhat assuage Pyongyang's anxieties about this dependence (indeed, this may have been a contributing motivation for the North's opening). However, if relations backslide even slightly to their former self, from Pyongyang's vantage point, the prospect of having to rely on its primary rival for future energy and food sustenance would render the status quo an unbearable and losing situation.

In a broader theoretical and historical vein, preemptive/preventive situations have also been ameliorated when the two parties are liberal democracies; when they want to avoid the reputational costs of being branded the aggressor; and when they have defensive-, rather than offense-based, military doctrines.[26] Again, in spite of the DPRK's recent diplomatic overtures to the outside world, longer-term trends in Pyongyang do not hint at any of these conditions. Given past acts of state-sponsored terrorism and rogue acts in violation of international norms, reputational concerns do not appear to factor into Pyongyang's policy calculations, effectively removing any additional stigma attached to lashing out or being perceived as the aggressor. Barring some unforseen internal transformation, North Korea will remain the type of illiberal state that history has shown not to be averse to initiating preventive hostility. And most ominous, the North's forward deployments of artillery, tanks, and personnel along the DMZ—which have not abated despite the recent inter-Korean thaw—reflect a preemption-friendly belief in the offense having the advantage.[27] Moreover, even a benign interpretation of the North's deployments as defensively intended does not mitigate preemptive nor preventive incentives to act. On the contrary, inferior forces deployed offensively (but for defensive reasons) are extremely prone to "use them or lose them" motivations if conflict appears imminent.[28]

Finally, for motivations to strike first to be compelling, there must be a non–status quo outcome envisioned as having a higher utility than doing nothing. The preemptor may exaggerate or idealize the utility of this alternative, but one must exist, otherwise the choice of striking first amounts to suicide. For example, in the Pacific War case, the Japanese non–status quo option was a surprise attack dealing initial heavy losses to the American Pacific fleet, combined with a quick strike into the Southwest Pacific that would deter the Americans from undertaking a protracted and costly war in Asia. Although this plan was ill-conceived, without the belief that this non–status quo outcome carried a higher expected utility than doing nothing, the Japanese attack on Pearl Harbor would have been conscious suicide. Ominously enough, one can envision a spectrum of such alternatives for the North. In a worst-case scenario, through long-range artillery barrages, missile strikes, or chemical weapons attacks deliberately non-American in target and short of all-out war, the North could seek to hold Seoul hostage with the hope of renegotiating a new status quo.[29] Again, the relevant point here is not the objective feasibility of such an action, but the belief in North Korea that acting is better than doing nothing, which promises slow and certain death.

LOSS AVERSION—THE DOUBLE-OR-NOTHING LOGIC

Another factor behind the North's logic of lashing out needs highlighting. As noted above, the conventional wisdom is that there is little threat of DPRK aggression because Pyongyang would not knowingly commit suicide. In short, the choices are: 1.) do not attack—accept the status quo, which provides certain short-run gains of regime survival and coexistence with the South (potentially in a nonconfrontational manner); or 2.) attack—change the status quo and opt for potentially greater but highly uncertain gains. Faced with these odds, any right-minded gambler will choose the former option, preferring certain gains to larger but highly uncertain ones.

However, the logic described above assumes a gains-motivated basis for action, and does not account for more risk-acceptant inclinations by states as their situation deteriorates. As behavioral and decision theories applied to international relations have found, state choice is not determinable through a priori net asset and gain-based utility calculations, but are context-dependent. Three tenets of prospect theory illuminate the North Korean case. First, how states "frame" a situation or "encode" a decision can drastically affect choice. For example, if I play golf expecting to shoot ten strokes below my handicap, but shoot only five strokes below, I see this as an inferior outcome rather than a positive improvement in my game. On the other hand, if I play with no prior expectations of a final score, and achieve the same five-below performance, my assessment of this outcome is substantially different. In both cases, the "frame" critically determines the evaluation regardless of the objective equivalence of the two situations. Second, states are generally averse to losses ("endowment effect"); they value what they have more than what they can achieve. For this reason, states generally fight to defend territory they already possess more than they would to acquire that same territory. Schoolyard fights break out over the defending of reputations rather than the increasing of them. The endowment effect was implicit in the domino theory of the Cold War because the motivation to fight in the periphery was more to avoid losing a chain of small allies to the enemy rather than seeking new states bandwagoning in one's favor.[30] Third, certain outcomes weigh more heavily in states' calculations than probable ones (certainty effect). This does not mean states always prefer certain outcomes to uncertain ones, but that their behavior is primarily motivated by the pursuit of certain gains or the avoidance of certain losses.[31]

Loss aversion and framing can give rise to risk-acceptant behavior entirely different from that based on gains-motivated, expected-utility calculations. As Janice Stein notes, the degree of risk political leaders are willing to incur over a policy is starkly different depending on the context: "Because people are generally averse to loss, whether an outcome is treated as a gain or a loss has a significant impact on the choice they make. Indeed, when an identical outcome is re-framed as a loss rather than a gain, people reverse their preference and make a different choice."[32] An illustration of the risky choice thesis is gambling. A risky double-or-nothing bet looks bad to a gambler with pocketed winnings; this same strategy, however, looks increasingly appealing to one on her last few dollars. In sum, the "decision frame" is critical to choice. This frame, in turn, is determined by the identification of a reference point and the coding of decisions in terms of gains or losses.[33]

ACTUATING PREEMPTIVE/PREVENTIVE SITUATIONS

Prospect theory specifies the conditions under which preemptive or preventive action can occur among similarly situated states.[34] There is general agreement that a preemptive or preventive situation is one in which the status quo is deemed unbearable. However, the theory is unclear on the causal mechanism that leads to the actualization of that situation—why do some states act under objectively preemptive/preventive conditions while others do not? Some have focused on the offense/defense balance as the key determinant, others on hostile images of the adversary, and others on regime-type.[35] However, empirical studies have found that many of these factors are not sufficient to explain the actualization of a situation conducive to striking first.[36]

Incorporating the framing of choice and decisions, one can deduce more specified propositions about the occurrence of preemption/prevention among similarly situated states (see table 8.1). If a state is potentially a target of attack, but frames the situation as a "winning" one, then it will generally be risk-averse to preemptive or preventive actions. Even though such actions of-

Table 8.1. Actualization of Preemptive/Preventive Action

Preemptive/Preventive situation with . . .	Domain of wins	Neutral	Domain of losses
Offense advantage	Cell 1: unlikely (indeterminate)	Cell 3: Likely	Cell 5: Highly Likely
Defense advantage	Cell 2: Highly unlikely	Cell 4: Unlikely	Cell 6: Very likely

fer the possibility of larger gains, the motivating factor for non-action is the threat such actions pose to current holdings. This incentive for nonaction would be reinforced by beliefs in defense having the advantage and long time-horizons (cell 2).[37] If a state is contemplating preemptive/preventive action and frames the situation as "neutral" (i.e., either through discrete or cumulative encoding, it sees the status quo as a nonlosing one), then it is still unlikely to take the risky choice of striking first and jeopardize current holdings. The disincentive to act in this situation is marginally less than if framed in the domain of wins, and thus less determinate. The critical factor determining choice in this situation is the offense/defense balance. If conquest is perceived as easy, then the occurrence of preemption/prevention is more likely (cell 3).

If a state perceives itself to be the potential target of attack and frames the situation in the domain of losses, then the likelihood of preemptive/preventive actualization is high (cells 5 and 6). Time-horizons are short; moreover, loss aversion in a losing situation results in risk-acceptant behavior akin to an "anything to stop the bleeding" mentality. A state is willing to accept the risk of preemptive/preventive war, which carries substantially disastrous but merely probable losses, in order to avoid near-certain losses in the present. The incentive to act is exponentially reinforced if offense is perceived to be advantageous (cell 5). Levy rightly points out a problem here regarding relative risk assessments. Whether a risk-acceptant state in the domain of losses sees war or doing nothing as more risky is not easily determinable.[38] While not wholly resolving this problem, I argue that one important criterion is the severity of the domain of losses. If a state sees itself in the domain of losses but hovers just above a subsistence level, then it may be marginally more risk averse (i.e., choose a mini-max strategy), and willing to take certain losses, provided they don't result in outcomes below the subsistence level. However, if the state is already below the subsistence level and in the domain of continuing losses, loss aversion, risk acceptance, and the incentive to act becomes acute.

NORTH KOREA'S DECISIONAL FRAME

A priori indicators by which to designate North Korea's decisional frame are: 1.) those ideational objectives that legitimate and celebrate the national identity, 2.) state of material well-being (i.e., economic and military), 3.) standing in the international community, and 4.) availability of allies.[39] An important barometer of a changing frame of reference is the perspective on time. If decisional frame indicators have positive values (i.e., ideational objectives being attained; satisfactory economic and military strength; garnering some external support), then a state is not in the domain of losses, manifested among other things in long time-horizons.

Whichever way Kim Jong Il may slice it, North Korea's decisional frame on the Korean peninsula is a losing one (cells 5 or 6).[40] The Dear Leader's reference point could be the status quo, in which case notwithstanding the slow trickle of aid and support from the outside world, the widening economic gap between North and South would leave him in a rapidly "losing" situation. Or, his reference point could be a future aspiration point such as unification with northern dominance—in which case the losing situation is more acute. While North Korea faced this window of vulnerability with the South during the Cold War, the motivation for preventive action was less salient as the situation was not nearly as desperate then.[41] Through the mid-1970s, the CIA calculated GNP per capita for the two Koreas as roughly equal.[42] Pyongyang's *juche* ideology had standing in the international community and won it membership in the Non-Aligned Movement while ROK applications were rejected (because of U.S. forces in Korea). The North had a sizeable military with quantitative edges over the South. DPRK infiltration of the South was so extensive that Kim Il Sung confidently stated in 1977 that he could insert or extract units anywhere, anytime (a claim that U.S. forces in Korea confidentially conceded as true).[43] In addition, from Pyongyang's perspective, the ROK hardly looked the model of stability in the 1960s and 1970s as its presidents were exiled, overthrown by coup and assassinated, and its external security guarantees looked, at best, tenuous based on ambivalent actions by successive U.S. administrations from Johnson to Carter.[44] By contrast, the North's livelihood was fully ensured by the security and economic patronage of the Soviet Union and China.

This situation gave rise to impressions in Pyongyang that with time, gaps could be closed. North Korea's decisional frame was at worst neutral, and more often than not, in the domain of wins (cells 2–4). Recently released documents from German Democratic Republic (GDR) (or East Germany) archives of confidential discussions between Erich Honecker and Kim Il Sung in December 1977 provide a rare window on Kim's private views. Kim expressed extreme confidence in the longevity of the DPRK regime. The economic gap favoring the South was not a concern because political instability and the withdrawal of U.S. troops (i.e., Carter plan) would eventually lead the South Korean people to choose *juche*. The communization of the Korean peninsula, the North Korean leader continued, would then lay the conditions for "stimulating the revolution in Japan."[45] As Oberdorfer recounts, Kim was so confident of the South's eventual demise that there was little the North needed to do to encourage this outcome—despite the South's economic advantages, DPRK time-horizons were long.

> [T]wo days after Park's assassination, Kim Il Sung addressed a military meeting, drawing a stark contrast between South Korea, "one half of our territory . . . under the occupation of the U.S. imperialists and reactionaries, landlords and capitalists," and the DPRK, where "our people are enjoying a happy life . . . without any worries about food, clothing, medical treatment and education." Kim announced, "There is no better 'paradise' and no better 'land of perfect bliss' than our country. . . ." While approving the elimination of "traitor" Park Chung hee, the North Korean leader cautiously told the military assembly, "*We must wait and see what change this will bring about in the revolutionary situation in South Korea.*" (Emphasis added).[46]

However, the trend dramatically changed in the 1990s. Perceptions of the status quo as a losing one became apparent between 1992 and 1994. It was around this time the DPRK suffered China's normalization with South Korea, Kim Il Sung's death, and the cumulative effects of decaying infrastructure, poor harvests, and energy shortages, manifest in consecutive years of negative economic growth. German unification had deep psychological and material impacts on North Korean confidence as the GDR (i.e., Honecker) had been a close confidante and consistent economic supporter. Abandonment by China (1992) and Russia (1990) was not only in economic but also, effectively, security patronage at a time when fuel shortages were undermining military readiness (in China's case, this was somewhat ameliorated by added military compensation by Beijing to Pyongyang). Western visitors to the Chinese border in 1997 reported increased self-help barter activities by local and provincial DPRK authorities, in defiance of the central government's control and directives.[47] A steady stream of diplomatic defections led Pyongyang to recall twelve ambassadors from foreign missions in 1997 and 1998. And at home, a growing number of public executions of prominent party officials suggest divisions in elite leadership circles.[48] These trends were unheard of during the Cold War; moreover, their instances have increased dramatically since 1993 according to South Korea legislative reports.[49] As one expert observed:

> By 1993, North Korea was a country without a national strategy. To be more precise, it had a national strategy—the same one it always had—but this was almost completely irrelevant to the problems at hand. The pressing problem at hand was regime survival.[50]

Noted Korea specialist Bruce Cumings puts it more graphically:

> Kim Il-sung's death came amid dire war threats [from the West] and inaugurated an unending stream of calamities: floods in 1995 and 1996, drought in 1997, even a tidal wave killing hundreds as August ended. . . . Pyongyang is in a triage

> mode right now, helping where it can, denying when it must, . . . This crisis is terrible, by far the worst since the Korean war ."[51]

Signs of the status quo viewed in the domain of losses are abundant. First, there is outright acknowledgment in DPRK statements that the status quo is substantially worse than any past reference point. Statements talk about "returning" to economic levels of the past (and then growing beyond these levels).[52] Second, in related fashion, themes of change and reform have proliferated in North Korean propaganda; while Kim's speeches in 1997 carried messages of continuity (e.g., maintaining certain "revolutionary traditions"), increasingly these were couched in conditional language that "reserv[es] the right for creative development" as the North experiences the "trials and tribulations in our construction of socialism."[53] Recent statements are more desperate in tone, showing a clear need for change. As the government-run newspaper *Rodong Sinmun* stated in a 2001 New Year's editorial:

> [T]he most important task to be accomplished with priority, precisely, is to effect fundamental innovations in the ideological viewpoint of people and their way of thinking, struggle ethos, and work attitude in such a way that meets the requirements of the new century. . . . It is impossible to advance the revolution even a step further if we should get complacent with our past achievements or be enslaved to outdated ideas and stick to the outmoded style and attitude in our work.[54]

Third, anecdotal evidence reinforces the notion that the status quo is a losing one. Highlighting Kim Jong Il's formal power ascension and the DPRK's fiftieth anniversary celebrations in September 1998 was an odd rebroadcasting of an old Kim Il Sung speech, symbolizing how celebration of the present and future could only be made with reference to better times in the past. Visiting congressional groups to North Korea in 1998 estimated one million people dead of starvation since the early 1990s.[55] The World Food Program reported in 2000 that the DPRK has the highest rate of malnutrition in East Asia, 62 percent of the population suffer from acute malnutrition and stunting, and 30 percent of the children between twelve and twenty-four months suffer from acute malnutrition.[56] The food rationing policy's Darwinian selection-like nature reflects increasingly short time horizons: the very young and very old are the last priorities.[57] Former DPRK ideologue Hwang Jang Yop's characterization is perhaps the most accurate and ominous: "It's like a land of darkness there. Most people think it's too painful to go on. They even think if it takes a war to bring change they are willing to start a war."[58]

CASES OF PREEMPTIVE LOGIC

Hostile actions taken by the DPRK during the 1990s clearly reflect this logic of preemptive action. For example, in 1995 the DPRK undertook a number of actions in the Joint Security Area (JSA) at Panmunjom that were in clear violation of the armistice. This included moving troops, well beyond the mutually agreed number, into the militarily sensitive JSA, removing uniform armbands designating the forces allowed into the area, as well as violating the minimal arms requirements (i.e., nothing beyond side arms). In August 1998, the North test-fired a ballistic missile over the Sea of Japan (Taepodong-I). Pyongyang claimed this to be a satellite launch, but it was also interpreted as an attempt to demonstrate a three-stage missile capability beyond what many intelligence analysts had previously predicted possible.

These were both clearly provocative and unsolicited actions, at the same time appearing devoid of a clear strategic calculation. In each case, these events were not part of a chain of escalating tensions but were isolated, almost random incidents.[59] Many saw these as reconfirming the view that the North was an unpredictable and dangerous adversary. Yet this puzzling behavior is explainable by the logic of preemptive action. In each case, Pyongyang sought to disrupt a status quo deemed highly unfavorable with the purpose of renegotiating a new status quo to its advantage. In the former case, this had to do with an attempt to debilitate the Military Armistice Commission and draw the United States into direct bilateral negotiations on a peace treaty, excluding the ROK.[60] In the latter case, the purpose, in part, was to overturn an emerging consensus in the intelligence community that the DPRK had reached technology ceilings in terms of its missile development (i.e., the *Rodong* missile), and would experience decreasing revenues from missile transfers. This launch, although a failed three-stage launch, disrupted this emergent "status quo" and elevated to the forefront the cessation of tests of this new program as a new issue of negotiation and compensation for Pyongyang.[61]

In a similar vein, one can imagine other such incidents in the future, where the North might lob several artillery shells or one chemically armed short-range missile into the South (deliberately non-American in target). A provocation that is too minor to prompt all-out war, but serious enough to raise the incentive for Seoul and Washington to give ground on one or another issue.

In sum, although the Cold War and post–Cold War both presented preventive/preemptive situations for North Korea, actualization of the former situation did not occur because North Korea's decisional frame was in the domain of gains. Despite the vulnerability gap favoring the South, time-horizons were long, and survival was never in question. The situation in the post–Cold War era, although superficially appearing similar, is fundamentally different. Survival has become the unwritten state objective, time is not on the North's side, and the decisional frame is firmly in the domain of losses (cells 5 or 6). Like the gambler who can't catch a break, the more North Korea frames today's situation as a losing one, the more appealing becomes the double-or-nothing option, and the greater the danger of preemptive action. Again, such an act would not be based on a rationale about winning, but one of avoiding further loss.

THE SUNSHINE POLICY AND THE DPRK'S DECISIONAL FRAME

Critics might concede the applicability of this analysis to North Korea for the past fifty years, but argue that it lacks relevance given events transpiring over the past eighteen months. Kim Dae Jung's "sunshine (or engagement) policy" provided the context in which the DPRK has sought improved relations with Seoul. This culminated with the unprecedented Korea summit (June 2000), and has since included family reunions, economic cooperation, and infrastructure rejuvenation.[62] For the first time since the death of Kim Il Sung in July 1994, Pyongyang ventured beyond its traditional Cold-War orbit of allies, opening diplomatic relations with almost every EU country (except France). The formerly reclusive, now garrulous Kim Jong Il has secured outside assistance in the form of food aid, medical and humanitarian supplies, and economic aid from international organizations and nongovernmental organizations (NGOs) to tide the country over through the extremely difficult years (the mid-1990s). The Dear Leader now entertains the prospect of political relations with the United States and Japan, and with this, the potential for large amounts of economic assistance from Tokyo and international financial institutions.[63] Pyongyang therefore favors the current status quo, critics might contend, in ways that render irrelevant the logic of preemptive action.[64] It has secured a level of subsistence from the outside through small diplomatic openings on its part. Moreover, it looks at these gains in absolute rather than relative terms vis-à-vis the gap with the South, hence reducing any anxieties about increasing inferiority.

There is no denying that the DPRK is in a better place today than it was between 1992 and 1998. Perhaps the two primary indicators of this are the food situation and Pyongyang's reduced diplomatic isolation relative to the past. According to the World Food Program (WFP), food shortages, for example, are less acute than they were in 1997 and 1998 across provinces.[65] Moreover, the economy has stopped the free fall in growth rates, and the regime appears to have made a stable political transition after Kim Il Sung's death in 1994. However, to argue that this new status quo is permanent is highly questionable. First, while famine-like conditions have abated, the absence of large-scale agricultural reform initiatives means that the mere symptoms rather than the underlying causes of the food shortages are being treated by the inflow of food assistance.[66] In addition, the long-term reliability of these annual inflows by internal organizations (IOs) and NGOs is high susceptible to donor fatigue, particularly as international attention shifts to food appeals in post-Taliban Afghanistan. Second, the attention and goodwill showered on the North in 2000 and 2001 has proved to be far from permanent. This initial iteration of diplomacy benefiting Pyongyang has been largely unilateral. In particular, the ROK, United States, and Japan's provision of various forms of assistance have been without concrete and meaningful reciprocal responses from Pyongyang; this in turn has increased domestic political pressure in all three capitols for making future concessions highly contingent. Finally, the combination of economic rationality in the South and the complete absence of internationally compliant legal institutions in the North also implies that the initial inflow of hard currency (e.g., Hyundai's Kumgang tours, as described in chapter 6) is far from reliable. Thus, what is apparent with the North's improved situation in 2000 and 2001 is not a new status quo, but a positive variation from the original one. This incremental change is welcome, but it is at the same time highly contingent and easily capable of backsliding.

Arguably, an important change connected with how the DPRK frames the status quo is the decreased likelihood of absorption as a scenario for unification. If absorption is completely irrelevant as a potential outcome, this would ameliorate DPRK visions of the status quo as unbearable (i.e., in the domain of losses), and reduce incentives for risk-taking behavior. However, again a distinction must be made between permanent changes to the status quo and temporary variations from it. While transient material conditions (i.e., DPRK's improved situation, ROK economic difficulties) might favor a no-absorption outcome, what matters from a DPRK decisional frame is the longer history of the ROK's stated intentions. Currently, these are enunciated in the "no-absorption" (or no unification) pledge of Kim Dae Jung's sunshine policy.[67] But this policy is as much an aberration as it is distinct in the history of South Korean unification policy, which since the establishment of the Republic in 1948 has held up unification (with Southern dominance) as the ideal objective. To assume from a DPRK perspective that the current South Korean president's view (well known as historically unique) would be the norm for any succeeding administration is difficult.[68]

"HAWK ENGAGEMENT"

Contrary to conventional logic, there are perfectly rational reasons for North Korea to choose to violate peace even if defeat is likely. Understanding the North Korean threat in terms of this logic highlights the misdirected focus of the DPRK engagement debate in Washington and Seoul. Hawks and doves oppose or support engagement based on their judgements about whether the North seeks to subvert the South or the degree to which it seeks reform. Instead, the criteria for choice should be the capacity of any strategy to circumvent situations in which the North 1.) sees the status quo as an unbearable and losing situation, 2.) sees an attack on it (or extinction) as imminent, or 3.) sees threatening behavior as better now than later.

In this light, coercion or isolation strategies are not appealing as a complement to basic deterrence/defense postures toward the DPRK. Noncommunication, threats, and intimidation only exacerbate preemptive/preventive situations by expanding the North's window of vulnerability, pushing the leadership further into framing the status quo in the domain of losses, and raising the costs of peace. On the other hand, conditional engagement (i.e., containment-plus-engagement) ameliorates preemptive and preventive situations. While maintaining necessary deterrent measures, it lengthens time horizons, reduces the threat of imminent attack, reduces the cost of the status quo, and can help change Pyongyang's frame of reference. Recent work on theories of influence concur with this basic point: "When the continuation of the status quo portends losses and is perceived as costly for a given state A, logically another state B can decrease the incentives for A to attack by adding to the value of that status quo, promising rewards for peaceful relations."[69]

Arguably, the choices made by the Perry review process in 1998 and 1999 followed this frame of thinking. As noted above, prior to the start of the congressionally mandated comprehensive study of DPRK policy in December 1998, North Korea undertook a series of limited hostile acts to disrupt a status quo deemed unfeasible (JSA incursions, missile tests, sea incursions). All were somewhat successful status quo–altering events (from a DPRK vantage point) because they put new issues and bargaining chips on the table for negotiation with the United States, South Korea, and Japan (i.e., armistice, in-kind compensation for missile controls, Northern Limitation Line [NLL]). But with the Perry review's recommendations for the United States and its allies to pursue engagement with the North (particularly after Secretary Perry's mission to Pyongyang in June 1999), holding open the possible inflow of economic funds, humanitarian aid, and political normalization, the train of limited hostile acts by the DPRK ceased. Perry's recommendations for engagement basically moved the DPRK out of the domain of losses and into a situation where it had a stake in the status quo. In this sense, the Bush administration's own policy review conclusions in favor of engagement are well-advised.[70] Contrary to these conclusions, initial discussions by Bush about cutting off dialogue with Pyongyang and revisiting the Agreed Framework ran the risk of pushing the North's decisional frame back to the logic of preemption (cells 5 and 6 instead of 3 and 4).

ENGAGEMENT AS THE EXIT STRATEGY

The lesson learned by the Clinton and Bush administrations is that the "default" prescription for North Korea today remains engagement. As this chapter shows, this is hardly a dove's recommendation in policy terms. The logic of preemption, prevention, and engagement flows deductively from rational deterrence theory.[71] The alternatives—containment-plus-isolation or containment-plus-coercion—only increase North Korea's rational incentives for hostility without victory. Conditional engagement initiatives carry their own risks and moral hazard in terms of unrequited cooperation by Pyongyang, but these are far less than the costs that would be incurred by a coercion/isolation strategy that backfired and led to war.

In the end, perhaps the strongest argument against engagement is normative. The North Korea regime and its practices are anathema to nearly every civilized value. The starving of children, the selling of daughters for cattle, and the physical handicaps that a generation of youth will bear due to a basic lack of nutrition and medicine all occur while the political regime and military survive in relative splendor.[72] Moreover, engagement would send the wrong message to North Korea and other rogue nations, reinforcing the hardliners' views that the West is conceding and giving others incentive to try similar things. As critics in Congress and among conservative circles in Korea and Japan argue, rather than transforming rogue regimes, engagement only reinforces their convictions to remain rogue.

Undoubtedly, seeking accommodation with rogue regimes is morally unappealing. In a sense, the choices were clearer and less difficult during the Cold War when the fight for Western values intersected with the fight against the adversary. But the Cold War is over. Regimes such as North Korea's should be regarded not as moral deviants to be reprimanded, but as security problems that need to be solved.[73] There are many who cannot accept this and even would be willing to risk war as the price of a more "moral" foreign policy. However, if the objective is achieving peaceful change, and solving (rather than fighting) the security problem, then the issue becomes one of explaining how engagement can be an acceptable alternative even to those in favor of isolation or coercion. Fortunately, there are at least five reasons that support such a stance.

First, engagement should be the desired strategy today because this is the best practical way to build a coalition for punishment tomorrow. A necessary precondition for coercing North Korea is the formation of a regional consensus that every opportunity to resolve the problem in a nonconfrontational manner has been exhausted. Without this consensus, implementing any form of coercion that actually puts pressure on the regime is unworkable. In 1994, there was resistance not only from China (who could veto a resolution for sanctions in the Security Council), but also from the U.S. allies (i.e., Japan, which was reluctant to curb remittances to the North from resident North Korean organizations) about proceeding prematurely to a sanctions policy.

Similarly, if the Agreed Framework were abandoned today, there is little likelihood that a consensus would be available for punitive action. On the other hand, pursuing engagement—the endgame of which would be to put the onus for taking any last chance for cooperation on North Korea—is the most effective way to build a coalition for punishment. In this sense, many of the criticisms of the Agreed Framework during the Bush policy review were misplaced. Among other cited problems, critics argued that the Framework was an open-ended appeasement policy that rewarded bad behavior, assumed (rather than verified) cooperative DPRK intentions, and lacked any clear exit strategy. In fact, U.S.-ROK-Japan good faith efforts at implementing the Agreed Framework are building the coalition for punishment if the North does not hold up its end of the agreement.[74] Rather than being devoid of an exit strategy, engagement and the Agreed Framework, in effect, are the exit strategy.

Second, today's carrots are tomorrow's most effective sticks. Sticks only work if North Korea has a stake in the status quo. When the North is in the domain of losses, then threatening more sticks is futile. For example, continuing to impose a decades-old embargo is unlikely to elicit a positive change in behavior. However, lifting sanctions, letting the North gain what little they can from new opportunities thus made available, and then using the possibility of reinstating sanctions as a potential stick later, is more likely to elicit changes in behavior. The idea would be first to push Pyongyang into the domain of gains for sticks to work. If they have a stake in the status quo—something they cannot lose—threats of punishment become effective. This dynamic could explain DPRK behavior on the detainment of an ROK tourist in June 1999 on alleged spy charges. The ROK retaliated by suspending further Kumgang mountain tours. The tours conducted by Hyundai represented a new and substantial source of hard currency for the North that was hardly worth losing over the propaganda value of capturing a South Korean "spy." The DPRK promptly released the tourist almost sheepishly after coercing a written confession. In this sense, the Hyundai tour, formerly the carrot, was also an effective stick in influencing North Korean behavior.

Third, conditional engagement is probably better than coercion at creating fissures among the DPRK regime elites. Policies of containment and coercion give the regime an unambiguous symbol around which to muster full support. Conditional engagement is more ambiguous. It confuses the target state's elite by challenging preconceived prejudices, and raises debates as to whether the engager's intentions are genuine or duplicitous. These debates in turn can create or exacerbate traditionalist/reformist, party/military, or generational leadership divisions, contributing to a crumbling of the regime from above.

Fourth, rather than prolong the rogue regime's existence (as commonly argued by the hawk), engagement can hasten its demise. North Korea faces the same reform dilemma of other illiberal regimes in the post–Cold War era: They need to open up to survive, yet in the process of opening up they unleash or cannot control the forces that ultimately lead to their demise. In this sense, engagement mechanisms like the Agreed Framework, inter-Korean trade, tourism, and investment bring into play the institutional and nongovernmental influences that nudge the North down the slippery slope of political reform. Anathema to the hawk, this strategy results in an interim improvement in the North's economic situation, but very much in line with the hawk's preferences, it also spawns the conditions for upheaval from below. As history has shown, revolutions and regime instability in downtrodden states are most likely not when conditions are at their worst, but when they begin to improve.

Fifth, should the hawk seek destruction of the North, engagement strategies offer better preparation for such an event. Proponents of Cold War–era containment-plus-isolation fixated on discouraging and, if necessary, repelling a Northern invasion, but they never really considered what to do after the North was defeated. Containment-plus-isolation was therefore a status quo policy that maintained the opaqueness of the DPRK regime and applied a simple but intimidating logic to tame it. Engagement, on the other hand, compels more proactive thinking about unification. It does not just black-box the North Korean state as isolation strategies do; rather, it promotes dialogue and information exchanges to increase transparency and reduce the eventual start-up costs of unification. The institutional ties between the two governments and economic development that grow out of engagement also help ease the costs of any future absorption process.

WHITHER THE CRITICS? HUMAN RIGHTS AND MISSILE DEFENSE

Many of the rationales for the preventive defense logic of engagement described above are plainly intuitive and perhaps such intuitions factored into the Bush policy review's conclusion in June 2001 to resume a process of engagement with the DPRK. Yet in the context of this chapter, the new Bush policy might face criticism on two counts. From the hard right, many would criticize engagement because it does not address the true victim, the North Korean people.[75] From the hard left, criticism might be that engagement is not credible because of the Bush administration's emphasis on missile defense and the need to maintain the DPRK as the poster child for National Missile Defense (NMD).

Many on the right see the DPRK problem in elegant and simple terms: end the regime, save the people. Nondialogue and hostility might therefore be seen as the most direct route to absorbing the North, but this overlooks perhaps the most important factor in the success of an absorption exercise—the North Korean population. Conventional wisdom is that after the evil DPRK regime is gone, northerners will view southerners as their saviors and elder brethren. This overly optimistic view underestimates the degree of enmity, noncontact, distrust, and bloodshed between the two regimes, a situation that does not augur well for social integration. If this is at all hard to fathom as a reaction by a northerner, just imagine how confident a southerner would feel about being absorbed under the "good graces" of a united North Korean government.[76] Given this, a policy of hard-line coercion and isolation that drove the Pyongyang leadership into the ground would also have the effect of alienating and frightening the northern populace, reinforcing decades of DPRK demonization of the United States and ROK. Engagement would convey a more compassionate image of Americans and South Koreans. It would start the process of unraveling half a century of negative indoctrination in the North, and in this manner, would lay the foundation for the southern polity and people to emerge as a credible receptacle of popular northern loyalty after the DPRK state collapses. Coercion may be more attractive to the hawk's dream of northern capitulation, but engagement better equips the hawk for her desired objective.

The Bush administration's unswerving enthusiasm for pressing forward with national and theater missile defense (TMD) systems, critics argue, are wholly at odds with an engagement policy with the North Koreans. NMD proponents have held out Pyongyang's missile threat as one of the primary rationales for the system. How can an administration therefore credibly propose engagement to solve a problem that it "needs"?

This has been a popular albeit poorly conceived criticism. It ignores the fact that supporting missile defense systems can actually strengthen the credibility and potential for success of engagement strategies vis-à-vis the DPRK. If one accepts the argument that engagement is most effective when it 1.) is undergirded by robust defense capabilities and 2.) communicates to the target clearly that engagement is a choice of the strong and not the expediency of the weak, then supporting missile defense is one way of effecting an enhanced engagement strategy on the Korean peninsula. Such a strategy would remain firmly committed to the path of engagement outlined in the sunshine policy and the Perry policy review (and now the Bush policy review) pushing Pyongyang further into the domain of gains, but it would also neutralize the one most likely avenue of coercive bargaining by the DPRK—the missile threat.

The type of system that might best handle the DPRK missile threat with the least negative consequences (i.e., for Chinese threat perceptions) concerns numerous subissues. But the point is that the conversations on missile defense and engagement strategies on North Korea should be linked. Deploying BMD systems alone as a stopgap measure against the North deals imperfectly at best with the missile threat but does little else to resolve the peninsula's tensions. Utilizing engagement to get at the deeper problem of transforming DPRK preferences and intentions is always subject to future acts of brinkmanship. The dilemma is apparent in the North's 1999 "temporary" moratorium on missile tests. Negotiated in exchange for an additional lifting of some U.S. economic sanctions, one could see the outcome as the fruit of a successful engagement strategy. But what is to prevent the North from trying to coerce in the future using the threat of rescinding its moratorium? Very little.

Linking the BMD and engagement conversations is, perhaps, the answer. Missile defense can make for an enhanced engagement strategy by the Bush administration. In combination with transparent and proactive engagement efforts by the U.S., Japan, and the ROK, missile defense (at least lower-tier systems supported by the ROK on the peninsula) at once can give strength, credibility, and insurance to engagement. It distinguishes engagement as a policy of the strong—one that cannot possibly be interpreted as appeasement or capitulation by Pyongyang or domestic critics in Washington and Seoul. At the same time, it avoids the potential pitfalls of nondialogue strategies which do little to solve proliferation problems presented by the regime. The success of engagement is not premised solely on conciliation but on a mix of conciliation and strength. Missile defense enhances—not undercuts or contradicts—engagement.

FIT POLICIES TO THREATS, NOT THREATS TO POLICIES

The policy imperative regarding North Korea is to be wary of Cold-War hangover. The Korean peninsula is still one of the last bastions of the bipolar conflict, but the internal and external circumstances surrounding the two regimes have changed dramatically since 1950. In spite of this, there is a stickiness inherent in decades of Cold-War thinking. Policymakers in Washington and Seoul fall into the trap of adhering to familiar policy templates and then, rather than reassessing the nature of the North Korean threat, simply assume the threat continues to fit with these templates. Fitting threats to policies rather than policies to threats in this manner is dangerous because the successful strategy that brought peace in one era could bring the exact opposite effect in another.

In the case of Korea, the most prudent strategy is one that adheres to a preventive defense logic of engagement. That is, policy should be directed at preventing situations in which the DPRK perceives the status quo as unbearable and therefore sees belligerence as the rational option even if there is little hope of victory. Coercion only exacerbates the North's double-or-nothing motives for striking first. Conditional engagement, on the other hand, reduces such incentives by giving Pyongyang a stake in the status quo and raising the benefits of peace (while at the same time maintaining robust deterrence capabilities). The preventive defense logic of engagement is not based on the assumption that DPRK preferences have changed toward peace, nor is it based on the hope that engagement can create such a change in preferences. Engagement enables the DPRK opportunities to prove to the outside world that it seeks integration, but if this fails, U.S.-ROK-Japan good faith efforts at engagement build the coalition for punishment. In this sense, engagement does not operate without a net. It is the exit strategy.

NOTES

1. For details and analysis of North Korea's diplomatic "blitz," see Samuel Kim, "North Korea in 2000: Surviving through High Hopes of Summit Diplomacy," *Asian Survey* 41, 1 (January-February 2001): 20–5.

2. The former argument is based in the notion that DPRK threatening behavior represents a classic security dilemma. Insecurity, particularly after the loss of its Cold-War patrons in the Soviet Union and China (after Beijing's normalization with the ROK in 1992), drives the North to aggression, hence engagement will offer the security assurances that will mollify DPRK behavior. The latter view calls for engagement because this is the only way to move Pyongyang away from traditional patterns of unpredictably aggressive behavior. Moreover, the regime's irrationality renders useless basic deterrence and defense strategies (which presume a degree of rationality on the part of the target state).

3. On prospect theory, see Daniel Kahneman and Amos Tversky, "Prospect Theory: An Analysis of Decision under Risk," *Econometrica* 47, 2 (March 1979): 263–91; and Kahneman and Tversky, "Rational Choice and the Framing of Decisions," *Journal of Business* 59, 4, part 2 (1986): S251–S278. For a good, readable introduction, see Jack Levy, "An Introduction to Prospect Theory," *Political Psychology* 13, 2 (1992): 171–86. The applications to international relations and political choice have been fairly recent. See Janice Gross Stein, ed., "International Cooperation and Loss Avoidance: Framing the Problem," in *Choosing to Co-operate: How States Avoid Loss* (Baltimore: Johns Hopkins University Press, 1993), 2–34; George Quattrone and Amos Tversky, "Contrasting Rational and Psychological Analyses of Political Choice," *American Political Science Review* 82, 3 (September 1988): 719–36; Levy, "An Introduction to Prospect Theory;" Charles Kupchan, *The Vulnerability of Empire* (Ithaca, NY: Cornell University Press, 1994); Robert Jervis, "Political Implications of Loss Aversion," *Political Psychology* 13, 2 (1992), 187–204; Jack Levy, "Prospect Theory and International Relations: Theoretical Applications and Analytical Problems," *Political Psychology* 13, 2 (1992): 283–310; Eldar Shafir, "Prospect Theory and Political Analysis: A Psychological Perspective," *Political Psychology* 13, 2 (1992): 311–22; and Y. Y. I. Vertzberger, *Risk Taking and Decision Making* (Stanford: Stanford University Press, 1998). There have been even fewer applications of prospect theory to specific cases. See Barbara Farnham, "Roosevelt and the Munich Crisis: Insights from Prospect Theory," *Political Psychology* 13,2 (1992): 205–35; Rose McDermott, "Prospect Theory in International Relations: The Iranian Hostage Rescue Mission," *Political Psychology* 13, 2 (1992): 237–63; Audrey McInerney, "Prospect Theory and Soviet Policy towards Syria, 1966–1967," *Political Psychology* 13, 2 (1992): 265–82; Paul Huth, D. S. Bennett, and C. Gelpi, "System Uncertainty, Risk Propensity, and International Conflict among the Great Powers," *Journal of Conflict Resolution* 36 (1992): 478–517; Gregory Gause, "Prospect Theory and Iraqi War Decisions," unpublished paper presented at the 1997 American Political Science Association (APSA), Washington D.C., August 28–31, 1997; and James Davis, *Threats and Promises* (Baltimore: Johns Hopkins University Press, 2000).

4. It should be emphasized that the use of preemptive war theory does not mean that North Korea will undertake a second attempt to overrun the peninsula. The "logic" of preemptive action is the valuable insight from this body of theory. The "act" need not be war, but could be a violent act of some sort (as described below).

5. Ashton Carter and William Perry, *Preventive Defense* (Washington, D.C.: The Brookings Institution, 1999), 14.

6. To reiterate, although strategies of engagement and containment are often juxtaposed, I use the term "engagement" in a conditional sense, meaning engagement instruments that are used in conjunction with—not in lieu of—basic containment strategies. Thus, for example, characterizing U.S. policy toward North Korea as engagement does not necessarily entail an abandonment of deterrent measures. In this sense, the spectrum of policy choice really ranges from unconditional containment (i.e., an unadulterated stick policy) to conditional engagement (i.e., a containment-plus-engagement or carrot-and-stick policy).

7. To argue the appeal of engagement to both doves and hawks is not meant to be flip or irresponsible. On the contrary, a responsible policy prescription is one that is implementable across a wide spectrum of views, and the latter clearly exists in the case of North Korea, given the regime's secrecy and the acute cognitive biases of those who observe it. In this regard, the implications of engagement are open-ended, but the point is that the policy still remains the best choice today as it prevents the emergence of a more unstable situation tomorrow vis-à-vis DPRK assessments and preemptive logic, discussed below. This implication of the policy should be palatable to both doves and hawks. The argument's other implication is to recognize the need to move beyond old Cold-War templates and reexamine the nature of the DPRK threat. This is because what was successful during the Cold War (containment-plus-isolation) may actually cause *more* instability today.

8. Jonathan Pollack and Chung Min Lee, *Preparing for Korean Unification: Scenarios and Implications* (Santa Monica, CA: RAND Corporation, 1999).

9. Robert Scalapino, *North Korea at a Crossroads*, Hoover Institution Essays on Public Policy, Stanford University, no. 73 (1997), 16–17. While the points of departure for Scalapino's work and this article are different, they arrive at similar conclusions regarding the need for engaging the North. Similarly, Michael O'Hanlon contends that North Korea's war initiation would be an "unwise gamble" or an "act of desperation." See Michael O'Hanlon, "Stopping a North Korean Invasion: Why Defending South Korea Is Easier than the Pentagon Thinks," *International Security* 22, 4 (1998): 138.

10. Marcus Noland, "Why North Korea Will Muddle Through," *Foreign Affairs* 76, 4 (1997): 105–18; Byung-joon Ahn, "The Man Who Would Be Kim," *Foreign Affairs* 73, 6 (1994): 94–108; and Nicholas Eberstadt, "Hastening Korean Unification," *Foreign Affairs* 76, 2 (1997): 77–92.

11. For representative examples of these bodies of theory, see Jack Levy, "Declining Power and the Preventive Motivation for War," *World Politics* 40, 1 (October 1987): 82–107; and Dan Reiter, "Exploding the Powderkeg Myth: Preemptive Wars Almost Never Happen," *International Security* 20, 2 (fall 1995): 5–34. Also see, Thomas Schelling, *The Strategy of Conflict* (Cambridge, MA: Harvard University Press, 1960); Thomas Schelling, *Arms and Influence* (New Haven: Yale University Press, 1966); Glenn Snyder, *Deterrence and Defense: Toward a Theory of National Security* (Princeton: Princeton University Press, 1961); Robert Jervis, "Cooperation under the Security Dilemma," *World Politics* 30 (January 1978); Stephen Van Evera, *The Causes of War* (Ph.D. dissertation, University of California, Berkeley, 1984); Jack Snyder, "Perceptions of the Security Dilemma in 1914," in *Psychology and Deterrence,* Robert Jervis, Richard Ned Lebow, and Janice Gross Stein, eds. (Baltimore: Johns Hopkins University Press, 1985), 153–79; Emerson M. S. Niou and Peter C. Ordeshook, "Preventive War and the Balance of Power: A Game Theoretic Approach," *Journal of Conflict Resolution* 31, 3 (summer 1987): 387–419; Randall Schweller, "Domestic Structure and Preventive War: Are Democracies More Pacific?" *World Politics* 44, 2 (January 1992): 235–69; Richard Ned Lebow, "Windows of Opportunity: Do States Jump through Them?" *International Security* 9, 1 (summer 1984): 147–86; Stephen Van Evera, "Offense, Defense, and the Causes of War," *In-*

ternational Security 22, 4 (spring 1998): 5–43; and Charles Glaser and Chaim Kaufmann, "What is the Offense-Defense Balance and How Can We Measure It?" *International Security* 22, 4 (spring 1998): 44–82.

12. Most scholars see the primary difference between the two as the time factor. The motivation for preemption is an imminent attack measured in days, while for prevention, threats are measured in years. The former also tends to take the form of surprise attacks, although not all surprise attacks are preemptive. See Reiter, "Exploding the Powder Keg Myth," 7; also see Levy, "Declining Power and the Preventive Motivation for War;" Jervis, "Cooperation under the Security Dilemma;" Richard K. Betts, *Surprise Attack: Lessons for Defense Planning* (Washington, D.C.: The Brookings Institution, 1982); and Robert Axelrod, "The Rational Timing of Surprise," *World Politics* 31, 2 (January 1979): 228–46. For a slightly different distinction, see Van Evera, *Causes of War.*

13. On power transitions, see Robert Gilpin, *War and Change in World Politics* (Cambridge: Cambridge University Press, 1981). Also see A. F. K. Organski, *World Politics* (New York: Knopf, 1968), chapter 14; Joshua Goldstein, *Long Cycles: Prosperity and War in the Modern Age* (New Haven: Yale University Press, 1988); George Modelski, "The Long Cycle of Global Politics and the Nation-State," *Comparative Studies in Society and History* 20 (April 1978): 214–35; William Thompson, *On Global War: Historical-Structural Approaches to World Politics* (Columbia: University of South Carolina, 1988); Paul Kennedy, *The Rise and Fall of the Great Powers: Economic Change and Military Conflict from 1500 to 2000* (New York: Random House, 1987); Jacek Kugler and A. F. K Organski, "The Power Transition: A Retrospective and Prospective Evaluation," in *Handbook of War Studies,* Manus I. Midlarsky, ed., (Boston: Unwin Hyman, 1989), 171–94; and Charles Kupchan, *The Vulnerability of Empire*.

14. Winston Churchill, *The Grand Alliance* (Boston: Houghton Mifflin, 1950), 603.

15. For applications to the Pacific War in 1941, see Bruce Russett, *Power and Continuity in World Politics* (San Francisco: Freeman, 1974), chapter 13; and Scott Sagan, "The Origins of the Pacific War," *Journal of Interdisciplinary History* 18 (spring 1988).

16. This was not the case during the early years of the Cold War as both Koreas adhered to a "unification by force" policy (*sônggong t'ongil*—literally, "unification by success"), or "march north" (*pukchin t'ongil*). The threat of ROK-initiated violence decreased under the Third and Fourth Republics as Park Chung Hee dropped the *pukchin t'ongil* for a formula seeking to beat the North on the economic and diplomatic front through export-led growth, heavy/chemical industry development, and an omnidirectional foreign policy. Why North Korea did not preempt during the Cold War is discussed below.

17. For economic data, see Bruce Cumings, *The Two Koreas*, Foreign Policy Association, Headline Series, no. 269 (May-June 1984), 65–6. The North Korean military grew from three hundred thousand to over one million troops over the two decades. See Nicholas Eberstadt, "'National Strategy' in North and South Korea" *NBR Analysis* 7, 5 (1996): 10, 12.

18. See Oberdorfer's recounting of conversations between Hwang and Selig Harrison in *The Two Koreas*, 401.

19. Inter-Korean matters have been subsumed nominally under the Party Central Committee. See "The DPRK Report," no. 14 (1998) at NAPSNet@nautilus.org.

20. "The DPRK Report," no. 7 (1997) at NAPSNet@nautilus.org. Also see Kim Jong Il's address at the fiftieth anniversary commemoration ceremony of Kim Il Sung University (December 1996), reprinted in *Wolgan Choson* (April 1997).

21. *Rodong Sinmun,* December 27, 2000, *FBIS-EAS*-2001-0117, December 27, 2000.

22. Eberstadt, "'National Strategy,'" 23.

23. On the South Korean side, for example, the purpose of the Vance mission in 1969 was to communicate to the South that the U.S. would not support unilateral retaliation by the South in response to a series of North Korean provocations in 1968.

24. Personal interview, high-level Chinese foreign ministry official with Asia portfolio, Washington D.C., October 1997.

25. For ROK plans to continue certain force modernization programs in spite of the economic crisis, see *Korea Herald,* June 8, 1998 ("Defense Ministry Pushes Destroyer Plan"); *Korea Herald,* September 22, 1998 ("Defense Ministry Proposes First-Ever Budget Cuts"); Sally Harris, "Coping with Pressure: South Korea's Defense Restructuring," *Korean Journal of Defense Analysis* 12, 2 (winter 2000): 207–30; and Victor Cha, "The Economic Crisis, Strategic Culture, and the Military Modernization of South Korea," *Armed Forces and Society* (forthcoming 2001).

26. On these arguments, see Schweller, "Domestic Structure and Preventive War;" Reiter, "Exploding the Powderkeg Myth," 25–8; and Van Evera, "Offense, Defense, and the Causes of War," 4–6.

27. For 2001 testimony on the improvements and augmentation to the DPRK military posture that has occurred at the same time that Pyongyang has sought detente with Seoul and the rest of the world, see the CINC UNC/CFC/USFK Posture Statement to U.S. Congress (General Schwartz) available at www.korea.army.mil/pao/news/index.htm (accessed 27 December 2001).

28. General James Clapper, Director of Defense Intelligence Agency (DIA) (1991 to 1994) and former chief of intelligence in Korea and Pacific commands, notes that the North's forward deployments may actually reflect a "best defense is a good offense" mentality to compensate for inferiorities in the relative military balance on the peninsula. In other words, the North does not necessarily believe that offense has the advantage but chooses to forward deploy because, as experienced in 1950, it would be incapable of sustaining supply routes with rear-area forces in the face of U.S. bombing runs. Clapper's analysis is cited in Leon Sigal, *Disarming Strangers: Nuclear Diplomacy with North Korea* (Princeton: Princeton University Press, 1998), 21.

29. Examples of past DPRK activity that are consonant with this logic are detailed below.

30. On these points, see Levy, "Prospect Theory and International Relations," 285; and Robert Jervis, "Domino Beliefs and Strategic Behavior," in Robert Jervis and Jack Snyder, eds. *Dominoes and Bandwagons* (New York: Oxford, 1991), 20–50. The endowment effect highlights the status quo bias of states. See Levy, "Prospect Theory and International Relations," 284; Robert Jervis, *The Meaning of the Nuclear Revo-*

lution (Ithaca, NY: Cornell University Press, 1989), 29–35; and Randall Schweller, "Neorealism's Status Quo Bias," *Security Studies* 5, 3 (1996).

31. As experiments by Kahneman and Tversky have shown, individuals prefer certain gains to uncertain but larger ones (or breaking even), and uncertain losses (or breaking even) to smaller but certain losses. Both of these findings run contrary to the predictions of expected utility theory ("Prospect Theory," 265–9).

32. Stein, "International Cooperation and Loss Avoidance," 14.

33. Reference points can either refer to the status quo or to an aspiration point (Levy, "Prospect Theory and International Relations, 285). Kahneman and Tversky generally see the reference point as chosen by the decision-maker at the beginning of the problem. However, the act of encoding, as Levy argues, can be discrete, that is, the reference point with respect to one's asset position at each choice; or cumulative, that is, the reference point and encoding of the choice within a string of choices (Levy, "An Introduction to Prospect Theory," 177). For recent work that further develops the concept of reference point as a subjective process rather than as an objectively neutral point, see William Boettcher, "Framing Foreign Policy Problems: A Study of Truman's Decision to Intervene in Korea," unpublished paper presented at the International Studies Association meeting, March 1998.

34. This is not the first attempt at linking propositions from prospect theory with those from preemptive/preventive theories of war; however it is a more specified drawing out of hypotheses. Links drawn between the two theories have been sketchy, emphasizing how loss aversion calculations can create more destabilizing situations than regular cost-benefit calculations. See Levy, "Prospect Theory and International Relations;" Jervis, *The Meaning of the Nuclear Revolution*, 171; Stein, "International Cooperation and Loss Avoidance," 21; and Jervis, "Political Implications of Loss Aversion." On how loss aversion contributes to cooperation, that is, when leaders identify small but certain losses from defection and larger but uncertain losses from cooperation, see Stein, "International Cooperation and Loss Avoidance, 22, and Michael Mastanduno, "Framing the Japan Problem," *International Journal* 44 (Spring 1989). Levy has studied how certain war situations (Franco-German, U.S.-Japan, U.S.-Iraq) were influenced by loss aversion. See "Declining Power and the Preventive Motivation for War;" and "Prospect Theory and International Relations," 287. Loss aversion has also been employed to explain the persuasiveness of the domino theory as a motivator of Cold War superpower confrontation. See Jervis, "Domino Beliefs and Strategic Behavior."

35. See Van Evera, "Offense, Defense;" Schelling, *Arms and Influence*; Levy, "Declining Power and the Preventive Motivation for War;" Jervis, "Cooperation under the Security Dilemma;" Robert Jervis, *Perception and Misperception in International Politics* (Princeton: Princeton University Press, 1976); and Schweller, "Domestic Structure and Preventive War."

36. Reiter's empirical study of interstate wars since 1816 shows the relative absence of preemptive war despite the existence of commonly accepted conditions for striking first ("Exploding the Powderkeg Myth").

37. If offense is perceived to have the advantage under the same conditions, the outcome is indeterminate, although it is unlikely that preemptive action will take place because of the threat such action would have on current gains.

38. Levy, "Prospect Theory and International Relations," 302–3.

39. One of the difficulties of applying prospect theory to international conflict decisions is the operationalization of the decisional frame. As Gause states, analysts often define the frame by the choice made by the subject. See "Prospect Theory and Iraqi War Decisions;" Levy, "Prospect Theory and International Relations;" and Shafir, "Prospect Theory and Political Analysis.") As a second-best solution, I choose a set of indicators that appear to be a relatively reasonable set of variables by which any country might evaluate its current situation. The problem of operationalization is compounded for this project because of the paucity of reliable data on North Korean perceptions.

40. Arguably, the influx of food aid and economic assistance that came with the recent smile diplomacy by the DPRK may have moved the regime into cells 3 or 4 where they frame the status quo as neutral (i.e., not a daily losing one). Even if this were the case, the point remains that any backsliding to the status quo *ex ante* would heighten the likelihood of DPRK action.

41. For the argument against preventive motivations for North Korean aggression during the Cold War, see David Kang, "Preventive War and North Korea," *Security Studies* 4, 2 (winter 1994/95): 330–63. Kang argues counterfactually that if preventive motivations are applicable to North Korea, then Pyongyang should have attempted to close the window of vulnerability long before the current status quo. I argue that the Cold War, while disadvantageous at times, was never viewed by the North in the domain of losses and thus preventive situations were not actualized. The post–Cold War situation, as described above, is fundamentally different.

42. Cumings, *Two Koreas,* 65–6.

43. Oberdorfer, *Two Koreas*, 100–1.

44. Respectively, these were the absence of U.S. retaliatory punishment for the January 1968 Blue House raid and USS *Pueblo* seizure; the Guam doctrine and Nixon's withdrawal of the seventh infantry division from Korea; the U.S. withdrawal from Vietnam in 1975 under Ford; and the 1977 Carter plan. See Victor Cha, *Alignment Despite Antagonism: The United States–Korea–Japan Security Triangle* (Stanford: Stanford University Press, 1999).

45. As cited in Oberdorfer, *Two Koreas*, 435. For these points generally, see 96–101 and 114–7.

46. Oberdorfer, *Two Koreas*, 115–6.

47. "North Korea's Decline and China's Strategic Dilemmas," *USIP Special Report*, October 1997.

48. *Korea Herald*, February 6, 1998 ("DPRK Recalls Twelve Ambassadors without Replacing Them"); and "The DPRK Report," no. 12 (1998) at NAPSNet@nautilus.org.

49. ROK National Assembly reports found that many more of the defectors in the 1990s were former government or party officials, and that the increase in numbers since 1993 do not include the unreported numbers (estimated between 2000 to 3000 annually) defecting through Russia and China (see *Kyodo Tsushin Nyusu Sokuho,* September 18, 1998, cited in Narushige Michishita, "Two Alliance after Peace on the Korean Peninsula," A/PARC Working Paper, Stanford University, May 7, 1999.)

50. Eberstadt, "'National Strategy,'" 14, 24.

51. Bruce Cumings, "Feeding the North Korea Myths," *The Nation,* September 29, 1997, 22–4.

52. *Nodong Sinmun,* December 27, 2000, 2 ("The Sagacious Leadership That Keeps Strengthening the People's Regime"), *FBIS-EAS*-2001-0117, December 27, 2000.

53. *Chosôn Ilbo,* March 20, 1997, reprint of Kim Jong Il's fiftieth anniversary speech at Kim Il Sung University; and "The DPRK Report," no. 7 (1997), at NAPSNet@nautilus.org.

54. *Rodong Sinmun,* January 9, 2001, 1 ("Let Us See and Solve All Problems from a New Viewpoint and a New Attitude"), *FBIS-EAS*-2001-0118, January 9, 2001.

55. *Jiji Tsushin Nyusu Sokuho*, November 18, 1998, cited in Michishita, "Two Alliance."

56. Cited in Kim, "North Korea in 2000," 27.

57. *London Times*, November 23 and 30, 1997 ("North Korea Chokes on Its Big Lie," and "Kim Shows Starving Nation No Mercy").

58. *Reuters*, June 15, 1998 ("Defector: Famine Killed 2.5 Million North Koreans").

59. The point here is not to deny that these acts took place in a general context of tensions, but that they were significantly more provocative and of a substantially different degree than the general level of tension might have predicted. In this sense, these acts were aberrations that were not easily explainable.

60. The North had been very dissatisfied with the larger role transferred to the South Koreans from the Americans in the Military Armistice Commission (MAC), which is the primary negotiation body for the armistice. To disrupt this, the North undertook clear armistice violations and refused to discuss these in the MAC, with the purpose of forcing the Americans to dialogue directly with them.

61. It should be remembered that the issue here is not whether these strategies are successful (in the JSA case, it was not, but in the Taepodong case, it was), but that there is a calculation that sees disrupting the status quo with an act of violence as rational.

62. On the sunshine policy, see Chung-in Moon and David Steinberg, eds., *Kim Dae-jung Government and Sunshine Policy* (Seoul: Yonsei University Press, 1999); and Hong Soon-young, "Thawing Korea's Cold War," *Foreign Affairs* (May-June 1999). On the Korea summit and its aftermath, see Sung-joo Han, "The Evolving Inter-Korean Relationship," *Journal of East Asian Studies* 1, 1 (February 2001): 155–78; Park Jong-Chul, "Challenges and Opportunities for the Two Koreas after the Summit," *Journal of East Asian Affairs* 14, 2 (Fall 2000): 301–27; Kwak Tae-Hwan, "The Korean Peace Process," *International Journal of Korean Unification Studies* 9, 1 (2000): 1–30; and Scott Snyder, "The Inter-Korean Summit and Implications for U.S. Policy," *Korean Journal of Defense Analysis* 12, 2 (winter 2000): 53–70.

63. See Selig Harrison, "The Missiles of North Korea," *World Policy Journal* (spring 2001); and Harrison, "Promoting a Soft Landing in North Korea," *Foreign Policy* 106 (spring 1997): 57–76.

64. See Samuel Kim, "North Korea in 2000," 12–29.

65. *World Food Program (WFP) Democratic People's Republic (DPR) Korea Update*, February 25, 2001, distributed by the World Food Program, P.O. Box 27, Munsudong, Pyongyang, 850-2-3817-639 (fax); *Washington Post*, September 5, 2000 (Doug Struck, "North Korea Back from the Brink").

66. In addition, according to the WFP, because 20 percent of counties still remain inaccessible and Pyongyang has not allowed an international nutritional survey since 1998, there still is no reasonably accurate sense of how much the situation has improved (*WFP DPR Korea Update*, February 2001).

67. This statement came officially at Kim's Berlin Declaration (March 10, 2000); see Kongdan Oh, "North Korea's Engagement: Implications for South Korea," in National Intelligence Council and Library of Congress, *North Korea's Engagement: Perspectives, Outlook, and Implications*, CR 2001-01 (May 2001).

68. Finally, even to concede that the recent improvements in the DPRK's food and economic situations are not transient, instead representing a new stable status quo and thereby putting Pyongyang in a less desperate situation than in the past, is to make, in effect, a similar argument. Such an argument acknowledges that the status quo *ex ante* was indeed in the domain of gains for the DPRK and that engagement policies during the Kim-Clinton era were critical in pulling the North out of this situation and creating a stake for it in the new status quo.

69. Davis, *Threats and Promises,* 5.

70. See "White House Statement on North Korea Policy Review," June 6, 2001, available at www.nautilus.org, and Secretary Powell–Foreign Minister Han Seung-Soo press conference transcript, June 7, 2001, available at www.usinfo.state.gov (accessed 12 July 2001). For fuller commentary, see Victor D. Cha, "Korea's Place in the Axis," *Foreign Affairs* 81, 3 (May-June 2002): 79–92.

71. Davis, *Threats and Promises*; and Barry Nalehuff, "Rational Deterrence in an Imperfect World," *World Politics* 43 (April 1991).

72. Elizabeth Rosenthal, "In North Korean Hunger, Legacy Is Stunted Children," *New York Times*, December 16, 1998.

73. For interesting observations on the American unwillingness to view itself as capable of negotiating with pariah states, see Sigal, *Disarming Strangers*.

74. A key element of such an exit strategy is having China view U.S.-ROK-Japan engagement efforts as complete and undertaken in good faith.

75. Jack Rendler, "The Last Worst Place on Earth," in Henry D. Sokolski, ed. *Planning for a Peaceful Korea* (Carlisle, PA: Strategic Studies Institute, 2001); and Nicholas Eberstadt, *The End of North Korea* (Washington D.C.: American Enterprise Institute, 2000).

76. For an interesting account that highlights some of the problems encountered by former North Korean defectors trying to assimilate into southern society, see Young-chul Chang's *Tangsindûli kûroke chalnattsôyo?* [Are you that much better than me?] (Seoul: Sahoe p'yông on, 1997).

Bibliography

Ahn, Byung-joon. "The Man Who Would Be Kim." *Foreign Affairs* 73, 6 (1994): 94–108.

Akaha, Tsuneo, ed. *The Future of North Korea.* London: Routledge, 2002.

Albright, David and Kevin O'Neill, eds. *Solving the North Korean Nuclear Puzzle*. Washington, D.C.: The Institute for Science and International Security, 2000.

Anquilla, John. *Dubious Battles: Aggression, Defeat, and the International System.* Washington, D.C.: Crane and Russak, 1992.

Arreguin-Toft, Ivan. "How the Weak Win Wars: A Theory of Asymmetric Conflict." *International Security* 26, 1 (summer 2001): 93–128.

Axelrod, Robert. "The Rational Timing of Surprise." *World Politics* 31, 2 (January 1979):228–46.

Balwin, David. "Power Analysis and World Politics: New Trends versus Old Tendencies." *World Politics* 31, 2 (January 1979): 161–94.

Barston, Ronald P. "The External Relations of Small States." In *Small States in International Relations,* eds. August Schou and Arne Olav Brundtland. Stockholm: Almqvist & Wiskell, 1971.

Bazhanov, Eugene (Evgeniy) and Natasha Bazhanov. "The Evolution of Russian-Korean Relations." *Asian Survey* 34, 9 (September 1994): 789–98.

Berger, Thomas U. "Unsheathing the Sword? Germany and Japan's Fractured Political-Military Cultures and the Problem of Burden Sharing." *World Affairs* 158 (spring 1996): 174–91.

Bernstein, Richard and Ross H. Monroe. *The Coming Conflict with China.* New York: Alfred A. Knopf, 1997.

Betts, Richard K. *Surprise Attack: Lessons for Defense Planning.* Washington, D.C.: The Brookings Institution, 1982.

———. "Wealth, Power, and Instability: East Asia and the United States after the Cold War." *International Security* 18, 3 (winter 1993/1994): 34–77.

Bleak, Philipp C. "Putin Signs New Military Doctrine, Fleshing Out New Security Concept." *Arms Control Today* 30, 4 (May 2000): 42.

Bloom, William. *Personal Identity, National Identity, and International Relations.* New York: Cambridge University Press, 1990.

Breslauer, George and Philip Tetlocks, eds. *Learning in U.S. and Soviet Foreign Policy.* Boulder, CO: Westview Press, 1991.

Brooks, Stephen G. "Dueling Realisms." *International Organizations* 51, 3 (summer 1997): 445–77.

Bulichev, Georgi. "Russia's Korea Policy: Toward a Conceptual Framework." *Far Eastern Affairs* 2 (2000): 3–12.

Bulichev, Georgi and Dmitry Kulkin. "Russia and South Korea: Some Thoughts on the First Decade of Relations." *Far Eastern Affairs* 5 (2000): 24–31.

Buzan, Barry. "Security, the State, the 'New World Order,' and Beyond." In *On Security,* ed. Ronnie D. Lipschutz. New York: Columbia University Press, 1995.

Buzan, Barry and Gerald Segal. "Rethinking East Asian Security." *Survival* 36, 2 (summer 1994): 3–21.

Calder, Kent. "Japanese Foreign Economic Policy Formation: Explaining the Reactive State." *World Politics* 40, 4 (July 1988): 517–41.

——. "The New Face of Northeast Asia." *Foreign Affairs* 80 1 (January-February 2001): 106–22.

Campbell, Kurt M. and Mitchell B. Reiss. "Korean Changes, Asian Challenges and the U.S. Role." *Survival* 43, 1 (spring 2001): 53–69.

Carter, Ashton B. and William Perry. *Preventive Defense: A New Security Strategy for America.* Washington, D.C.: The Brookings Institution, 1999.

Cha, Victor D. *Alignment Despite Antagonism: The United States–Korea–Japan Security Triangle.* Stanford, CA: Stanford University Press, 1999.

——. "Is There Still a Rational North Korean Option for War?" *Security Dialogue* 29, 4 (1998): 477–90.

——. "Engaging China: Seoul-Beijing Detente and Korean Security." *Survival* 41, 1 (spring 1999): 73–98.

——. "Engaging North Korea Credibly." *Survival* 42, 2 (summer 2000): 136–55.

——. "The Ultimate Oxymoron: Japan's Engagement with North Korea." *North Korea's Engagement: Perspectives, Outlook, and Implications*, Conference Report to the National Intelligence Council. Washington, D.C. (CR 2001-01, May 2001), 73–85.

Christensen, Thomas. "Posing Problems without Catching Up: China's Rise and Challenges for U.S. Security Policy." *International Security* 25, 4 (spring 2001): 5–40.

Cruz, Consuelo. "Identity and Persuasion: How Nations Remember Their Pasts and Make Their Futures." *World Politics* 52 (April 2000): 275–312.

Cumings, Bruce. *The Two Koreas*, Headline Series no. 269. New York: Foreign Policy Association, 1984.

——. "Feeding the North Korea Myths." *The Nation* (September 29, 1997), 22–4.

——. "Toward a Comprehensive Settlement of the Korea Problem." *Current History* 98, 632 (December 1999): 403–8.

Davis, James. *Threats and Promises.* Baltimore: The Johns Hopkins University Press, 2000.

Deng, Yong. "Chinese Perceptions of U.S. Power and Strategy." *Asian Affairs* 28, 3 (fall 2001): 150–5.

Deudney, Daniel. "Dividing Realism: Structural Realism versus Security Materialism on Nuclear Security and Proliferation." *Security Studies* 2, 3/4 (spring/summer 1993): 7–36.

Dittmar, Lowell and Samuel Kim, eds. *China's Quest for National Identity.* Ithaca, NY: Cornell University Press, 1993.

Downs, Chuck. *Over the Line: North Korea's Negotiating Strategy.* Washington, D.C.: The AEI Press, 1999.

Drobysheva, Irina. "Primorskii Krai Concerned about Russian-Korean Rail Link." *Russian Regional Investor* 3, 10 (May 23, 2001), available at www.iews.org.

Dujarric, Robert. "North Korea: Risks and Rewards of Engagement." *Journal of International Affairs* 54, 2 (spring 2001): 465–87.

Eberstadt, Nicholas. "How Much Money Goes from Japan to North Korea?" *Asian Survey* 36, 5 (May 1996): 523–42.

——. "'National Strategy' in North and South Korea." *NBR Analysis* 7, 5 (1996).

——. "Hastening Korean Unification." *Foreign Affairs* 72, 2 (March-April 1997): 77–92.

——. "Prospects for U.S,-DPRK Economic Relations." *Korea and World Affairs* 21, 4 (winter 1997): 534–67.

——. "North Korea's Unification Policy: 1948–1996." In *North Korean Foreign Relations*, ed. Samuel S. Kim. New York: Oxford University Press, 1998.

——. *The End of North Korea.* Washington, D.C.: The American Enterprise Institute Press, 2000.

Eberstadt, Nicholas and Richard J. Ellings, eds. *Korea's Future and the Great Powers.* Seattle, WA: University of Washington Press, 2001.

Farnham, Barbara. "Roosevelt and the Munich Crisis: Insights from Prospect Theory." *Political Psychology* 13, 2 (1992): 205–35.

Friedberg, Aaron L. "Ripe for Rivalry: Prospects for Peace in a Multipolar Asia." *International Security* 18, 3 (winter 1993/1994): 5–33.

——. "Will Europe's Past Be Asia's Future?" *Survival* 42, 3 (autumn 2000): 147–59.

Gaimusho (Japanese Ministry of Foreign Affairs). *Gaiko Seisho (The Blue Paper)*, no. 32 (1988).

Garrett, Banning and Bonnie Glaser. "Looking across the Yalu: Chinese Assessments of North Korea." *Asian Survey* 35, 6 (June 1995): 528–45.

Gause, Gregory. "Prospect Theory and Iraqi War Decisions." Unpublished paper presented at the annual meeting of the American Political Science Association, August 28–31, 1997.

Gilpin, Robert. *War and Change in World Politics.* Cambridge: Cambridge University Press, 1981.

Glaser, Charles and Chaim Kaufmann. "What Is the Offense-Defense Balance and How Can We Measure It?" *International Security* 22, 4 (spring 1998): 44–82.

——. "Realists as Optimists: Cooperation as Self-Help." *International Security* 19, 3 (winter 1994/1995): 50–90.

Goldstein, Joshua. *Long Cycles: Prosperity and War in the Modern Age*. New Haven: Yale University, 1988.

Grigor, Ronald. "Provisional Stabilities: The Politics of Identities in Post-Soviet Eurasia." *International Security* 24, 3 (winter 1999/2000): 139–78.

Habeeb, William. *Power and Tactics in International Negotiation: How Week Nations Bargain with Strong Nations*. Baltimore: The Johns Hopkins University Press, 1988.

Hall, Rodney Bruce. *National Collective Identity: Social Constructs and International Systems*. New York: Columbia University Press, 1999.

Han, Sung Joo. "The Evolving Inter-Korean Relationship." *Journal of East Asian Studies* 1, 1 (February 2001): 155–78.

Harris, Sally. "Coping with Pressure: South Korea's Defense Restructuring." *Korean Journal of Defense Analysis* 12, 2 (winter 2000): 207–30.

Harrison, Selig S. "Promoting a Soft Landing in North Korea." *Foreign Policy* 106 (spring 1997): 57–76.

——. "Time to Leave Korea?" *Foreign Affairs* 80, 2 (March-April 2001): 62–78.

——. "The Missiles of North Korea." *World Policy Journal* 17, 3 (fall 2000): 13–24.

Hart, Tom. "The PRC-DPRK Rapprochement and China's Dilemma in Korea." *Asian Perspective* 25, 3 (2001): 247–59.

Hasegawa, Hiroshi. "Kome Jito Kenjo no Fukaki Anto" (Political Infighting for Rice Aid). *Aera* (June 12, 1995): 19–22.

Hayes, Peter. *Pacific Powderkeg: American Nuclear Dilemmas in Korea.* Lexington, MA: Lexington Books, 1991.

Hayes, Peter, Lyuba Zarsky, and Walden Bello. *American Lake: Nuclear Peril in the Pacific.* New York: Penguin Books, 1986.

Heginbotham, Eric and Richard Samuels. "Mercantile Realism and Japanese Foreign Policy." *International Security* 22, 4 (spring 1998): 171–203.

Hong, Soon-young. "Thawing Korea's Cold War." *Foreign Affairs* 78, 3 (May-June 1999): 8–12.

Hong Wan Suk. Geostrategiya Rossii I severo-vostochnaya Aziya. [Russia's geostrategy and Northeast Asia] Moscow: Nauchnaya Kniga, 1998.

Huntington, Samuel P. *The Clash of Civilizations and the Remaking of World Order.* New York: Simon and Schuster, 1996.

——. "The Lonely Superpower." *Foreign Affairs* 78, 2 (March-April 1999): 35–49.

Huth, Paul, D. S. Bennett, and C. Gelpi. "System Uncertainty, Risk Propensity, and International Conflict among the Great Powers." *Journal of Conflict Resolution* 36, 3 (1992): 478–517.

Hwang, Eui-gak. *The Korean Economies.* Oxford: Clarendon Press, 1993.

James, Harold. *A German Identity: 1770–1990.* New York: Routledge Books, 1989.

Jervis, Robert. "Cooperation under the Security Dilemma," *World Politics* 30 (January 1978): 167–214.

——. *The Meaning of the Nuclear Revolution.* Ithaca, NY: Cornell University Press, 1989.

——. "The Future of World Politics: Will It Resemble the Past?" *International Security* 16, 3 (winter 1991/1992): 39–73.

——. "Political Implications of Loss Aversion." *Political Psychology* 13, 2 (1992): 187–204.

Ji, You. "China and North Korea: A Fragile Relationship of Strategic Convenience." *Journal of Contemporary China* 10, 28 (August 2001): 387–98.

Johnston, Alastair Iain. "China's New 'Old Thinking': The Concept of Limited Deterrence." *International Security* 20, 5 (1995/1996): 5–42.

——. "Engaging Myths: Misconceptions about China and Its Global Role." *Harvard Asia Pacific Review* (winter 1997/1998): 9–12.

Johnston, Alastair Iain and Robert Ross, eds. *Engaging China: The Management of an Emerging Power.* London and New York: Routledge, 1999.

Joo Seung-Ho. "Russian Policy on Korean Unification in the Post–Cold War Era." *Pacific Affairs* (spring 1996): 32–38.

——. "Russia and Korea: The Summit and After." Paper presented at the Forty-Second Annual Convention of the International Studies Association, Chicago, February 20–23, 2001.

Kahneman, Daniel and Amos Tversky. "Prospect Theory: An Analysis of Decision under Risk." *Econometrica* 47, 2 (March 1979): 263–91.

Kang, C. S. Eliot. "The Four-Party Peace Talks: Lost without a Map." *Comparative Strategy* 17 (1998): 327–44.

——. "North Korea and the U.S. Grand Strategy." *Comparative Strategy* 21, 1 (January-March 2001): 25-43.

Kang, David. "Preventive War and North Korea." *Security Studies* 4, 2 (winter 1994/1995): 330–63.

——. "North Korea: Deterrence through Danger." In *Asian Security Practice: Material and Ideational Influences,* ed. Muthiah Alagapa. Stanford, CA: Stanford University Press, 1998.

Katzenstein, Peter, ed. *The Culture of National Security: Norms and Identity in World Politics*. New York: Columbia University Press, 1996.

Kato, Koichi. "Kitachosen o sekyokuteki ni shien subekida: Kato Koichi, Jiminto Kanshicho nikiku" (We should help North Korea earnestly: Interview with Kato Koichi). *Kendai Koria* (1995): 16–21.

Kennedy, Paul. *The Rise and Fall of the Great Powers: Economic Change and Military Conflict from 1500 to 2000.* New York: Random House, 1987.

Keohane, Robert. *International Institutions and State Power: Essays in International Relations Theory.* Boulder, CO: Westview Press, 1989.

Kim, Dalchoong and Chung-in Moon, eds. *History, Cognition, and Peace in East Asia.* Seoul: Yonsei University Press, 1997.

Kim, Jang-han. "North Korea's Economy and the Prospect of its Overseas Economic Policy in 2000." January 3, 2001, available at www.kotra.co.kr/nk.

Kim, Samuel S. "North Korea in 1994: Brinkmanship, Breakdown, and Breakthrough," *Asian Survey* 35, 1 (January 1995): 13–27.

——. "The Dialectics of China's North Korea Policy in a Changing Post–Cold War World." *Asian Perspective* 18, 2 (fall/winter 1994): 5–36.

——. "North Korea and the United Nations." *International Journal of Korean Studies* 1, 1 (spring 1997): 77–105.

——. "China as a Great Power." *Current History* 96, 611 (September 1997): 246–51.

——. ed. *North Korean Foreign Relations in the Post–Cold War Era,* New York: Oxford University Press, 1998.

——. ed. *China and the World: Chinese Foreign Policy Faces the New Millennium.* Boulder, CO: Westview Press, 1998.

——. "The Roles of the Major Powers." In *Patterns of Inter-Korean Relations,* ed. Bae Ho Hahn and Chae-Jin Lee. Seoul: The Sejong Institute, 1999.

——. ed. *Korea's Globalization.* New York: Cambridge University Press, 2000.

——. ed. *East Asia and Globalization.* Lanham, MD: Rowman & Littlefield Publishers, 2000.

——. "The Making of China's Korea Policy in the Era of Reform." In *The Making of Chinese Foreign and Security Policy in the Era of Reform, 1978–2000,* ed. David M. Lampton. Stanford, CA: Stanford University Press, 2001.

——. "North Korea in 2000: Surviving through High Hopes of Summit Diplomacy," *Asian Survey* 41, 1 (January/February 2001): 12–29.

——. ed. *The North Korean System in the Post–Cold War Era.* New York: Palgrave, 2001.

——. "China, Japan, and Russia in Inter-Korean Relations." In *Korea Briefing 2000–2001: First Steps Toward Reconciliation and Reunification,* eds. Kongdan Oh and Ralph Hassigs. Armonk, NY: M. E. Sharpe, 2002.

Kim, Taeho. "Strategic Relations between Beijing and Pyongyang: Growing Strains and Lingering Ties." In *China's Military Faces the Future*, eds. James R. Lilley and David Shambaugh. Armonk, NY: M. E. Sharpe, 1999.

Koh, B. C. "U.S.-Japan Security Cooperation and the Two Koreas." In *Korean Security Dynamics in Transition,* eds. Kyung-Ae Park and Dalchoong Kim. New York: Palgrave, 2001.

Kotch, John B. "Korea's Multinational Diplomacy and U.S.-Korea Relations: The Challenge of Change in the Twenty-First Century. " *The Journal of East Asian Affairs* 14, 1 (spring/summer 2000): 135–58.

Krasner, Stephen D., ed. *International Regimes.* Ithaca, NY: Cornell University Press, 1983.

Krause, Jill and Neil Renwick, eds. *Identities in International Relations.* New York: St. Martin's Press, 1996.

Kugler, Jacek and A. F. K Organsk. "The Power Transition: A Retrospective and Prospective Evaluation." In *Handbook of War Studies*, ed. Manus I. Midlarsky. Boston: Unwin Hyman, 1989.

Kupchan, Charles. *The Vulnerability of Empire.* Ithaca, NY: Cornell University Press, 1994.

Kwak, Tae-Hwan. "The Korean Peace Process." *International Journal of Korean Unification Studies* 9, 1 (2000): 1–30.

Lapid, Yosef and Friedrich Kratochwil, eds. *The Return of Culture and Identity in IR Theory.* Boulder, CO: Lynne Rienner Publishers, 1996.

Lebow, Richard Ned. *Between Peace and War: The Nature of International Crisis.* Baltimore: The Johns Hopkins University Press, 1981.

——. "Windows of Opportunity: Do States Jump through Them?" *International Security* 9, 1 (summer 1984): 147–86.

Lee, Chong-suk. "Puk-e-so bon Han-il Hyupjung kwa Cho-il Hoidam" (South Korea–Japan treaty from the eyes of North Korea and the North Korea–Japan normalization talks), *Yuksa Bipyung* (historical review) 28 (1995): 57–9.

Lee, W. D. *Bukil Kukkyogyosup kwa Ilbon eui Daebuk Jungchek* (The North Korea–Japan normalization talks and Japan's North Korea policy). Seoul: SNU IAS, 1996.

Levin, Norman D. "Feel Their Pain (If You Like), But Watch Their Actions." *Survival* 38, 4 (winter 1996/1997): 41–3.

Levy, Jack. "Declining Power and the Preventive Motivation for War." *World Politics* 40, 1 (October 1987): 82–107.

——. "An Introduction to Prospect Theory." *Political Psychology* 13, 2 (1992): 171–86.

——. "Prospect Theory and International Relations: Theoretical Applications and Analytical Problems." *Political Psychology* 13, 2 (1992): 283–310.

Li, Vladimir. *Rossiya i Koreya v geopolitike evraziiskogo Vostoka* (Russia and Korea in the geopolitics of the Eurasian east). Moscow: Nauchnaya Kniga, 2000.

Liang Qiao and Wang Xianghui. *Chaoxian Zhan* (Unlimited War). Beijing: People's Liberation Army Cultural Press, 1999.

Mack, Andrew. "Why Big Nations Lose Small Wars: The Politics of Asymmetric Conflict." *World Politics* 27, 2 (January 1975): 175–200.

——. "The Nuclear Crisis on the Korean Peninsula." *Asian Survey* 33, 4 (April 1993): 339–59.

Manning, Robert A. "The United States and the Endgame in Korea: Assessment, Scenarios, and Implications." *Asian Survey* 37, 7 (July 1997): 597–608.

——. "The Enigma of the North." *The Wilson Quarterly* 23, 3 (summer 1999): 72–80.

Manyin, Mark. "North Korea–Japan Relations: The Normalization Talks and the Compensation/Reparation Issue." *CRS Report for Congress* (April 21, 2001) Washington, D.C.: Congressional Research Services.

Mastanduno, Michael. "Preserving the Unipolar Moment: Realist Theories and U.S. Grand Strategy after the Cold War" *International Security* 21, 4 (spring 1997): 49–88.

Mazarr, Michael J. "Going Just a Little Nuclear." *International Security* 20, 2 (fall 1995): 92–122.

McDermott, Rose. "Prospect Theory in International Relations: The Iranian Hostage Rescue Mission." *Political Psychology* 13, 2 (1992): 237–63.

McInerney, Audrey. "Prospect Theory and Soviet Policy towards Syria, 1966–1967." *Political Psychology* 13, 2 (1992): 265–82.

McVadon, Eric A. "Chinese Military Strategy for the Korean Peninsula." In *China's Military Faces the Future*, eds. James R. Lilley and David Shambaugh. Armonk, NY: M. E. Sharpe, 1999.

———. "China's Goals and Strategies for the Korean Peninsula. " In *Planning for a Peaceful Korea*, ed. Henry D. Sokolski. Carlisle, PA: Strategic Studies Institute, 2001.

Mearsheimer, John. "Back to the Future: Instability in Europe after the Cold War." *International Security* 15, 1 (summer 1990): 5–56.

Meyer, Peggy Falkenheim. "Gorbachev and Post-Gorbachev Policy toward the Korean Peninsula." *Asian Survey* 37, 8 (August 1992): 757–72.

Michell, Anthony. "The Current North Korean Economy." In *Economic Integration of the Korean Peninsula,* ed. Marcus Noland. Washington, D.C.: Institute for International Economics, 1998.

Michishita, Narushige. "Two Alliance after Peace on the Korean Peninsula." A/PARC Working Paper, Stanford University, May 7, 1999.

Mikheev, Vasilii V. "Russian Policy towards [the] Korean Peninsula after Yeltsin's Reelection as President." *The Journal of East Asian Affairs* 11, 2 (summer/fall 1997): 348–77.

Ministry of Defense. *White Paper*. Seoul, Korea: Ministry of Defense, Republic of Korea, 1999.

———. *White Paper*. Seoul, Korea: Ministry of Defense, Republic of Korea, 2000.

Modelski, George. "The Long Cycle of Global Politics and the Nation-State." *Comparative Studies in Society and History* 20 (April 1978): 214–35.

Moltz, James Clay and Alexandre Y. Mansourov, eds. *The North Korean Nuclear Program: Security, Strategy, and New Perspectives from Russia*. New York and London: Routledge, 2000.

Moon, Chung-in. "Korea and Asian Security in the Twenty-First Century." *Asian Voices: Promoting Dialogue between the U.S. and Asia*. Washington, D.C.: Sasakawa Peace Foundation USA, 2000.

Moon, Chung-in and David Steinberg, eds. *Kim Dae Jung Government and Sunshine Policy* Seoul: Yonsei University Press, 1999.

Nalehuff, Barry. "Rational Deterrence in an Imperfect World." *World Politics* 43, 3 (April 1991): 313–35.

Natios, Andrew S. *The Great North Korean Famine: Famine, Politics, and Foreign Policy.* Washington, D.C.: United States Institute of Peace Press, 2001.

Noland, Marcus. "Why North Korea Will Muddle Through." *Foreign Affairs* 76, 4 (1997): 105–18.

———. "The External Economic Relations of North Korea and Prospects for Reform." In *North Korean Foreign Relations*, ed. Samuel S. Kim. Hong Kong: Oxford University Press, 1998.

———. *Avoiding the Apocalypse: The Future of the Two Koreas* (Washington, D.C: Institute for International Economics, 2000).

———. "The Economic Situation in North Korea." In *The Two Koreas and the United States*, ed. Wonmo Dong. Armonk, NY: M. E. Sharpe, 2000.

Noland, Marcus, Sherman Robinson, and Monica Scatasta. "Modeling North Korean Economic Reform." *Journal of Asian Economics* 8 (1997): 115–38.

Noland, Marcus, Sherman Robinson, and LiGang Liu. "The Economics of Korean Unification." *Journal of Policy Reform* 3 (1999): 255–99.

——. "Modeling Korean Unification." *Journal of Comparative Economics* 28, 2 (2000): 400–21.

Noland, Marcus, Sherman Robinson, and Tao Wang. "Rigorous Speculation: The Collapse and Revival of the North Korean Economy." *World Development* 28, 10 (2000): 1767–87.

"North Korea's Decline and China's Strategic Dilemmas." *USIP Special Report* (October 1997).

Oh, Kongdan. "North Korea's Engagement: Implications for South Korea," In *North Korea's Engagement: Perspectives, Outlook, and Implications.* National Intelligence Council and Library of Congress, CR 2001-01 (May 2001).

Oh, Kongdan and Ralph Hassig. "North Korea between Collapse and Reform." *Asian Survey* 39, 2 (March/April 1999): 287–309.

O'Hanlon, Michael. "Stopping a North Korean Invasion: Why Defending South Korea Is Easier Than the Pentagon Thinks." *International Security* 22, 4 (spring 1998): 135–70.

Okonogi, Masao. *Nihon to Kitachosen: Korekara no Konen* (Japan and North Korea: Five years from now). Tokyo: PHP Press, 1991.

Organski, A. F. K. *World Politics*. New York: Knopf, 1968.

Oye, Kenneth A. "Explaining Cooperation under Anarchy: Hypotheses and Strategies." *World Politics* 38, 1 (October 1985): 1–24.

Park, Han S. "The Nature and Evolution of the Inter-Korean Legitimacy War." In *Korean Security Dynamics in Transition*, eds. Kyung-Ae Park and Dalchoong Kim. New York: Palgrave, 2001.

Park, Jong-Chul. "Challenges and Opportunities for the Two Koreas after the Summit." *Journal of East Asian Affairs* 14, 2 (fall 2000): 301–27.

Park, Kyung-Ae and Dalchoong Kim, eds. *Korean Security Dynamics in Transition*. New York: Palgrave, 2001.

Park, Sang Hoon. "North Korea and the Challenge to the U.S.–South Korean Alliance." *Survival* 36, 2 (summer 1994): 78–91.

Pastor, Robert A. ed. *A Century's Journey: How the Great Powers Shape the World.* New York: Basic Books, 1999.

Paul, T. V. *Asymmetric Conflicts: War Initiation by Weaker Powers.* New York: Cambridge University Press, 1994.

Perl, Raphael. *North Korean Drug Trafficking: Allegations and Issues in Congress.* Congressional Research Service, March 9, 1999.

Pharr, Susan. "Japan's Defensive Foreign Policy and the Politics of Burden Sharing." In *Japan's Foreign Policy after the Cold War: Coping with Change*, ed. Gerald Curtis. Armonk, NY: M. E. Sharpe, 1993.

Pollack, Jonathan and Chung Min Lee. *Preparing for Korean Unification: Scenarios and Implications.* Santa Monica, CA: RAND Corporation, 1999.

Posen, Barry R. and Andrew L. Ross. "Competing Visions for U.S. Grand Strategy." *International Security* 21, 3 (winter 1996/1997): 44–50.

Prizel, Ilya. *National Identity and Foreign Policy: Nationalism and Leadership in Poland, Russia and Ukraine*. New York: Cambridge University Press, 1998.

Qiao, Liang and Wang Xianghui. *Chaoxian Zhan* (Unlimited War). Beijing: People's Liberation Army Cultural Press, 1999.

Quattrone, George and Amos Tversky. "Contrasting Rational and Psychological Analyses of Political Choice." *American Political Science Review* 82, 3 (September 1988): 719–36.

Ray, James Lee. "The Democratic Path to Peace." *Journal of Democracy* 8, 2 (April 1997): 49–64.

Reiss, Mitchell. *Bridled Ambition: Why Countries Constrain Their Nuclear Abilities*. Washington, D.C.: Wilson Center Press, 1995: 231–320.

Reiter, Dan. "Exploding the Powderkeg Myth: Preemptive Wars Almost Never Happen." *International Security* 20, 2 (fall 1995): 5–34.

Rendler, Jack. "The Last Worst Place on Earth." In *Planning for a Peaceful Korea*, ed. Henry D. Sokolski. Carlisle, PA: Strategic Studies Institute, 2001.

"Review of United States Policy toward North Korea: Findings and Recommendations." William J. Perry, Department of State, October 12, 1999.

Rice, Condoleezza. "Promoting the National Interest." *Foreign Affairs* 79, 1 (January/February 2000): 45–62.

Ross, Robert S. "The Geography of the Peace: East Asia in the Twenty-First Century." *International Security* 23, 4 (spring 1999): 81–118.

Roy, Denny. "North Korea as an Alienated State." *Survival* 38, 4 (winter 1996/1997): 22–36.

Rozman, Gilbert. "Flawed Regionalism: Reconceptualizing Northeast Asia in the 1990s." *Pacific Review* 11, 1 (1998): 1–27.

——. "Mutual Perceptions among the Great Powers in Northeast Asia" In *Politics and Economics in Northeast Asia: Nationalism and Regionalism* in *Contention*, ed. Tsuneo, Akaha. New York: St. Martin's Press, 1999.

Rubinstein, Alvin Z. *Imperial Decline: Russia's Changing Role in Asia*. Durham, NC: Duke University Press, 1997.

Russett, Bruce. *Power and Continuity in World Politics*. San Francisco: Freeman, 1974.

——. *Grasping the Democratic Peace: Principles for a Post–Cold War World.* Princeton, NJ: Princeton University Press, 1993.

Russett, Bruce and John O'Neal. *Triangulating Peace: Democracy, Interdependence, and International Organizations.* New York: Norton, 2001.

Sagan, Scott. "The Origins of the Pacific War." *Journal of Interdisciplinary History* 18 (spring 1988): 893–922.

Scalapino, Robert. *North Korea at a Crossroads.* Hoover Institution Essays on Public Policy, Stanford University, no. 73 (1997).

Schelling, Thomas. *The Strategy of Conflict.* Cambridge: Harvard University Press, 1960.

——. *Arms and Influence.* New Haven, CT: Yale University Press, 1966.

Schweller, Randall. "Domestic Structure and Preventive War: Are Democracies More Pacific?" *World Politics* 44, 2 (January 1992): 235–69.

——. "Neorealism's Status Quo Bias." *Security Studies* 5, 3 (spring 1996): 90–121.

Segal, Gerald. "Does China Matter?" *Foreign Affairs* 78, 5 (September/October 1999): 24–36.

Shafir, Eldar. "Prospect Theory and Political Analysis: A Psychological Perspective." *Political Psychology* 13, 2 (1992): 311–22.

Shigemura, Toshimitsu. "Gaiko o Asonda Yotou Houchotan Soudou" (The governing parties' delegation to North Korea to ridicule Japan's foreign policy). *Chuogoron*. (June 1995): 99–105.

Sigal, Leon V. " Who Is Fighting Peace in Korea? An Undiplomatic History." *World Policy Journal* 14, 2 (summer 1997): 44–58.

———. *Disarming Strangers: Nuclear Diplomacy with North Korea.* Princeton, NJ: Princeton University Press, 1998.

Snyder, Glenn. *Deterrence and Defense: Toward a Theory of National Security.* Princeton, NJ: Princeton University Press, 1961.

Snyder, Jack. "Perceptions of the Security Dilemma in 1914." In *Psychology and Deterrence*, eds. Robert Jervis, Richard Ned Lebow, and Janice Gross Stein. Baltimore: Johns Hopkins University Press, 1985.

Snyder, Scott. *Negotiating on the Edge: North Korean Negotiating Behavior*. Washington, D.C.: United States Institute of Peace Press, 1999.

———. "Pyongyang's Pressure." *The Washington Quarterly* 23, 3 (summer 2000): 163–70.

———. "The Inter-Korean Summit and Implications for U.S. Policy." *Korean Journal of Defense Analysis* 12, 2 (winter 2000): 53–70.

———. "North Korea's Challenge of Regime Survival: Internal Problems and Implications for the Future." *Pacific Affairs* 73, 4 (winter 2000/2001): 517–33.

Sokolski, Henry D., ed. *Planning for a Peaceful Korea*. Carlisle, PA: Strategic Studies Institute, 2001.

Song, Dexing. "Lengzhan hou DongbeiYa anquan xingshe de bianhua" (Changes in the post–Cold War Northeast Asian security situation). *Xiandai guoji guanxi* (Contemporary International Relations) 9 (1998): 34–8.

Stein, Janice Gross. "International Co-operation and Loss Avoidance: Framing the Problem." In *Choosing to Co-operate: How States Avoid Loss*, ed. Janice Stein. Baltimore: The Johns Hopkins University Press, 1993.

Suh, Dae-Sook, and Chae-Jin Lee, eds. *North Korea after Kim Il Sung.* Boulder, CO: Lynne Rienner Publishers, 1998.

Tanaka, Akira. "Kitashosen Kome wa Heiwa Boke" (Rice aid toward North Korea is just a Disguise). *Shokun*, 1995, 68–77.

Taylor, William J. Jr. "The Korean Peninsula at the Crossroads: Which Way?" In *The Two Koreas and the United States: Issues of Peace, Security, and Economic Cooperation*. ed. Wonmo Dong. Armonk, NY: M. E. Sharp, 2000.

Thompson, William. *On Global War: Historical-Structural Approaches to World Politics.* Columbia, S.C.: University of South Carolina, 1988.

Tkachenko, Vadim. "Russian-Korean Cooperation to Preserve the Peace." *Far Eastern Affairs* 2 (1999): 23–35.

Tversky, Amos and Daniel Kahneman. "Rational Choice and the Framing of Decisions." *Journal of Business* 59, 4, part 2 (1986): S251–78.

U.S. Secretary of Defense William Cohen's "2000 Report to Congress: Military Situation on the Korean Peninsula, September 12, 2000," available at http://defenselink.mil/news/Sept2000/korea09122000.html (accessed 10 December 2000).

Van Ness, Peter. "Globalization and Security in East Asia." In *East Asia and Globalization,* ed. Samuel S. Kim. Lanham, MD: Rowman & Littlefield Publishers, 2000.

Vertzberger, Y. Y. I. *Risk Taking and Decision Making.* Stanford, CA: Stanford University Press, 1998.

Von Hippel, David and Peter Hayes. "DPRK Energy Sector: Current Status and Scenarios for 2000 and 2005." In *Economic Integration of the Korean Peninsula*, ed. Marcus Noland. Washington, D.C.: Institute for International Economics, 1998.

Wallander, Celeste. "Russia's New Security Concept." *Arms Control Today* 30, 1 (January/ February 2000): 15–20.

——. "Wary of the West: Russian Security Policy at the Millennium." *Arms Control Today* 30, 2 (March 2000): 7–12.

Walt, Stephen M. "Alliance Formation and the Balance of World Power." *International Security* 9, 4 (spring 1985): 208–47.

——. *The Origins of Alliance.* Ithaca, NY: Cornell University Press, 1987.

Waltz, Kenneth R. "The Emerging Structure of International Politics." *International Security* 18, 2 (fall 1993): 44–79.

Wendt, Alexander. "Anarchy Is What States Make of It: The Social Construction of Power Politics." *International Organization* 46, 2 (spring 1992): 391–425.

——. *Social Theory of International Politics*. New York: Cambridge University Press, 1999.

Williams, James H., Peter Hayes, and David Von Hippel. "Fuel and Famine: North Korea's Rural Energy Crisis." Paper presented to the Pentagon Study (Group on Japan and Northeast Asia), Washington, D.C., October 22, 1999.

Wit, Joel. "The United States and North Korea." *Brookings Policy Brief*, no. 74 (March 2001) available at www.brookings.edu/comm/policybriefs/pb074/pb74.pdf (accessed 15 January 2002).

——. "North Korea: The Leader of the Pack." *The Washington Quarterly* 24, 1 (winter 2001): 77–92.

Wohlforth, William C. "The Stability of a Unipolar World." *International Security* 24, 1 (summer 1999): 5–41.

Wolf, Charles Jr., et al. *Long-Term Economic and Military Trends, 1994–2015: The United States and Asia.* Santa Monica, CA: RAND Corporation, 1995.

World Bank. *World Development Report 2002.* New York: Oxford University Press, 2001.

Wu, Xinbo. "Managing the Korean Issue: A Chinese Perspective." *Korea and World Affairs* 24, (spring 2000): 79–91.

Yamamoto, Okashi. "Nichicho Fuseijo Kankeishi" (Abnormal relationship between Japan and North Korea). In *Nichicho Kankei: So no Rekishi to Genzai* (The Japan–North Korea Relationship: Its History and the Present), ed. Sekai. Special Issue, 1992.

Yang, K. W. "Bukil Kukyo Jungsanghwa Gyosup: 1991–1995" (The normalization talks between North Korea and Japan). In *Tongil Hwangkyung kwa Tongil Kyoyuk* (The environment and education for unification), ed. Tongilwon (National Board of Unification), 1995.

Yi, Xiaoxiong. "Dynamics of China's South Korea Policy: Assertive Nationalism, Beijing's Changing Strategic Evaluation of the United States and the Korea Factor." *Asian Perspective* 24, 1 (2000): 71–102.

Yu, Shaohua. "Chaoxian Bandao Xingshi de Fazhan yu Qianjing" (The evolving situation and future prospects of the Korean Peninsula), *Guoji Wenti Yanjiu* [International Studies] 4 (1997): 12–16.

Zabrovskaya, Larisa. *Rossiya i KNDR: Opyt proshlogo I perspektivy budushchego* (1990-e Gody) [Russia and the DPRK: Past experience and future perspectives (1990s)]. Vladivostok: Dal'nauka, 1998.

——. "The 1961 USSR-DPRK Treaty and Signing of a New Russia–North Korean Treaty." *Korea and World Affairs* (fall 2000): 440–52.

Ziegler, Charles E. *Foreign Policy and East Asia: Learning and Adaptation in the Gorbachev Era*. Cambridge: Cambridge University Press, 1993.

Zoellick, Robert B. "A Republican Foreign Policy." *Foreign Affairs* 79, 1 (January/February 2000): 63–78.

Zou, Yunhua. "Zhanqu Daodan Fangyu yu Quanqiu he Diqu Anquan de Guanxi" (The relationship between the theater missile defense and the global and regional security). *Guoji Wentia Yanjiu* (International Studies) 1 (1998): 27–9.

Index

About the Editors and Contributors

ABOUT THE EDITORS

Samuel S. Kim, formerly a Fulbright professor at the Foreign Affairs Institute, Beijing, China (1985–1986) and a professor at Princeton University (1986–1993), teaches in the department of political science and is a senior research scholar at the East Asian Institute, Columbia University. He holds an M.I.A. and Ph.D. from Columbia. Kim is the author or editor of eighteen books on Northeast-Asian international relations and world order studies, including, most recently, *China and the World: Chinese Foreign Policy Faces the New Millennium* (ed.,Westview Press, 1998); *Korea's Globalization* (ed., Cambridge University Press, 2000); *The North Korean Political System in the Post–Cold War Era* (ed., Palgrave, 2001) and *The Two Koreas in the Global Community* (Cambridge University Press, forthcoming). He has published more than one hundred fifty articles in edited volumes and leading international relations journals, including *American Journal of International Law, China Quarterly, International Interactions, International Journal, International Organization, Journal of Peace Research, World Politics, and World Policy Journal*.

Tai Hwan Lee is Director of Regional Studies Program and former Director of Foreign Policy and Security Studies at the Sejong Institute, Seoul, Korea. He received his B.A. from Seoul National University, and earned an M.A.L.D. from The Fletcher School of Law and Diplomacy and a Ph.D. from the University of Southern California. He has served as a policy analyst in the Ministry of Foreign Affairs and a policy advisor to the Ministry of National Defense in Korea. He was a visiting fellow at the Foreign Affairs College,

Beijing (1995). He is the author or coauthor of several books, including *Politics of Energy Policy in Post-Mao China* (Seoul: Asiatic Research Center, Korea University 1995), *Internationalization and Globalization: Korea, China, Japan* (Seoul: Jipmundang, 2000) (in Korean). He is the editor of several books in Korean, including *Domestic Politics and Foreign Policy of Major Powers in Northeast Asia* (Seoul: The Sejong Institute, 1998), *Security and Foreign Policies of a Unified Korea* (Seoul: The Sejong Institute, 1999), and *Environmental Cooperation in Northeast Asia* (Seoul: The Sejong Institute, 2002). He has been in charge of organizing the annual Sejong–China Institute of Contemporary International Relations (CICIR) conference in Beijing and editing the proceedings. He is editor in chief of the journal *Current Issues and Policies* and an editor of *National Strategy* (in Korean).

ABOUT THE CONTRIBUTORS

Victor D. Cha is associate professor of government and D. S. Song-Korea Foundation Chair in the Edmund Walsh School of Foreign Service, Georgetown University. He is the author of *Alignment Despite Antagonism: The United States–Korea–Japan Security Triangle* (Stanford, CA: Stanford University Press, 1999), which won the 2000 Ohira Book Prize, and he has written articles on international relations and East Asia in journals including *Survival*, *International Security*, *International Studies Quarterly*, *Orbis*, *Foreign Affairs, Political Science Quarterly,* and *Asian Survey*. Professor Cha was a former John M. Olin National Security Fellow at Harvard University, two-time Fulbright Scholar, and Hoover National Fellow at Stanford. He serves as an independent consultant to the U.S. Department of Defense (Office of the Secretary of Defense), and has been a guest analyst on Asia issues for various media including *CNN*, *National Public Radio*, *New York Times*, *Washington Post*, and *Time*. He currently directs a new project at Georgetown, "The Future of American Alliances in Asia."

C. S. Eliot Kang is an associate professor of political science at Northern Illinois University. He received his Ph.D. from Yale. He also studied at Princeton and received his A.B., *summa cum laude*, from Cornell. He has taught at the University of Pennsylvania and was a research fellow in at The Brookings Institution. He was also an International Affairs Fellow of the Council on Foreign Relations and a visiting fellow at the Japan Institute of International Affairs. His professional background includes working for the investment banking firm of Dillon, Read, & Co., Inc. Specializing in security and economic issues of Northeast Asia, he has published numerous book chapters and articles in publications such as *International Organization*, *Comparative Strategy*, and *World Affairs*.

Myonwoo Lee is vice president of the Sejong Institute. He earned an M.A. and Ph.D. from Ohio State University. Lee has edited several volumes, including *The Surrounding Four Powers, 1996–1997: An Analysis of Political Elites* (Seoul: The Sejong Institute, 1998); *A Study of Japanese NGOs Activities* (Seoul: The Sejong Institute, 1996); *Political Changes and Policy Changes in Japan* (Seoul: The Sejong Institute, 1996); and, in Korean, coauthored *Japan's Rightists* (Seoul: Joongshim, 2000) and *Korean-Japanese Relations in the Post–Cold War Era* (Seoul: Jiphyunjon, 1998). He currently works on the comparative study of Korea and Japan on the themes of IT industry and economic crisis.

Robert A. Manning is currently Senior Counselor for Energy, Technology, and Science Policy for the Department of State since October 2001. Prior to that he was C. V. Starr Senior Fellow and Director of Asian Studies at the Council on Foreign Relations. Chapter 2 is an updated draft of a paper originally presented to the International Studies Association prior to his joining the Department of State. The views expressed herein are solely those of the author, not of the Department of State or any other U.S. government agency. Manning is author of "The Asian Energy Factor: Myths and Dilemmas on Energy, Security, and the Pacific Future," (Palgrave/St. Martins Press, 2000) and coauthor of *China, Nuclear Weapons, and Arms Control: A Preliminary Assessment* (Council on Foreign Relations Press, 2000), and has edited or contributed to more than a dozen volumes as well as to leading journals including *Foreign Affairs, Foreign Policy Survival, Asian Survey,* and *The Wilson Quarterly*. He has been director of the CFR-sponsored independent Task Forces, *Testing North Korea: Policy in a New Era* and *The United States and Southeast Asia: An Agenda for the New Administration*. He is also on the executive board of the Council for Security Cooperation in the Asia-Pacific (CSCAP).

Marcus Noland is a senior fellow at the Institute for International Economics and an associate of the International Food Policy Research Institute. He earned a Ph.D. from Johns Hopkins University. He was a senior economist at the Council of Economic Advisers in the executive office of the President of the United States, and has held research or teaching positions at Johns Hopkins University, the University of Southern California, Tokyo University, Saitama University, the University of Ghana, the Korea Development Institute, and the East-West Center. Noland has been the recipient of fellowships sponsored by the Japan Society for the Promotion of Science, the Council on Foreign Relations, the Council for the International Exchange of Scholars, and the Pohang Iron and Steel Corporation (POSCO). He has served as an occasional consultant to organizations such as the World Bank and the National Intelligence Council, and has testified before the U.S. Congress on numerous occasions. He has written extensively on the political economies of North and South Korea, including *Avoiding the Apocalypse: The Future of the Two Koreas* (Washington, D.C.: Institute for International Economics, 2000).

Elizabeth Wishnick is an associate of the East Asian Institute at Columbia University, and earned a Ph.D. from Columbia. In 2002 and 2003 she will be a Fulbright Visiting Professor at Lingnan University, Hong Kong. She is the author of *Mending Fences: The Evolution of Moscow's China Policy from Brezhnev to Yeltsin* (Seattle: University of Washington Press, 2001) and of numerous articles on great power relations and regional development in Northeast Asia that have appeared in journals such as *Asian Survey, SAIS Review, ERINA Report, Journal of East Asian Affairs,* and *Issues and Studies.* The results of her two-year study on center-regional differences in Russia's Asia policy were published as *NBR Analysis* in March 2002. She has taught at Yale College, Barnard College, and Columbia University, and has been a research fellow at Taiwan's Academia Sinica, the Hoover Institution, and the Davis Center at Harvard University.